VAGUENESS AND LAW

Vagueness and Law

Philosophical and Legal Perspectives

Edited by

GEERT KEIL

Professor of Philosophy, Humboldt University Berlin

and

RALF POSCHER

Professor of Public Law and Legal Philosophy,
Albert-Ludwigs-University of Freiburg

OXFORD
UNIVERSITY PRESS

OXFORD

UNIVERSITY PRESS

Great Clarendon Street, Oxford, OX2 6DP,
United Kingdom

Oxford University Press is a department of the University of Oxford.
It furthers the University's objective of excellence in research, scholarship,
and education by publishing worldwide. Oxford is a registered trade mark of
Oxford University Press in the UK and in certain other countries

Published in the United States of America by Oxford University Press
198 Madison Avenue, New York, NY 10016, United States of America

British Library Cataloguing in Publication Data
Data available

Library of Congress Control Number: 2016953196

ISBN 978–0–19–878288–9

Printed and bound by
CPI Group (UK) Ltd, Croydon, CR0 4YY

Acknowledgements

This book emerged from the research project *Dealing Reasonably with Blurred Boundaries: Vagueness and Indeterminacy as a Challenge for Philosophy and Law*. The project spanned four years and was supported by a research grant from the Volkswagen Foundation within the funding initiative 'Key Issues in the Humanities'. The main aims of the project were to identify and systematize phenomena of vagueness and indeterminacy in different fields of application, to examine their semantics, ontology, and epistemology, and to develop procedures of dealing reasonably with blurred boundaries. Another output of this project is the volume *Vagueness in Psychiatry*, published in parallel with the present book by Oxford University Press (Keil et al. 2016).

We are indebted to Marc Andree Weber, who commented on all chapters and assisted us with the final editing and preparation of the manuscript. Eric J. Engstrom meticulously copy-edited the introduction and two chapters (8 and 9). David Lanius read a draft of the introduction and made a number of helpful suggestions.

Throughout the editing and publication period, it was an immense pleasure to work with Nicole Leyland, Natasha Flemming, and Elinor Shields at Oxford University Press.

Contents

I. THEORIES OF VAGUENESS AND THEIR IMPACT ON JURISPRUDENCE

II. VAGUENESS PHENOMENA IN LAW

III. DEALING WITH VAGUENESS IN LAW

List of Contributors

Hrafn Asgeirsson is Senior Lecturer in Law and Philosophy at the University of Surrey School of Law.

Brian H. Bix is Frederick W. Thomas Professor of Law and Philosophy at the University of Minnesota.

Leo Katz is the Frank Carano Professor of Law at the University of Pennsylvania Law School.

Geert Keil is a Professor of Philosophy at Humboldt University of Berlin.

Adam J. Kolber is Professor of Law at Brooklyn Law School.

Nikola Kompa is a Professor of Philosophy at the University of Osnabrück.

Andrei Marmor is Jacob Gould Schurman Professor of Philosophy and Law at the Cornell Law School.

Michael S. Moore holds the Charles R. Walgreen, Jr Chair at the University of Illinois; he is Professor of Law, Professor of Philosophy, Professor in the Center for Advanced Study, and Co-Director of the Program in Law and Philosophy.

Ralf Poscher is a Professor of Public Law and Legal Philosophy, Albert-Ludwigs-University of Freiburg.

Diana Raffman is a Professor of Philosophy at the University of Toronto.

Frederick Schauer is David and Mary Harrison Distinguished Professor of Law at the University of Virginia.

Stephen Schiffer is Silver Professor of Philosophy at New York University.

Lawrence M. Solan is the Don Forchelli Professor of Law and Director of Graduate Education at Brooklyn Law School.

Roy Sorensen is a Professor of Philosophy at Washington University in St Louis.

Jeremy Waldron is University Professor in the School of Law at New York University.

Marc Andree Weber is Postdoctoral Researcher at the Institute for Political Science and Philosophy of Law, Albert-Ludwigs-University of Freiburg.

Vagueness and Law

Philosophical and Legal Perspectives

Geert Keil and Ralf Poscher

Vagueness of meaning is a pervasive feature of natural language, a common concern of philosophers and legal scholars, and a theoretical challenge to both. In the philosophy of language and logic, vagueness has become one of the hottest topics of the past two decades. A number of theories of vagueness have been developed that are largely unknown outside academic philosophy. These theories, however, show little or no concern for socially relevant examples. Philosophers aim to understand what vagueness *is*, what the phenomenon teaches us about the working of language, how it can be accommodated in a systematic theory of meaning, and how the logical paradoxes arising from vagueness can be dealt with. Legal scholars, on the other hand, are interested in the *implications* that vagueness has for law-making, adjudication, and legal interpretation. Regrettably, 'to date, these two investigations of vagueness—in philosophical logic and the philosophy of law—have been largely independent of one another' (Soames 2012, p. 95).

This book brings together leading scholars who are working on the topic of vagueness in philosophy and law. It not only collects essays in the respective fields but also depicts how philosophers conceive of vagueness in law from their theoretical perspective and how legal theorists make use of philosophical theories of vagueness. The contributions aim to strengthen the theoretical bridges between philosophy and law to the benefit of both fields.

There are few fields other than law in which the various aspects of the theoretical discussion on vagueness encounter such a rich number of real-world examples. Almost every socially relevant question that involves drawing a boundary eventually becomes the object of legal adjudication. Law is the bottleneck through which social issues are ultimately pressed. The domain of law is an ideal testing ground for the fruitfulness or even viability of the conceptual distinctions, strategies, and solutions of different theoretical approaches to vagueness. While legal theory and interpretation will probably not yield new solutions to the sorites paradox, they may develop and implement procedures for dealing reasonably with vague language and provide tools to decide hard cases in non-arbitrary ways *without* drawing sharp boundaries.

What, on the other hand, can legal scholars learn from philosophers of language? Not much, some suspect. Stephen Schiffer once wrote that 'philosophical theories of vagueness, even if true, have nothing to offer jurisprudential concerns about vagueness. Once she is reminded of certain platitudes about vagueness, the legal theorist needs no further help from philosophers of language and logic' (Schiffer 2001, p. 421).[1] There are reasons, however, that suggest greater need for collaboration. One reason is that legal theory has, aside from a few recent exceptions (Poscher 2012, Marmor 2014), paid little attention to the differences between the various *kinds* of linguistic indeterminacy that are grouped under the heading of 'vagueness', let alone to the various theories that try to account for these phenomena. Although the challenge that vagueness poses to legal interpretation has long been recognized, few legal scholars are prepared to say exactly what distinguishes soritical vagueness from Waismann's 'open texture', combinatorial vagueness, or ambiguity, and to explain why the differences matter for legal interpretation. Nor are they inclined to examine the intricate philosophical question of how the semantic aspects of vagueness relate to its *metaphysical* aspects, i.e. how vagueness in language relates to continuity phenomena in the world. Timothy Endicott's pioneering monograph *Vagueness in Law* has prepared the ground for a fruitful cooperation between philosophers of language and legal scholars. Much, however, remains to be done.

In sum, law is at once both a rich source of various vagueness phenomena and a highly relevant testing ground for theories of vagueness. Are some theories of vagueness particularly well suited to describing how vagueness is dealt with in the law? Can theories of vagueness suggest solutions to pressing questions that arise from vagueness in law? Will the conceptual distinctions between various kinds of vagueness and linguistic indeterminacy prove useful for clearing up issues in the methodology of legal interpretation?

1. Semantic Vagueness

Vagueness is first and foremost a semantic property of linguistic expressions. Vague terms such as 'heap', 'bald', 'rich', or 'red' draw no sharp boundary between their extension and their anti-extension. They tolerate marginal changes, admit borderline cases, give rise to the paradox of the heap ('sorites paradox'), and thus challenge bivalence, i.e. the view that every sentence or proposition is either true or false. A number of theories of vagueness have been developed in the philosophy of language and logic, the most important ones being supervaluationism, contextualism, many-valued logic and degree theories, epistemic theories, and incoherentist or nihilistic theories.[2] There is a vast literature that discusses the logical, semantic, pragmatic, epistemic, and metaphysical aspects of vagueness. Linguists and philosophers have investigated what distinguishes 'soritical' vagueness from other kinds of linguistic indeterminacy, such as ambiguity, generality, open texture, and family resemblance concepts.

---

[1] Schiffer's position in the current volume shows far more nuance than his 2001 article.
[2] For an overview, see Williamson 1994, Keefe and Smith 1997, Keefe 2000, Sorensen 2001, Graff and Williamson 2002, Shapiro 2006, Ronzitti 2011, Raffman 2014, Hyde 2014, and Sorensen 2016.

Philosophers have also distinguished different *kinds* of vagueness. Kinds of vagueness describe different linguistic phenomena rather than different classes of terms. Many natural language expressions exhibit more than one kind of vagueness. At the heart of the philosophical debate is *vagueness of degree*, also called *soritical* or *quantitative* vagueness. A predicate is soritically vague if its intension draws no sharp line with respect to some gradable property of the object or class of objects to which it is supposed to apply. Soritical vagueness consists in 'the lack of a precise cut-off point along some dimension' (Alston 1964, p. 87). Such predicates are 'semantically tolerant' of marginal changes in the key parameters of their application.[3] Their tolerance, however, is limited to an unspecified range of values, so that quantitatively vague predicates give rise to borderline cases. Colour terms provide classic examples: a ripe tomato is clearly red, a green tomato is clearly not red, but during its ripening a tomato passes through shades of colour that resist clear classification. Needless to say, there is also no sharp line between clear cases of 'red' and borderline cases of 'red'. Soritically vague predicates typically exhibit *higher-order vagueness*: the borderline area has fuzzy boundaries, if any, so that the term 'borderline case' has itself borderline cases.

Vague predicates like 'heap', 'red', or 'bald' can be used to 'prove' by a series of incremental arguments—if 1,000 grains of sand make up a heap, then so do 999 grains, etc.—that a single grain of sand makes up a heap, that a green tomato is red, or that someone with a full head of hair is bald. The sorites paradox can be traced back to the ancient philosopher Eubulides of Miletus, who used the examples 'heap' (Greek: *soros*) and 'bald man'. The problem with soritical reasoning is that the conclusion is patently false, while it is notoriously difficult to pinpoint the fallacy. This is why the problem of the heap is more aptly called a *paradox* than a fallacy: 'Seemingly impeccable reasoning from seemingly impeccable premises yields a patent falsehood' (Raffman 1994, p. 42).

Soritical or quantitative vagueness is distinct from *qualitative* vagueness, also called *combinatorial* vagueness. This second kind of vagueness 'stems from an indeterminacy as to just what combination of conditions is sufficient or necessary for the application of the term' (Alston 1964, pp. 87–8). Classical examples include 'religion', 'game', or 'disease'. For such concepts, we have not fully made up our minds about which properties an object must possess in order to fall under the term or concept. The question of whether Buddhism counts as a religion—in spite of it lacking features that other religions share, such as a belief in god(s)—is not a matter of degree. The indeterminacy stems instead from the number of possible or even established combinations of conditions, and the lack of a set of conditions that are both necessary and jointly sufficient for the correct application of the term 'religion'.

Soritical and combinatorial vagueness often overlap. Standard examples of combinatorial vagueness also exhibit soritical vagueness because conditions can be fulfilled to a greater or lesser degree. Inversely, standard examples of apparently

---

[3] Cf. Wright 1975, p. 335 and Raffman 1994, p. 41.

one-dimensional vague terms actually have more than one dimension: whether or not a collection of grains is a heap depends not only on their number but also on their arrangement. The same holds for baldness (see Weber, ch. 8 this volume). In soritical reasoning, speakers abstract away from these further dimensions but need not deny their existence. Treating a term as solely soritically vague is legitimate in contexts where the other dimensions are held constant.

The term 'multidimensional vagueness' is sometimes used synonymously with 'combinatorial vagueness'. It may be useful, however, to reserve it for a third, more complex phenomenon that can be illustrated by the legal term 'neglect'. This term is multidimensionally vague insofar as (i) there are a number of elements that are potentially relevant for classifying a certain case as neglect; and (ii) at least some of them admit of degrees, such as how long the child was left unattended, in which environment, and how old or mature the child was, to mention only the most obvious elements. Furthermore, (iii) these elements, various combinations of which can constitute neglect, are *incommensurable* because 'no common denominator would allow a quantitative comparison of the various constitutive elements on a single evaluative scale' (Marmor 2014, p. 89).

Multidimensional vagueness is often found in 'essentially contested concepts' in the sense of Gallie (1956). The concept 'democracy' is a case in point. Not only is it unclear what combination of properties must hold for it to be attributable to a state, it is likewise uncertain to what degree certain properties (such as election cycles) have to be fulfilled and how excesses in one dimension can offset deficiencies or even absences in others.

Soritical vagueness, the combinatorial openness of cluster concepts and the incommensurability of constitutive elements are distinct phenomena that concepts can exhibit. They can be kept apart analytically even if they are intertwined in many natural language terms.

2. Semantic Vagueness and 'Vagueness' in the World

The conventional view has it that all vagueness is semantic or representational. However, the omnipresence of vagueness in natural languages prompts the question of whether the semantic phenomenon reflects a corresponding non-linguistic feature of the represented reality. In recent years, a growing minority of philosophers have suggested that there is an 'ontological' or 'metaphysical' kind of vagueness, either in addition to semantic vagueness or in elucidation, or even in replacement of it.[4]

Now the term 'vague' has such heavy semantic connotations that it sounds odd to apply it to non-representational items. Accordingly, it has been held that 'the notion that things might actually *be* vague, as well as being vaguely described, is not properly intelligible' (Dummett 1975, p. 111). The question is whether the linguistic infelicity reflects some deeper mismatch. So let us change the wording: few

---

[4] For an overview, see Keil 2013. The present section draws on this article.

would deny that physical objects can have 'fuzzy', 'blurry', or 'unsharp' boundaries, both spatially and temporally. As soon as we change the wording from 'vague' to 'blurred' and its cognates, the impression of categorial absurdity vanishes.

Many real-world objects and events exhibit a kind of 'seamlessness' that is not an artefact of linguistic representations and classifications. In this volume, the chapters by Schiffer, Raffman, Poscher, Kompa, Katz, and Kolber touch on the issue of natural continuities. For example, *clouds* consist of swarms of water droplets whose density gradually diminishes towards the periphery of the cloud. The robust fact that clouds don't have sharp edges supervenes on the way that matter is distributed in space-time. Imagine, by contrast, a world in which all physical objects have simple geometrical forms and a limited number of further discrete features—sharp edges, hard surfaces, a fixed number of distinct shapes and colours. Imagine a *Lego world*: just Lego bricks and the void. It goes without saying that language would have evolved differently in a Lego world.

At the same time, 'cloud' is a semantically vague predicate. A pivotal question in the debate on 'metaphysical vagueness' is how the vagueness of linguistic expressions and the fuzziness of spatio-temporal boundaries relate to one another. In the dispute between a representational and a metaphysical understanding of vagueness, 'the semantic theorist holds that indeterminacy afflicts not objects themselves but objects as represented; the metaphysical theorist denies precisely this' (Eklund 2013, p. 171). Do semantic vagueness and ontic seamlessness *compete* as explanations for the speaker's uncertainty about what to say? In the literature, claims are frequently made about vagueness being 'due to', holding 'by virtue of', or 'deriving from' some non-semantic source. Semantic theorists have an easy answer to this source question: while a physical object like Mount Everest 'may have fuzzy spatial boundaries (…), [i]t is open to us to identify the ultimate source of Everest's fuzzy boundaries as our vague sortal, *mountain*' (Garrett 1991, p. 350). This sounds like an attractive approach to take: the general term 'mountain' is a *sortal* term, or a *count noun*. Unlike mass nouns such as 'sugar', count nouns allow us to *individuate* and count objects. It is only the sortal character of the predicate 'mountain' that allows us to determine where, in a chain of mountains, the first mountain ends and the next one begins. 'Mountain', however, is a *vague* sortal term, and Everest, so the argument goes, cannot have sharper spatial boundaries than the term 'mountain' allows competent speakers to draw.

Let us rehearse a pivotal difference between sortal and non-sortal ontologies. For Aristotle, '*being an individual* goes with *being of a substantial kind F*' (Furth 1988, p. 205). Aristotelian 'first substances', i.e. concrete particulars, are always of a certain kind: they are *constitutionally offy*, as Austin might have said. For Aristotle, any first substance (*prōtē ousía*) is a well-individuated particular of a certain natural kind, the principle of individuation being included in our mastery of the kind term. By contrast, the basic category in Quine's non-sortal ontology is that of a 'physical object'. A physical object is defined as 'the aggregate material content of any portion of space-time, however ragged and discontinuous' (Quine 1976, p. 497). Physical objects do not come in kinds and hence do not pose problems of classification or individuation. They have crystal-clear identity conditions: physical objects are 'identical if and only if spatiotemporally coextensive' (Quine 1985, p. 167).

The boundaries of physical objects cannot be fuzzy because any set of arbitrarily chosen spatio-temporal coordinates singles out some physical object. Note also that physical objects cannot be counted. The question as to how many physical objects there are in my home office has no answer, pending some sortal classification of the objects. Pencils, books, and atoms are countable, physical objects are not because 'physical object' is not a sortal term.

Regarding the question of whether objects as such can have fuzzy boundaries, we submit that the deep divide is between two competing understandings—or types— of ontology: between a sortal ontology of Aristotelian substances and a non-sortal ontology of Quinean physical objects. As regards vagueness, Quine argues that since the 'liberal notion of physical object spares us the pointless task of demarcating bodies' (Quine 1976, p. 497), the undisputed vagueness of sortal classifications can be kept out of ontology—in Quine's austere sense of 'ontology'. In a non-sortal ontology of unspecified physical objects, demarcation problems do not arise, hence vagueness gains no traction.

The importance of sortality for the debate on vague objects has only recently come into sharper focus. The reason is probably that our broadly Aristotelian common-sense ontology of sortally specified objects is built into the categorial structure of natural languages, while non-sortal ontologies are the constructions of philosophers and physicists.

In our common-sense ontology of mountains and clouds, bald heads, and heaps, vagueness is ubiquitous. This has given rise to the question of what the ultimate source of vagueness is: our representations or the things themselves, the language or the world? We wonder, however, whether the source question has a clear meaning, let alone a clear answer. The best one can say is that the relationship between semantic vagueness and ontic seamlessness is dialectical, because natural languages did not evolve in a Lego-world. An analogy might be helpful to illustrate the dialectics at work. Think of language as a tool: sugar tongs are perfect tools for gripping sugar cubes. But if you try and fail to grip powdered sugar with sugar tongs, then who is to blame, the sugar or the tongs?

3. Semantic and Communicative Vagueness

Vagueness also has conversational and pragmatic aspects. Above we stated that vagueness is a semantic property of linguistic expressions. This is true for the technical use of the term by philosophers of language, but it does not capture all ordinary uses. In ordinary language, the word 'vague' is often used dismissively. Vague hints, vague promises, or vague announcements are airy and nebulous, in the sense that the speaker is deliberately evasive or less specific than contextually appropriate. By speaking vaguely, intentions can be hidden and information withheld.[5]

---

[5] Cf. Soames 2012, pp. 95–6: 'In ordinary life, a remark is often considered vague if the information it provides is insufficiently specific to advance the accepted conversational purpose (especially when the speaker is expected to possess that information).'

Marmor calls this pragmatic kind of vagueness, i.e. this lack of informativity in a given context, 'conversational vagueness'. He makes it clear that semantic and conversational vagueness are independent of one another: 'Just as an expression can be conversationally vague in a given context without using vague terms, an expression can be precise even when it uses a vague term applied to a borderline case' (Marmor 2014, p. 91).

It seems more apt to say that, in such cases, being vague is not a property of the linguistic expression in the first place but rather qualifies *what the speakers does* with his words. At least it is more instructive to draw the distinction that way. Plausibly, a word and a speaker's conduct cannot both be vague in exactly the same sense of the term. We submit that in cases of conversational or communicative vagueness the term is used *adverbially* rather than adjectively. When a person is described as *speaking vaguely*, the adverb is used to qualify the speaker's communicative behaviour, which can be assessed quite independently of the semantic properties of the words she uses. Joan Baez' bittersweet memory, 'You were so good with words and at keeping things vague' (*Diamonds and Rust*, 1975), is a comment on Bob Dylan's linguistic behaviour rather than on the expressions he used. Communicative vagueness is a form of deliberate underspecification.

Semantic vagueness and communicative underspecification are distinct but related phenomena. *Intentionalist* accounts of vagueness try to *explain* semantic vagueness with recourse to speakers' communicative intentions.[6] Intentionalism is a reductive form of a *pragmatic* approach to vagueness. Generally, pragmatic approaches argue that a number of properties that semantic theories attribute to linguistic expressions are misattributed and need to be taken with a pinch of salt. Consider 'providing information' and 'drawing boundaries': Marmor says that 'expressions can be vague in the information they provide' (Marmor 2014, p. 90), but it is doubtful whether providing information is an expression's job in the first place. Pragmatic approaches argue that providing or withholding information is something that speakers do and is only derivatively attributable to the linguistic means they use.[7] Again, vague predicates, semantic theories say, fail to draw sharp boundaries. Is drawing boundaries a predicate's job in the first place, rather than something that speakers do, or fail to do, when they use predicates to classify cases? Wittgenstein, who held that meaning supervenes on use, took such a pragmatic perspective on vagueness. In his famous remarks on the combinatorial vagueness of the concept of 'game', he insists that drawing boundaries is first and foremost a human activity: 'What still counts as a game and what no longer does? Can you give the boundary? No. You can draw one; for none has so far been drawn. (…) To repeat, we can draw a boundary—for a special purpose' (Wittgenstein 1953/2001, §§ 68, 69).

---

[6] Cf. Poscher, ch. 3 this volume.

[7] In other places, Marmor attributes the activity of 'conveying information' to speakers: 'Speakers can use a vague term, even if applied to a semantically borderline case, to convey information that is precise enough in the specific context of the conversation' (Marmor 2014, p. 93).

Conversations unfold between speakers and their addressees. While Wittgensteinian conventionalists hold that meaning is or supervenes on rule-governed use, Donald Davidson argues that 'the notion of meaning depends entirely upon successful cases of communication. That is, where a person intends to be interpreted in a certain way and is' (Davidson and Glüer 1995, p. 81). Speakers who intend to be understood must take their addressees' presumed hermeneutic resources into account. Still, good intentions leave ample room for getting one's wires crossed. For example, listeners may have difficulties grasping the content that the speaker intended to convey because some element of the contextual background of the utterance is not shared.[8] In law, such interpretative challenges are of great practical import because of the considerable gap between the context of legislation and the addressees' knowledge of it. Even for legal experts, it can be impossible to reconstruct the intentions of the legislator—not only because of the paucity of legislative materials, but also because of the sometimes historically removed circumstances of legislation. Even if precise intentions could be revealed by legal experts through extensive contextual research, the interpretative challenges raise the normative question of whether legislative intentions that are hidden from the layman's eye should be relevant for the determination of legal content. Giving the law content that does not reveal itself to its addressees seems to contradict not only the law's aspiration to be public but also its central function of guiding people's behaviour.

When exploring the potential virtues and vices of vagueness in law, we must keep the difference between semantic and conversational aspects in mind: is the respective indeterminacy or underspecification a semantic property of linguistic expressions or is it a feature of a speaker's—for example, the legislator's—communicative behaviour? Or is it perhaps even due to poor interaction or communicative barriers between speakers and addressees?

4. Vagueness in Law: Vice or Virtue?

Vague expressions are omnipresent in natural language and their use in legal texts is virtually inevitable. Hence, the law has to live with at least a certain amount of vagueness. Given that vagueness is an undeniable trait of natural language and its legal expansion, it is advisable to distinguish the *phenomenon* of vagueness from the particular *challenges* that it poses to jurisdiction, legislation, and the rule of law.

If a law is phrased in vague terms, the question of whether it applies to a particular case often lacks a determinate answer. When does a punishment become 'cruel and unusual', when does a person exercise 'reasonable care', what behaviour

---

[8] Cf. Marmor, ch. 6 this volume.

qualifies as 'neglect', what bail is 'excessive'? Legal rules also contain words that are less obviously vague:

> Consider, for example, a term like 'entering' the premises, which forms part of the definition of burglary. Suppose that the defendant broke the window and had his arm through the boundary of the premises in question: did he enter the building? And what if only his finger got through? Or only some instrument he was using to break the window?
>
> (Marmor 2014, p. 87)

Vagueness challenges legal analogues to the principle of bivalence, i.e. the principles that legal rules are either valid or invalid, that actions are either legal or illegal, that the elements of a crime are present or not, legal interpretations correct or false, defendants guilty or innocent, judicial decisions right or wrong. In law, the challenge is even more serious than in most ordinary conversational contexts because bivalence is not optional. Judges have to deliver a decision even in cases in which the law is vague. Vagueness and other kinds of legal indeterminacy pose a serious threat to the very legitimacy of the law's all-or-nothing practice. Given the omnipresence of vagueness, is there any rational justification for juridical bivalence apart from taking it as a merely technical device to avoid a denial of justice? In philosophical theories of vagueness, however, it is a matter of controversy whether vagueness forces us to abandon bivalence. How much does the significance of juridical bivalence depend on which theoretical approach to vagueness is chosen? Bivalence is but one example of how competing philosophical and linguistic accounts of vagueness may influence the ways we deal with vague legislative language.

H.L.A. Hart captured a widespread attitude towards vagueness in law when he stated that 'uncertainty at the borderline is the price to be paid for the use of general classifying terms' (Hart 1961/2012, p. 128). His remark related to Friedrich Waismann's idea of the 'open texture' of language, but it applies to soritical and combinatorial vagueness as well. Vagueness in all of its kinds is a pervasive aspect of law, but it is also inimical to some of the law's core values. One of the fundamental pillars of the rule of law is legal certainty. The determinacy of written law facilitates jurisdiction, makes the law predictable, and enables people to use it as a guide. In a stylized account, the legislature is supposed to make laws and the courts are supposed to apply and enforce them. If the law is vague and thus indeterminate, how should the courts decide on borderline cases without slipping into the role of the legislature?[9] Vagueness, irrespective of its sources, poses a threat to legal and political ideals: not only to legal certainty and predictability but also to the separation of powers. In borderline cases, the law seems to be indeterminate and thus incapable of upholding its core rule-of-law values. It seems the law would have to avoid vagueness at all costs. The 'void-for-vagueness' doctrine in American constitutional law even invalidates legal norms that are too vague. Vagueness seems to decrease the rule of law and to increase the rule of men.

---

[9] Cf. Solan, ch. 10 this volume, and Bix, ch. 11 this volume.

On the other hand, a number of legal theorists have highlighted the *value* of vagueness in law with respect to the ideal of justice: vague legislative language gives judges discretion, which they can use to do justice to the peculiarities of the case (Endicott 2011). The flip side is that judges can use their discretion for other purposes as well, for example for the kind of interpretative hubris that Jeremy Bentham polemicized against: '[W]hen the judge dares to arrogate to himself the power of interpreting the laws, that is to say, of substituting his will for that of the legislator, every thing is arbitrary—no one can foresee the course which his caprice may take' (Bentham 1843/1962, p. 325). Roy Sorensen even surmises that vagueness makes judges lie in order to hide their powers (ch. 14 in this volume). The dilemma is obvious. Vaguely worded regulations leave room for interpretation, allocate power to the courts, and allow judges to consider individual circumstances. The exercise of discretion is an integral part of the court's role, but any discretion can be used capriciously. So, how much and which kind of discretion is too much? What exactly is the value of vagueness for law, and when does vagueness become detrimental to the rule of law?

Another strand in the debate on the value of vagueness in law concerns the effects on the primary *addressees* of the law. Jeremy Waldron sees an ethical value in vagueness in that it engages the citizens to whom the law is addressed as thoughtful and responsible subjects. Whereas determinate laws simply requires the obedience of its addressees, vague or otherwise underspecified laws engage them as moral agents. Such laws demand that they exercise their own judgement in precisifying a vague standard in a given situation and taking responsibility for their choice. In republican terms, vague laws seem to engage them as citizens rather than as mere subjects of the law.[10]

In discussions about the potential value of vagueness in law, it has not always been clear whether the values associated with vagueness are really merits of vagueness as opposed to merits of other features of language, such as generality, multidimensionality, open texture, or context sensitivity. Sorensen, for example, argues that some values that are credited to vagueness are actually functions of *generality*. General terms that cover many things with a single word are highly useful in law because they are open-ended and allow for projection to other cases. No long disjunctive list of specific entries could do the same work that the terms 'torture' or 'vehicle' do (Sorensen 2001, pp. 406–7). But terms can be general without being vague. 'Prime number', for example, is general but not vague. It remains an open question whether or not the alleged value of vagueness is misattributed,[11] so that vagueness in law is 'a price to be paid' (Hart 1961/2012, p. 128) rather than a virtue. The debate on the value of vagueness is further complicated by the fact that vagueness itself is a vague notion. Some of the attributional differences might be due to lack of clarity about whether multidimensionality, open texture, or context sensitivity are just aspects of vagueness or are distinct from vagueness proper.

---

[10] Cf. Waldron 2011 as well as his contribution to this volume, ch. 15.
[11] Cf. Kompa, ch. 9 this volume.

5. Vagueness and Arbitrariness

Let us take a closer look at the flip side of judicial discretion, i.e. the arbitrariness of judges. Although there are many kinds of arbitrariness, their common denominator is plausibly that '[a]rbitrariness is a lack of reason' (Endicott 2014, p. 49). Stated more precisely: 'An arbitrary decision in general is one that is not distinguished, by reasons in favour of it, from an unreasoned choice. In the special sense in which arbitrariness is a departure from the rule of law, a decision is arbitrary whenever the law itself ought to demand a justification other than the fact that the decision maker made it, and there is no such justification' (ibid., p. 70). Arbitrary decisions constitute a departure from the rule of law because they violate the principle that reasons must be given.

A more specific form of arbitrariness is to violate *the principle of equal treatment* without adequate reason. Equality requires that like cases be treated alike and unlike cases differently. When lawgivers or courts infringe upon the principle of equal treatment without adequate reason, they also violate, by the same token, the principle that prohibits arbitrary action on the part of the state.

Now the phenomenon of soritical vagueness points to a persistent tension that is associated with a conflict of aims and that arises with the need to avoid both kinds of arbitrariness. Let us explain. The weak spot of the principle of equal treatment is that, for some features of real-world cases, exact likeness in the legally relevant respect is rare or virtually impossible. In order to be applicable in such cases, the rule to treat like cases alike must be interpreted less strictly. What it reasonably demands is that cases that are *sufficiently similar* in relevant respects be treated alike. Similarity, however, is a matter of degree, and similar cases can be arranged in a sorites series.[12] Technically speaking, similarity is not a transitive relation: Tiny differences can 'add up' to vast ones, even if the cases are perceptually indiscriminable when presented pairwise.[13] Still, courts are forced to decide. If they stipulate an arbitrary cut-off point in order so settle the case, they violate the principle that reasons must be given.

Applying the rule of equal treatment to sequences of incrementally similar cases amounts to soritical reasoning and hence yields absurd results. Here are two legal examples illustrating this point:[14]

(a) The first is Endicott's case of the million raves (discussed by Raffman in ch. 2, this volume):

The Criminal Justice and Public Order Act empowers the police to direct organizers of 'raves' to shut down their sound equipment [if] 'amplified music is played during the night

---

[12] See Jónsson 2009, pp. 194–5, for the view that the principle of treating like cases alike invites the arrangement of similar cases in sorites series.

[13] The literature on the sorites paradox has taught us about 'the nontransitivity of marginal difference: a series of insignificant differences "add up" to a significant one' (Raffman 1994, p. 42).

[14] A third pertinent case is German jurisdiction on *coercion* as prohibited by the German Criminal Code (StGB § 240). Von Savigny 1991 has adduced an historical series of High Court decisions, stretching from 1880 to 1984, that gradually extended, via soritical reasoning, the definitional elements of 'violence' and 'the use of force' to finally include a peaceful sit-in that blocked the street.

[and] is likely to cause serious distress to the inhabitants of the locality'. [It is] easy to imagine clear cases of a 'rave' as defined in the Act. It seems that there will also be borderline cases, chiefly because of the vagueness of 'serious distress'. Somewhere between the silent and the seismic, there is music to which the police power is not clearly applicable, and not clearly inapplicable.

Imagine one million rave organizers charged with disobeying a police order to shut down their music. All appear in the same court one after the other. The first defendant [played music] at a deafening volume, and he is convicted. [...] [E]ach successive rave organizer played the music at an imperceptibly lower volume—until the one millionth rave organizer played it at a hush that undeniably caused no distress to anyone. He will be acquitted. But if the decrement in volume in each case is trivial, it seems that no particular conviction ought to be the last. [...] Finding the organizer guilty in one case and not in the next case seems arbitrary.

(Endicott 2000, pp. 57–8)

Note that the predicament also holds for Dworkins' ideal judge Hercules (Dworkin 1986, p. 239) who knows all relevant facts, has superhuman intellectual powers, and grasps all questions of legal interpretation in their complexity:

I propose that the case of the million raves would cause a crisis, in which Hercules would have to make decisions that he cannot justify in principle. [...] Why should an imperceptible difference in volume make a polar difference to the legal outcome?

(Endicott 2000, pp. 161–2)

Note further that the soriticality of the series reduces ad absurdum the principle that like or infinitesimally similar cases must be treated alike:

Not only must any particular stopping place in a sorites series be arbitrary, but because the tolerance of vague predicates appears to lead to paradox, it seems impossible for Hercules to observe the fundamental tenet that like cases should be treated alike. On pain of absurdity, for example of convicting all of the rave organizers, he must stop applying the predicate 'serious distress' at some point before the end of the series. In so doing, he must install a sharp boundary.

(Raffman, this volume, p. 59)

Note, thirdly, that by choosing some arbitrary stopping-place, Hercules violates the principle that reasons must be given. He adjudicates arbitrarily in the sense of not being able to ground his decision on any reason inherent to the case:

A court should be able to justify its decisions, and how can a trivial change in the music justify the difference between conviction and acquittal? If like cases should be treated alike, then the legal treatment of two cases should not be materially different when there is no material difference between them.

(Endicott 2000, p. 58)

(b) A second case in point is the IQ score threshold for death-row offenders in the United States. In *Atkins v. Virginia*,[15] the U.S. Supreme Court ruled that executing

---

[15] *Atkins v. Virginia*, 536 U.S. 304 (2002).

individuals with intellectual disabilities (then known as 'mental retardation') violates the Eight Amendment of the U.S. Constitution that forbids cruel and unusual punishment. The court, however, did not give a definition of when someone counts as being intellectually disabled, leaving it to the individual states to establish their own criteria, provided that they generally conform to accepted clinical definitions. A number of states, including Virginia and Florida, set a bright-line threshold requirement for determining intellectual disability: an IQ of 70 or below makes a person ineligible for the death penalty, whereas persons with an IQ of 71 can be sent to death row.

Cases such as Atkins provide an extreme example of the disturbing consequences of drawing a line in a continuum, even if we set aside the controversies over the reliability and validity of IQ tests. Mental abilities are gradable properties, 'mental retardation' is a soritically vague notion, and a difference of one point on the IQ scale is negligibly small and invites soritical reasoning. (We'll spare our readers the thought experiment of lining up a million intellectually disabled death-row inmates in a sorites series.) Virginia and Florida turned a blind eye to all these worries, ignored vagueness, and attached binary consequences to the IQ cut-off score. In Atkins cases, the question of where to draw the line in a continuum has turned into a matter of life and death. It comes as no surprise that executing a person who just barely misses the stipulated, arbitrarily precise threshold of a highly contentious criterion was regarded as unconstitutional by the U.S. Supreme Court.[16]

To sum up: the principle that reasons must be given forbids the stipulation of arbitrary boundaries. In borderline cases, however, no resources for making a reason-based decision seem to be available, not even for Hercules. How should judges react in this situation? What is the lesson to be drawn from Hercules' predicament? Do theories of legal interpretation and adjudication dispose of additional resources? Can philosophical theories of vagueness help?

The authors of this book take different stances on these questions. Diana Raffman does not even share Endicott's diagnosis that Hercules' predicament is due to the quantitative vagueness of terms like 'serious distress': 'The problem of having to draw arbitrary boundaries between like cases owes not to the vagueness of the legal language, but to the law's inability to make use of that vagueness' (p. 61). While ordinary speakers do not need to draw boundaries between incrementally different cases thanks to vague predicates that license them to go either way, courts 'are trapped in the predicament Endicott describes' because they need stable decisions (p. 62). Roy Sorensen holds that while ordinary speakers can suspend judgement in the face of vagueness, judges are cornered into prevarication, or even lying. Adam Kolber takes a different perspective, advising legislatures to 'smooth out' the law by introducing more fine-grained regulations and linking them to gradual changes in output. Leo Katz and Ralf Poscher insist on the inevitability of arbitrary decisions with respect to the substance of at least some legal issues. However, this does not imply that Hercules must have reached his wit's end.

---

[16] See *Hall v. Florida*, 134 S. Ct. 1986 (2014).

Even if an arbitrary decision with respect to the substance of the issues has to be taken, there might be good second-order reasons for embracing arbitrarily drawn sharp boundaries, like delivering legal peace in the case at hand and legal certainty for those to come.

6. Guide to Contents

The chapters are organized into three parts. The first part of the book addresses the import of different theories of vagueness for the law. As far as philosophers have engaged with the law in the past, their first impressions were sometimes sceptical. A case in point is Stephen Schiffer's assessment, quoted above, that 'the legal theorist needs no further help from philosophers of language and logic' (Schiffer 2001, p. 421). In the present volume, Schiffer arrives at a more nuanced assessment. His and the other chapters in the first part refer to a wide range of approaches, from supervaluationism to contextualism, degree-theoretic accounts, intentionalism, and epistemicism, and explore the fundamental question of whether the law can learn anything from engaging with the various theories of vagueness.

Stephen Schiffer addresses the question head-on. Jurisprudential issues of vagueness tend to be broadly normative, whereas philosophical issues are not. So why expect philosophical theories of vagueness to be relevant to issues of vagueness in law? On closer inspection, a number of implications can be identified. Schiffer shows that vagueness has some profound effects on meaning that bear on judicial interpretation. In particular, he argues that an adequate semantics that accommodates the features of 'penumbral shift' and 'penumbral ignorance' reveals flaws of originalism with respect to constitutional law and of textualism in law in general.

Diana Raffman exposes a predicament that jurisdiction finds itself in when adjudicating borderline cases. Vagueness of language is commonly supposed to be a source of difficulty for the law insofar as it is a source of indeterminacy, and indeterminacy results in borderline or 'hard' cases. Raffman argues that in legal cases where soritical vagueness is present, specifically where the court appears obliged to draw arbitrary boundaries between cases that are only incrementally different, the difficulty derives not from the vagueness of the language in which the law is expressed, but rather from the relationship between the law and the continuous, seamless character of the phenomena—properties, actions, states of affairs, etc.—to which it must apply. Raffman argues that soritical vagueness precisely provides the resources to *avoid* drawing sharp boundaries in a continuous environment, because it allows speakers to go either way. The law, however, since it demands 'sharp' decisions, cannot make use of those resources. Only ordinary speakers can make use of them, and so the legal difficulties remain.

Ralf Poscher takes a look at vagueness and law from an intentionalist perspective. If meaning ultimately resides in the intentions of speakers, vagueness must have its origin in these intentions. This intentionalist account resonates with a rising interest in intentionalism in legal theory, where it figures prominently in the debate about legislative intent. The chapter tries to broaden this interest by applying intentionalism to the specific—but for legal methodology central—phenomenon of vagueness. After laying out the general structure of an intentionalist reconstruction of vagueness, the chapter sketches its consequences for the different aspects of the vagueness discussion such as the sorites paradoxes, higher-order vagueness, or the relationship between truth and vagueness. The law is especially apt to illustrate the values of vagueness, which are reflected in the institutional framework of the legal system.

Hrafn Asgeirsson turns the tables on the relationship between theories of vagueness and the law. Instead of asking what the law can learn from philosophical conceptions of vagueness, he wonders whether legal practice could adjudicate between theories of vagueness. He refers to Scott Soames, who has recently argued that the fact that lawmakers and other legal practitioners regard vagueness as having a valuable power-delegating function gives us good reason to favour one theory of vagueness over another. If Soames is right, then facts about legal practice can, in an important sense, adjudicate between rival theories of vagueness. Asgeirsson argues that due to what he calls the 'Gappiness Problem'—raised by recent critics of the 'communicative-content theory of law'—we have to give up the one premise of Soames' argument that he seems to take to be uncontroversial: that the legal content of a statute or constitutional clause is identical with, or constituted by, its communicative content. He provides a sketch of his own account of legal content and shows how it provides a response to the Gappiness Problem. This account, however, does not suffice to vindicate Soames' argument—a point he deems generalizable.

Michael S. Moore defends a realist semantics for the law that largely rules out semantic vagueness on the basis of the law's objectivity. The objectivity thesis says that singular propositions of law, which are decisive of particular cases, have determinative, mind-independent truth-values. Objectivity thus understood rules out ontological and semantic but not epistemic vagueness. Strong versions of the objectivity thesis hold that there is an answer to even the hardest of hard cases, difficult though it may be to ascertain what that answer is. Moore deems the strong objectivity thesis plausible on a 'realist' semantic theory that draws on Putnam's insights about how natural kind terms refer. Such a realist semantics minimizes indeterminacy and allows for meaningful (albeit radical) disagreements between speakers. These two general advantages are translated into comparable advantages for such semantics if used in law. Finally, Moore applies the realist semantics to law itself and defends the possibility and desirability of legal theory about law (and not just the law itself) being objective.

The chapters in the second part of the book address various kinds of vagueness and how vagueness relates to other phenomena such as context sensitivity. In law, the concept of vagueness is often employed somewhat loosely in the sense of general indeterminacy, and different kinds of vagueness are not distinguished from one another. All the contributions in the second section make the case that it is worthwhile for the law to be more precise about the notion of vagueness, its subspecies, and their relation to cognate linguistic phenomena. The authors suggest that greater awareness of the varieties of vagueness and indeterminacy phenomena can make lawyers aware either of specific issues that they have heretofore overlooked or of specific solutions and their benefits and costs.

Andrei Marmor develops the idea that conversational (or pragmatic) vagueness is distinct from semantic vagueness and largely independent of it. An expression is conversationally vague when its contribution to the particular conversation in question is not entirely clear, mostly due to a borderline application of the expression's relevance to its context. Contrariwise, an expression can be precise in the context of a conversation even if it employs a borderline application of a semantically vague term. In the first part of the chapter Marmor explains these distinctions and their theoretical foundations. He shows that conversational vagueness is prevalent in law, where legal context often makes semantically precise expressions conversationally vague in the context of their legal application. He insists that conversational vagueness leads to legal indeterminacy even if everything about the pragmatic context of legislation were known.

Frederick Schauer discusses a vagueness phenomenon that is seldom dealt with: second-order vagueness, not to be confused with higher-order vagueness. Most of the philosophical literature on vagueness starts with the identification of the term whose vagueness is at issue—'tall', 'short', 'bald', 'tadpole', etc. But in legal interpretation, an additional problem arises because it is not always obvious which term in a legal text, or even which legal text, is the operative one. Hart's idea of a rule of recognition conceptualizes the way in which some second-order rule is necessary to identify which first-order rule is applicable to some form of conduct, but it is often the case that the second-order rule itself exhibits various forms of vagueness. When that is so, vagueness appears as a distinct problem with important but often unrecognized implications for the law.

Marc Andree Weber turns his attention to legal definitions. He argues, perhaps surprisingly, that only scientific or artificial expressions can be soritically vague (in his technical sense of 'soritical vagueness'), whereas the vagueness of natural language expressions is always of the combinatorial kind. A non-trivial consequence of this is that legal definitions that precisify natural language concepts not only add aspects of meaning to existing expressions but also effectively change the meanings of these expressions. As for the law, Weber suggests that we should avoid precisifying ordinary concepts with the help of legal definitions to the extent that we wish legal language to be in line with natural language. Aligning legal with natural language, he further argues, allows us to deal with gaps and loopholes in our laws at the very moment we become aware of them, reducing the need for post facto legislative repairs.

Nikola Kompa concentrates on a different distinction: the one between vagueness and context sensitivity. Most, if not all, general terms of natural languages are vague. Vague terms are commonly characterized by their failure to draw—sharp—boundaries. Consequently, any boundary drawn is bound to be arbitrary. Yet legal practice ought to comply with a principle of non-arbitrariness. Kompa argues that although vagueness introduces arbitrariness, this does not pose a problem for legal interpretation. What proves to be challenging, but perhaps also valuable, is the context sensitivity of linguistic interpretation in general. Kompa first puts forth a criterion for distinguishing vagueness from context sensitivity, and then addresses the question of how and to what extent context sensitivity affects legal interpretation. Yet, since vagueness remains even if all context sensitivity has been accounted for, she also suggests how one might legitimately draw a boundary despite vagueness.

The third part of the book takes on the pragmatic aspects of vagueness in law. The chapters give different answers to the question of how to deal with vagueness in law and with the professional, political, moral, and ethical issues it gives rise to. Some authors highlight the inevitability of a certain degree of legal arbitrariness that vague legislative language induces. They also point to the moral and political implications of legal indeterminacy. Other contributions show ways to either accommodate vagueness in law or to bring its potentially positive effects into focus. Vagueness is even regarded as a catalyst for engaging the addressees of the law in practical and moral deliberation.

Lawrence M. Solan addresses concerns about the excessive exercise of judicial discretion. Legal theorists and judges have attempted to develop methods for dealing with vague laws that will bring uniformity to legal analysis. He discusses competing approaches to the resolution of vagueness, several of which were proposed by the late Justice Antonin Scalia of the U.S. Supreme Court. They include defaulting to the ordinary meaning, relying on coherence, whether as an independent value or as a proxy for what the legislature intended, and resorting to the law's purpose. Each of these approaches has its merits. However, Solan argues, each is most appropriate in different situations, and no theory has been developed that can distinguish between situations. Without such a theory, he concludes, we will have to live with uncertainty in the resolution of vague laws as a cost of attempting to govern ourselves through a close linguistic reading of enacted laws.

Brian H. Bix looks at the role of vagueness and other forms of indeterminacy within a larger context of legal reasoning and decision making, emphasizing in particular the way that legal actors on occasion ignore or override semantic meaning in their interpretation and application of (vague, ambiguous, or semantically certain) terms in legal texts. When legal academics focus on theories of meaning and reference, they too often overemphasize the importance of these topics, as well as the ability of better knowledge about them to resolve all difficulties in legal interpretation. Bix points to the authority of judges, and perhaps also their moral, political, or legal duty to apply the law in ways that may diverge from the meaning, or meanings, of the legal texts considered on their own. He highlights that meaning and reference are important to law and legal reasoning, as are political and moral choice.

Leo Katz seeks to identify one of the root causes of non-epistemic uncertainty and explains why the law produces discontinuities that cannot be eliminated by more scalar regulations. He argues that many moral structures are inherently discontinuous. At the same time, the particular way in which these moral structures map onto the real world is loose and not strictly determinate. This results in bright-line rules whose discontinuous character is morally required, although the locations of its continuities are not required to be in any particular place. To make this more concrete, Katz considers Tversky and Kahneman's famous prospect theory. The discontinuous treatment of gains and losses is arguably morally required, but the location of the inflection point is notoriously indeterminate. This produces a discontinuity that cannot be eliminated by making relevant legal and moral categories more scalar.

Adam Kolber takes the opposite view, arguing that the deleterious effects of legal vagueness can be reduced by making the law less all-or-nothing. Many laws draw a sharp distinction along a spectrum. For example, the reasonableness of defensive force can vary, but courts focus on whether a defendant was sufficiently reasonable rather than on how reasonable he was. Such line drawing can have harsh effects. These effects can be ameliorated by 'smoothing' the law so that the consequences of a violation depend not on crossing some sharp boundary but on a feature that varies along a spectrum. Kolber challenges Katz's view that attempts to make the law less all-or-nothing are doomed to fail. He argues that it is not only possible but also often desirable to smooth the law. While there are costs that must be weighed against the benefits, he advocates looking for good opportunities to make the law smoother than it is now.

For *Roy Sorensen* there is no way of ensuring integrity when dealing with vagueness in law. His chapter is a sequel to his seminal 2001 paper *Vagueness Has No Function in Law*, where he argued that borderline cases necessitate judicial insincerity. Truth tellers, Sorensen holds, cope with the uncertainties associated with vagueness by suspending judgement or by hedging. Judges forswear these options. They vow to provide verdicts that are specific, decisive, and timely. Having renounced key alternatives to lying, judges are often cornered into prevarication. The deception is justified by the need to settle conflicts—the correctness of the settlement being only of secondary importance. Accordingly, verdicts are wrapped in the protective majesty of the law. As a side effect, judges receive no praise for their willingness to dirty their hands. Sorensen describes two sources of judicial prevarication corresponding to the two senses of 'vague'—soritical vagueness and underspecifity. The performative aspect of verdicts provides a means of unifying the sources.

Even if vagueness poses an ethical dilemma for judges, *Jeremy Waldron* argues that this dilemma can be balanced by a virtue that unspecific regulations have with regard to the *addressees* of the law. One form of indeterminacy that is commonly called 'vagueness' stems from the use of value predicates like 'reasonable' and 'excessive'. A case can be made that the use of such vague value predicates represents a distinctive way of guiding action—a mode of guiding action that may be more respectful of intelligent agency than the use of more determinate predicates in legal rules. Terms like 'reasonable' help to encourage thoughtfulness and reflection on the part of those who are called upon to apply the law. On the other hand, it may be difficult to align or coordinate the self-application of such norms with their secondary application by law enforcement officials and judges. They work best where there is substantial reason to expect such alignment, worst where there is good reason not to.

References

Alston, William P. 1964. *Philosophy of Language*. Englewood Cliffs (NJ): Prentice-Hall.

Bentham, Jeremy. 1843/1962. 'Principles of the Civil Code'. In *The Works of Jeremy Bentham*, Vol. 1, edited by John Bowring, 297–364. New York: Russell & Russell.

Davidson, Donald and Kathrin Glüer. 1995. 'Relations and Transitions—An Interview with Donald Davidson'. *Dialectica* 49(1): 75–86.

Dummett, Michael. 1975. 'Wang's Paradox'. *Synthese* 30(3–4): 301–24. Reprinted in and quoted from *Vagueness: A Reader*, edited by Rosanna Keefe and Peter Smith, 99–118. Cambridge (MA): MIT Press.

Dworkin, Ronald M. 1986. *Law's Empire*. Oxford: Hart Publishing.

Eklund, Matti. 2013. 'Metaphysical Vagueness and Metaphysical Indeterminacy'. *Metaphysica* 14(2): 165–79.

Endicott, Timothy. 2000. *Vagueness in Law*. Oxford: Oxford University Press.

Endicott, Timothy. 2011 [first published in 2005]. 'The Value of Vagueness'. In *Philosophical Foundations of Language in the Law*, edited by Andrei Marmor and Scott Soames, 14–30. Oxford: Oxford University Press.

Endicott, Timothy. 2014. 'Arbitrariness'. *Canadian Journal of Law and Jurisprudence* 27(1): 49–71.

Furth, Montgomery. 1988. *Substance, Form and Psyche: An Aristotelian Metaphysics*. Cambridge: Cambridge University Press.

Gallie, Walter B. 1956. 'Essentially Contested Concepts'. *Proceedings of the Aristotelian Society* 56: 167–98.

Garrett, Brian. 1991. 'Vague Identity and Vague Objects'. *Noûs* 25(3): 341–51.

Graff, Delia and Timothy Williamson (eds). 2002. *Vagueness*. Aldershot: Ashgate.

Hart, H.L.A. 1961/2012. *The Concept of Law*, 3rd edn. Oxford: Oxford University Press.

Hyde, Dominic. 2014. 'Sorites Paradox'. In *The Stanford Encyclopedia of Philosophy (Winter 2014 Edition)*, edited by Edward N. Zalta. Available at: <http://plato.stanford.edu/archives/win2014/entries/sorites-paradox/>.

Jónsson, Ólafur P. 2009. 'Vagueness, Interpretation, and the Law'. *Legal Theory* 15(3): 193–214.

Keefe, Rosanna. 2000. *Theories of Vagueness*. Cambridge: Cambridge University Press.

Keefe, Rosanna and Peter Smith (eds). 1997. *Vagueness: A Reader*. Cambridge (MA): MIT Press.

Keil, Geert. 2013. 'Vagueness and Ontology'. *Metaphysica* 14(2): 149–64.

Keil, Geert, Lara Keuck, and Rico Hauswald (eds). 2016. *Vagueness in Psychiatry*. Oxford: Oxford University Press.

Marmor, Andrei. 2014. 'Varieties of Vagueness in the Law'. In *The Language of Law*, 85–106. Oxford: Oxford University Press.

Poscher, Ralf. 2012. 'Ambiguity and Vagueness in Legal Interpretation'. In *The Oxford Handbook of Language and Law*, edited by Lawrence Solan and Peter Tiersma, 128–44. Oxford: Oxford University Press.

Quine, W.V.O. 1976. 'Whither Physical Objects?' In *Essays in Memory of Imre Lakatos*, edited by Robert S. Cohen, Paul K. Feyerabend, and Marx W. Wartofsky, 497–504. Dordrecht: Springer.

Quine, W.V.O. 1985. 'Events and Reification'. In *Actions and Events: Perspectives on the Philosophy of Donald Davidson*, edited by Ernest LePore and Brian McLaughlin, 162–71. Oxford: Blackwell.

Raffman, Diana. 1994. 'Vagueness Without Paradox'. *The Philosophical Review* 103(1): 41–74.

Raffman, Diana. 2014. *Unruly Words. A Study of Vague Language*. New York: Oxford University Press.

Ronzitti, Giuseppina (ed.). 2011. *Vagueness: A Guide*. Dordrecht: Springer.

Schiffer, Stephen. 2001. 'A Little Help From Your Friends?' *Legal Theory* 7(4): 421–31.

Shapiro, Stewart. 2006. *Vagueness in Context*. Oxford: Oxford University Press.

Soames, Scott. 2012. 'Vagueness and the Law'. In *The Routledge Companion to Philosophy of Law*, edited by Andrei Marmor, 95–108. New York: Routledge.

Sorensen, Roy. 2001. 'Vagueness Has No Function in Law'. *Legal Theory* 7(4): 385–415.

Sorensen, Roy. 2016. 'Vagueness'. In *The Stanford Encyclopedia of Philosophy (Winter 2013 Edition)*, edited by Edward N. Zalta. Available at: <http://plato.stanford.edu/archives/spr2016/entries/vagueness/>.

von Savigny, Eike. 1991. 'Passive Disobedience as Violence: Reflections on German High Court Decisions'. In *Justice, Law, and Violence*, edited by James B. Brady and Newton Garver, 53–64. Philadelphia (IL): Temple University Press.

Waldron, Jeremy. 2011. 'Vagueness and the Guidance of Action'. In *Philosophical Foundations of Language in the Law*, edited by Andrei Marmor and Scott Soames, 58–82. Oxford: Oxford University Press.

Williamson, Timothy. 1994. *Vagueness*. London: Routledge.

Wittgenstein, Ludwig. 1953/2001. *Philosophical Investigations*. Translated by G.E.M. Anscombe. Oxford: Basil Blackwell.

Wright, Crispin. 1975. 'On the Coherence of Vague Predicates'. *Synthèse* 30(3): 325–65.

PART I

THEORIES OF VAGUENESS
AND THEIR IMPACT
ON JURISPRUDENCE

1

Philosophical and Jurisprudential Issues of Vagueness

Stephen Schiffer

1. Philosophical Issues of Vagueness

Philosophers seek an account of what vagueness is that resolves the sorites paradox, a conundrum that has troubled philosophers since the fourth century BC.
'Sorites' derives from the Greek word for heap, 'soros', and the original 'paradox of
the heap' turned on the apparently plausible but application-destroying assumption that if *n* grains of (say) sand do, or don't, make a heap, then one grain more
or less would make no difference to whether it is, or isn't, a heap. But essentially
the same paradox can be run on any, or virtually any,[1] vague term, as the paradox
turns on two related appearances that every vague term presents. The first is that
there is no precise division to be identified between the things to which the term
applies and the things to which it doesn't apply, and therefore no precise division
to be identified between the conditions that would make a vague sentence true
and those that would make it false. The second appearance explains the first; it's
that vague terms appear to be what Crispin Wright called *tolerant* (Wright 1976),
in the sense that, if a vague term applies, or doesn't apply, to a thing *x*, then it
applies, or doesn't apply, to any other thing that differs only minutely from *x* with
respect to that feature of *x* which secures the term's application, or non-application, to *x*. Because the same kind of paradox can be generated using virtually any
vague term, 'sorites paradox' has long been used in philosophy as a label for any
paradox of that kind.

Paradoxes are usefully illustrated as inferences that give three incompatible
appearances: that they are valid (i.e. have conclusions that can't be false if their
premises are true); that their premises are true; and that their conclusions are not
true. Inferences that present *sorites* paradoxes can take any one of a few forms, but in
every one of those inferences either one or more of its premises or its conclusion will

---

[1] It's not entirely clear that one could construct a sorites paradox that turned on the vagueness of,
say, 'chair' or 'horse'.

exploit the two paradox-generating appearances of every vague term. For example, the following inference presents a sorites paradox.

SI (1) A nine-year-old human female is a girl.
(2) A forty-year-old human female is not a girl.
(3) ∴ For some number *n*, an *n*-year-old human female is a girl, but a human female one second older than that isn't a girl.

SI presents a paradox because it appears to be valid (it is, after all, valid if the least number principle is valid); its premises certainly seem true; and, since it's very difficult to see how one second can make the difference between being a girl and not being a girl, it's very difficult to see how its conclusion can be true. And since the paradox SI presents is owed to the two features that the vague term 'girl' shares with every other vague term, SI presents a sorites paradox.

Since the sorites turns on the two trouble-making appearances that all vague terms present, one should expect that, to whatever extent the sorites has a resolution, it will come from an account of what vagueness is. Saying what vagueness is requires saying what sorts of things may be vague and in what their vagueness consists. It is generally recognized that concepts and linguistic expressions of just about every syntactic category may be vague (connectives such as 'and' and 'or' may be an exception), but there is an important debate, to be touched on later, about whether vagueness is wholly a feature of language and thought or whether extra-linguistic objects and properties may also be vague. It's also generally recognized that to be vague is to admit of borderline cases. For example, 'red' is vague because it's possible for something to be a borderline case of a thing to which 'red' applies—that is to say, a thing to which 'red' neither determinately applies nor determinately doesn't apply[2]—and if Mount Everest is a vague thing, then it's vague because there are times that are borderline cases of times at which the mountain came into existence and places that are borderline cases of places on the mountain. Every philosophical theory of vagueness offers an account of what it is to be a borderline case, and uses that account to proffer its view on how the sorites should be resolved. It's also taken to be a defining feature of vagueness that, if a term φ is vague, then so is ⌜borderline φ⌝, and this entails that there are no precise determinate boundaries at any order of vagueness.

At issue in every theory is whether or not the *law of excluded middle* (every instance of '*S* or not-*S*' is a logical truth) and the *principle of bivalence* (every statement is true or false) are correct. For suppose Ralph is borderline bald, neither determinately bald nor determinately not bald. Then, no matter how much one knows about the hair situation on Ralph's scalp and no matter how masterful one's use of 'bald', it's impossible to know that Ralph is bald and impossible to know that he isn't bald, and that makes it tempting to conclude that there is no fact of the matter as to whether or not he is bald, which in turn calls into question both excluded middle and bivalence. The law of excluded middle is a mainstay of classical logic

---

[2] My use of 'determinate' is pretheoretic and thus leaves open whether a proposition's being indeterminate entails that it's neither true nor false.

and the principle of bivalence is a mainstay of classical semantics. Those who reject excluded middle typically propose some non-classical logic as the correct logic for vague language, and those who reject bivalence typically propose some non-classical semantics, which may say that there are only two truth-values, truth and falsity, but that borderline statements have no truth-value, or they may propose that there are three or more truth-values, or that truth and falsity come in degrees measured by real numbers in the interval [0, 1]. There are also those who insist that excluded middle and bivalence hold for borderline statements, and these theorists devote most of their resources to trying to swat away the counterintuitive consequences of their position. Every position on vagueness must also contend with other questions that ineluctably arise in the attempt to say what vagueness is—for example, questions about higher-order vagueness (borderline borderline cases, or borderline borderline borderline cases, or...), or about the appropriate propositional attitude to have towards a proposition one takes to be borderline, or about similarities between the sorites paradox and semantic paradoxes such as the liar.

Although the problem of vagueness has been with philosophers for about 2,400 years, the number of words they have written on it in the past thirty or so years far exceeds the number they wrote on it in the 2,370 or so years before then. This is in part due to the realization that the sorites can't be dismissed as an amusing brain teaser or as a defect of vernacular language that poses no serious threat to the semantical or logical issues with which logicians and philosophers of language should be concerned, but also to the ever-increasing use of formal techniques in analytical philosophy. There are many theories of vagueness—indeed, it is difficult to suppose there is any position in logical space on vagueness where one or more philosophers are not to be found exercising all the ingenuity they can muster. None of these theories comes close to being recognized as the correct theory of vagueness. Here, simply by way of illustration, are three prominent examples of theories of vagueness.

The *epistemicist* accepts classical logic and bivalence. Because he accepts bivalence, he would say that, notwithstanding Ava's being a borderline case of a thing to which 'girl' applies, 'Ava is a girl' is either true or else false, and thus that it's either a fact that Ava is a girl or else a fact that she's not a girl; and because he accepts classical logic and bivalence and also knows that a nine-year-old human female is a girl but that a forty-year-old human female isn't a girl, he also accepts that there is a number n such that an n-year-old human female is a girl but an $n.0000000317097919838$-year-old human female—i.e. a human female one second older than n years old—isn't a girl, and so for this theorist the sorites inference SI is sound. But if there is such a number n and it's either a fact that Ava is a girl or a fact that she's not a girl, notwithstanding that she is a borderline case of a thing to which 'girl' applies, then wherein lies the vagueness of 'girl'? To this the epistemicist answers that it lies in the explanation of why it's impossible to know what the cut-off number or the truth-value of a borderline statement is, where epistemicists may differ on what they take that explanation to be.[3] For the epistemicist, vagueness is a kind of irremediable ignorance.

---

[3] See e.g. Sorenson 1988 and Williamson 1994.

The *supervaluationist* aims to deny bivalence but to accept excluded middle in a way that enables her to accept *both* that there is a number n such that a human female n years old is a girl but one $n.0000000317097919838$ years old isn't a girl *and* that no number n is such that the statement *that a human female n years old is a girl but one who is $n.0000000317097919838$ years old isn't a girl* is true.[4] The trick is to be accomplished with her account of truth. For the supervaluationist, a statement is true just in case it's true in every admissible precisification of the language, false just in case it's false in every admissible precisification of the language, and neither true nor false just in case there is an admissible precisification of the language in which it's true and one in which it's false. A *precisification* of a language L is an assignment of denotations to the expressions of L that makes every statement in L bivalent (i.e. true or false), and a precisification of L is *admissible* just in case it respects certain analytical connections among the expressions of L and assigns to the denotation of each expression everything to which the expression determinately applies, nothing to which it determinately doesn't apply, and then divides the remaining cases in any arbitrary way. So consider borderline bald Harold. Since Harold is a borderline case of a thing in the denotation of 'bald', there will be an admissible precisification in which 'Harold is bald' is true and an admissible precisification in which it's false, and therefore 'Harold is bald' will be neither true nor false. But although it's neither true nor false, the instance of excluded middle 'Harold is bald or Harold is not bald' will be true, notwithstanding that neither of its disjuncts is true, for in every admissible precisification of English one of its disjuncts will be true, albeit not the same disjunct in every admissible precisification. Similarly, the sentence 'There is a number n such that a human female n years old is a girl but one $n.0000000317097919838$ years old isn't a girl' will be true, for in every admissible precisification there will be some number that makes the sentence true, but no number will be the one that makes it true in every admissible precisification.

The *degree-of-truth theorist* recognizes 'degrees of truth' intermediate between complete truth and complete falsity, and she measures these degrees by real numbers in the interval $[0, 1]$, where a statement is true to degree 0 if it's false *tout court* and true to degree 1 if it's true *tout court*. Borderline statements are true and false to positive degrees that sum to 1. The degree to which a borderline statement is true is a measure of its place in the statement's penumbra. For example, if the hair situation on borderline Harold's scalp more closely resembles the hair situation on the scalp of a man who is determinately bald than it resembles that on the scalp of a man who is determinately not bald, then the degree to which 'Harold is bald' is true will be greater than the degree to which it is false. Degree-of-truth theorists may differ on the rules they accept for determining the degrees of truth of complex sentences and on the logic they take vague language to require. Many who apply a degree-theoretic notion of truth to vagueness adopt a degree-functional account of the connectives due to Łukasiewicz in which, for example, the degree of truth

---

[4] See e.g. Fine 1975.

of a conjunction is the lowest degree of its conjuncts, and the degree of truth of a disjunction is the highest degree of its disjuncts (Łukasiewicz and Tarski 1956). That semantics requires a non-classical logic, for on it excluded middle and non-contradiction fail: if $T(p)$ and $T(\neg p)$ are both 0.5, then $T(p \lor \neg p)$ and $T(p \& \neg p)$ are also 0.5. On a Łukasiewiczian continuum-valued fuzzy logic SI is invalid, for while its premises are true to degree 1, its conclusion is true to a degree close to 0.

2. Jurisprudential Issues of Vagueness

These tend to be broadly normative. One issue is when, if ever, vagueness in law is desirable. Since virtually every sentence anyone produces (outside of mathematics) is vague to some degree or other, vagueness in law is unavoidable. Nevertheless, it may always be asked of any statute or other legal text whether a formulation of it that was less or more vague would have been better. It seems obvious to me that some texts would benefit, while others would suffer, from being made more precise. For example, there are good reasons why certain statutes should be ruled 'void for vagueness': no one could know that acts of oral or anal sex between consenting adults were crimes just from knowing there was a law criminalizing 'abominable and detestable crimes against nature'. On the other hand, any attempt to replace the 'beyond reasonable doubt' charge to the jury in criminal cases with an explicit criterion for a doubt's being reasonable would surely be disastrous, and the framers of the Bill of Rights did well not to try to be more precise than they were in writing that 'excessive bail shall not be required, nor excessive fines imposed, nor cruel and unusual punishments inflicted'. Whether philosophers or jurisprudes can come up with useful general conditions for when vagueness in law is, or isn't, desirable, is a further question.

Another big question concerns what judges should do in the face of indeterminacy of this, that, or the other kind. The judge's duty is to 'uphold the law', but what should be her duty when in a given case it is indeterminate what it would be to uphold the law, even when the judge has availed herself of all the judicial decisions, legal principles, and writings deemed relevant to determining when the law applies and when it doesn't apply? This is in every case a normative question, as is the further question of what sorts of considerations are appropriate for a judge to consider in trying to answer those questions. There is considerable debate in philosophy about the factual status of normative questions of every kind, and no philosophical theory of any kind, let alone one about vagueness, holds the key to answering them.

3. The Relevance of Philosophical Theories of Vagueness to Jurisprudential Issues of Vagueness

Philosophical and jurisprudential issues of vagueness are very different, so why should anyone think that philosophical theories of vagueness are relevant to issues of vagueness in the law? No one should think that, I argued in an earlier article on the topics of this chapter. There I concluded that 'philosophical theories of vagueness, even if true, have nothing to offer jurisprudential concerns about vagueness. Once she is reminded of certain platitudes about vagueness, the legal theorist needs no further help from philosophers of language and logic' (Schiffer 2001, p. 421).[5] By that I did *not* mean that philosophers who work on vagueness have no contribution to make to jurisprudential issues of vagueness, or that works such as Timothy Endicott's *Vagueness in Law* (Endicott 2000) don't make important contributions. At the beginning of this chapter I said that 'philosophers seek an account of what vagueness is that resolves the sorites paradox', where, I explained, such theories often propose a specific semantics or logic for vague language, and I offered epistemicism, supervaluationism, and degree-theoretic accounts of vagueness as three examples of the sort of theories I had in mind. It was to such theories that I was alluding when I said philosophical theories of vagueness had nothing to offer jurisprudential concerns about vagueness. The judge who must decide what to do about a case to which a particular law neither determinately applies nor determinately doesn't apply won't be helped by learning that a Łukasiewiczian continuum-valued fuzzy logic was the correct logic to use in evaluating vague arguments. Nor will the judge be helped by knowing that epistemicism was correct and that therefore it was either a fact that the law in question applied or else a fact that it didn't apply, when she also knew it was metaphysically impossible for her or anyone else to know what the fact of the matter was. As far as she should be concerned, it should make no difference whether there is no fact of the matter or there is but it's impossible to know what it is.

In a commentary on my 2001, Kent Greenawalt said that he agreed with me 'that philosophical theories of vagueness have no direct practical implications for how judges decide borderline cases; judges face a normative question what to do. However,' he continued, 'a judge who embraces a particular philosophical theory of vagueness may be influenced in how he conceptualizes determinations of difficult legal issues, and this conceptualization may affect the judge's method of decision' (Greenawalt 2001, p. 433). Towards the end of his article, Greenawalt makes clear what he has in mind. Suppose we have two judges, *X* and *Y*, who are equally aware

- that it's typically the case that sundry laws, legal principles, judicial and administrative precedents, legal writings, etc., may be relevant to determining what the correct resolution of a given legal issue is,

---

[5] By 'platitudes about vagueness' I meant features of vagueness that nearly all theorists take to be data that constrain their theories of vagueness. These 'platitudes' include, but aren't exhausted by, such things as that virtually every expression is vague; that, while some expressions may be more or less vague than others, owing to the limitations of our perceptual and cognitive faculties, it's impossible to replace our vague terms and concepts with ones that aren't vague to any degree; that a vague utterance may be determinately true or determinately false; that if a thing is borderline *F*, then it's conceptually impossible to know that it's *F* or that it's not *F*; and that being vague is distinct from being ambiguous, unspecific, uncertain, unclear, or indeterminate (the counterfactual sentence 'If Verdi and Wagner had been compatriots, Verdi would have been German' is indeterminate quite apart from the vagueness of 'compatriot' and 'German'). Other such 'platitudes' will be mentioned later when I discuss what I call penumbral profiles.

- that there is, nevertheless, in principle always the possibility that, no matter how much legal material is taken into account, it will be indeterminate what the correct legal resolution of the issue is, but

- that a judge can't simply declare the issue not to have a determinate legal solution and be done with it, but must in every case decide the issue in *some* way,

but who differ in the following respect:

- judge *X* rejects bivalence and believes that if an answer to a legal issue is neither determinately true nor determinately false, then it's also neither true nor false,

whereas

- judge *Y* accepts bivalence for all statements and thus believes that even if an answer to a legal issue is neither determinately true nor determinately false, it's still either true or false—except that it's impossible for anyone to discover which answer is true when none is determinately true.

Given the descriptions of judges *X* and *Y*, what differences in their methods of making judicial decisions does Greenawalt think we should find between *X* and *Y* as a result of the different theories of indeterminate issues they hold?

It's not entirely clear. It would support Greenawalt's claim that a judge's method of deciding legal issues may be affected by the philosophical theory of vagueness he accepts if we should expect the following difference between *X* and *Y*: when *X* concludes that a legal issue has no determinately correct answer, he also concludes that the law has 'run out', and that he must 'turn to non-legal materials to resolve the case, taking account of both a desirable result and a sound legal rule for future cases' (Greenawalt 2001, p. 443). But when *Y* concludes that a legal issue has no determinately correct answer, knowing that it nevertheless has a correct answer, he's likely to keep trying to find out what that correct answer is. But *that* can't be what Greenawalt intends: it would be utterly irrational of *Y* to keep searching for the correct answer when he knows there is no determinately correct answer, for it's his view that it's impossible for anyone to know what the correct answer is when that answer isn't determinately correct. Since *Y* must rule on the issue even if it's impossible for him to know what the correct ruling would be, he is in exactly the same position *X* is in when he concludes that there is no fact of the matter as to what the correct decision is. *Y* would be every bit as compelled as *X* to 'turn to non-legal materials to resolve the case, taking account of both a desirable result and a sound legal rule for future cases'.

Greenawalt's text suggests that the point he had in mind was a difference that would arise between *X* and *Y* when either 'confronts an issue she thinks is very difficult; she is not sure how to resolve it' (Greenawalt 2001, p. 443). He suggests that judge *X*, who holds that an issue has no correct resolution if it doesn't have a determinately correct resolution, 'is likely to assume that when she finds an issue to be very difficult' that it has no correct resolution, and that she may 'properly turn to non-legal materials to resolve the case', whereas judge *Y*, who thinks that a legal issue has a correct answer even when it's indeterminate what that answer is, will behave differently when confronted with a very difficult legal issue:

> Schiffer speaks of theorists who suppose that applications of vague concepts are either true or false as conceiving indeterminacy as a kind of 'irremediable ignorance', but it is just in this respect that a judge is crucially different from the person deciding whether someone at the border is bald. She has inexhaustible legal materials, and her judgment is important enough to warrant hard work. If she keeps studying all the materials, the judge may approach closer to what 'the law requires'. The person gauging baldness has no further inquiry to make. ... The judge is *not* likely to throw up her hands, declare her irremediable ignorance about what the law requires, and proceed to decide on the same bases as the judge who is persuaded she must reach outside the law because the law has no correct answer.
>
> (Greenawalt 2001, pp. 443–4)

I find this puzzling. Is the point supposed to be that judge *Y* will have a better appreciation of all that bears on when a resolution is legally correct? That can't be right, for it was stipulated that *X* and *Y* are equally aware of all that must be taken into account. Is the point supposed to be that *X* will be inclined to think that there are more indeterminate legal issues than *Y* thinks there are? There is nothing to warrant that: *X* and *Y* differ on what constitutes indeterminacy, not on how frequently it is to be found. Is the point supposed to be that, confronted with the same difficult legal issue, *X* will be quicker than *Y* to assume it has no determinately correct resolution? Again, however, that can't be right; there is no reason whatever why *X* should seek a determinately correct resolution any less assiduously than *Y* would. Greenawalt has not made good his claim to show that, and how accepting a particular philosophical theory of vagueness can affect the methodology by which a judge makes legal decisions.

4. Penumbral Shift and Penumbral Ignorance

Now I will suggest that there is a way technical philosophical work on vagueness may be relevant to understanding what judicial interpretation can and can't be. This source of relevance wasn't mentioned in my 2001 work because I wasn't then adequately aware of it. At the beginning of this chapter I said that philosophers seek an account of what vagueness is that resolves the sorites paradox. I continue to believe that it's irrelevant to jurisprudential issues of vagueness which such theories are, or are not, correct. But two under-appreciated features of every vague expression bear importantly on issues of judicial interpretation. I call the two features *Penumbral Shift* and *Penumbral Ignorance*. In this section I will explain what they are and discuss one surprising effect they have on the semantics of vague expressions.[6] In the

---

[6] There are other surprising effects that I won't be able to discuss in this chapter. For example, it's assumed by many philosophers of language that an expression's having meaning consists in there being something that it means, but in future work I will argue that Penumbral Shift and Penumbral Ignorance show that, while vague expressions have meaning, there can't be things that are their meanings.

next and final section, section 5, I will illustrate the relevance of Penumbral Shift and Penumbral Ignorance to issues of judicial interpretation by bringing those features explicitly to bear on one particular theory of judicial interpretation, Supreme Court Justice Antonin Scalia's textualism.

Before I can explain Penumbral Shift and Penumbral Ignorance I need first to explain the notion of a *penumbral profile*, and I also need to say something about how I will understand the type/token distinction. Every literally—as opposed to, say, metaphorically—uttered token of every vague expression has a penumbral profile. Two predicate tokens have the same penumbral profile provided it's necessarily the case that, if either token is true/false of a thing, then so is the other; if either token is such that it's indeterminate whether it's true/false of a thing, then so is the other; if either token is such that it's indeterminate whether it's indeterminate whether it's true/false of a thing, then so is the other; and so on. Two singular term tokens have the same penumbral profile provided it's necessarily the case that if one token refers to a thing, then so does the other; if it's indeterminate whether one token refers to a thing, then it's also indeterminate whether the other token refers to it; if it's indeterminate whether it's indeterminate whether one token refers to a thing, then it's also indeterminate whether it's indeterminate whether the other token refers to that thing; and so on. And two sentence tokens have the same penumbral profile provided it's necessarily the case that if either is such that it's true/false, so is the other; if either is such that it's indeterminate whether it's true/false, then so is the other; if either is such that it's indeterminate whether it's indeterminate whether it's true/false, then so is the other; and so on.

I turn now to how I will understand the type/token distinction. I want to say, for example, that the sentence *type* 'She never married him' expresses no proposition and therefore has no truth-value, but that *tokens* of that sentence type may express propositions and therefore have truth-values. For example, a particular token of that sentence type will express the proposition that Lou Salomé never married Friedrich Nietzsche if, in producing that token, the speaker referred to Salomé with his uttered token of 'she', referred to Nietzsche with his uttered token of 'him' and in uttering the sentence meant that the former never married the latter. But what exactly is an expression token? Physical realizations of expressions—say, realizations in sound or ink—are tokens, but one's understanding of what an expression token is can't be limited to such physical realizations if one wants the notion of an expression token in order say such things as that it's only tokens of indexical sentence types, and never the sentence types themselves, that can have truth-values. For suppose the sentence 'She never married him' occurs in a book about Lou Salomé. Books, like expressions, also admit of a type/token distinction. When you say 'The four books on the table are mine', you're talking about book tokens, which are physical objects, but when you say 'I wrote four books', you're talking about book types, which are abstract entities. Now the sentence 'She never married him' on page 184 of the book is, like the book it's in, an abstract entity; yet it expresses a proposition, the proposition that Lou Salomé never married Nietzsche. Should we say that that abstract entity isn't identical with the sentence type 'She never married him', since that abstract entity, unlike the first, expresses no proposition, or should we qualify what was said about the sentence type and now say that indexical sentence types can express propositions *relative to certain occurrences*? A problem with saying the latter is that the abstract entity that is the book about Lou Salomé itself stands in a certain relation to another abstract entity consisting of the same words in the same order but in which the sentence 'She never married him' doesn't express a proposition and so doesn't have a truth-value. That abstract entity is simply the sequence of expression types that occur in the book, and that entity isn't identical to the book, for the sequence of expression types existed long before the book came into existence in, say, 1996. Anyway, I don't really want to get embroiled in these sorts of issues, and I don't have to, since the bottom line seems clear enough: the sentence 'She never married him' in the book expresses the proposition it does because of its relation to intentions the author of the book had in writing it. Henceforth when I speak of expression tokens I should be taken to mean instantiations, physical or abstract, of expression types that count as instantiations of those expression types by virtue of the intentions their authors had in producing them. Actually, for most of this section one may, for all that matters, take expression tokens to be actually produced sounds or marks; the use of 'expression token' in reference to abstract entities such as books comes into play when I turn in the next section to issues about the semantic contents of statutes and constitutions.

So much for my two preliminaries. *Penumbral Shift* is the fact that the penumbral profiles of a vague expression's tokens may shift somewhat from one token of the expression to another; that is to say, two tokens of any vague expression may have somewhat different penumbral profiles. For example, asked who snatched her purse, Thelma replies, 'A bald guy wearing a grey sweatshirt and track pants', and her utterance may be determinately true notwithstanding the fact that the man who snatched her purse shaves his head but would otherwise have a luxuriant head of hair. But in a conversation about hereditary baldness, the purse snatcher's sister might correct a remark by saying, 'No; he's not bald, he just shaves his head', and that utterance, in that context, would count as determinately true. In still another context the question is raised whether a man who shaved his head would be bald if no one would take him to be bald if he stopped shaving his head and let his hair grow out, and in that context it might be true to say, 'That's undetermined by the use of "bald" in everyday speech; such a man would be neither determinately bald nor determinately not bald.' In a community in which people typically marry before the age of twenty, an utterance of 'He's a bachelor' may count as true when said of an unmarried eighteen-year-old male, whereas in a conversation among New Yorkers, where for both men and women the average age for a first marriage is between thirty and thirty-five, an utterance of 'He's a bachelor' would most likely not count as definitely true when said of an unmarried eighteen-year-old male, and may even count as false. 'Midtown' is the name of a vaguely defined section of Manhattan. If you are in Times Square you are definitely in Midtown. If you now travel in a straight line in any direction you will eventually definitely not be in Midtown, but at no point will you have crossed an invisible line on one side of which you are definitely in Midtown and on the other side of which you are definitely not in Midtown. An utterance of 'Jack works in Midtown' would very likely count as true if Jack is a lawyer whose firm is located at Park Avenue and Sixtieth Street. But an utterance of 'Fiona lives in Midtown' is more likely to count as false or as neither determinately true nor determinately false if she lives in an elegant co-op apartment at Park Avenue and Sixtieth Street.

The penumbral profiles of two tokens of a vague expression can differ by only so much, but there can be no saying precisely how much is too much, for, as the sorites paradox teaches us, with vague expressions there are no precise boundaries to be drawn at any order of vagueness. The expression 'tall man' (meaning *tall for a man*), for example, is vague, but every literally uttered token of that expression must be true of a man 2 metres tall and false of a man 1.7 metres tall. Yet no number *j* can be identified as the smallest number such that every literally uttered token of 'tall man' will be true of a man whose height is equal to or greater than *j* metres, and no number *k* can be identified as the largest number such that every literally uttered token of 'tall man' is false of a man whose height is equal to or less than *k*. The fact that virtually every vague expression has applications that are guaranteed to be correct is crucial to our ability to communicate effectively with vague language. My guess is that indeterminacy isn't usually an issue with non-general statements of fact, such as utterances of 'Mike is tall', 'His child is a girl', 'She lives in Harlem', etc. Indeterminacy is much more likely to be an issue when a vague generalization is confronted with cases the speaker hadn't or couldn't have contemplated, such as, perhaps, an utterance in 1866 of 'No State shall make or enforce any law which shall abridge the privileges or immunities of citizens of the United States; nor shall any State deprive any person of life, liberty, or property, without due process of law; nor deny to any person within its jurisdiction the equal protection of the laws.'

Penumbral Ignorance is the fact that speakers, and those who understand what they say, neither know what the penumbral profiles of their vague utterances are nor what determines them. Bob asks Jane whether Frank has any children, and she replies, 'Yes; he has two girls.' Jane knows that her utterance is determinately true because she knows Frank has exactly two offspring, both determinately female, one seven years old, the other five years old. Both Jane and Bob understand Jane's utterance as well as they understand any utterance. Now 'girl' is vague: it's impossible for anyone to identify a number *n* such that a female child is a girl until she is *n* days old but not a girl thereafter. There are also physical and psychological properties that may make an individual neither determinately female nor determinately not female. Suppose Bob and Jane—neither of whom is a philosopher, both of whom are intelligent native speakers of English—are now asked whether 'girl', as just then uttered by Jane, would apply to an eighteen-year-old human female, or to a person with two X chromosomes but who had developed hormonally as a male. There is no telling what Jane or Bob would say in response, but whatever they would say would have no special authority. It is simply not a requirement on Jane's use of 'girl' or on her and Bob's understanding of her utterance that they be able to say of an arbitrarily chosen possible individual whether or not that individual would be a borderline instance—or a borderline borderline instance, or . . .—of a thing to which the token of 'girl' uttered by Jane applied. Nor need they know. A careful speaker won't apply a vague term to a thing unless she is confident that the term determinately applies to it, and she has no reason to ponder *recherché* possible cases that have nothing to do with her concerns in making her utterance. Although speakers don't know what the penumbral profiles of their vague utterances are, they may of course know particular facts about those profiles. For example, there may be three simultaneous utterances of 'Leroy is celibate', one true, one false, and one borderline true/false, and for each of these utterances there may be a suitably informed witness who knows the truth status of the utterance she witnessed. It is, of course, no surprise that ordinary speakers not only don't know what the penumbral profiles of their utterances are, but also have no idea what determines them. It's perhaps somewhat surprising, however, that no theorist knows what determines them either. That isn't to say that nothing is known. When a vague utterance is made and facts emerge that induce the speaker and her hearer to agree that what was said was neither determinately true nor determinately false, that, all else being equal, may suffice for what was said actually to have that status. But suppose we have an indisputably true token of, say, the vague sentence 'Sabine is a very wealthy Berliner' and then after the fact the question is raised whether the speaker and his hearer would have taken the uttered token of 'very wealthy Berliner' to be true of Sabine if she had been worth only n euros, where being worth that amount isn't one of the amounts that every token of 'very wealthy Berliner' must be true of or false of in order to count as a literally uttered token of that expression. Such counterfactuals, like an utterance of 'She would be happy if she hadn't married Fritz', virtually never have determinate truth-values, and for that reason we probably need to say that it's indeterminate how the speaker and hearer would have regarded the truth status of the token of 'Sabine is a very wealthy Berliner' in that counterfactual situation, and therefore indeterminate what truth status it would have relative to that situation.

Penumbral Shift and Penumbral Ignorance have a surprising effect on reports of what was said in utterances of vague sentences, which effect generates a puzzle for a widely accepted theory of those reports. The view—call it the Standard View—is that, if in uttering a sentence σ a person x says that S, then a report of what x said in uttering σ is correct only if it reports x as having said that S. If we assume, as I will for expository convenience, that the things we say are propositions of some stripe or other, then the Standard View may be put by saying that a saying report of the form 'A said that S' is true just in case the referent of the 'A' term said the proposition to which the 'that S' term refers. That characterization of the Standard View is OK, so far as it goes, but to go further with it requires a view about the things to which tokens of vague singular terms refer and the properties expressed by tokens of vague predicates. Suppose, for example, that on Saturday Al and Betty are walking on the beach when Al points in the direction of some dunes and says,

(1) That area is secluded.

To what does the token of 'that area' refer, and what does the token of 'secluded' express? That question can't be answered without taking a stand on the issue of ontic vagueness. That issue is a contest between a view I will call *No-Vagueness-in-the-World* and a view I will call *Vagueness-in-the-World*.

No-Vagueness-in-the-World claims that nothing outside of language and thought is vague: there are neither vague properties nor vague things; every property and thing is absolutely precise: every physical object has precise conditions of individuation, and every property has precise conditions of application that everything either satisfies or fails to satisfy. Consequently, the vagueness of a predicate token doesn't consist in its expressing a vague property, and the vagueness of a singular-term token doesn't consist in its referring to a vague object. What, then, does it consist in? That depends on which No-Vagueness-in-the-World theorist one asks. The epistemic theorist would say that the token of 'that area' uttered by Al refers to a precisely defined area of the beach and that the token of 'secluded' refers to a precisely defined property. For the epistemicist, what makes the tokens of 'that area' and 'secluded' vague is that it's impossible to know the precise area that is the referent of the token of 'that area' or the precise property that is the property expressed by the token of 'secluded'. No-Vagueness-in-the-World isn't a feasible option if its truth depends on its conjunction with the epistemic theory. There are various problems with the epistemic theory, but I take the following to be the most serious.[7] Perhaps no one can say in non-semantic terms what determines the thing to which an utterance refers or the property it expresses, but I believe we know enough about how those semantic values are determined to know that it's extremely implausible that their determinants could determine everything referred to and every property expressed to be more precise than any scientific measuring device could possibly determine it to be. I shall assume that the epistemic theory isn't an option, and that therefore, given No-Vagueness-in-the-World, nothing is determinately the referent of a vague singular-term token or determinately the property expressed by a vague predicate token.

A more prudent route for the No-Vagueness-in-the-World theorist to take would be to say that, while no precise area can be such that it's determinately the referent of the token of 'that area' Al produced when he uttered (1), uncountably many precise areas may each be such that it is indeterminate whether it's the token's referent, or indeterminate whether it is indeterminate whether it's the token's referent, or indeterminate whether it is indeterminate whether it is indeterminate whether it's the token's referent, and so on. Call this vast array the *content array for the token of 'that area'*. As regards vague predicates, the more prudent No-Vagueness-in-the-World theorist will say that, while no precise property can be such that it's determinately the property expressed by the token of 'secluded' Al uttered, uncountably many precise properties may each be such that it is indeterminate whether it's the property expressed by the token, or indeterminate whether it is indeterminate whether it's the property expressed by the token, and so on. Call this vast array the *content array for the token of 'secluded'*; the content arrays for the expression tokens contained in a sentence token will in the obvious way determine a content array of precise propositions for the sentence token itself. We should also expect

[7] I discuss objections to epistemicism in several publications. See especially Schiffer 1999 and 2003, pp. 181–7. Timothy Williamson responds to Schiffer 1999 in Williamson 1999.

the No-Vagueness-in-the-World theorist to take a broadly supervaluationist line on
the truth conditions of the token of (1) ('That area is secluded') Al uttered, in the
following way. For every area α in the content array for the token of 'that area' and
every property φ in the content array for the token of 'secluded', the pair $<\alpha, \varphi>$
may be taken to represent a singular proposition that is true iff α has φ, false iff α
doesn't have φ. Then the token of (1) is true iff each of those propositions is true,
false iff each of them is false; and if some of those propositions are true while others
are false, then the token of (1) will be neither true nor false, or it will be indeterminate whether it's neither true nor false, or indeterminate whether it is indeterminate
whether it's neither true nor false, etc., depending on intricacies of higher-order
vagueness that I won't now venture into. There are, however, two further things
that should be said. The first is that the penumbral profiles of the token of 'that
area' and of 'secluded' together with the syntax of (1) (I'll assume that is determinate) will determine the penumbral profile of the token of the sentence (1), and
the truth status of the token determined by the singular propositions in its content
array must of course be consistent with the token's penumbral profile. For example, if the sentence token's penumbral profile has it that the obtaining of a certain
state of affairs would constitute a borderline case of the token's being true, then the
content array of singular propositions determined for the token must entail that it
is indeterminate whether the token is true if the state of affairs in question obtains.
We may say that, if the content array for a vague expression token determines it
to have a certain penumbral profile, then that is also the array's penumbral profile.
The penumbral profile of a vague expression token's content array must match that
of the token whose content array it is. The second thing that should be said is that,
since Penumbral Ignorance entails that it's impossible to know what any expression token's penumbral profile is, then, given No-Vagueness-in-the-World, it's also
impossible to know what the penumbral profile of a token's content array is, and
therefore impossible to know what its content array is. Of course, that needn't
prevent us from knowing that a vague utterance is true or that it's false, or even, if
conditions are right, that it's indeterminate whether it's true or whether it's false.

Vagueness-in-the-World claims that there are vague objects and properties, in
addition to whatever precise objects and properties there may be. Vague objects
and properties are objects and properties that themselves have penumbral profiles.
For example, if a certain location is a borderline instance of a location that is in a
certain vague area, then that is a feature of the area's penumbral profile, and if a
thing is a borderline instance of a certain vague property, then that is a feature of
the property's penumbral profile. If No-Vagueness-in-the-World is correct, then,
as regards Al's utterance of (1) ('That area is secluded'), no precise area is available to be the content of the uttered token of 'that area', no precise property is
available to be the content of the uttered token of 'secluded', and, consequently,
no precise proposition is available to be the content of the uttered token of (1).
But if Vagueness-in-the-World is correct, then there is a vague area available to be
the content of the uttered token of 'that area', there is a vague property available
to be the content of the uttered token of 'secluded', and, consequently, there is a
vague proposition available to be the content of the uttered token of (1). These are,

respectively, the vague area whose penumbral profile matches that of the token of 'that area', the vague property whose penumbral profile matches that of the token of 'secluded', and the vague proposition whose penumbral profile matches that of the token of (1). For suppose, say, that a vague property φ has a penumbral profile that matches that of a vague predicate token τ. Then τ is true of a thing x iff x has φ; it's indeterminate whether τ is true of x iff it's indeterminate whether x has φ; and so on. Since the content of a predicate token is that property, if any, whose application to a thing determines the predicate's application to it (in the sense that the application status of the property to a thing entails the application status of the predicate to that thing), the fact that φ and τ have matching penumbral profiles would seem sufficient for us to deem φ the content of τ.

For every vague object or property there will be an array of precise objects or properties that determines the same penumbral profile, and vice versa, and it's arguably merely a matter of convention whether we say, for example, that the token of 'secluded' Al uttered has as its content that array of precise properties whose penumbral profile matches the token's or that it has as its content that vague property whose penumbral profile matches the token's. Because it will considerably simplify the exposition of what is to follow, I will henceforth assume that every token of a vague singular term that doesn't fail altogether to refer (e.g. 'Atlantis') refers to a vague entity whose penumbral profile matches its penumbral profile and that every vague predicate token expresses a vague property whose penumbral profile matches its penumbral profile. I think it will be pretty obvious how the conclusions I come to relative to Vagueness-in-the-World would be matched, *mutatis mutandis*, by the conclusions I would come to relative to No-Vagueness-in-the-World, but the reader sceptical of the claimed equivalence may simply read me as at best having shown what follows relative to Vagueness-in-the-World.

Now we may return to the puzzle Penumbral Shift and Penumbral Ignorance create for the Standard View of saying reports.

On Saturday, as he and Betty are walking on the beach, Al points in a certain direction and utters (1) ('That area is secluded'). Let α be the vague area whose penumbral profile matches that of the uttered token of 'that area' and is therefore the referent of that token, and let φ be the vague property whose penumbral profile matches that of the uttered token of 'secluded' and is therefore the property expressed by that token. Then the uttered token of (1) expresses the vague proposition $<\alpha, \varphi>$, thereby making that proposition the proposition Al said in uttering (1). Now suppose that on Sunday Betty and Carl are walking along the same stretch of Beach, and at roughly the place where Al made his remark the day before to Betty, Betty points in the direction Al pointed in and says to Carl,

(2) Yesterday, Al said that that area was secluded.

We are all very familiar with that sort of saying report, and we should have no trouble accepting that Betty's utterance is true—or at least that native speakers of English familiar with the circumstances of Al's utterance of (1) on Saturday and of Betty's utterance of (2) on Sunday would unhesitatingly take Betty's utterance to be true. The fact that we readily accept that Betty's utterance may be true creates a problem for the Standard View. For the application of the Standard View to Betty's utterance of (2) entails that her utterance of (2) was true only if the token of the that-clause she uttered—viz. 'that that area is secluded'—referred to <α, φ>, the proposition we're supposing Al to have said, and that in turn entails that the token of 'that area' Betty uttered referred to the vague area α and that the token of 'secluded' she uttered expressed the vague property φ. At the same time, Penumbral Shift and Penumbral Ignorance virtually guarantee that the token of the that-clause Betty uttered won't refer to <α, φ>. For the that-clause token referred to that proposition only if the referent of the token of 'that area' it contained was α, the same vague area that was the referent of the token of 'that area' Al uttered, and only if the property expressed by the token of 'secluded' it, the that-clause token, contained was φ, the same vague property expressed by the token of 'secluded' Al uttered. But Penumbral Shift on its own should lead us to expect that the penumbral profiles of the tokens of 'that area' and 'secluded' Betty uttered are at least somewhat different from those of the tokens of those expressions Al uttered, and that therefore the contents of Betty's tokens will themselves be somewhat different from the contents of Al's tokens. Then, on top of that, Penumbral Ignorance secures that, while Betty might have said that her intention in uttering 'that area' was to refer to the area to which Al referred the day before, she couldn't have intended to refer to α, for, not knowing α's penumbral profile, she had no way of distinguishing that vague area from the uncountably many very similar vague areas with which it overlapped, and similar reasoning shows that she couldn't have intended her utterance of 'secluded' to express φ. So let α' and φ' be the vague area and the vague property, respectively, whose penumbral profiles match those of the tokens of 'that area' and 'secluded', respectively, that Betty uttered, thereby making <α', φ'> the referent of the that-clause token Betty uttered. Since <α', φ'> $\neq$ <α, φ>, Betty's utterance is false if the Standard View is correct.

Our dilemma, then, is this. On the one hand, saying that the Standard View is correct (and that therefore Betty's utterance of (2) is false) would be problematic, for we would then have to accept a very unappealing error theory, in that it seems obvious to us that many saying reports of the form 'A said that S' are true, but given Penumbral Shift, Penumbral Ignorance, and the fact that the expressions in virtually every that-clause are vague to at least some extent, if we say that the Standard View is correct, then we would have to say that virtually every saying report is false. On the other hand, it would also be problematic to say that Betty's utterance of (2) is true, even though the token of the that-clause she uttered refers to the proposition <α', φ'>. For (2) evidently says that <α', φ'> was the proposition Al said when he uttered (1), and how could that be when the determinants of that proposition weren't operative in the context of Al's utterance but only in the context of Betty's utterance? It is not feasible in this chapter to inventory all the positions in logical space that might be offered as solutions to this dilemma and then to assess their relative merits and demerits, but I should think our first choice would be for a solution that allows us to say both that some close relative of the Standard View is correct and that Betty's utterance of (2) may be true, even though the penumbral profiles of the tokens of 'that area' and 'secluded' she uttered differed somewhat from the penumbral profiles of the tokens of those terms Al uttered.

It's not immediately clear to me how that could work out unless something like one of the following two views was correct.

The more conservative of the two views says that a token of a sentence of the form

(3) *A* said that *P*,

which, for our purposes, we may take to be equivalent to 'The content of *A*'s utterance was the proposition that *P*', doesn't have the truth condition its surface grammar might lead one to think it has. That truth condition is that:

(3) is true iff *A* stands in the having-said relation to the proposition that *P*.[8]

If (3) had that truth condition, it's logical form would be

$$S(A, p),$$

where *S* is the relation expressed by 'said' in (3) and *p* = the proposition that *P*. But the truth condition (3) actually has, the present suggestion goes, is that:

(3) is true iff, for some proposition *q*, *A* stands in the having-said relation to *q* and the proposition that *P* is similar to *q* in such-and-such contextually relevant respects,

which would give (3) a logical form we might represent as:

$$\exists q (S(A, q) \,\&\, (p \approx q)),$$

where '≈' stands for a contextually determined resemblance relation. On this proposal, then, Betty's utterance of (2) ('Al said that that area was secluded') was true if the proposition Al said was similar enough to the proposition to which the token of the that-clause Betty uttered referred, where what counts as being 'similar enough' depends on such things as the conversational point of Betty's utterance. A simpler way of expressing the view being proposed would be to say that saying reports of form (3) contain a hidden *roughly* operator, where the nature and degree of roughness in effect determine how similar the proposition referred to in the saying report must be to the proposition actually said.

The second, less conservative, way out of the pickle the Standard View finds itself in thanks to Penumbral Shift and Penumbral Ignorance might be put in the following way. When we look just at Al's utterance of (1) it seems feasible to say that the content of Al's utterance, and thus what he said, is <α, φ>, but when we look at Betty's utterance we find reason to say that Al said the similar but distinct proposition <α', φ'>. The key assumption underlying this dilemma is that vague expression tokens have their contents absolutely, without relativization to anything. But suppose vague expression tokens don't have their contents absolutely, but only relative to *contexts of interpretation*, where such contexts are contexts in which judgements may be made about the contents of utterances made in other

---

[8] '*A* stands in the having-said relation to the proposition that *P*' is shorthand for 'the referent of the "*A*" term stands in the relation expressed by the token of "said" to the proposition that is the referent of the "that *P*" term.'

contexts of interpretation. If we accept that sort of relativity, then we should also want to say that Betty's utterance of (2) contains an implicit reference to her context of interpretation. We should then understand the revised Standard View to say that Betty's utterance is true relative to her context of interpretation just in case the content of Al's utterance relative to *that* context is the vague proposition that is the referent relative to that same context of the that-clause token Betty uttered. Since the penumbral profile of an expression token can't differ from the penumbral profile of its content,[9] it would also follow that an expression token's penumbral profile was itself relative to a context of interpretation. It should be noticed that the relativity posited by the present suggestion is pretty tame, for it is constrained in the same way differences in the penumbral profiles of tokens of a vague expression are constrained. For example, in no context of interpretation can a property be the property expressed by a token of 'girl' relative to that context unless it's necessarily the case that the property is instantiated by every human female no older than twelve years old. There is one advantage that this proposal has over the more conservative proposal that preceded it, although I'm uncertain how much weight the advantage should be given. Suppose that, instead of having simply uttered (2), Betty had uttered

(4) Yesterday, Al said that that area was secluded; but I don't think that's definitely true. It's at best indeterminate whether it's secluded.

It seems to me that if Carl agrees with Betty that the area in question is at best borderline secluded, then he would, and should, further agree with Betty that what Al said the day before wasn't definitely true, even though the penumbral profile the token of (1) ('That area is secluded') had in Al's context determined a proposition that was true. If that really is a feature of the way we speak which a theory of vague language should accommodate, then that favours the second of the two proposals, for only that proposal permits there to be a way Al's utterance may be said to be true and a way it may be said to be neither definitely true nor definitely false.

Each of the proposals just sketched is, of course, in need of further elaboration. They won't get it here. I offer these sketches primarily by way of illustrating some of the vagaries of interpretation created by Penumbral Shift and Penumbral Ignorance. It is those vagaries that have relevance to theories of judicial interpretation, to which topic I now turn.

5. Penumbral Shift, Penumbral Ignorance, and Judicial Interpretation

As the verb 'to interpret' is used in law, two interpretative acts are typically involved in a judge's interpretation of a law-promulgating text (a *text*, for short)—principally,

---

[9] As we have already noted, if, e.g., the penumbral profile of a predicate token is such that it's indeterminate whether the token is true of a certain thing, then it must also be the case that it's indeterminate whether that thing instantiates the property expressed by the token.

a statute, regulation, or written constitution. The first interpretative act is to decide what is to count as the law promulgated by the text, and, once that is decided, the second interpretative act is to decide how that law applies to a particular case or cases, particularly to cases to be decided by the judge's court. Theories of judicial interpretation are normative theories of how judges ought to perform interpretative acts of the first kind, and those theories are taken to determine, or at least constrain, interpretative acts of the second kind. In this final section I will illustrate the bearing of what I have so far said in this chapter to issues of judicial interpretation by discussing its bearing on one particular theory of judicial interpretation, Supreme Court Justice Antonin Scalia's *textualism*, sometimes called *originalism* in its application to the U.S. Constitution. The discussion of textualism will make salient an entirely unsurprising condition that must be met by any theory of judicial interpretation that hopes to be plausible.

Common law is law based on the principle of *stare decisis*, the principle that 'a decision made in one case will be followed in the next' (Scalia 1997, p. 7). For a judge to decide whether a decision reached in another case is binding on the case before her, she must first discern the principle of that prior decision, where that requires deciding in what respects her case must be similar to the decided case in order for the decision reached in that case to be binding on her case. Discerning the principle established by a court's decision 'is an art, or a game, rather than a science, because what constitutes the "holding" of an earlier case is not well defined and can be adjusted to suit the occasion' (Scalia 1997, p. 8). Because of this scope for creativity on the part of the judge, common law judges have considerable scope within which to create law. Federal courts, however, are not governed by common law, for 'every issue of law resolved by a federal judge involves interpretation of text—the text of a regulation, or of a statute, or of the Constitution' (Scalia 1997, p. 13). Although, he says, he has 'no quarrel with the common law and its process', Scalia does 'question whether the *attitude* of the common-law judge—the mind-set that asks, "What is the most desirable resolution of this case, and how can any impediments to the achievement of that result be evaded?"—is appropriate for most of the work that [federal judges do]' (Scalia 1997, p. 13). Scalia intends his textualism to be an antidote to the attitude he deplores. Textualism holds that jurists should take the law promulgated by a text to be determined by, and only by, 'the meaning the text had when it was created'. As a theory of constitutional interpretation, textualism is called *originalism* because it holds that judicial interpretations of the Constitution should be determined by, and only by, the 'original meaning' of the Constitution, which is to say, 'the meaning [the Constitution] had when it was adopted'.[10] Before we can assess how Penumbral Shift and Penumbral Ignorance might affect textualism we must first know to what 'the meaning a text had at the time it was created' is supposed to refer.

Evidently, it refers to a meaning a text may have at one time but not at another time, and such meanings can only be the meanings of expression *types*. The meaning

[10] Remarks Scalia delivered at the Woodrow Wilson International Center for Scholars in Washington, D.C., on 14 March 2005.

of the word type 'decimate' has changed over time, for it once meant 'to kill one in ten'. But if we're talking about the 'meaning' of a particular token of 'decimate', one can mean only the content of that token, or the meaning the type of which it's a token had at the time the token was produced, and neither of those two things can change over time. But if the 'meaning a text had at a given time' refers to the meanings of the sentence types tokened in the text, then it is impossible for that meaning to determine any law. That is because a law must specify a condition for something's being in conformity with the law, and no sentence type can specify such a condition. No sentence type can specify such a condition because if it did the condition would have to be expressed by a predicate type, or conjunction of predicate types, contained in the sentence. Yet predicates in law-promulgating texts will invariably be vague to at least some degree, and therefore if they expressed properties, those properties would be vague properties, and Penumbral Shift entails that no vague predicate *type* (or conjunction of them) can express any vague property. For, necessarily, if a predicate type expressed a property, then that property would be the content of every literally uttered token of the predicate,[11] but Penumbral Shift entails that literally uttered tokens of a vague predicate may express somewhat different properties, properties with somewhat different penumbral profiles.[12] So, if textualism is to have any chance of being correct, 'the meaning the text had when it was created' must refer to the propositional content expressed by the sentence tokens produced by the authors of the text (in the extended sense of 'token' stipulated above at the beginning of section 4, and that is a content that is constrained but never determined by the meanings of the tokened sentences. I say this, however, not as an objection to Scalia, but merely to show how textualism's talk of 'meaning'

[11] For example, to say that the predicate 'prime number' expresses the property of being a prime number is for all intents and purposes to say that the predicate means that property; but if that is what 'prime number' means, then every literally uttered token of 'prime number' must express the property of being a prime number, for otherwise it wouldn't have been literally uttered.

[12] In other words, Penumbral Shift entails that no vague property can be the meaning of a vague predicate. That is of some importance apart from present concerns, not least because it refutes an often-heard palliative about vagueness (e.g. Mark Sainsbury appeals to the palliative in Sainsbury 1996). The palliative is supposed to show that vagueness requires no special accommodation in, and poses no threat to, compositional truth or meaning theories. For example, a theorist might say that the meaning ascription

(G) 'Girl' means the property of being a girl

is perfectly true as it stands, notwithstanding the vagueness of 'girl', and this because, as the used occurrence of 'girl' in (G) simply inherits its vagueness from that of (G)'s quoted occurrence of 'girl', the vagueness of the used occurrence is the same as the vagueness of the quoted occurrence. Penumbral Shift, however, shows such a claim to be false, for a consequence of Penumbral Shift is that the sentence *type* (G) no more expresses a proposition or has a truth-value than does the sentence type 'She didn't do it to him.' Penumbral Shift also shows something considerably more disturbing to those who hope to take theoretical comfort in the palliative, namely, that, while *tokens* of (G) will express propositions and so have truth-values, *every one of those propositions, and therefore every token of (G), must be false.* To see this, let γ be the vague property that is the content of the unquoted token of 'girl' in the displayed token of (G). γ will have a penumbral profile that matches that of the token of 'girl' whose content it is. Since tokens of that occurrence of 'girl' in other tokens of (G) may, and certainly will, have other penumbral profiles, those tokens won't have γ as their content. At the same time, the referent of the token of 'girl' in the sentence token (G) is the word *type* 'girl', and therefore the displayed token of (G) is true only if the word type 'girl' means γ, which would require γ to be the content of every token of 'girl'—and that, we know, is precluded by Penumbral Shift.

must be understood if it is not to be dismissible as false right off the bat. And while Scalia does say some pretty confused things about meaning (after all, he's a judge, not a semanticist),[13] he also emphasizes the importance of 'context' ('Nothing but conventions and contexts cause a symbol or sound to convey a particular idea'; Scalia and Garner 2012, section on 'Related-Statutes Canon'), and, some of what he writes can be correct only if understood to be about the contents of expression tokens. A good example of that is his explanation of why he dissented from the Supreme Court's holding in *Smith v. United States*.[14] At issue in that case was a statute that provided for an increased gaol term if 'during and in relation to [a] drug trafficking crime [the defendant] uses…a firearm'. The defendant 'used' a gun in a drug trafficking crime in that he offered a drug dealer an unloaded gun in exchange for a certain quantity of cocaine. The Court held that the defendant was subject to the increased gaol time, because he had 'used a firearm during and in relation to a drug trafficking crime'. In his dissent Scalia made an objection which a philosopher of language might have put by saying that a sentence type of the form '*A* used an *X*' no more expresses a proposition, and therefore no more has a truth-value, than does the sentence type 'Bill is tall': just as in a literal utterance of 'Bill is tall' there must be a comparison class *C* such that in uttering the sentence the speaker meant that Bill was tall for a *C* (e.g. an eight-year-old boy or an NBA forward), so in a literal utterance of 'Smith used a firearm' there must be something *X* that a firearm might be used to do such that in uttering the sentence the speaker meant that Smith used a firearm to *X* (e.g. threaten a rival or drive a nail). It seemed clear to Scalia that the proposition expressed by the statute was that a defendant who used a firearm to *shoot or threaten to shoot* his victim in the commission of a drug-trafficking crime would be subject to an increased gaol term. As Scalia observed, 'when you ask someone, "Do you use a cane?" you are not inquiring whether he has hung his grandfather's antique cane as a decoration in the hallway' (Scalia 1997, p. 24).

Should we, then, understand textualism to be the doctrine that jurists ought to interpret the law promulgated by a text to be nothing more nor less than what the text says, its propositional content? That is close to what it needs to be, but it needs a little more refining. Although there are many issues about the nature of the propositional contents of vague sentence tokens, only one of those issues—the issue of arrays of precise propositions versus vague propositions—has been discussed in this chapter. Nevertheless, I believe, and will assume, that a textualist neither puts herself at a disadvantage nor gives herself an advantage by adopting the working hypothesis that those contents are vague propositions whose penumbral profiles match those of the sentence tokens whose contents they are (either absolutely or relative to a context of interpretation or some other parameter). It may, however, seem that it

---

[13] In one of his discussions of meaning, Scalia says that 'King Lear would still be King Lear if it were produced by the random typing of a thousand monkeys over a thousand years. And a Bob Hope joke would still be funny if it were sculpted in sand by the action of the desert wind' (Scalia and Garner 2012, section on 'Textualism and Its Challengers'; references are to Kindle publication of the book, which doesn't give original page numbers).

[14] *Smith v. United States*, 508 U.S. 223 (1993).

matters a lot to the textualist which account of saying reports (= accounts of what texts say) is correct. For instance, the textualist will clearly want to distance herself from the two theories of saying reports that emerged in the wake of the dilemma Penumbral Shift and Penumbral Ignorance create for the Standard View of saying reports, for both those theories give interpretative weight to the interests of those interpreting a text, and that must be anathema to the textualist. Fortunately for the textualist, she needn't, and shouldn't, get embroiled in the details of the semantics of statements reporting what a text says. Her theory shouldn't turn on which semantic theory turns out to be the best fit for those reports. Her theory needs, quite simply, to be that a judge ought to take the law promulgated by a legal text to be given by, and only by, the set of vague propositions whose penumbral profiles match those had by the sentence tokens that comprise the text in the context in which those tokens were produced.[15] Unfortunately for the textualist, although that is the best formulation of her theory, it is nevertheless a formulation that the textualist should reject; for not only would its acceptance by judges *not* be an antidote to the 'mind-set that asks, "What is the most desirable resolution of this case, and how can any impediments to the achievement of that result be evaded?" ', its acceptance would actually *encourage* that mind-set. Let me explain.

The problem for the textualist is that he not only has Penumbral Shift and Penumbral Ignorance to contend with; he has them *plus* (what we may call) *Judicial Necessity* to contend with. When someone says something we judge not to have a determinate truth-value, it's no big deal: we judge that what they said has no determinate truth-value and move on. Judicial Necessity is the fact that that is a luxury judges don't have. More exactly, Judicial Necessity applies to federal judges who must decide cases involving the interpretation of legal texts; it is the fact that a judge hearing such a case never has the option of not deciding the case because it's indeterminate whether the law in question applies to it. Even if a judge knows that the relevant law has no determinate application to the case she is hearing, she must still officially 'decide' either that the law does apply to the case or that it doesn't apply to it.[16] Now, *even one who is unaware of Penumbral Shift and Penumbral Ignorance* should expect that a judge who is a textualist—say, a Supreme Court Justice (call her *X*)—will not infrequently find herself in the following sort of bind:

1. The Court is hearing a case in which the issue is whether a certain statute *S* is in violation of a certain amendment *A* to the Constitution. It's clear to *X* and to many other jurists that, regardless of what one ought to understand the *law* promulgated by *A* to be, *A*'s *propositional content* has no determinate application to *S*. (Perhaps *X* is one of the Supreme Court Justices hearing *District of Columbia v. Heller*. In that case the Court had to decide whether or not the District of Columbia's Firearms Control Regulations Act of 1975

---

[15] Please keep in mind that as I'm using 'token', the word applies to abstract occurrences of sentences in abstract works that may or may not themselves have physical tokens, such as a book, all copies of which have been destroyed, or a long-forgotten statute, no copies of which still exist.

[16] To rule that a statute is 'void for vagueness' is to rule that in the case being heard no law promulgated by the statute was violated because the statute promulgated no legally binding law.

was in violation of the Second Amendment to the Constitution. The act prohibited D.C. residents other than law enforcement officers or members of the military from possessing handguns, unless that handgun had been registered under the District's registration law and was then reregistered within sixty days after the act went into effect. The Second Amendment to the Constitution, adopted in 1791, reads: 'A well regulated Militia, being necessary to the security of a free State, the right of the people to keep and bear Arms, shall not be infringed.')

2. Since X is a textualist *and* believes that A's propositional content has no determinate application to S, X must further believe that statute S is neither determinately in violation of the law promulgated by A nor determinately not in violation of it.

3. Nevertheless, Judicial Necessity requires that X either vote that S is in violation of the law promulgated by A or else vote that S is not in violation of that law. Therefore, not only will her vote be hypocritical, in that it won't represent what she believes, it will also be a vote that could only have been made on the basis of considerations other than what by her lights the law requires, and in that sense X's vote must be decided by considerations other than A's propositional content—say, by general principles of morality or public policy, or whatever else might help X to decide which outcome would have the best consequences.

One doesn't need Penumbral Shift and Penumbral Ignorance to make the point that the *propositional contents* of texts will not infrequently fail to deliver determinate verdicts on legal issues that fall within their purview. That point can be made just on the basis of what most philosophers who work on vagueness take for granted about it. The importance of Penumbral Shift and Penumbral Ignorance for textualism, and for theories of judicial interpretation generally, is that they should make one appreciate how many cases there would be in which a judge would have to believe that it was indeterminate how the law promulgated by a text applied in those cases, if that law had to be determined solely by the propositional content of the text. This is made even more apparent when one also takes into account two ancillary facts about the kinds of texts judges are required to interpret. First, these are very often texts in which quite vague predicates must be applied to cases that are outside the safe zone of cases with respect to which every token of a predicate must apply/fail to apply simply by virtue of being a token of that predicate; and second, although we don't know exactly what determines the penumbral profiles of tokens of vague expressions, we do seem to know that some weight attaches to the judgments speakers make when their generalizations are tested by cases they hadn't anticipated when they made those generalizations. The problem is that counterfactual judgments about what judgments speakers would have made if their generalizations had been confronted with this, that, or the other kind of unexpected case are mostly indeterminate, and because of the indeterminacy of those counterfactuals one seeking to know the application status of a generalization with respect to such a case is bound to judge the application status to be indeterminate. In fact, I submit that this sort of indeterminacy is manifested in most of the cases in which the Supreme Court's decision is reached by a vote whose split just happens to coincide with a split in the political ideology of the Justices.

No one who agrees with the points just made can coherently call himself a textualist. For to agree about the frequent indeterminacy of application of generalizations in the propositional contents of legal texts is perforce to recognize that often the decisions reached by federal judges can't be based *only* on the propositional contents of the legal texts they must interpret but must be based in part on considerations pertaining to the moral and ideological consequences of their decisions, and once the importance of such considerations are recognized, what will there be, really, to distinguish the view of the textualist from the view of a theorist such as Ronald Dworkin,[17] a prime example of the sort of legal theorist Scalia says has the attitude of the common-law judge, 'the mind-set that asks, "What is the most desirable resolution of this case, and how can any impediments to the achievement of that result be evaded?" '

Scalia has expounded on textualism in many places, culminating with the publication in 2012 of *Reading Law: The Interpretation of Legal Texts*, a book (co-authored with Bryan Garner) of well over 500 pages. One would expect to find in these writings *some* awareness of the dangers vagueness poses for textualism. In fact, however, one finds virtually no such awareness, and in the Introduction to that book one even finds Scalia saying he hopes his book will demonstrate that 'most interpretive questions have a right answer'—although he doesn't tell us the nature of that demonstration and it's very clear that the book demonstrates no such thing. I think there may be a few reasons—in addition to the entirely understandable reason that he isn't very aware of the ubiquity of vagueness or of its trouble-making features—why Scalia doesn't think the textualist judge will find himself in the sort of dilemma Penumbral Shift, Penumbral Ignorance, and Judicial Necessity predict he should find himself in. First, like most of us he can be disingenuous or self-deceiving about the meanings he finds, or about the ideological considerations that are instrumental to his finding the meanings he finds. (In *District of Columbia v. Heller*, mentioned above, the Court voted by five to four that the District's Firearms Control Regulations Act of 1975 violated the Second Amendment ('A well regulated Militia, being necessary to the security of a free State, the right of the people to keep and bear Arms, shall not be infringed') and was therefore unconstitutional. The Opinion of the Court was delivered by Justice Scalia, and in it he wrote that 'The Amendment's prefatory clause announces a purpose, but does not limit or expand the scope of the second part, the operative clause.' OK, so if I say 'Having noticed there was no milk in the house, I went to the supermarket', what I said is true if I noticed there was no milk in the house today but went to the supermarket three weeks ago.) Second, Scalia seems to share the attitude, prevalent in legal writings on judicial interpretation, that vagueness in, say, the text of a statute isn't something that might result in the statute's being indeterminate in its application to certain

17 See e.g. Dworkin 1996.

cases but merely something one must work around to get a 'fair reading' of the text which eliminates the vagueness, as though the vagueness of a text might not be an ineliminable feature of its content. Third, Scalia is often too quick to infer from the fact that speakers at a certain time applied a term to certain things that their application of the term to those things was correct, rather than the result of their mistaken belief that the term applied to those things. Fourth, when all is said and done, Scalia doesn't really accept the textualism he claims to own, the view that a judge ought to understand the law promulgated by a text to be determined by, and only by, 'the meaning the text had at the time it was created'. In the Preface to *Reading Law*, after saying that judges ought to consider the meaning of a text to be the sole determinant of the law promulgated by the text, Scalia asks how that meaning is to be determined, and his answer is that 'nothing but conventions and contexts cause a symbol or sound to convey a particular idea'. But then he immediately adds that there are also 'jurisprudential conventions that make legal interpretation more than just a linguistic exercise'. The jurisprudential conventions to which he alludes are so-called *canons of interpretation*, of which the book lists seventy. Then, lest he be accused of having mischaracterized textualism, he quickly adds that 'properly regarded, [these canons] are not "rules" of interpretation in any strict sense but presumptions about what an intelligently produced text conveys'.[18] That does fairly describe several of the canons. For example, the 'Conjunctive/Disjunctive Canon' is that '*and* joins a conjunctive list, *or* a disjunctive list—but with negatives, plurals, and various specific wordings there are nuances' and the 'Punctuation Canon' is that 'punctuation is a permissible indicator of meaning'. Other canons, however, are clearly not platitudes consistent with the claim that the law promulgated by a text is determined by, and only by, the propositional content of that text, and some of these canons can be brought to bear when it would be indeterminate how a particular law applied to a given case if the law promulgated by the text really were wholly determined by the text's propositional content. Examples include the *Rule of Lenity* ('Ambiguity [which in legal writings usually encompasses vagueness] in a statute defining a crime or imposing a penalty should be resolved in the defendant's favor'); the *Constitutional-Doubt Canon* ('A statute should be interpreted in a way that avoids placing its constitutionality in doubt'); the *Related-Statutes Canon* ('Statutes *in pari materia* are to be interpreted together, as though they were one law'); and the *Prior-Construction Canon* ('If a statute uses words or phrases that have already received authoritative construction by the jurisdiction's court of last resort, or even uniform construction by inferior courts or a responsible administrative agency, they are to be understood according to that construction'). Depending on the authority courts permit them to have them, such canons might decrease the number of cases in which a law has no determinate application, but there would still remain many cases in which a textualist judge *should* find himself in the kind of dilemma Penumbral Shift, Penumbral Ignorance, and Judicial Necessity will often

---

[18] Scalia and Garner 2012, in the section 'Sound Principles of Interpretation'. All the remaining quotations are also from this section.

create for any textualist judge capable of knowing when the propositional content of the text he must apply to his case has no determinate application to that case. It might also be noted that, while certain of the canons of interpretation will result in certain laws having a determinate application which they wouldn't have had but for those canons, it's also the case that those canons force the textualist who acknowledges them to admit the relevance of moral and policy principles in determining what the law should be, for it is in those principles that the canons in question find their justification. The entirely unsurprising upshot of the foregoing discussion of textualism is that no theory of judicial interpretation can hope to be plausible unless it recognizes the legitimate—indeed, inescapable—reliance on moral and other normative considerations in the making of judicial decisions.[19]

References

Dworkin, Ronald. 1996. *Freedom's Law: The Moral Reading of the American Constitution.* Cambridge (MA): Harvard University Press.

Endicott, Timothy. 2000. *Vagueness in Law.* Oxford: Oxford University Press.

Fine, Kit. 1975. 'Vagueness, Truth and Logic'. *Synthese* 30(3): 265–300.

Greenawalt, Kent. 2001. 'Vagueness and Judicial Responses to Legal Indeterminacy'. *Legal Theory* 7(4): 433–45.

Łukasiewicz, Jan and Alfred Tarski. 1956. 'Investigations into the Sentential Calculus'. In Alfred Tarski, *Logic, Semantics, Metamathematics*, translated by J.H. Woodger, 38–59. Oxford: Clarendon Press.

Sainsbury, Mark. 1996. 'Concepts Without Boundaries'. In *Vagueness: A Reader*, edited by Rosanna Keefe and Peter Smith, 251–64. Cambridge (MA): MIT Press.

Scalia, Antonin. 1997. *A Matter of Interpretation: Federal Courts and the Law.* Princeton: Princeton University Press.

Scalia, Antonin and Garner, Bryan A. 2012. *Reading Law: The Interpretation of Legal Texts.* St Paul (MN): Thomson/West.

Schiffer, Stephen. 1999. 'The Epistemic Theory of Vagueness'. *Noûs* 33(s13): 481–503.

Schiffer, Stephen. 2001. 'A Little Help From Your Friends?' *Legal Theory* 7(4): 421–32.

Schiffer, Stephen. 2003. *The Things We Mean.* Oxford: Oxford University Press.

Sorensen, Roy A. 1988. *Blindspots.* Oxford: Clarendon Press.

Williamson, Timothy. 1994. *Vagueness.* London: Routledge.

Williamson, Timothy. 1999. 'Schiffer on the Epistemic Theory of Vagueness'. *Noûs* 33(s13): 505–17.

Wright, Crispin. 1976. 'Language-Mastery and the Sorites Paradox'. In *Truth and Meanings: Essays in Semantics*, edited by Gareth Evans and John McDowell, 223–47. Oxford: Clarendon Press.

[19] This chapter derives from a talk I gave at the conference on 'Vagueness in Law' held at New York University in March 2013. It benefited from the discussion following my talk, and from the astute observations of my commentator, Andree Weber. A version of it was also given as a talk at Tel Aviv University in December 2014, and the discussion following that talk was also beneficial.

2

Vagueness in Law

Placing the Blame Where It's Due

Diana Raffman

1.

Linguistic vagueness is often viewed as causing trouble for the law. For instance, in the U.S. Supreme Court's majority opinion in *Grayned v. City of Rockford*,[1] Justice Thurgood Marshall writes:

Vague laws offend several important values. First, because we assume that man is free to steer between lawful and unlawful conduct, we insist that laws give the person of ordinary intelligence a reasonable opportunity to know what is prohibited, so that he may act accordingly. Vague laws may trap the innocent by not providing fair warnings. Second, if arbitrary and discriminatory enforcement is to be prevented, laws must provide explicit standards for those who apply them. A vague law impermissibly delegates basic policy matters to policemen, judges, and juries for resolution on an *ad hoc* and subjective basis, with the attendant dangers of arbitrary and discriminatory applications.

(*Grayned*, pp. 108–9)

Vagueness is standardly understood as the possession of blurred boundaries of application, where the 'blur' is supposed to consist in the existence (or possibility) of borderline cases of a term's application. Borderline cases are thought to be a chief source of legal indeterminacy, and legal indeterminacy may force judges to make decisions arbitrarily.[2] Timothy Endicott writes:

Vagueness is a snare for legal theorists. They have grappled fitfully with an enigma it creates for legal theory—or, at least, for any theory that portrays courts as applying the law. If the law is formulated in vague language, what does a court do in a borderline case? If it is not clear what the law requires in such a case, how can a court apply the law? It almost seems as if there is no law for the case, and yet there is a legal provision that claims to tell people their rights and duties.

(Endicott 2000, p. 57)

---

[1] 408 U.S. 104 (1972).
[2] See Bix 2004, pp. 97–8, for some different conceptions of legal indeterminacy. See Raffman 2005 and 2014, ch. 2, for arguments that borderline cases are not in fact definitive of vagueness.

Vagueness in law: Placing the Blame Where it's Due. First Edition. Diana Raffman. © Diana Raffman 2016.
Published 2016 by Oxford University Press.

Roy Sorensen paints a particularly bleak picture:

> Judges cannot discover the correct answer to a question about an absolute borderline case because no one can. When a judge regards *x* as an absolute borderline F, he can no longer even try to learn whether *x* is F. He is stuck. The judge is not permitted just to confess his ignorance. The judge is obliged to answer. Therefore, he is obliged to answer insincerely.
>
> (Sorensen 2001, p. 400)[3]

Legal theorists who discuss borderline cases and indeterminacy often take the type of vagueness at issue to be soritical, i.e. the type associated with the notorious sorites paradox. 'Old', 'adult', 'mentally handicapped', 'seriously distressing', and 'cruel punishment' are prime examples of soritically vague terms. For a simple example to start, consider a series of ages proceeding from an age at which a person is clearly old, say eighty-five years, to an age at which a person is clearly not-old,[4] say ten years, and suppose that each age is one day younger than the last. (Assume a single fixed context, e.g. Canadians in 1990.) Since a single day cannot make the difference between being old and being not-old, it seems we can construct the following argument:

> Eighty-five years is an old age.
> If eighty-five years is an old age, then eighty-five-years-minus-one-day is an old age.
> If eighty-five-years-minus-one-day is an old age, then eighty-five-years-minus-two-days
>   is an old age.
> Etc.
> Therefore, ten years is an old age.

This is the sorites paradox: seemingly impeccable reasoning from seemingly impeccable premises yields an absurd result. An analogous puzzle is thought to arise for any word that has blurred boundaries. The conditional premises in the paradoxical argument are meant to express the intuition that a vague term like 'old' is *tolerant*: it tolerates incremental changes in the dimension(s) (here, age) decisive of its application (Wright 1976).

The proper diagnosis of the paradox—what has gone wrong in the argument?—is a matter of persistent controversy, and I am not going to go into that here.[5] But the device of a sorites series will play an important role in my discussion. I said that legal theorists working on problems of vagueness and indeterminacy in the law often take the species of vagueness at issue to be soritical. Here is Andrei Marmor, employing a variant of H.L.A. Hart's classic example:

A city ordinance stipulates that 'No motor vehicles are allowed in the park.' Now, we know what motor vehicles are; the determinate extension is pretty clear. But suppose that the question arises whether a bicycle powered by a small electric engine also counts as a 'motor

---

[3] Sorensen uses here the term 'absolute borderline case' to refer to soritical borderline cases; see the next paragraph above. The present paper is much informed by Sorensen's, despite reaching a different conclusion.
[4] Here and throughout, 'not-Φ' will mean whatever 'not Φ' means; I use the hyphen only to avoid scope ambiguities.
[5] I propose a diagnosis in the course of developing a theory of vagueness in Raffman 2014.

vehicle' for the purposes of this ordinance and thus [is] prohibited from entering the park. Can we say whether an electric bicycle is a motor vehicle or not? The answer would seem to be that from a semantic perspective it can go either way. It would not seem to be mistaken to say that it is, nor would it be a mistake to say that it isn't.

Furthermore, it is easy to see how we get a sorites sequence here: Suppose we say that an electric bicycle is not a motor vehicle. Then what about a motorized wheelchair? A golf cart powered by an electric engine? A golf cart powered by a regular engine? A small scooter? And so on and so forth.

(Marmor 2012, p. 9)[6]

Endicott elaborates an example designed by Mark Sainsbury (1995, pp. 26 and 38) in which 'someone makes a pearl-sized lump of pearl [material]' (Endicott 2000, p. 39). The question immediately at issue for Endicott is whether the lump would be a borderline case of a pearl; but for present purposes I am interested in the series he constructs, meant to be a sorites series, in order to justify an affirmative answer:

We could place [the lump] in a sorites series from clear cases of the positive extension of 'pearl' to clear cases of its negative extension.... Start with a paradigm pearl. Then imagine an almost fully developed pearl taken from an oyster and given a very thin coating of pearl material. Then imagine a very slightly less developed pearl taken from an oyster and given a very slightly thicker coating of pearl material.... That process can be continued until we reach [the lump], and it can be continued past [the lump] by gradually altering the composition of the material, until we end up with something that is clearly not a pearl.

(Endicott 2000, p. 41 n. 20)

Another example from Endicott will be important later in our discussion:

We can use the regulation of music in Britain to illustrate the problem. The Criminal Justice and Public Order Act empowers the police to direct organizers of 'raves' to shut down their sound equipment, and creates an offence of refusing to do so. The power applies to 'a gathering... at which amplified music is played during the night... and is such as... is likely to cause serious distress to the inhabitants of the locality.'... [It is] easy to imagine clear cases of a 'rave' as defined in the Act. It seems that there will also be borderline cases, chiefly because of the vagueness of 'serious distress.' Somewhere between the silent and the seismic, there is music to which the police power is not clearly applicable, and not clearly inapplicable.

Imagine one million rave organizers charged with disobeying a police order to shut down their music. All appear in the same court one after the other. The first defendant [played music] at a deafening volume, and he is convicted. All the defendants played the same music in the same way under the same conditions, except that each successive rave organizer played the music at an imperceptibly lower volume—until the one millionth rave organizer played

[6] Here I quote from the original 2012 draft of this paper published as USC Legal Studies Research Paper No. 12–8. The version of the paper now available (under the same title) at <http://papers.ssrn.com/sol3/papers.cfm?abstract_id=2039076> is a subsequent revision (2013) that no longer includes the example of a motorized wheelchair. (The paper also appears as ch. 4 of Marmor 2014.) I cite the original 2012 version simply because a wheelchair is easy to represent pictorially; see the discussion in section 3 below. Nothing essential to my argument turns on this.

it at a hush that undeniably caused no distress to anyone. He will be acquitted. But if the decrement in volume in each case is trivial, it seems that no particular conviction ought to be the last....Finding the organizer guilty in one case and not in the next case seems arbitrary....A court should be able to justify its decisions, and how can a trivial change in the music justify the difference between conviction and acquittal? If like cases should be treated alike, then the legal treatment of two cases should not be materially different when there is no material difference between them.

(Endicott 2000, pp. 57–8)

I will say more about these examples shortly.

In what follows I will argue that in legal cases where soritical vagueness is present, specifically where the court appears obliged to draw arbitrary boundaries between cases that are only incrementally different, the difficulty derives not from the vagueness of the language in which the law is expressed, but rather from the relationship between the law and the continuous, seamless character of the actions and states of affairs to which it is applied.[7] Contrary to appearances, soritical vagueness provides the resources to *avoid* drawing sharp boundaries in a continuous environment. But by its nature, the law cannot make use of those resources. Only ordinary speakers can make use of them, and so the legal difficulties remain.

Before turning to my central argument, I need to distinguish two sources of legal indeterminacy that differ importantly from soritical vagueness but are often run together with it.[8] This will help to isolate the species of vagueness that concerns us.

2.

The two non-soritical sources of legal indeterminacy I have in mind are *open texture* and *essential contestedness*. I'll begin by characterizing soritical vagueness in greater detail so that the contrast with the other two notions comes out clearly.

(i) **Soritical vagueness.** According to the standard philosophical picture, soritically vague terms have blurred boundaries of application: there is no clear division between the ages that are old and the ages that are not, or between the punishments that are cruel and the punishments that are not. The 'blur' is typically thought to consist in possession of borderline cases—the 'iffy' items in a sorites series that lie between the clear cases at the endpoints. Less roughly, borderline cases for a vague term 'Φ' are items (e.g. ages) with respect to which it is *indeterminate* whether they are Φ. Maybe sixty-five years, for example, is a borderline old age, lying between the determinately old ages and the determinately not-old ages but not classifiable with either. In general, borderline cases are *neither determinately Φ nor determinately*

---

[7] The term 'seamless' used in this context comes from Sainsbury 1990.

[8] I am hardly the first to notice the muddle on this score (*cf.* e.g. Endicott 2000, especially ch. 3, Sorensen 2001, Waldron 2002, Bix 1993, Marmor 2005, Schauer 2011, Poscher 2012); but my sorting of it may shed a different light on the role of vagueness in legal language.

not-Φ—neither determinately old nor determinately not-old, neither determinately cruel nor determinately not-cruel.⁹

I defend a different view of borderline cases (Raffman 2005 and 2014, ch. 2). In
the present context, its most important element is the claim that any item that can
competently be classified as borderline Φ can also competently be classified as Φ
and as not-Φ;¹⁰ I'll express this idea by saying that any item that can competently be
classified as borderline Φ is *variable* with respect to the predicates at issue (*viz.*, 'Φ',
'not-Φ', 'borderline Φ').¹¹ A crucial feature of this variability is the arbitrariness to
which it gives rise: there can be no reason, no argument in the nature of the case, for
classifying a variable item as borderline (or as Φ, or as not-Φ) rather than as Φ (borderline, not-Φ) or as not-Φ (Φ, borderline). By the same token, a competent speaker
classifying each age in our series *seriatim* could stop applying 'old' at any of a number
of places: the word 'old' admits of multiple equally competent, arbitrarily different
stopping places. (Of course, any permissible stopping place will lie in the region
of borderline or variable cases, not in the determinate regions near the endpoints.)
Different speakers will stop at different places, and each individual speaker will stop
at different places on different runs along the series. The differences are arbitrary in
the sense that there can be no reason, in the nature of the case, to stop applying 'old'
at any *particular* age. (If there can be such a reason, then the series in question is not
a sorites series; the difference between adjacent items is too large.)

Presumably speakers are aware of the arbitrariness: they are aware that they could
have stopped elsewhere. Consequently there is no question of argument and no
question of error: when speakers diverge in their stopping places, they don't, or
anyway shouldn't, argue with each other or think each other mistaken; and when
I vary in my stopping places from one occasion to the next, I don't think that I am
correcting my prior use each time. In such cases there is mere divergence, not genuine disagreement, where by 'disagreement' I mean roughly a divergence in which
argument is appropriate, i.e. reasons can be given, and mistakes are possible.

A distinction between sense and reference will help to separate soritical vagueness from open texture and essential contestedness. Soritical vagueness, possession
of blurred boundaries of application, is an aspect of the *reference* of a vague word:

---

⁹ Also, since neither '*x* is Φ' nor '*x* is not Φ' is true of a borderline case, so the standard story goes,
bivalence is violated and sentences referring to borderline cases are neither true nor false but rather
indeterminate in truth-value. In the legal-theoretic literature, see e.g. Raz 1979 for this view. As I see it,
indeterminacy, legal or otherwise, is not properly characterized in terms of a failure of bivalence, but
I cannot pursue that question here. At present I am concerned only with *sources* of legal indeterminacy.

¹⁰ Actually, on the analysis I develop in Raffman 2005 and 2014, ch. 2, borderline cases are not
defined in terms of contradictory predicates like 'old' and 'not-old'; rather, they are defined in terms
of incompatible predicates such as 'old' and 'middle-aged', or 'old' and 'young'. This difference isn't
germane to my discussion here, though, so for present purposes I go along with the standard analysis.
(For some good examples of incompatible predicates, see the passage from Waldron 2002 quoted at
the end of section 4 below.)

¹¹ Some philosophers of language *define* borderline cases as items that are variable in this way (e.g.
Shapiro 2006). I think that goes too far; rather, any item that can competently be classified as borderline is variable. ('Variable' here is a metalinguistic theoretical term.) The latter claim entails that a
classification of 'borderline' is never *required*; therefore, I contend, there can be no clear or determinate
borderline cases. See Raffman 2005, 2010, and 2014, ch. 2, for elaboration.

the question is whether a word like 'old' or 'seriously distressing' applies in a given borderline case. The associated indeterminacy consists in the existence of multiple equally permissible answers to that question (multiple permissible stopping places in a sorites series). It's not that the sense or meaning analysis of a vague word is indeterminate or otherwise unclear; its sense may *be* indeterminate, but that is an independent fact, not an element, or even a result, of its vagueness.[12]

(ii) **Open texture.** Let me say straightaway that my characterizations of open texture and essential contestedness will be superficial; just how these features of language, in particular legal language, should be understood is a matter of on-going discussion among legal theorists, and exploring those issues would take us off our path.[13] For present purposes I will say just enough about these two phenomena to make clear the relevant ways in which they differ from soritical vagueness.

In his book *Law, Language, and Legal Indeterminacy*, Brian Bix discusses Hart's famous fictional rule 'No vehicles in the park'. Hart wrote:

There will … be plain cases constantly recurring in similar contexts to which general expressions are clearly applicable ('If anything is a vehicle a motor-car is one') but there will also be cases where it is not clear whether they apply or not. ('Does "vehicle" used here include bicycles, airplanes, roller skates?')

(Hart 1961/1994, p. 126)

Now Bix:

We begin with the plain case or the paradigm (the car) and then consider a list of criteria which allow us to begin to evaluate how similar a purported extension would be. For example, like a car, roller-skates make noise (but not nearly as much) and they threaten safety and order (though ... on a much lower scale). [On the other hand,] roller-skates are far smaller than cars and ... do not pollute the air [like cars]. There are both similarities and dissimilarities; some criteria are fulfilled, others are not. In Hart's language, 'there are reasons both for and against our use of a general term.' This is the 'open texture' of rules, that particular situations arise that we are not thinking of when proffering the rule and which are different in some ways from the situation we had in mind (the paradigm) at that time.

(Bix 1993, p. 9)[14]

Bix's remarks reveal at least two important differences between open texture and soritical vagueness. First, notice that the 'criteria' he cites are different dimensions on which the similarity of roller skates to cars can be assessed—noisiness, size, dangerousness, etc. Skates are like cars on some dimensions and different on others; some

---

[12] You might think that if sense determines reference, then there must be something relevantly 'multiple' or otherwise indeterminate about the sense of a vague expression as well as its reference. It's not clear to me how such a view would apply to terms like 'tall' or 'old' or 'blue' as opposed to multi-dimensional terms like 'vehicle' or 'nice' or 'reasonable'; but even if it is correct, it changes nothing essential to my account of vagueness in legal or ordinary language.

[13] For an introduction to that debate, see again Sorensen 2001.

[14] For Waismann, who introduced the term (Waismann 1945), open texture is the permanent possibility of unforeseen, possibly unforeseeable (e.g. wildly implausible) cases with respect to which it is unclear whether a given concept applies. Hart's use of the term seems to have been somewhat inconsistent; see Schauer 2011 for illuminating discussion.

properties of skates, like their noisiness, provide reason to classify them together with cars, while other properties, like their size, provide reason not to. If I understand correctly, the thought is that it's indeterminate whether skates are vehicles because it's indeterminate whether (e.g.) having a certain relatively large size is essential to being a vehicle.[15] In contrast, in a soritical borderline case, a single feature is describable both as Φ and as not-Φ: a single age of sixty-five years is describable both as old and as not-old. Thus the roller skates, with their multiple potentially decisive features, are essentially different from soritical borderline cases.[16]

Notice also Bix's talk of reasons. He quotes Hart as asserting that 'there are reasons both for and against our use of a general term', for example, reasons both for and against classifying roller skates along with cars as vehicles. With respect to soritical borderline cases, however, there can be no such reasons: there can be no reason, in the nature of the case, for classifying sixty-five as old rather than borderline or not-old—in general, no reasons for stopping at any *particular* age. Bix writes:

> Hart wrote that by his notion of judicial discretion he did not mean that the judge's decision would be merely arbitrary. [In *The Concept of Law*] he had written that in the filling in of 'open texture,' judges display 'judicial virtues' (for example, impartiality and reliance on neutral principles) in a legislative task.... Discretion is a negative freedom, an absence of constraint, but not necessarily (or usually) an absolute freedom.
>
> (Bix 1993, pp. 26–7)[17]

We find nothing analogous to such discretion in our 'decisions' to stop at any particular place in a sorites series. The scare quotes around 'decisions' in the preceding sentence are meant to underscore the contrast between classification of a soritical borderline case, on the one hand, and decision making in the presence of open texture, on the other. Only in the most attenuated sense do I *decide* how to classify the variable items in the series; rather, some psychological mechanism, some norm-free subpersonal part of me, puts them into one category or another. From the viewpoint of semantics (*a fortiori* of the law) my classifications of soritical borderline cases are, within a certain range of alternatives, random. Most important of all, whereas the indeterminacy of open texture is resolvable by appeal to such factors as the intentions of the framers of a law, or what is best morally or politically

---

[15] Philosophers of language sometimes talk about soritical borderline cases in similar fashion. Here is Lynda Burns, for example:

> [W]e should blame [the] hesitation [characteristic of borderline cases] on the recognition of the more cautious observers of aspects of the object which make it deserving of the predicate, and other aspects which make it less than so deserving. That is, these objects present us, or can present us, with equivocal information. They have the potential to impress us with features which make them describable as F, and other features which should make us describe them as non-F: this is what makes the predicate F vague.
>
> (Burns 1995, p. 31)

I think Burns' characterization is mistaken, for the reason given above.

[16] As far as I can tell, open texture as characterized above is the phenomenon that often goes by the name 'multidimensional vagueness' in the philosophical literature. Endicott introduces the term 'extravagantly vague' for this kind of vagueness (Endicott 2011, pp. 24–5).

[17] See Schauer 2011 for an argument that language is not open-textured in the way Hart envisioned.

for the society in question, or what fits best with established theory in other areas, the indeterminacy of soritical borderlines is not resolvable at all. We can arbitrarily precisify, but that is a far cry from resolution in the sense intended here.

Appeal to a sense/reference distinction may shed light here as well. The open texture of 'vehicle' is an indeterminacy not in the term's reference, but in its sense. Insofar as its decisive dimensions of application are unclear, its sense or meaning analysis—its definition, if you like—is indeterminate. Hence if the roller skates are indeterminate with respect to being a vehicle, they are indeterminate in a sense importantly different from that of soritical borderlines. The latter reflect an indeterminacy (multiplicity) in the reference of a vague term, not the sense.

(iii) Essentially contested concepts. On at least one usual understanding, essential contestedness too is an indeterminacy with respect to the dimensions that decide the application of a term (concept). However, essentially contested concepts are normative concepts, and whereas the disagreement engendered by open texture is restricted to the transitional items near the boundaries of neighbouring categories, essentially contested concepts provoke disagreement even about cases that all sides take to be clear. Jeremy Waldron explains:

> [T]he term 'essentially' refers to the *location* of the disagreement or indeterminacy; it is contestation at the core, not just at the borderlines or penumbra, of a concept. We all know about vagueness and legal indeterminacy based on vagueness: some things are green, some are blue; but on the borderlines there are blue/green cases of uncertainty. This and allied phenomena like 'open texture' are quite familiar in jurisprudence. By contrast, [an essentially contested concept] evokes disagreement not only about marginal cases... but also about paradigm or core cases.
>
> (Waldron 2002, pp. 148–9)

For example, debates over the moral permissibility of abortion often focus on cases that both sides take to be clear: the 'pro-life' side holds that a conceptus clearly is, while the 'pro-choice' side holds that a conceptus clearly is not, a person with a right to life. In contrast, divergences resulting from the soritical vagueness of 'person' are restricted to transitional items (e.g. gestational stages) in the progression from a non-person to a person. This is what makes the latter divergence arbitrary, and the giving of reasons inappropriate, and mistakes impossible. It is *mere* divergence. Moreover, application of a vague word is intra-subjectively, not just inter-subjectively, variable: each speaker will vary arbitrarily in her stopping places in a sorites series for 'person', and will not (or at least should not) suppose, on any particular occasion, that she is correcting her past use. In the abortion debate, on the other hand, each side thinks that opposing views are defective.

3.

Of the three examples cited above—'No motor vehicles in the park', the pearl-sized lump of pearl material, and the case of the million raves—only the last employs a sorites series; it illustrates the tolerance of the predicate 'serious distress' over incremental differences in volume. In Marmor's series for 'motor vehicle', on the other hand, adjacent items are not incrementally different in the way required for a sorites series. (For convenience and clarity in what follows, I am going to adjust Marmor's example and work with the predicate 'vehicle', as in Hart's original scenario, and the series in Figure 2.1 below). We have no reason to think that, in ordinary English, the predicate 'vehicle' tolerates the difference (whatever exactly it may be) between (e.g.) a golf cart and a bicycle, or between a wheelchair and a pair of roller skates. Indeed, we don't even know the dimension(s) on which that difference is to be defined.[18]

To be sure, we can imagine the *shape* of a golf cart transforming gradually into the shape of a bicycle, and from there into the shape of a wheelchair. But that would show at most that a shape incrementally (e.g. indiscriminably) different from a golf cart (bicycle) shape is itself a golf cart (bicycle) shape. It would show nothing about the tolerance of 'vehicle'.[19] To be soritical, the series would need to satisfy at least two requirements: (1) it would need to be defined with respect to a dimension (or dimensions) on which 'vehicle' tolerates incremental differences, i.e. a dimension on which anything incrementally different from a vehicle is itself a vehicle; and (2) it would need to contain a golf cart, a bicycle, and a wheelchair among other things. Granted, you could gradually transform (e.g.) a golf cart into a bicycle, piece by piece; for example, you could first remove the steering wheel, then one (or more) of the seats, then the accelerator and brake pedals, then two of the wheels, etc., and then add handlebar, bicycle seat, and so forth, and end up with at least a funny-looking bicycle. But again this series of contraptions would not be a sorites series, for there is no guarantee, *a fortiori* no intuitive guarantee, that 'vehicle' tolerates removal of (e.g.) a steering wheel, or seats, or pedals. There is no reason to think that 'vehicle' is tolerant to changes that big and functionally relevant.

Perhaps we can construct a sorites series for 'vehicle' if we descend to, say, the molecular level. Maybe we can go from a golf cart to a bicycle by removing molecules one by one from the golf cart. But how exactly would this work? It can't be that we remove molecules one by one from the golf cart until we arrive at a bicycle, in the way we could remove hairs from a hairy head until we arrive at a bald one.

Figure 2.1 Sorites series for 'vehicle'?

[18] After finishing this chapter I discovered that Scott Anderson notes in passing the implausibility of the idea that 'vehicle' is soritical (Anderson 2006, p. 107).
[19] Notice that there is no such thing as the shape of a vehicle *per se*, i.e., no vehicle shape analogous to a golf cart or bicycle shape.

Maybe the idea would be that we remove molecules from the golf cart until we reach an assemblage of molecules that can then be transformed into a bicycle by *adding* molecules one by one. But even if that idea makes sense (I can't tell), what could determine the order in which the molecules are removed and then added? Would any old order do? (Again, I don't know.) More importantly, we have no reason to suppose, and certainly no intuition, that 'vehicle' tolerates removal of a single molecule; for all we know, the removal of some single molecule would make the difference between a contraption's being able, and not being able, to carry an electric current, or to support the weight of passengers and/or cargo. Furthermore, in all likelihood we would arrive at an assemblage of molecules that is definitely not-a-vehicle well before arriving at a bicycle; whereas the bicycle is supposed to be an intermediate (borderline) case.

Certainly one could construct a sorites series progressing in size from (e.g.) a car (determinately a vehicle) to a toy car (determinately not a vehicle, in the sense relevant to the prohibition). We can imagine that the toy is a perfect, two-inch long replica of the car.[20] The difference in size between adjacent stages in the series could be made sufficiently small that the tolerance requirement is met and no particular item is the last vehicle in the series. Both inter- and intrasubjective variations in our stopping places would persist. However, such a series would not contain a wheelchair or a bicycle or a golf cart.

Our second proposed example of soritical vagueness was Endicott's series for 'pearl'. In fact, neither the pre-lump portion of this series nor the post-lump portion is a sorites series. On the one hand there is no obvious reason to suppose that if something is a pearl, then something slightly less developed with a coating of pearl material is also a pearl. Presumably the latter item, although a perfect physical duplicate of a pearl, could fail to be a pearl for lack of the requisite biological history. On the other hand we cannot assume that 'pearl' tolerates even slight differences of material constitution: why think that something with a chemistry slightly different from that of a pearl must be a pearl? Maybe having a certain biochemical constitution is essential to being a pearl. So in neither portion of the series is 'pearl' tolerant. The lump may illustrate the open texture of 'pearl', but not any vagueness.[21] Competent speakers—maybe scientists—will diverge as to the proper classification of the lump, but their divergence will be a genuine disagreement. They will give reasons for their respective views, will not hold them arbitrarily, and will challenge opposing views.

My purpose in considering the 'vehicle' and 'pearl' examples has been to show that the constraints on a sorites series are surprisingly strict. My argument in the remainder of this chapter concerns only soritical vagueness, not open texture or essential contestedness. With the differences among these sources of indeterminacy

---

[20] Maybe the gas tank is filled with an eyedropper. Hart discusses an example quite like this one (Hart 1961/1994, p. 129), but he thinks it would be indeterminate whether the toy car is a vehicle.

[21] I argue elsewhere that natural kind terms are probably not soritically vague; see Raffman 2014, ch. 4, § 4.6.

clarified (enough for my purposes, at least), I want now to consider just how the soritical vagueness of legal language is supposed to cause trouble for the law.

4.

Soritical vagueness is often seen as a threat to the rule of law. In particular, apparently any application of a soritically vague legal predicate to a borderline (variable) case must be arbitrary, and this may seem to cast doubt on the integrity of judicial decision making. Endicott formulates the problem in terms of Ronald Dworkin's ideal judge Hercules:

> I propose that the case of the million raves would cause a crisis, in which Hercules would have to make decisions that he cannot justify in principle.... His conception [of serious distress] aims to be principled. But what scheme of principle... could account for a statement of the requirements of the law according to which one [rave] organizer in our series is convicted and the next is acquitted? How can Hercules treat x_i in the same way as x_0, and treat x_{i+1} the same way as $x_{1,000,000}$, when x_i and x_{i+1} have done materially the same thing? Why should an imperceptible difference in volume make a polar difference to the legal outcome? An interpretation on which there is a sharp boundary will suffer in the dimension of justification, because it will lack integrity: there will be no consistency in principle between a conviction and an acquittal for materially equivalent conduct. Yet, faced with the series of defendants, Hercules himself can come up with no other result.... Real judges do not ordinarily face a case like the case of the million raves. But that case only *brings to light* the problem that Hercules would face in *every* case in which the requirements of the law can be stated in vague language.
>
> (Endicott 2000, pp. 161–2)[22]

Not only must any particular stopping place in a sorites series be arbitrary, but because the tolerance of vague predicates appears to lead to paradox, it seems impossible for Hercules to observe the fundamental tenet that like cases should be treated alike. On pain of absurdity, for example of convicting all of the rave organizers, he must stop applying the predicate 'serious distress' at some point before the end of the series. In so doing, he must install a sharp boundary.[23]

Compelling as the latter line of reasoning may be, I believe it is based upon a misconception of soritical vagueness. To be sure, Hercules and his 'ordinary' brethren on the bench would face exactly the problem Endicott describes—but not because of any features of the language in which the law is expressed, vague or otherwise. Let me explain.

Results of a psycholinguistic experiment on ordinary speakers' use of vague words suggest that they are able to classify the items in a sorites series, *seriatim*, without

---

[22] It's curious that Endicott blames Hercules' problem on the vagueness of the language, for he himself correctly notes that replacing 'serious distress' with a precisified analogue would be of no help. A law specifying a precise loudness as the first distressing one would draw a line as sharp and arbitrary as any that Hercules might draw.

[23] For some interesting arguments against the requirement that like cases be treated alike, see Marmor 2005.

installing a boundary.[24] The vagueness of the predicates they employ is largely what enables them to do this. Suppose that an ordinary speaker proceeds along our sorites series of ages and shifts from 'old' to 'borderline' at sixty-two years. If we then query him about the preceding ages he just classified as old, *viz.*, sixty-three-years-minus-364-days, sixty-three-years-minus-363-days, sixty-three-years-minus-362-days, and so forth, he will now be disposed to classify at least some of those ages as borderline also, although he classified them as old only moments before. Perhaps he will now say 'borderline' as far back as, say, sixty-five-years-minus-121-days before shifting back to 'old' at sixty-five-years-minus-120-days, in a repeat of the same pattern in the opposite direction. Intuitively: when the speaker first classifies sixty-two years as borderline, it's not as if the preceding age(s) still seem old; instead, it's as if a string of ages shift their category simultaneously, so that consecutive ages never seem category-different at the same time. (Similarly for the later switch from 'borderline' back to 'old'.) By the time the speaker shifts to 'borderline', he is already in the midst of variable ages that can competently be called 'old' and competently be called 'borderline' and competently be called 'not-old'. So the idea that his classifications should be fluid in this way is not so surprising.

In a different, related task the speaker is asked to consider neighbouring ages in the series *seriatim* but pairwise. In that case he will classify both members of each pair in the same way; he will not place consecutive (paired) ages in different categories. For example, if he starts with the pair eighty-five years/eighty-five-years-minus-one-day, he will classify both ages (individually) as old or both as borderline or both as not-old; similarly for the pair eighty-five-years-minus-one-day/ eighty-five-years-minus-two-days, and the pair eighty-five-years-minus-two-days/ eighty-five-years-minus-three-days, and so forth. (In effect the speaker will confirm *seriatim* each of the conditionals in the sorites paradox.) At each step of the way, he will treat like ages alike. This, I suggest, is the right way to understand tolerance: an expression is tolerant insofar as it applies equally to incrementally different items *considered simultaneously*, i.e. pairwise.[25]

How can each conditional in the paradox be true, given that the series progresses from (pairs of) old ages to (pairs of) not-old ages? Since he is competent, our speaker will begin by classifying each member of each pair of ages as old; but as always, at some point before the end of the series he must stop applying 'old' and make some other response—say, 'borderline old'. Since the members of each pair receive the same classification, his shift from 'old' to 'borderline old' must occur *between pairs*. Hence, since each pair of ages shares one member with the preceding pair and one with the succeeding pair, i.e. successive pairs overlap in one age,

---

[24] See Raffman 2014, ch. 5. The experiment discussed there involved judgements of a sorites series of hue stimuli; here I am supposing that we can generalize to the case of non-perceptual predicates like 'old' and 'seriously distressing'. Of course, such a generalization could be questioned, but given the intuitive plausibility of the major premise of the paradox for non-perceptual as well as perceptual vague terms, I am optimistic that it will hold up. I provide further defence for it in the chapter just cited, especially §5.3.

[25] This may be to construe tolerance as a pragmatic rather than semantic feature of an expression; see Raffman 2014, ch. 5, especially § 5.6.

it follows that some age in the series must shift its category membership from 'old' in its first pairing to 'borderline' in its second. (We have already granted that the classification of transitional items in a sorites series is variable; what I'm proposing now is just a specific instance of that variation.) This shift in category membership of an individual age enables the speaker to treat like ages alike without sliding down the slope to absurdity.

Of course, any sorites series contains *permissible stopping places*; otherwise, competence with a vague predicate would require its application to all of the items therein. It is vital to distinguish (mere) permissible stopping places from boundaries. By 'permissible stopping place' I mean simply any place at which a competent speaker, classifying the items in a sorites series *seriatim*, could permissibly stop applying the predicate in question; there will be multiple such places. Unlike a boundary, stopping places have no legislative force; stopping at a particular place does not signify that other stopping places are incompetent or incorrect, or even legitimately questionable. (All theorists of vagueness acknowledge the existence of permissible stopping places.)

The two experimental tasks described above reveal a crucial variability in the ordinary use of vague words. If I am right, this variability (freedom, if you like) makes it possible for competent speakers to shift categories (predicates) in a sorites series without installing a boundary between adjacent, incrementally different items. In this way, the vagueness of these terms enables speakers to apply them to the seamless, continuous world around us. And, of course, this is just what judges, even Hercules, cannot do. A judge's ruling is and must be stable (at least until a successful appeal).[26] The problem of having to draw arbitrary boundaries between like cases owes not to the vagueness of the legal language, but to the law's inability to make use of that vagueness.

Jeremy Waldron correctly notes the special difficulty of decision making about cases whose crucial features belong to a continuum; but like Endicott, he places the blame on the language:

> Problems of vagueness will arise whenever we confront a continuum with terminology that has, or aspires to have, a bivalent logic. On the one hand...humans range imperceptibly in age from zero to more than a hundred years old; on the other hand, surely it is either true or false, at a given time, that Sam is a youth and not an adult. And so on for all sorts of terms: 'short' and 'tall' classifying persons on the continuum of height; 'village,' 'town,' and 'city' classifying communities on the continuum of population; 'rich' and 'poor' classifying individuals on continua of wealth and income; 'careful,' 'negligent,' and 'reckless' classifying behavior on a continuum of attentiveness.

(Waldron 1994, pp. 516–17)

You might think the problem would be ameliorated, if not solved, by employing infinitely many truth-values or degrees of truth in order to accommodate the continua at issue. But then arbitrary boundaries would exist between the two members of *every* pair of incrementally different cases; the members of every pair would

---

[26] See Endicott 2000, especially pp. 192–3.

receive different evaluations. The problem would be worse, not better. This suggests that bivalence in the language is not the culprit in the cases at issue. Rather, the source of the trouble is the law's need for stable rulings. Judicial decision making cannot be fluid in the manner of ordinary speakers' applications of vague words.

If my account of the use of vague words by ordinary speakers in a sorites series is at least roughly right, then to that extent it is not the vagueness of legal predicates that creates problems for the law. Rather, needing sharp and stable decisions, the court is unable to make use of the vagueness of its own language, and consequently is forced to draw arbitrary boundaries between incrementally different cases. Far from violating the principle that like cases should be treated alike, the vagueness of vague terms helps us to adhere to it. Whereas ordinary speakers are able to exploit the vagueness of their words to avoid unwanted boundaries, and so to treat like things alike, the courts are trapped in the predicament Endicott describes.

References

Anderson, Scott A. 2006. *Legal Indeterminacy in Context*. Doctoral dissertation, Ohio State University.

Bix, Brian H. 1993. *Law, Language, and Legal Indeterminacy*. New York: Oxford University Press.

Bix, Brian H. 2004. *A Dictionary of Legal Theory*. New York: Oxford University Press.

Burns, Lynda. 1995. 'Something to Do with Vagueness'. *The Southern Journal of Philosophy* 33(Supplement): 23–47.

Endicott, Timothy. 2000. *Vagueness in Law*. Oxford: Oxford University Press.

Endicott, Timothy. 2011. 'Vagueness and Law'. In *Handbook on Vagueness*, edited by G. Ronzitti, 171–91. London: Springer Verlag.

Hart, H.L.A. 1958. 'Positivism and the Separation of Law and Morality'. *Harvard Law Review* 71(4): 593–629.

Hart, H.L.A., 1961/1994. *The Concept of Law*, 2nd edn. Oxford: Oxford University Press.

Marmor, Andrei. 2005. 'Should Like Cases Be Treated Alike?' *Legal Theory* 11(1): 27–38.

Marmor, Andrei. 2012. 'Varieties of Vagueness in the Law'. USC Legal Studies Research Paper No. 12–8; revised 2013.

Marmor, Andrei. 2014. *The Language of Law*. Oxford: Oxford University Press.

Poscher, Ralf. 2012. 'Ambiguity and Vagueness in Legal Interpretation'. In *The Oxford Handbook of Language and Law*, edited by Lawrence Solan and Peter Tiersma, 128–44. Oxford: Oxford University Press.

Raffman, Diana. 2005. 'Borderline Cases and Bivalence'. *The Philosophical Review* 114(1): 1–31.

Raffman, Diana. 2010. 'Demoting Higher-Order Vagueness'. In *Cuts and Clouds: Vagueness, Its Nature and Its Logic*, edited by Richard Dietz and Sebastiano Moruzzi, 509–22. Oxford: Oxford University Press.

Raffman, Diana. 2014. *Unruly Words: A Study of Vague Language*. New York: Oxford University Press.

Raz, Joseph. 1979. 'Legal Reasons, Sources, and Gaps'. In *The Authority of Law*, 53–77. Oxford: Oxford University Press.

Sainsbury, Mark. 1990. 'Concepts Without Boundaries'. Inaugural Lecture, King's College London. Reprinted in *Vagueness: A Reader*, edited by Rosanna Keefe and Peter Smith, 251–64. Cambridge (MA): MIT Press, 1997.

Sainsbury, Mark. 1995. *Paradoxes*, 2nd edn. Cambridge: Cambridge University Press.

Schauer, Frederick. 2011. 'On the Open Texture of Law'. *Virginia Public Law and Legal Theory* Research Paper No. 2011–35. Available at SSRN: <http://ssrn.com/abstract=1926926> or <http://dx.doi.org/10.2139/ssrn.1926926>.

Shapiro, Stewart. 2006. *Vagueness in Context*. Oxford: Oxford University Press.

Sorensen, Roy. 2001. 'Vagueness Has No Function in Law'. *Legal Theory* 7(4): 387–417.

Waismann, Friedrich. 1945. 'Verifiability'. *Proceedings of the Aristotelian Society*, Supp. Vol. 19: 119–50.

Waldron, Jeremy. 1994. 'Vagueness in Law and Language: Some Philosophical Issues'. *California Law Review* 82(3): 509–40.

Waldron, Jeremy. 2002. 'Is the Rule of Law an Essentially Contested Concept (in Florida)?' *Law and Philosophy* 21(2): 137–64.

3

An Intentionalist Account of Vagueness

A Legal Perspective

Ralf Poscher

The debate on vagueness has become a rich and diversified topic whose different aspects are only infrequently discussed from the viewpoint of a more general perspective on language and communication. In the following I wish to explore the potential of an intentionalist approach—roughly along the lines of Grice[1] and Davidson[2]—to the different aspects of vagueness. Intentionalist approaches to language might not be able to clarify all its mysteries,[3] but they nevertheless contribute to its understanding and allow us to put the remaining issues into perspective.[4] This chapter hopes to achieve a similar goal for the discussion of vagueness. I believe that some light at least can be shed on its issues and that some of the issues not resolved by an intentionalist perspective can be more clearly defined, or at least localized.

For law, the intentionalist perspective has been of particular interest since intentionalist approaches to the law became central to methodological discussions in the field[5]—most prominently in the debates around originalist

---

[1] Cf. Grice 1989; on the development of Grice's intentionalist program see Neale 1992, p. 509.

[2] Cf. Davidson 1986, Davidson 1993, and Davidson 1994. On Davidson's reception of Grice see Avramides 2001 and Cook 2009.

[3] Cf. Davidson and Glüer 1995, p. 83:

> But I don't think you can define the notion of linguistic meaning on the basis of intentions; it's a necessary condition, but it's not sufficient. And even if you could define meaning on the basis of intention, I wouldn't be very interested, because intention seems to me at least as hard to explain as meaning.

See also McGinn 2015, pp. 201–2. On the differences between Davidson and Grice, see J. Cook 2009, pp. 567–70.

[4] For recent general critiques of intentionalist accounts see Azzouni 2013, pp. 265–320. His perceptual account relies heavily on the conscious phenomenology of semantic experiences. Intentionalist accounts should, however, be able to accommodate much of the 'data' when subconscious inferences are taken into account—a possibility not finally eschewed but regarded as 'empirically unlikely' by Azzouni 2013 (p. 289). See also Lepore and Stone 2015, who do still accept the fundamental importance of 'direct' communicative intentions but try to broaden the importance of conventional meaning. For a first adaption of this approach for law see Matczak 2016.

[5] Cf. Alexander and Prakash 2004, Fish 2005, Fish 2008, Fish 2011, Neale 2008, Ekins 2012, ch. 7, as well as, differentiated with respect to different legal acts, Solum 2013.

---

approaches to constitutional law[6] or in the discussion on legislative intent in general.[7] Though these discussions also point to vagueness as one of the main sources of legal indeterminacy motivating recourse to the intentions of the legislator, they do not specifically relate intentionalism to vagueness. The chapter will thus attempt to explore the further potential of an intentionalist perspective for law and its theoretical issues. The reference to the law also highlights how some of the functional features of vagueness underlined by the intentionalist perspective are mirrored in legal discussions and in the institutional set-up of the law.

In doing so a standard critique levelled against intentionalism in law must be set aside. In law the usefulness of an intentionalist perspective is often questioned with respect to the mechanisms of modern law-making,[8] which involves large collective bodies such as parliaments, and other representative assemblies such as city councils. From an intentionalist perspective, the involvement of these collective bodies raises the issue of collective intentionality, which is a separate topic in the theory of action.[9] This debate cannot be taken up here. It can, however, be set aside for three reasons. First, though today at least the more important legislative acts are mostly passed by collective bodies, this is not a necessary feature of the law and not even ubiquitous in contemporary legal systems. Even in contemporary legal systems many laws are issued by individual agents like presidents, ministers, mayors, commissioners, chiefs of police, or other heads of administrative bodies that issue executive orders or administrative regulations of various kinds. Second, given our ubiquitous talk about collective agents and their intentions, the issue raised is less whether we can sensibly do so, but rather how to reconstruct it sparing our ontology of dubious collective minds. Given that there are promising reductive accounts in the theory of action and agency,[10] the chapter will presuppose that one of these will also play out for the law and the collective bodies involved in the process of modern law-making—although the details that have to be worked out are anything but trivial.[11] Third, in an intentionalist perspective there can be no meaning without intentions. Legislative acts can thus only acquire meaning by at least presupposing intentions connected to them—even those of a fictitious legislator.

The chapter will proceed by outlining the general idea of an intentionalist approach to vagueness, while noting its implications for law. It presents the basic elements of an intentionalist approach in sections 1–7 and draws out its implications for different issues of vagueness and vagueness in law in section 8.

---

[6] Cf. e.g. Campos 1996, Greene 2012, and van Patten 1987.

[7] For a decidedly intentionalist approach see e.g. Ekins 2012, ch. 7.

[8] Cf. Hurd 1990 and Waldron 1995.   [9] Cf. e.g. Chant et al. 2014.

[10] See e.g. (with difference in the way collective intentions are reconstructed) Gilbert 1989, (especially pp. 197–200), Gilbert 2000 (especially pp. 1–31), Searle 1990, and Bratman 1999, pp. 125–9 and 142–61.

[11] Cf. in the more recent literature Ekins 2012, Nourse 2012, Nourse 2014, and Poscher forthcoming.

1. Vagueness and Intentions

Vagueness is a phenomenon of non-natural meaning. Natural indicators or signs, as Grice called them, might be inconclusive, but they are not vague. If there is a smoke plume over the forest, it might come from an incipient forest fire or the chimney of the nearby lodge. The 'natural meaning' of the smoke is inconclusive, but not vague. It was one of Grice's fundamental insights that non-natural meaning is tied to intentions (Grice 1989, pp. 92 and 217–23). Whereas natural signs take their 'meaning' from causal relations between an object and its environment, non-natural signs acquire their meaning through the communicative intentions that a speaker or author connects with an utterance. Non-natural meaning is an intentional phenomenon. Meaning is tied to intentions. There is no meaning without at least the presupposition of intentions.[12] The famous lines drawn in the sand by the waves that resemble letters[13] do not have any meaning. We can assign meaning to them only by presupposing some kind of hypothetical speaker.[14] If the waves form the signs 'I love you', we might presuppose an ordinary kind of context like a couple on a romantic walk and one of them stating her or his affection. If vagueness is an aspect of the meaning of non-natural signs and non-natural signs acquire their meaning only through the intentions utterers attach to them, then vagueness must ultimately reside in the intentions of utterers.

2. Speakers and Semantic Meaning

Vagueness is further a phenomenon of both: the pragmatic meaning of utterance tokens and the semantic meaning of utterances types, or of speakers' and sentence meaning in the terms of Grice.[15] But whereas the discussion on vagueness very often focuses on the semantic meaning of terms like 'bald', 'tall', or 'heap', an intentionalist account of meaning has to start with speakers' meaning or the meaning of utterance tokens.

In very basic communicative scenarios the speaker's intentions are all there is to the meaning of a non-natural sign. Consider the example with which Grandy and Warner illustrate the Gricean approach:

[I]magine you are stopped at night at an intersection, when the driver in an oncoming car flashes her lights. You reason as follows: 'Why is she doing that? Oh, she must intend me to

---

[12] Cf. Davidson 1994, p. 120: 'So in the end, the sole source of linguistic meaning is the intentional production of tokens of sentences.' On the presupposition of fictive authors and intentions, cf. Marmor 2005; cf. also Poscher forthcoming.
[13] Cf. Knapp and Michaels 1982, pp. 727–8. For the law, cf. Fish 2008.
[14] See Alexander and Prakash 2004, p. 987 n. 25.
[15] Other languages even have different words for the two concepts: e.g. in German 'Meinen' and 'Bedeutung' (see Kemmerling 2015, p. 235).

believe that my lights are not on. If she has that intention, it must be that my lights are not on. So, they are not.' To summarize:

The driver flashes her lights intending
1. that you believe that your lights are not on;
2. that you recognize her intention (1);
3. that this recognition be part of your reason for believing that your lights are not on.

(Grandy and Warner 2013)[16]

The meaning of the flashes depends solely on the empirical fact that the driver had a certain communicative intention. If it turned out that the car with flashing lights was driven by some drunken students trying to dazzle other drivers for fun, the flashes would have no meaning at all.

Semantic meaning comes into play when we employ certain signs standardly to convey the same communicative intentions—communicative intentions understood in Davidson's sense of intentions to get 'across to someone else what you have in mind by means of words that they interpret (understand) as you want them to' (Davidson 1994, p. 120). The terms and syntactical combinations of terms of our natural language are signs to which speakers standardly or typically or averagely attach certain communicative intentions. In an intentionalist perspective, the semantic or conventional meaning of expressions—in the case of individual terms their lexical meaning—is a function of speakers' meaning of a multitude of utterance tokens. Conventional, lexical, or semantic meaning supervenes on some kind of average, core, or paradigm connection that the utterers of a certain language community usually establish between an intention type and a specific utterance type. Semantic meaning is thus some kind of aggregate of speakers' meaning.[17] In an intentionalist perspective, semantic meaning is lexical in character. Its content is subject to empirical investigation, as pursued by lexicographers for ages and by computer linguists through the big data analysis of large textual corpora in our own time.

Semantic meaning plays a facilitating role in communication.[18] On the one hand, it gives the speaker a set of signs that he can rely on to be understood by his audience; on the other hand, semantic meaning is usually the stepping-stone for our inferences about a speaker's intentions, because we infer that she connected the intentions standardly connected with an utterance type with her utterance token. But speakers are not tied to the semantic meaning of signs when they make use of them, as long as they can be confident that there are enough contextual clues to infer the intentions they connect with their use of a

---

[16] Cf. also Warner 2001, p. ix.

[17] See Grice 1989, pp. 127–8, 220. On the similarity of Grice and Davidson on this point, see Cook 2009, p. 567. Even authors who embrace a semanticist approach to meaning see speaker's meaning as its ultimate source. See Salmon 2005, p. 324.

[18] This corresponds to the view that language is not conventional at its core; conventions have a mere facilitating role in language. See Davidson 1984, pp. 278–9 and Kemmerling 2015, p. 231.

term.[19] Neologisms and malapropisms are probably the best cases in point. When in Thomas Mann's *Zauberberg* (1924/2002, ch. 7: 'Mynheer Peeperkorn', p. 835) Mrs Stöhr calls Mr Peeperkorn a 'money-magnet' we are able to understand that she means a 'magnate'. Ironic usage, Gricean implicatures, and metaphors are slightly more complex. Here what Davidson called the 'first meaning' often still corresponds to the semantic meaning, and it is only on the basis of the—conventional—first meaning that the hearer can infer what the speaker intends to 'get across'.[20] But in these cases too what the speaker tries to 'get across' does not correspond to the semantic meaning of the words employed. The term 'hot' can be used to communicate that a dish is cold, if used under the appropriate circumstances with the proper ironic intonation. In law this raises the normative question of which kind of meaning should prevail when the intentions of the legislator deviate from the semantic meaning of the expressions employed. But the very fact that this question can be raised presupposes a distinction between speakers' meaning and semantic meaning.

Vagueness can be a property of both speakers' and semantic meaning. However, they are not independent of each other, but share a dialectical relation.[21] On the one hand, semantic meaning supervenes on a diachronic and synchronic multitude of speakers' meanings. On the other hand, the individual speaker relies on semantic meaning to form and express her intentions. The semantic meaning of the terms an individual speaker employs is not at his disposal. Terms with their semantic meaning are like tools that a speaker can employ to form and communicate her intentions. Like any tool they restrict what can be achieved with them. Pliers can be used to hammer in nails, but we cannot pinch with a hammer. If a speaker employs a semantically vague term, she can usually only use it to communicate a vague content. If she asks for 'a large glass of water', she can only be vague with regard to the exact number of millilitres the glass must hold. Even if she wanted exactly 500 ml—barring special circumstances—the speaker could not express this intention with the term 'large glass'. Rational speakers cannot—consciously—intend the impossible (Davidson 1989, p. 147). They usually cannot intend to communicate a precise content with a semantically vague term, since the addressee would not be able to infer it. Speakers cannot make use of terms like the infamous Humpty-Dumpty from Alice in Wonderland, who insisted: 'When *I* use a word...it means just what I choose it to mean—neither more nor less' (Carroll 1872, p. 72). In contrast to what Humpty-Dumpty believes, speakers must at least

[19] Cf. famously Grice 1989, pp. 24ff., 34, 39, on linguistic implicatures, and Davidson 1986, on malaproprisms.
[20] See Talmage 1994. The notion of 'first meaning' provides Davidson, with 'a deeper notion of what words, when spoken in context, mean; and like the shallow notion of correct usage, we want to distinguish between what a speaker, on a given occasion, means, and what his words mean' (Davidson 1986, p. 91)—and this even for an idiolect, since a malapropism or neologism could also be used ironically, metaphorically.
[21] I am especially thankful to Geert Keil for pressing me on this dialectic, even though my treatment of it might not fully do justice to his critique.

hope that the addressees of their communication can infer their intention from the terms employed.[22]

Only if special contextual circumstances permit can semantically vague terms be used to communicate precise intentions and vice versa. If the menu in a restaurant offers two sizes of beer—300 ml and 500 ml—ordering a 'large beer' can express the precise intention of ordering 500 ml of beer.[23] Speakers have to use a term that allows them to successfully communicate their intentions. Semantically vague terms require special context to communicate precise intentions. This, however, does not change the fact that it is the intention of the speaker that gives vague or precise meaning to an utterance and that the vagueness and precision of the semantic meaning of a term supervenes on the communicative intentions of speakers in a diachronic and synchronic fashion. If most restaurants offered only the two sizes of beer—or if the law required them to offer only the two sizes—the term 'large beer' could become semantically precise. In much the same way, semantically precise terms are sometimes used to communicate vague intentions. Someone might complain 'It will take a year to finish this task', to indicate that it will be time-consuming, without being precise about the exact time it will take.[24]

3. Vagueness of Speakers' Meaning

Whereas large parts of the vagueness discussion focus on semantic meaning and the vagueness of terms, an intentionalist approach suggests a change of perspective that concentrates on the vagueness of speakers' meaning. If meaning ultimately resides in the intentions of speakers, the same must be true of vagueness as one

[22] On Davidson's account, much speaks in favour of the radical interpreter as the relevant standard (see Talmage 1996, pp. 541–4). What the radical interpreter requires is some kind of consistency of use. Since cases of unsuccessful communication are parasitic on successful ones, Davidson himself was not too concerned with the question of whether the mere intention of such consistency would suffice (see Talmage 1996), or whether it must have already been set into a consistent practice (see Glüer 2013, n. 25). On cases in which the speaker failed to be understood, Davidson remarked:

> What should we say of the many cases in which a speaker expects, or hopes, to be understood in a certain way but isn't? I can't see that it matters. If we bear in mind that the notion of meaning is a theoretical concept which can't explain communication but depends on it, we can harmlessly relate it to successful communication in whatever ways we find convenient. So, if a speaker reasonably believes he will be interpreted in a certain way, and speaks with the intention of being so understood, we may choose to say he means what (in the primary sense) he would have meant if he had been understood as he expected and intended.

(Davidson 1994, p. 121)

[23] In these colloquial contexts there are further issues to be addressed. 'Large beer' would give us primarily a sharp lower boundary—498 ml would miss the mark. As for the upper boundary questions of granularity (cf. Keil 2010) come into play—504 ml would be regarded as large, too, but 2000 ml could be rejected as too large. But there are scenarios in which even these issues are ruled out—as in boxing, where fighters are grouped in weight classes and heavyweight fighters have to weigh at least X kg to be referred to as 'large fighters'.

[24] On similar constellations, see Marmor, ch. 6 this volume.

of its features. Thus an intentionalist approach must start with a discussion of the vagueness of utterance tokens.

Since a sign cannot have non-natural meaning unless a speaker connects communicative intentions with it, it can only have meaning *insofar as* a speaker connects communicative intentions with it. If a speaker only forms an imprecise, vague intention, the utterance he attaches it to can only have an imprecise, vague speaker's meaning, too. If a police officer orders a bystander and potential witness to an accident to stay 'in the vicinity' of the police car, the *command* is vague, since it does not specify where the vicinity ends. He would be baffled if asked the exact distance he had in mind. The reason why his utterance has only a vague speaker's meaning is that the officer did not bother to contemplate an exact distance. He employed the lexically vague term 'vicinity' for precisely that reason.

Our language, however, does not condemn us to form vague intentions. Especially with our system of numbers and metrics it provides us with sufficient means to form precise intentions. Numbers and metrics, however, are not the only means of arriving at precise delimitations. The etymology of the demarcation term 'deadline' provides a fitting—though gruesome—example for establishing precise delimitation without the use of metrics.[25]

The term was coined during the American Civil War. It became infamous through a POW-camp, where the prisoners were held in stockades with a 'deadline' running along its inside. According to a Report by the Secretary of War the camp commander 'established said dead line, which was...marked by...strips of [boards nailed] upon the tops of...stakes or posts, he...instructed the prison-guard stationed around the top of said stockade to fire upon and kill any of the prisoners aforesaid who might touch, fall upon, pass over, or under, or across the said "dead line" '.[26] The boards and robes made the 'deadline' precise without relying on metrics or numbers.

In the less drastic and benign case of the police officer, instead of forming a rough-and-ready intention as to the location of the bystander, he could have established a physical line with crime scene tape or elaborated on an exact distance in metres and centimetres from a fixed point of reference like the bumper of the police car, or relied on geodata from his smartphone. But for obvious reasons he did not bother. A rough-and-ready designation of the area using the vague term 'vicinity' was good enough for the practical purpose of securing the scene of the accident and keeping track of the bystander as a possible witness. Speakers have a choice. They can form intentions that are unspecific with respect to the exact borders of a phenomenon they are aimed at or they can form a precise intention. Our language

---

[25] See Allen 2000 as well as the entry 'Deadline' in the Online Etymology Dictionary, available at: <http://www.etymonline.com/index.php?term=deadline&allowed_in_frame=0>.

[26] 'Trial of Henry Wirtz' (U.S. 40th Congress, 2nd Session. 1867–1868. House Executive Document No. 23, 7 December 1867, p. 4). After the war the commander, Wirtz, was sentenced to death by a union army tribunal and hanged in Washington at the present site of the U.S. Supreme Court. Historians consider the trial against Wirtz as one of the first modern war crime trials and a precursor of the Nürnberg trials (see Paul Finkelman, available at: <http://www.c-span.org/video/?319092-6/discussion-military-trial-henry-wirz>).

provides them with the vague concepts to do the former and the conceptual instruments to do the latter.

In terms of precision our language works in two ways. It provides us with terms like 'vicinity', 'bald', 'tall', or 'heap' that we can use in a rough-and-ready fashion, and with a different set of terms that give us—alongside practices of measurement or delimitation—the means to be precise should the need arise.[27] Whether we have already developed practices of measurement or delimitation seems largely contingent and is not central to the vagueness debate. The paradigms it pertains to—like tallness, number of grains or hairs, etc.—are even typically such that there are terms and practices of precision at hand.

It goes without saying that we find the same mechanisms and their combinations in the law. The law can require drivers to drive at a reasonable speed or set a fixed speed limit of 55 mph or both—set a numerically fixed speed limit and demand that the speed within this limit is adjusted to circumstances according to some vague reasonableness standard.[28]

4. Vagueness of Language and 'Vagueness of the World'

Given the way the world presents itself to us phenomenologically, this twofold character of our linguistic means with regard to precision seems to be a good fit. At the macro level the world presents itself to us with discrete objects—like a chair or a table—but also with continuous phenomena like horizons, the blurred boundaries between the valley and the foot of the mountain, clouds, etc. —and more fundamentally the continuity of space and time. It also confronts us with generic continua in the different shades of coloured objects that blur into each other, the infinitesimally small differences in the size of objects delivering a continuum of sizes, lengths, and weights. In a world that presented itself only in discrete ways—in a Lego- or Minecraft-world (Keil 2013)—there would be neither a need for vague concepts nor concepts of precisification.[29] Precise concepts that are related to the different but always discrete phenomena of the world would be enough. But given the continuous phenomena of our world, we have to deal with them in our conceptual apparatus.

Theoretically we could have developed a conceptual apparatus that would only allow for the formation of precise intentions. With respect to the continuous

[27] Even if precisifications for standard examples of vagueness are easily found, this does not imply that we have developed practices of precision or measurement with regard to every phenomenon. For many phenomena there might not be such practices at hand. But for the systematic point on vagueness it is a contingent point whether we have already established a practice of precision.

[28] See Waldron, ch. 15 this volume.

[29] Discreteness alone would not suffice. It would not only have to be a world in which the objects always present themselves as discrete as they do in our macro-level surroundings of tables and chairs on the individual level; to avoid vagueness they would also have to be 'discrete' on a generic level, i.e. they would have to be like natural kinds of chemical elements or biological species. For the law already, Hart 1961/2012, p. 128, contemplated a similar scenario.

phenomena of the world, we could have come up with precise segmentations of colours, sizes, time-frames, etc. But there would have been serious downsides to such a Lego- or Minecraft-language for our non-Lego- or Minecraft-world. We would only be able to form an intention after determining precise boundaries in the continua we encountered. In most cases, however, the precisification effort to come up with such precise segmentations is not necessary, or even contrary, to the further purposes that we pursue with our communicative intentions. If a hunter wants to warn a member of the hunting party about a lion lurking in the high grass, the time it would take to exactly determine the position of the animal could get his fellow hunter killed. So it is easy to see why we would develop vague concepts like 'in the vicinity of the high grass' to cope with continua.[30]

On the other hand, precision is sometimes needed, as in commercial transactions or engineering. To cope with continuous phenomena in these cases we have developed precise concepts such as numbers and measurements alongside artefacts such as scales, yardsticks, and the standard metre to complement them. Further, certain forms of generalization are probably only possible with the help of vague concepts like the different reasonableness standards employed in the law. Though generalization and vagueness should not be confused,[31] the law also depends on *vague* generalizations, because it would be impossible to come up with precise generalizations for any instance of, for example, the standard of the reasonable man.

With this twofold conceptual apparatus we thus get the best of both worlds with regard to the continuous phenomena of our world. Our conceptual apparatus gives us a pragmatic choice with regard to our intentions: we can make them precise or leave them vague. Correspondingly, speakers can choose whether to develop a vague or precise communicative intention and thus whether to give their utterance a vague or precise speaker's meaning. As already shown, the law makes ample use of both options and combines them in multiple ways. In particular, it can also stack them one upon the other—as in environmental law, when the statute prohibits hazardous emissions and the administrative regulation sets a threshold value in micrograms.[32]

5. Vagueness as One Form of Underspecification of Intentions

In an intentionalist reconstruction it is quite obvious what vagueness consists in and why it is a feature of speaker's meaning. Vagueness of speakers' meaning resides

---

[30] Wittgenstein was right to reject Frege's claim that a vague concept would be as useless as designating an area with vague boundaries. Forming vague intentions can even have specific advantages over forming a precise one (Wittgenstein 1958, PI 71).

[31] See Sorensen 1988, Sorensen 2001, p. 406, and Waldron 1994, p. 522.

[32] For instance, Bundes-Immissionsschutzgesetz (BImSchG) [Federal Immission Control Act], § 1, ¶ 1, § 48, ¶ 1, No. 1 and Technische Anleitung zur Reinhaltung der Luft (TA-Luft) [Technical Instructions on Air Quality Control] in Germany; Clean Air Act, sec. 108, sec. 109, and National Ambient Air Quality Standards (NAAQS) in the United States.

in the underspecification of the speaker's intentions with regard to some continuous phenomenon of the world. What is underspecified is the precise border of a segment of a continuous phenomenon that the intentions of speakers are directed at. Vagueness of speakers' meaning thus consists in the underspecification of their intentions with regard to borderlines within a continuum.

The failure to precisify borderlines, however, is just one way in which intentions can be underspecified. Especially in legal methodological debate, there is an acute sense that vagueness is only one of the issues that can leave the law underspecified. Regulatory intentions, like any other, can be underspecified in all kinds of ways. Intentions can be underspecified with respect to any property of an object or a person—not just continuous ones. We can underspecify persons by their nationality, their marital status, their number of living biological parents, etc. We can underspecify animals by their species, cars by their licensing year, their number of registered seats, etc. A German law can extend a certain social security benefit to foreigners and leave it underspecified whether it is to be extended only to European Union citizens or also to foreigners from countries associated with the European Union or even to any foreigner. Other laws can be underspecified by ambiguity. For example, a membership statute might provide for a reduction in fees for 'children' of members and be underspecified whether it is understood as a privilege for youngsters or as sort of group rebate restricted to families. In law underspecification can also arise through conflicting regulations when it is left open which of two or more statutes should prevail.

Underspecification does not pose any deep philosophical conundrums, if we focus on the intentions of the speaker or in the case of the law of the legislator. With regard to what is underspecified, there is simply no intention and thus no speaker's meaning to be had. Asking for speaker's meaning with regard to aspects of her intention that are underspecified is futile. If the speaker has formed an intention to buy a car, but not specified whether she wants to buy a Mercedes or a BMW, the question of whether she wants to buy a Mercedes or a BMW has no answer. If the legislator has no intention with regard to which of two conflicting statutes is to prevail, the question of which he intended to prevail will be without answer. To insist on an answer would be pointless. The only correct answer is that the speaker has not yet developed an intention as to the brand of the car she intends to buy and the legislator has not developed an intention as to which of the two statutes should be applied. In law this is where legal construction comes into play[33] to draw on general legal principles such as *lex posterior derogat legi priori* or *lex specialis derogat legi generali*.

That underspecification leaves what is underspecified undetermined is an analytical truth, not a philosophical riddle. This is also true of underspecification with regard to the precise borderline in a continuum. If the speaker has formed the more precise intention to buy a red car, but has not run through the different shades in the spectrum between red and yellow to determine which shade she prefers, her

---

[33] For the hermeneutic specifics of legal construction, see Poscher forthcoming.

intention is underspecified in much the same way as with regard to the brand. The same holds for the legislator who has settled for a reasonableness approach to speed limits and not bothered to fix a numerical speed limit. In an intentionalist perspective, vagueness of communicative utterances is theoretically transparent in much the same way as other kinds of underspecification. Since there are no intentions with respect to the precise borderline in the continuum of shades between red and orange or in the continuum of reasonable and unreasonable speeds, there is no specific borderline to be had. Since a speaker's meaning is tied to her communicative intentions, there is no speaker's meaning to be had if she did not develop them. The question of whether the speaker meant a certain borderline shade of red is just as senseless as the question of whether he meant a Mercedes or a BMW or whether the legislator, who was not aware of the collision, meant the one or the other statute to prevail. They are senseless because the intention contains no propositional content in this respect.[34] It would be like asking whether someone who said nothing is right.

6. The Pragmatic Character of Vagueness

The intentionalist reconstruction of vague speakers' meaning reveals the pragmatic character of vagueness. What causes speakers' meaning to be vague is the vagueness of their communicative intentions. They are vague, because speakers have to make a choice regarding the precisification of their intentions. This is true of any kind of precisification, be it concerned with borderlines in a continuum or with other aspects of the intention.

Precisifying intentions entails decision- and opportunity-costs (Poscher 2012, pp. 143–4).[35] Speakers must gather more information, consume time, and resources to determine the exact shades of red that they prefer for their new car, just as they must to determine a brand. More often than not such efforts will be unnecessary, since the choice of car will depend not only on the colour, but on many other factors such as price, brand, horsepower, safety, etc. The red cars that make the shortlist will probably all sport a paradigmatic shade of red, so that no further precisification is needed. But even if a decision on a borderline case is easy to take, premature precisifications might incur opportunity costs. Refraining from precisification allows us to postpone a decision on borderline cases to a later time, when information might have improved. Even if a car in a borderline shade of red makes it onto the shortlist, it seems advantageous to decide on it when the trade-offs between the redness of the cars and their price, horsepower, fuel efficiency are known. More often than not the decision- and opportunity-costs of a precisification are misspent

---

[34] Cf. Keil 2010, p. 71.

[35] At least in part the savings in decision and opportunity costs are mirrored in the values of vagueness described in Endicott 2005 from the perspective of the addressees of the law. Asgeirsson 2012, pp. 304–15, relatives some of the values that Endicott identified. On Scott Soames's similar power-conferring argument, see Asgeirsson 2012, ch. 4.

or even in conflict with the purpose of the communication—as in the case of the warning about the lion in the high grass.

Just considering the number of issues that modern legislation has to regulate it is easy to see why the same holds for legislators. They would be overwhelmed by the decision- and opportunity-costs incurred were they even to try to precisify every regulation. The legislator must use vague terms to unload the burden of precisification first onto the courts, which will deal with it by means of legal construction on a case-by-case basis. Though precisification is in most cases not a live option, it must be stressed that we have the conceptual and practical means to establish precise borders in the continua of our macro-level everyday world. The choice of whether to draw a sharp borderline in a continuum is of a pragmatic character and forced on us neither by the nature of the world nor by the nature of our language.

If we choose to draw a precise borderline in a continuum, the decision as to where it should be drawn will be driven by pragmatic considerations, too. In less fine-grained continua some further purpose of the speaker might determine a precise boundary. A carpenter who has to fill a hole in a wall with wooden slats might have slats in his truck that range in length from 60 to 120 cm in 5 cm increments. After a first look at the hole he might tell his apprentice to fetch some of the large slats from the truck. He picks a vague expression, because his apprentice is smart and has a good eye. The apprentice will bring an abundance of slats, some slightly too short and some perhaps too long, but enough of each length to fix the hole. The carpenter could have been more precise by measuring the hole. By measuring the hole he could have come up with the precise segment—and number—of slats needed. After measuring the hole he could have asked his apprentice to bring him slats ranging from 95 to 115 cm, and this precisification would be fully determined by the purpose of fixing the hole.

In law this resembles a situation in which the legislator provides a statute with a vague standard, which—in light of its purpose—could be more specific, and leaves the specification to the executive or an administrative agency. The regulation of food additives serves to protect against the unhealthy consumption of chemicals. Though an exact amount could be given for at least some additives, the legislator might not bother to work out a catalogue but just forbid 'unsafe amounts' of additives and leave the specification to be determined by a public health agency, which is also more suited to adjust the precise regulation to new empirical findings.

In more fine-grained continua, however, the precisification can become arbitrary[36] with regard to the further purpose, but be governed by some secondary pragmatic reasons. If our carpenter were to build a shelf, it would probably not matter for all practical purposes concerning the use of the shelf, whether it were—in the continuum of lengths—199 or 200 or 201 cm long. Nevertheless he would probably

---

[36] For Raffman 2014, p. 108 and *passim*, the arbitrariness of assigning a vague predicate or its proximate incompatible to borderline cases is a defining feature of vagueness.

not order his apprentice to build a 'long' shelf, but to make a 200 cm shelf. The precisification of exactly 200 would be arbitrary with respect to the utility of the shelf, but driven by secondary considerations such as the greater ease with which we remember round numbers.

The law often has to deal with continua of this kind, especially in the dimension of time. For all practical purposes it does not matter whether a prison sentence for a crime is one year or one year and one, two, or three days. But here the round number principle comes to bear as well. The arbitrariness of fixing the border at an exact number in cases such as these has even been acknowledged in a recent election law case before the German constitutional court. The court had to decide on the limit of the number of surplus representatives that emerge from the complicated combination of proportional and majority voting principles in German election law. It fixed the limit at half the number of representatives that it takes to form a parliamentary group, i.e. fifteen. In discussing the reasons for picking this precise number, the court conceded: 'The senate realizes that there cannot be given a reason for the exact number of 15 overhang seats.... But under these special circumstances it is the task of the court to specify the requirements of equality to the system of seat assignment in a way that the legislature is able to design the election code on a reliable foundation.'[37]

In yet other cases there might not even be secondary reasons of this kind; only the precisification as such has pragmatic advantages. If the subway runs on a seven-minute schedule it might make no difference for all practical purposes if a couple take the train at 7.49, 7.56, or 8.03 h. If they wish to travel together, however, they would be ill-advised to agree to meet in an 'eightish' train or a train around 8.00 h. Which precisification they pick is arbitrary, but picking one is necessary to ensure a joint ride.

Whether we precisify our intentions and where we locate the precisification if we have reasons to precisify are both purely pragmatic questions. More often than not speakers and legislators have good pragmatic reasons to shun the precisification tools that would allow them to form precise intentions. They have good reasons to make ample use of vague concepts to form vague communicative intentions, which cause their utterances to be vague. But nothing in the structure of our language or in the structure of the world excludes precisification, even if it can sometimes only be of an arbitrary kind. Vagueness of speaker's meaning is a thoroughly pragmatic phenomenon.

However, it should be stressed that the individual pragmatic disposability of vagueness only pertains to the vagueness of speaker's meaning. Even though semantic meaning arises through a diachronic and synchronic aggregation of a multitude of speakers' meanings, the individual speaker cannot dispose over semantic meaning and usually only has an infinitesimal influence on it by her own use of terms. The speaker, however, can rely on the semantic meaning of terms and context as tools to form and communicate either vague or precise intentions.

---

[37] 2 BvE 9/11 et al. [2012] BVerfGE 131, 316, p. 370 (para. 144) (translation by the author).

7. Vagueness of Semantic Meaning

If speakers could somehow—miraculously—muster the costs of precision and only form synchronized, precise, communicative intentions there would be no vagueness of semantic meaning. But as this is impossible for pragmatic reasons, it becomes apparent how semantic vagueness arises, since semantic meaning supervenes on an aggregation of speakers' meanings (see section 2). First, vagueness of semantic meaning can have the same source as vagueness of speaker's meaning. All speakers using a specific term might have no determinate intention with regard to a borderline case, either because the case has never presented itself or there has never been a need to discriminate it. If for some reason wooden slats always came in only two sizes—one and two metres—there would never have been a reason for any speaker to precisify his intention connected with the term 'large slat' with respect to one and-a-half-metre-long slats. With regard to one-and-a-half-metre-long slats semantic meaning would be as vague as any speaker's meaning.

Second, even if each speaker has a precise intention in her use of a term, semantic vagueness could still arise, when their precise communicative intentions diverge. If our carpenter had only one- and two-metre slats and his colleague had only two- and four-metre slates, the semantic meaning of 'large slat' would be vague with respect to two-metre slats due to the inconsistencies of communicative intentions that each connects with the same utterance type. Even on this tiny scale, vagueness might arise through diverging speakers' intentions with regard to the same expression ('large slat'); it is easy to imagine how such divergences can produce semantic vagueness on the level of a whole language community. Third, there may be contextual factors—like the implicit indices attached to the different usages of 'large' and 'small'—that make it difficult to pin down what kind of average, core, or standard type of intentions semantics refer to, even if there are determinate intentions in each context. Selecting 'tall students' for a basketball team might produce different results than selecting them for a soccer team, even though the group is the same. Thus, context theories of vagueness stress the importance of context in connection with semantic vagueness (e.g. Raffman 1996, Shapiro 2006), but context is not the only factor. This explains the line held against them: '[V]agueness remains even when the context is fixed' (Williamson 1994, p. 215).[38]

Since all three factors may obtain in various combinations and to different degrees, we see why sematic meaning will tend to be more vague than speaker's meaning: if semantic meaning is an aggregate of the communicative intentions that speakers connect with the same type of signs, then the underspecifications of each speaker's meaning, diverging precisifications, and contexts will aggregate as well. A speaker can form her intentions in accordance with the semantic meaning of a term, leaving it as precise and imprecise as the semantics of the terms employed. She can also form a more precise intention and provide enough clues for

---

[38] For a contextualist defence, see Åkerman and Greenough 2010.

the addressees for the heightened degree of precision by the context of her utterance token. Pudding is a semantic borderline case of 'solid'. But if the speaker asked to be handed something 'solid' to throw at someone, in the context of a practical joke, the addressee of the request can infer from the context that she included the pudding on the table in her intention.

In law this relation between speaker's and semantic meaning resembles this structure. The classic legal canons of interpretation operate under the assumption that the semantic meaning of the law can be precisified through legislative intent.[39] This does not imply that there is always something to be gained. Most of the time, the legislative intention is not more precise than the semantics, or even if it were more precise it is impossible to reconstruct. Even when a more precise legislative intention can be discovered, the normative question of its import with regard to rule-of-law values, which favour semantic meaning, have to be addressed. Nevertheless, all these are familiar issues of legal methodology and build on the intentionalist assumption that in cases of semantic vagueness the intentions of the speaker can precisify what is meant.

8. Implications for Classic Vagueness Topics

In the following the implications of an intentionalist reconstruction of vagueness will be outlined for some major topics in the vagueness discussion. For each topic there is a highly specialized debate, some of which could almost fill a small library. It is impossible to do justice to the different positions, let alone to their nuances. Instead, the following will outline the direction of an answer that is implied by an intentionalist account of vagueness and will necessarily do so with a broad brush, leaving many of the details to be filled in. The purpose is not to provide definitive and detailed answers to every issue, but rather to give some plausibility to the intentionalist account, by outlining in what spirit some of the major issues in the vagueness debate could be addressed.

8.1 Sorites paradoxes

One of the most discussed vagueness issues are the sorites paradoxes. They rely on the tolerance principle according to which a minute difference in quantity does not change the quality of an entity. The classic heap paradox runs as follows:

> Premise 1: 10,000 grains of sand are a heap.
> Premise 2: A collection of grains of sand that is a heap minus one grain is still a heap.
> Conclusion: 9,999 grains of sand are a heap.

After 9,999 iterations of the syllogism we are left with the false conclusion that one grain of sand is a heap. It seems that vague terms lead us to nonsensical claims such as that one grain of sand is a heap of sand, because in the continuum of grains from

---

[39] See von Savigny 1840/1867, pp. 171–2 and Larenz 1991, pp. 317–18 and 328–33. See also Bobbit 1982, pp. 9–25.

10,000 to one there is no iteration of the syllogism at which we would be able to stop the regression.

From an intentionalist perspective one would have to ask what kind of intentions a speaker attached to a vague term that is susceptible to a sorites series. What we find would be intentions of a certain granularity.[40] If we go back to our speaker who said that she wanted to buy a red car, we would find a 'colour-intention' of a granularity that distinguishes between ranges of paradigm cases of red, yellow, orange, blue, and green. At this level of granularity paradigm cases of orange might be considered as borderline cases for which she did not make up her mind as to whether they would still fulfil her desire for a 'red' car. If she were confronted with a series of cars in fine-grained shades between yellow and dark red, we would simply not find an intention with respect to a choice at that level of granularity. As far as her sensual discriminatory capacities go, she could newly develop an intention also for this level of granularity, but she still would have to do so—with all the intricacies that develop at the borders of our discriminatory capacities.[41]

So on the one hand, she would not have developed an intention for a specific borderline at the granularity of a sorites series; on the other hand, she would have an intention at a more coarse-grained level with respect at least to paradigm cases of the red–yellow spectrum.[42] This explains why we can discriminate with confidence at the more coarse-grained level, but run into trouble at the finer-grained one. It is not only that we have not made up our mind where the boundaries should lie in a more fine-grained series, but we have not even developed an idea how we should tackle the task, since the task is a very different one from the one we are facing in the coarse-grained case. In the coarse-grained cases we can usually rely on substantive reasons like our colour preferences, but in sufficiently fine-grained sorites series we have to make arbitrary decisions on purely stipulative boundaries.[43] At the different levels of granularity we encounter different borderline issues. At a more coarse-grained level there might be a category for which we have not made up our mind with respect to the purposes we pursue. In the case of expressing the wish to buy a red car, the speaker might not have made up her mind whether an orange one would still satisfy her colour preferences. She would still have to weigh her reasons—maybe only in face of a concrete car, when the deviation from paradigm cases of red can be weighed against other factors. At the fine-grained level of a sorites series she would have to revert to a coin or a dice to draw an arbitrary boundary. Thus at the fine-grained level of the sorites series there is no intention of the speaker to be had. Asking what kind it is, is just senseless in the sense explained above (see section 5).

The difference in granularity and the different kind of decision making that comes with it corresponds to the generally very pragmatic handling of sorites issues

---

[40] The idea of a granularity index is another point that I owe to the comments of Geert Keil, who analysed its importance for vagueness in Keil 2010.

[41] Raffman 2014, pp. 146–9, found empirical evidence for a hysteresis effect in the way we handle sorites series in a so-called forced march experiment, in which subjects were asked to qualify colour patches shifting incrementally in hue from blue to green.

[42] Cf. the similarity model of Endicott 2000, pp. 155–7, stressing the centrality of paradigm cases.

[43] See Raffman 2014, p. 108 and *passim*, on arbitrariness as a characteristic for soritical vagueness.

in the law. There are—as far as I can see—hardly any serious sorites discussions in law, not even in those conflicts where the underlying continuum is at the centre of the debate. The law generally operates at a level of granularity at which substantive reasons matter. In the constitutional discussion on abortion the continuum of the development of human individual takes centre stage. Though constitutional debates on abortion are among the most heated, the issue is not where exactly to draw the line in a fine-grained continuum. The debate centres on whether abortion should be legal at all, legal within the first three months, or whether there should be a ban solely on late-stage abortions. There has never been a debate about whether it should be three months or three months plus or minus one, two, or three days. The law focuses at a coarse-grained level of granularity and knows that the very fine-grained decisions that the sorites argument aims at are arbitrary with respect to the substantive issue. It settles them with secondary pragmatic reason like the advantages of full or round numbers (see section 6)—usually without any controversy.

8.2 Higher-order vagueness

A troubling feature of vagueness is its fractal nature: not only are there borderline cases for vague terms, but there are borderline cases of borderline cases. In this regard, vagueness is different from Sainsbury's stipulated term 'minor' according to which 'minor' applies to people under seventeen and not to people over eighteen (Sainsbury 2001, p. 38). The term is indeterminate with regard to seventeen-year-olds, but has precise boundaries which delimit this borderline case. There are even some instances of such non-standard cases of vagueness in law. German criminal law forbids drunk driving by a regulation that prohibits driving a vehicle when 'unable to drive safely due to the consumption of alcohol' (StGB, § 316). The courts precisified the vague expression in the following way: it does not apply to alcohol blood concentrations of less than 0.3‰; it always applies to alcohol blood concentrations of more than 1.1‰ (absolute inability to drive) and has to be considered on the basis of further circumstances on a case-by-case basis for alcohol blood concentrations between 0.3‰ and 1.1‰.

Occurrences of such non-standard vague terms with precise boundaries, however, are a rare exception in real-life environments. In standard cases of vagueness, speakers and legislators do not even bother to establish clear-cut systematic borderlines for borderline cases. In continua they not only refrain from forming an intention for borderline cases, but do not even bother to establish a borderline between positive, negative, and borderline cases. They even leave the borderlines that divide borderline from non-borderline cases undetermined. Under the '*act-claire-doctrine*' developed for TFEU, Art. 267 European Union law requires the courts of last instance of member states to refer every question on which European Union law is not 'obvious' to the Court of the European Union.[44] But there is a whole case law on the borderline cases of an *acte claire*.

---

[44] 283/81 *CILFIT* [1982] Report 3415, paras 13–16.

The reasons for this are very similar to those that keep speakers from precision in the first place: the decision and opportunity costs incurred. These might even be higher for precisifying exact borderlines for borderline cases, since we would have two borderlines to draw instead of one. However, as with the sorites series, the speaker's intention will be allocated at a higher level of granularity. On this coarse-grained level the finer-grained levels on which higher-order vagueness relies do not exist. Just as in a coarse-grained representation of France as a hexagon—to take an example from Austin 1962, 143—the finer-grained shapes of the French border do not exist. If cases are presented at the finer-grained level of higher-order borderline cases—as in the case of a sorites series—there are no intentions of the speaker to be had and thus no meaning.

8.3 Vagueness, truth, and logic

In an intentionalist perspective, vagueness is akin to counterfactuals and fiction in that the intentions that bestow meaning on non-natural signs are incomplete. Unlike reality, fiction is not ontologically dense. Fiction only describes certain aspects of a fictive world, relies on unstated background assumptions to fill in some of the rest, and leaves other aspects undetermined. To take David Lewis's example of Sherlock Holmes: Conan Doyle explicitly let us know that Sherlock Holmes lived in 221B Baker Street; he did so before the implicit background assumption that 221B Baker was located in a city which shared, if not otherwise described, the features of his contemporary London, and left many features of his fictive world, such as the blood type of Inspector Lestrade, undetermined. With regard to the undetermined aspects of fictions there are no truths: 'Is the world of Sherlock Holmes a world where Holmes has an even or an odd number of hairs on his head at the moment when he first meets Watson? What is Inspector Lestrade's blood type? It is absurd to suppose that these questions about the world of Sherlock Holmes have answers' (Lewis 1978, p. 42). They do not have an answer, because the text does not hold any truth-apt propositional content in this respect.

Like fictions, intentions are not ontologically dense: '[A]n intention cannot specify all the characteristics of the intended act that are relevant to its desirability. No matter how elaborately detailed an intention is' (Davidson 1985, p. 197). Intentions only pertain to certain aspects of their objects. Let us return to our example of the speaker who communicates her intention to buy a car. Her intention is specific in that she does not want to buy a motorcycle, and she might even specify it with regard to further aspects such as colour, but there are aspects such as brand with regard to which it is not specified. In this case, just as there is no answer as to the blood type of Inspector Lastrade, there is no answer as to the brand our speaker intends to buy. The same holds for borderline cases of the vague aspects of her intention like the borderline shades of red as far as the colour of the car is concerned. With respect to these borderline cases the communicative intention does not provide a truth-apt propositional content. There is no answer to the question. In an intentionalist perspective, borderline cases have no truth-value, just as some propositions about fictions have no truth-value. They have no truth-value because the text lacks truth-apt propositional content in this respect.

Thus in law communicative interpretations with respect to the intent of the legislator have no truth-value with respect to borderline cases that the legislator did not include in his positive or negative intentions. These intentional voids have to be filled by legal construction. Whether the methodological standards for legal construction provide a basis for truth claims is beyond the scope of the intentionalist account.[45]

As for logic, which deals with truth, it suggests that the proper logical reconstruction of vagueness could seek guidance from attempts to develop a logic for counterfactuals and fictions. An intentionalist account of vagueness is compatible with any logical system that allows for underspecification, whether it works with three (Tye 1994), fuzzy (Goguen 1969), or supervaluational (Fine 1975, Keefe 2000, pp. 152–220) truth-values—even though a focus on truth-apt propositional content suggests that good old bivalence may very well suffice (Keil 2010). An intentionalist account has no cards in this game and it may well be that different logical systems fit vagueness equally well or that each of them presents some different internal difficulty. But that should be of no concern for an intentionalist account of vagueness: first, it is a problem of logic and not of a theory of a phenomenon if logic does not fit the phenomenon; second, underspecification is not a special issue that logic has with vagueness. Dealing with underspecification is a more general logical issue, as is evident in the logical discussion on counterfactuals and fiction.

8.4 Vagueness of individuation and of classification

Vagueness takes different forms. Two distinct ones are vagueness of individuation and vagueness of classification.[46] Vagueness of individuation concerns the precise delimitation of an object. Vagueness affects predicates and singular terms.[47] Some objects present themselves as discrete, like a chair in an otherwise empty room. But other objects present themselves as continuous with other parts of the world. If our world were a Lego- or Minecraft-World, in which mountains rose like pyramids in ninety-degree blocks over flat valleys, Mount Everest would have a precise delimitation. But in the world as it is it is anything but obvious where Mount Everest begins in the continuous landscape of the Himalayas.

Vagueness of classification arises because some objects in our world come in fine-grained sizes, degrees, and shades. If people came only in two sizes, 1.5 and 2 metres in height, there would be no vagueness issue with regard to who we consider a short and who a tall person. Instead, in our world people come in all sizes in between. The continuity of sizes people come in makes the classification of short and tall persons susceptible to vagueness.

---

[45] On the truth-aptness of legal construction, see Poscher forthcoming.
[46] See e.g. Alston 1967, pp. 219–20.   [47] See e.g. Quine 1960/2013, p. 114.

In an intentionalist perspective, there are no structural differences between vagueness of individuation and classification. In both cases precision can in principle be achieved. A speaker could delimit Mount Everest in the Himalayas by some more or less arbitrary physical boundary on the ground or using geodata, etc. He could also draw a sharp boundary between short and tall persons by picking—more or less arbitrarily—a height around 1.75 metres or any other measurement according to his purpose—for example, something well above the median, if he wanted to recruit a basketball team. In both cases speakers could form and communicate their intentions accordingly, but in most cases there is no need to incur the decision- and opportunity-costs involved in precise demarcation and classification. In most contexts forming a rough-and-ready intention will suffice. However, in those cases in which the expenditure is justified speakers will precisify their intentions. If a border conflict in the Himalayas were to be resolved by relying on the 'foot of Mount Everest' as the border between two countries, they would come up with a precise demarcation under international law. The same holds for classifications: if diamonds were traded in heaps, we would have as precise a concept of 'heap' as we have of carats. In an intentionalist perspective there is as little mystery to vagueness of individuation as there is to vagueness of classification.

8.5 Quantitative and combinatorial vagueness

Systematizing different forms of vagueness brings another distinction into play, that between quantitative vagueness on the one hand and combinatorial (Alston 1967, pp. 219–20) vagueness on the other. Much of the debate on vagueness is devoted to continuous phenomena of the world. It focuses on how vague expressions relate to these continua and their failure to single out a sharp borderline in some spatial, temporal, numerical, or otherwise quantitative continuum in an individual phenomenon or between phenomena under a classification. It is concerned with quantitative issues like how many grains of sand form a heap, how many hairs it takes to not be considered bald, etc. There is, however, another type of issue discussed under the heading of vagueness, which is distinct, as it cannot be explained by the occurrence of continua. In these cases, vagueness arises from an underspecification with respect to qualitative aspects of a phenomenon that a term relates to.[48] In a German court case the question arose whether a glass brick is a window in the sense of the law.[49] The vagueness of 'window' with regard to glass bricks does not concern drawing a sharp boundary in a continuum, but rather the discontinuous relation in which the term 'window' stands to the combination of properties like translucence, transparency, and openability.

Combinatorial vagueness involves issues of family resemblance (Wittgenstein 1958, § 67), prototype (Rosch 1975 and Rosch 1978, pp. 35–41) or stereotype (Putnam 1975, pp. 148–52 and 247–69) theory and essentially contested concepts (Gallie 1956). From an intentionalist perspective it does not matter whether these

---

[48] See the introduction to this volume, as well as Sorenson, ch. 14 this volume.
[49] BGH, NJW 1960, pp. 292–3.

phenomena are treated under the heading of combinatorial vagueness or any other label. They share with quantitative vagueness the fact that they are created by the underspecification of the intentions of speakers, who have not formed an intention with regard to the inclusion or exclusion of certain objects—such as the glass bricks with regard to the communicative intentions connected with the term 'window'. As in cases of quantitative vagueness, though, they could have made up their minds and formed intentions with regard to the inclusion or exclusion of glass bricks. If an emergency regulation requires a certain number of 'windows' on every floor of a building to secure evacuation routes the legislator has not only excluded glass bricks from its intentions, but also provided a context that allows for their reconstruction.

The reasons why speakers refrain from forming combinatorially precise intentions are the same as in cases of quantitative vagueness, too. The decision- and opportunity-costs of precisification can be at least as high as in cases of quantitative vagueness. It can be as laborious to make up one's mind about all the necessary and sufficient properties of the window one intends to talk about, as it is to draw a precise borderline in a continuum. The opportunity costs of doing so prematurely might even be higher for combinatorial aspects. This might explain why in law most disputes seem to concern combinatorial rather than quantitative vagueness. They more frequently concern the properties required to be legally considered a political party, an enterprise, a vehicle, etc. than the degree to which a well-specified property must be present.

It is further understandable that both types of underspecification are regarded as related issues, since combinatorial and quantitative vagueness are often intertwined, giving rise to multidimensional vagueness (Raffman 2014, pp. 28–9 and 109). For multidimensional concepts it might on the one hand be underspecified what kind of qualities it has to comprise and also to which degree a certain quality has to be developed and whether and how far a quantitative surplus in one dimension can compensate for a shortcoming in another, which brings all issues connected with incommensurability into play. When the legislator employs a concept like 'democracy'—for example, in a regulation limiting the export of arms to 'democratic' states—it might not have made up its mind how the different dimensions of government like accountability, bottom-up decision making, inclusiveness, temporal restriction of political power and guarantees of civil liberties have to relate, to what degree they have to be fulfilled, and whether and how far a surplus in one dimension can compensate for deficiencies in another. It might just form its intention on the basis of what it considers paradigm cases of democracies.

An intentionalist account of vagueness can thus explain why quantitative, combinatorial, and multidimensional cases of underspecification are discussed under the same heading, but has to take no stand on whether that is a wise terminological choice. Independent of the terminological choice an intentionalist account of vagueness can explain both phenomena as different[50] but related kinds of underspecification of communicative intentions.

---

[50] Cf. Raffman 2014, p. 108: 'multidimensional vagueness is a closer relative to ambiguity than to vagueness'.

8.6 Vagueness and epistemology

Already from the exposition of the intentionalist approach to vagueness it becomes apparent that vagueness is not in substance a question of epistemology.[51] Since meaning is tied to intentions there can only be meaning insofar as there are intentions to rely on. Where there are no intentions there is no non-natural meaning of signs. Since the intentionalist account reconstructs vagueness as a lack of intentions with regard to the precise boundaries of a phenomenon, there is no meaning to be had with regard to precision—thus there is nothing to know. The question of what a speaker meant by an utterance with regard to a borderline case he has not included in or excluded from his intention is as senseless as those in Lewis's examples of fictions.

That vagueness is not an epistemological issue in substance does not mean that there are no epistemological issues with regard to vagueness. How can we find out whether a certain case was included or excluded in the intention of the speaker? There are at least three issues connected with this epistemological question.

First, there is the interpretative question of how the addressee of an utterance can decipher the communicative intentions of the speaker and its limits. In general this pertains to the issue of knowledge of other minds.[52] Interpreters must infer the intentions of the author of an utterance and their limits by drawing on semantics and their knowledge of observable context. Inferences are mostly straightforward, sometimes difficult, and sometimes impossible to draw with sufficient epistemic confidence. But that it might be difficult or even impossible to reconstruct the communicative intentions of a speaker is a general issue of communicative interpretation and not specific to intentions regarding borderline cases. They arise for precise intentions in just the same way. If the apprentice of a carpenter in Germany finds a note to prepare 2 x 1 boards for a customer in England, he might not be able to find out whether the carpenter meant 2 x 1 metres or 2 x 1 yards, if the carpenter is out of town or deceased. In law these epistemic issues are even more complicated for the legislative acts of collective bodies such as parliaments. Relying on reductive accounts of collective intentions, the epistemic issues are multiplied by a multitude of individual intentions involved. These specific issues concerning legislative acts of collective bodies are set aside in this chapter. They have to be addressed in a theoretical reconstruction of collective legislative intent. But however they are solved, they do not pertain specifically to vagueness, but to all kinds of legislative underdeterminacy.

A second issue concerns the gap between the abstractness of generic intentions and the concrete objects that they pertain to (Gadamer 1989, p. 310). This issue is central to law, since in law generic legal regulations have to be applied to concrete cases. If the legislator requires drivers to stop at red lights, it surely does not have every concrete red light in the country in its mind. The issue of how generic

---

[51] The intentionalist approach thus runs counter to epistemic theories of vagueness such as those provided in Williamson 1994, especially pp. 185–247, and Sorenson 1988, e.g. pp. 365–9.

[52] For an overview of the discussion on other minds, see Hyslop 2014.

concepts relate to concrete cases, however, is again not specific to vagueness. It involves the theoretical issue of rule following and presents itself not only for borderline but also for core cases of concepts and for vague and precise concepts alike.[53] Even if the speaker has not formed the vague intention to look for a 'tall' player for her basketball team, but for a player 'over 2 m tall', it remains to be explained in which sense her intention also includes a certain 2.10 m player she did not even know existed. However the theoretical issue that involves the rule-following debate might be resolved, it will in some sense have to rely on our dispositions[54] to react with confirmation when presented with a concrete case of a red light or a certain 2.10 m player. By the same token, whether a concrete case is a borderline case of a generic intention has to rely in some way on the speaker's disposition to react with indecision when presented with a concrete borderline case, or to use Grice's formulation, if it is a case 'in which one just does not know whether to apply the expression or withhold it, and one's not knowing is not due to ignorance of the facts' (Grice 1989, p. 177). Indecision can be just as much a dispositional reaction as affirmation or rejection when confronted with a specific case under a generic intention. Whether someone intended to buy a specific car with a certain reddish shade, when he announced that he wanted to buy a red car, can in principle be tested by his relevant dispositions. Relating concrete borderline cases to abstract vague intentions involves the same theoretical issues of rule following that we are confronted with in the application of precise and nonstandard vague terms. However central to law these theoretical issues are and however difficult they might turn out to be, they are not specific to vagueness.

A third issue pertains to the stability of intentions with regard to borderline cases. It might not only be difficult for the interpreter to reconstruct the communicative intentions of the speaker, but also for the speaker himself. If the buyer who wants to buy a red car is confronted with an especially favourable offer in a shade between paradigm cases of red and orange, he might himself be uncertain whether he intended such a shade all along or whether his colour intentions changed when presented with the favourable offer. But again, issues like these are probably typical for vague intentions, but can arise with regard to precise ones as well. If the buyer formed the intention to buy a car with airbags, he might be in the same position with regard to side-airbags as to a borderline colour shade. The instability of intentions and the unreliability of memory are epistemic hurdles to the reconstruction of communicative intentions even from a first-person perspective. They can become specifically challenging and sometimes even insurmountable in law, which often relies on the collective intentions of large legislative bodies. But again, they are not specific to vagueness and just indicate the predicament of any epistemology that is geared towards potentially epistemically transcendent truths.

---

[53] On its role in so-called 'easy cases' in law, see Poscher 2015, especially pp. 288–91.
[54] Pettit 1996, pp. 86–97, stresses the dispositional element of any attempt to reconstruct our rule-following practices; for an overview of the rule-following discussion, cf. Kusch 2006.

8.7 The value of vagueness

At first sight, vagueness seems like a deficiency of language—a deficiency in precision. But many authors have supported the thesis that despite this first appearance there has to be some value in vagueness. It was Roy Sorenson who poured some water into the wine of praise. He convincingly showed that some values associated with vagueness were not due to vagueness, but to other features of language. Thus vagueness was associated with our ability to make classifying statements. H.L.A. Hart, for example, thought that 'uncertainty at the borderline is the price to be paid for the use of general classifying terms' (Hart 1961/2012, p. 128). Sorenson rightly pointed out that the generality of terms is distinct from, and not necessarily associated with, vagueness, the value of vagueness thus does not reside in allowing for generality. An intentionalist account of vagueness could not agree more, since it would even support that—at least theoretically—any type of classification can be rendered either vague or precise. However, it parts ways with Sorensen insofar as he insists that vagueness has no function at all (Sorensen 2001, pp. 406–13).

As should have become apparent, vagueness enables us to avoid the decision- and opportunity-costs incurred by precisifying our intentions prematurely with regard to the exact boundaries within a continuum or the exact qualities of the designate object (see section 6). Though generalization also has the benefit of saving decision- and opportunity-costs, vagueness adds to the benefit of generalization. Generalizations can be combined with precision or vagueness. 'Physical object with a density > 700 p' is general with respect to the size of the object. It can be rendered less general and precise by adding a precise measure like 'and > 1 metre in size'. It can, however, also be rendered less general and vague by adding a vague size requirement like 'macro level'. The latter saves the effort of fixing an exact size of the physical objects one is concerned with and it does not come with generality as such. That vagueness has a distinct function also becomes apparent in that it has the same cost-saving benefits when applied to the individuation of objects in a continuum, where generalization is not involved at all. Vagueness is a specific form of underspecification that pertains to the borderlines in continua whether the continua concern classes or individuals. It serves to save the decision- and opportunity-costs that would be incurred by—premature—precisification. In the face of continua in the world, vagueness allows for a faster development of intentions and their communication than a thoroughly precise vocabulary would. Therein lies the value of vagueness.

In law the interplay of legislation, administrative bodies and courts can be understood as machinery geared towards a division of labour that tries to optimize the distribution of the decision- and opportunity-costs entailed by precision.[55] The legislator does not have the resources of time or knowledge to design precise regulations for every future case. It will focus its intention at a fairly coarse-grained level

---

[55] See Poscher 2012, pp. 143–4. Cf. also Endicott 2011, pp. 22–4 and Asgeirsson 2012, pp. 304–15.

of granularity, which covers paradigm cases it wants to regulate, and uses vague terms that encompass them. The legislator typically leaves precisification either to administrative bodies, which will detail it with more fine-grained or sometimes even precise regulations, or directly to the courts, which deliver them incrementally on a case-by-case basis. Sometimes even paradigm cases of which the legislator is aware might only be addressed with a vague expression to allow for what Schmitt called dilatory formal compromises, to terminologically overcome political stalemates, and to defer decisions to the courts (Schmitt 1928/2008, pp. 85–7). Like communication in general, the law cannot dispense with vagueness. As in life in general, in law too it is vital to form and communicate intentions without incurring—often self-defeating—decision- and opportunity-costs. Much of the law's institutional design can even be understood to make the most of the value that vagueness has to offer.

References

Åkerman, Jonas and Patrick Greenough. 2010. 'Hold the Context Fixed—Vagueness Still Remains'. In *Cuts and Clouds*, edited by Richard Dietz and Sebastiano Moruzzi, 275–88. Oxford: Oxford University Press.

Alexander, Larry and Saikrishna Prakash. 2004. '"Is That English You're Speaking?" Why Intention Free Interpretation is an Impossibility'. *San Diego Law Review* 41(3): 967–95.

Allen, Robert (ed.). 2000. *The New Penguin English Dictionary*. London: Penguin Books.

Alston, William P. 1967. 'Vagueness'. In *The Encyclopedia of Philosophy Vol. 8*, edited by Paul Edwards, 218–21. New York: Macmillan.

Asgeirsson, Hrafn. 2012. 'Vagueness, Comparative Value, and the "Lawmakers' Challenge"'. *Archiv für Rechts- und Sozialphilosophie* 98(3): 299–316.

Austin, John Langshaw. 1962. *Sense and Sensibilia*, reconstructed from the manuscript notes by G.J. Warnock, Oxford: Oxford University Press.

Avramides, Anita. 2001. 'Davidson, Grice, and the Social Aspects of Language'. In *Paul Grice's Heritage. Semiotic and Cognitive Studies Vol. 9*, edited by Giovanna Cosenza, 115–38. Bologna: Brepols.

Azzouni, Jody. 2013. *Semantic Perception. How the Illusion of a Common Language Arises and Persists*. New York: Oxford University Press.

Bobbitt, Philip. 1982. *Constitutional Fate: Theory of the Constitution*. Oxford: Oxford University Press.

Bratman, Michael. 1999. *Faces of Intention. Selected Essays on Intention and Agency*. Cambridge: Cambridge University Press.

Campos, Paul. 1996. 'A Text Is Just a Text'. *Harvard Journal of Law & Public Policy* 19(2): 327–33.

Carroll, Lewis. 1872. *Through the Looking-Glass*. Raleigh (NC): Hayes Barton Press.

Chant, Sara Rachel, Frank Hindriks, and Gerhard Preyer (eds). 2014. *From Individual to Collective Intentionality*. New York: Oxford University Press.

Cook, John. 2009. 'Is Davidson a Gricean?' *Dialogue* 48(3): 557–75.

Davidson, Donald. 1984. 'Communication and Convention'. *Synthese* 59(1): 3–17. Reprinted in and cited from Donald Davidson. 2009. *Inquiries into Truth and Interpretation*, 265–80. Oxford: Clarendon Press.

Davidson, Donald. 1985. 'Replies to Essays I–IX'. In *Essays on Davidson. Actions and Events*, edited by Bruce Vermazen and Merril B. Hintikka, 195–229. New York: Oxford University Press.

Davidson, Donald. 1986. 'A Nice Derangement of Epitaphs'. In *Philosophical Grounds of Rationality*, edited by Richard E. Grandy and Richard Warner, 157–74. Oxford: Oxford University Press. Reprinted in and quoted from Richard E. Grandy and Richard Warner. 2005. *Truth, Language, and History*, 89–107. Oxford: Clarendon Press.

Davidson, Donald. 1989. 'James Joyce and Humpty Dumpty'. *Proceedings of the Norwegian Academy of Science and Letters*, 54–66. Reprinted in and cited from Donald Davidson. 2005. *Truth, Language, and History*, 143–57. Oxford: Clarendon Press.

Davidson, Donald. 1993. 'Locating Literary Language'. In *Literary Theory after Davidson*, edited by Reed Way Dasenbrock, 295–308. University Park (PA): Pennsylvania State University Press. Reprinted in and cited from Donald Davidson. 2005. *Truth, Language, and History*, 167–81. Oxford: Clarendon Press.

Davidson, Donald. 1994. 'The Social Aspect of Language'. In *The Philosophy of Michael Dummett*, edited by Brian McGuinness and Gianluigi Olivieri, 1–16. Dordrecht: Kluwer Academic Publishers. Reprinted in and quoted from Donald Davidson. 2005. *Truth, Language, and History*, 109–25. Oxford: Clarendon Press.

Davidson, Donald and Kathrin Glüer. 1995. 'Relations and Transitions—An Interview with Donald Davidson'. *Dialectica* 49(1): 75–86.

Ekins, Richard. 2012. *The Nature of Legislative Intent*. Oxford: Oxford University Press.

Endicott, Timothy. 2000. *Vagueness in Law*. Oxford: Oxford University Press.

Endicott, Timothy. 2005. 'The Value of Vagueness'. In *Vagueness in Normative Texts*, edited by Vijay K. Bhatia, Jan Engberg, Maurizio Gotti, and Dorothee Heller, 27–48. Bern: Peter Lang. Reprinted in and cited from Andrei Marmor and Scott Soames (eds). 2011. *Philosophical Foundations of Language in the Law*, 14–30. Oxford: Oxford University Press.

Fine, Kit. 1975. 'Vagueness, Truth and Logic' *Synthese* 30(3): 265–300. Reprinted in and cited from Rosanna Keefe and Peter Smith (eds). 1997. *Vagueness: A Reader*, 119–50. Cambridge (MA): MIT Press.

Fish, Stanley. 2005. 'There Is No Textualist Position'. *San Diego Law Review* 42(2): 629–50.

Fish, Stanley. 2008. 'Intention Is All There Is: A Critical Analysis of Aharon Barak's Purposive Interpretation in Law'. *Cardozo Law Review* 29(3): 1109–46.

Fish, Stanley. 2011. 'The Intentionalist Thesis Once More'. In *The Challenge of Originalism*, edited by Grant Huscroft and Bradley W. Miller, 99–119. Cambridge: Cambridge University Press.

Gadamer, Hans-Georg. 1989. *Truth and Method*, 2nd edn. Translated from the German by Joel Weinsheimer and Donald Marshall. New York: Continuum.

Gallie, Walter B. 1956. 'Essentially Contested Concepts'. *Proceedings of the Aristotelian Society* 56: 167–98.

Gilbert, Margaret. 1989. *On Social Facts*. London: Routledge.

Gilbert, Margaret. 2000. *Sociality and Responsibility*. Lanham (MD): Rowman & Littlefield.

Glüer, Kathrin. 2013. 'Convention and Meaning'. In: *A Companion to Donald Davidson*, edited by Ernest Lepore and Kirk Ludwig, 339–60. Chichester: Wiley Blackwell.

Goguen, Joseph A. 1969. 'The Logic of Inexact Concepts'. *Synthese* 19(3): 325–73.

Grandy, Richard E. and Richard Warner. 2013. 'Paul Grice'. In *The Stanford Encyclopedia of Philosophy (Fall 2013 Edition)*, edited by Edward N. Zalta. Available at: <http://plato. stanford.edu/archives/fall2013/entries/grice/>.

Greene, Jamal. 2012. 'The Case for Original Intent'. *The George Washington Law Review* 80(6): 1683–1706.

Grice, H.P. 1989. *Studies in the Way of Words*. Cambridge (MA): Harvard University Press.

Hart, H.L.A. 1961/2012. *The Concept of Law*, 3rd edn. Oxford: Oxford University Press.

Hurd, Heidi M. 1990. 'Sovereignty in Silence'. *Yale Law Journal* 99(5), 945–1028.

Hyslop, Alec. 2014. 'Other Minds'. In *The Stanford Encyclopedia of Philosophy (Spring 2014 Edition)*, edited by Edward N. Zalta. Available at: <http://plato.stanford.edu/archives/spr2014/entries/other-minds/>.

Keefe, Rosanna. 2000. *Theories of Vagueness*. Cambridge: Cambridge University Press.

Keil, Geert. 2010. 'Halbglatzen statt Halbwahrheiten. Über Vagheit, Wahrheits- und Auflösungsgrade'. In *Wahrheit, Bedeutung, Existenz*, edited by Martin Grajner und Adolf Rami, 57–86. Frankfurt: Ontos.

Keil, Geert. 2013. 'Introduction: Vagueness and Ontology'. *Metaphysica* 14(2): 149–64.

Kemmerling, Andreas. 2015. 'Meinen'. In *Handbuch Sprachphilosophie*, edited by Nikola Kompa, 227–37. Stuttgart: Metzler.

Knapp, Steven and Walter Benn Michaels. 1982. 'Against Theory'. *Critical Inquiry* 8(4): 723–42.

Kusch, Martin. 2006. *A Sceptical Guide to Meaning and Rules. Defending Kripke's Wittgenstein*. Chesham: Acumen.

Larenz, Karl. 1991. *Methodenlehre der Rechtswissenschaft*, 6th edn. Berlin: Springer.

Lepore, Ernest and Matthew Stone. 2015. *Imagination and Convention. Distinguishing Grammar and Inference in Language*. Oxford: Oxford University Press.

Lewis, David. 1978. 'Truth in Fiction'. *American Philosophical Quarterly* 15(1): 37–46. Reprinted in David Lewis. 1983. *Philosophical Papers, Vol. 1*, 261–75. Oxford: Oxford University Press.

Mann, Thomas. 1924/2002. *Der Zauberberg*. Frankfurt am Main: S. Fischer.

Marmor, Andrei. 2005. *Interpretation and Legal Theory*, 2nd edn. Oxford: Hart Publishing.

Matczak, Marcin. 2016. *Does Legal Interpretation Need Paul Grice? Reflections on Lepore and Stone's Imagination and Convention*. Available at: <http://ssrn.com/abstract=2716629 or http://dx.doi.org/10.2139/ssrn.2716629>.

McGinn, Colin. 2015. *Philosophy of Language. The Classics Explained*. Cambridge (MA): MIT Press.

Neale, Stephen. 1992. 'Paul Grice and the Philosophy of Language'. *Linguistics & Philosophy* 15(5): 509–59.

Neale, Stephen. 2008. 'Textualism with Intent'. Manuscript for Discussion at the Law Faculty, University of Oxford, with the author.

Nourse, Victoria. 2012. 'A Decision Theory of Statutory Interpretation: Legislative History by the Rules'. *Yale Law Journal* 122(1): 70–152.

Nourse, Victoria. 2014. 'Elementary Statutory Interpretation: Rethinking Legislative Intent and History'. *Boston College Law Review* 55(5): 1613–58.

Pettit, Philip. 1996. *The Common Mind. An Essay on Psychology, Society, and Politics (with a New Postscript)*. New York: Oxford University Press.

Poscher, Ralf. 2012 'Ambiguity and Vagueness in Legal Interpretation'. In *The Oxford Handbook of Language and Law*, edited by Lawrence Solan and Peter Tiersma, 128–44. Oxford: Oxford University Press.

Poscher, Ralf. 2015. 'Interpretation and Rule Following in Law'. In *Problems of Normativity, Rules and Rules-Following*, edited by Michal Araszkiewicz, Pawel Banas, Tomasz Gizbert-Studnicki, and Krzysztof Pleszka, 281–93. Cham: Springer.

Poscher, Ralf. Forthcoming. 'The Hermeneutic Character of Legal Construction'. In *Law's Hermeneutics. Other Investigations*, edited by Simone Glanert and Fabien Girard. London: Routledge.

Poscher, Ralf. Forthcoming. 2017, 'The Normative Construction of Legislative Intent'. *Droit & Philosophie, Annuaire de l'Institut Michel Villey*, Vol. IX.

Putnam, Hilary. 1975. *Mind, Language and Reality*. Cambridge: Cambridge University Press.

Quine, W.V.O. 1960/2013. *Word and Object*. Cambridge (MA): MIT Press.

Raffman, Diana. 1996. 'Vagueness and Context-Relativity'. *Philosophical Studies* 81(2): 175–92.

Raffman, Diana. 2014. *Unruly Words. A Study of Vague Language*. Oxford: Oxford University Press.

Rosch, Eleanor. 1975. 'Cognitive Representations of Semantic Categories'. *Journal of Experimental Psychology: General* 104(3): 192–233.

Rosch, Eleanor. 1978. 'Principles of Categorization'. In *Cognition and Categorization*, edited by Eleanor Rosch and Barbara Lloyd, 27–48. Hillsdale (NJ): Erlbaum.

Sainsbury, Mark. 2001. *Paradoxes*. Cambridge: Cambridge University Press.

Salmon, Nathan. 2005. 'Two Conceptions of Semantics'. In *Semantics versus Pragmatics*, edited by Zoltán Gendler Szabó, 317–28. Oxford: Oxford University Press.

Schmitt, Carl. 1928/2008. *Constitutional Theory*. Translated from the German by Jeffrey Seitzer. Durham: Duke University Press.

Searle, John. 1990. 'Collective Intentions and Actions'. In *Intentions in Communication*, edited by Philip R. Cohen, Jerry Morgan, and Martha E. Pollack, 401–15. Cambridge (MA): MIT Press.

Shapiro, Stewart. 2006. *Vagueness in Context*. New York: Oxford University Press.

Solum, Lawrence. 2013. 'Communicative Content and Legal Content'. *Notre Dame Law Review* 89(2): 479–520.

Sorensen, Roy A. 1988. *Blindspots*. Oxford: Clarendon Press.

Sorensen, Roy. 2001. 'Vagueness Has No Function in Law'. *Legal Theory* 7(4): 385–415.

Talmage, Catherine J.L. 1994. 'Literal Meaning, Conventional Meaning and First Meaning'. *Erkenntnis* 40(2): 213–25.

Talmage, Catherine J.L. 1996. 'Davidson and Humpty Dumpty'. *Noûs* 30(4): 537–44.

Tye, Michel. 1994. 'Sorites Paradoxes and the Semantics of Vagueness'. In *Philosophical Perspectives, Vol. 8. Logic and Language*, edited by James Tomberlin, 189–206. Atascadero (CA): Ridgeview Publishing. Reprinted in Rosanna Keefe and Peter Smith (eds). 1999. *Vagueness: A Reader*, 281–93. Cambridge (MA): MIT Press.

Van Patten, Jonathan. 1987. 'The Partisan Battle over the Constitution: Meese's Jurisprudence of Original Intention and Brennan's Theory of Contemporary Ratification'. *Marquette Law Review* 70(3): 389–421.

von Savigny, Friedrich Karl 1840/1867. *System of the Modern Roman Law*. Translated from the German by William Holloway. Madras: Higginbotham.

Waldron, Jeremy. 1994. 'Vagueness in Law and Language. Some Philosophical Issues'. *California Law Review* 82(3): 509–40.

Waldron, Jeremy. 1995. 'Legislators' Intentions and Unintentional Legislation'. In *Law and Interpretation. Essays in Legal Philosophy*, edited by Andrei Marmor, 329–56. Oxford:

Oxford University Press. Reprinted in Andrei Marmor. 2004. *Law and Disagreement*, 119–146. Oxford: Oxford University Press.

Warner, Richard. 2001. 'Introduction: Grice on Reasons and Rationality'. In H.P. Grice. 2001. *Aspects of Reason*, edited by Richard Warner, vii–xxxviii. New York: Oxford University Press.

Williamson, Timothy. 1994. *Vagueness*. London: Routledge.

Wittgenstein, Ludwig. 1958. *Philosophical Investigations*. Translated from the German by G.E.M. Anscombe. Oxford: Blackwell.

4

Can Legal Practice Adjudicate
Between Theories of Vagueness?

Hrafn Asgeirsson

Scott Soames has recently argued that the fact that lawmakers and other legal practitioners regard vagueness as having a valuable power-delegating function in the law, evidenced by actual legislative practice, gives us good reason to favour one theory of vagueness—the *partial-definition/context-sensitive theory*—over another—the *epistemic theory*.[1] The reason, Soames says, is that for a significant set of cases, the former helps explain this function, whereas the latter does not. If Soames is right, then facts about legal practice can in an important sense adjudicate between rival theories of vagueness, which is an exciting conclusion, both from the point of view of philosophy of law and philosophy of language. The argument is also likely to generate considerable optimism about what else we might expect to learn about language by looking at the law.

The purpose of this chapter is to significantly temper any such expectations, by arguing that we have to give up the one premise of Soames's argument that he seems to take to be uncontroversial: that the legal content of a statute or constitutional clause is identical with, or constituted by, its communicative content. Following Mark Greenberg, we can call this a version of the *communicative-content theory of law*.[2]

Recently, the communicative-content theory has come under serious pressure from several philosophers of law and legal scholars—including Greenberg, Lawrence Solum, and Dale Smith—who point out that legal textbooks are full of examples in which there appears to be some clear difference between the communicative content of a statute or constitutional clause and its legal content. I argue that the problem raised by these examples gives us good reason to reject certain versions of the theory, including Soames's, but go on to provide a preliminary sketch of my own account of legal content—the *Pro Tanto view*, as I call it—and show how it avoids the problem by allowing us to explain away the apparent 'gaps' in a principled and unified way.

---

[1] See Soames 2012.   [2] See Greenberg 2011b, pp. 217 ff.

Can Legal Practice Adjudicate Between Theories of Vagueness? Hrafn Asgeirsson. First Edition. Hrafn Asgeirsson 2016. Published 2016 by Oxford University Press.

Despite being a version of the communicative-content theory of law, however, the Pro Tanto view does not suffice to vindicate Soames's argument for the partial-definition/context-sensitive theory of vagueness, which I examine in some detail in the latter half of the chapter. Since legal content is neither identical with nor constituted by communicative content, facts about legal practice do not, after all, seem to be able to adjudicate between rival theories of vagueness—at least not in the way envisioned by Soames. Discussing, briefly, the cases of *Maurice v. Judd* and *Bronston v. United States*, I conclude by arguing that my point about Soames's argument is generalizable: due to the fairly complex relationship between language and law, we should be quite cautious about drawing general conclusions about language on the basis of facts about legal practice.

1. The Communicative-Content Theory of Law and Its (Recent) Critics

In outline, Soames's argument for the partial-definition/context-sensitive theory of vagueness (hereinafter the 'PD/CS theory') runs as follows. His starting point is the observation that we seem to have good reason to believe that the value of vagueness in the law consists—in large part—in the fact that, under certain circumstances, it is a good idea for lawmakers to formulate laws in vague terms and thereby facilitate their incremental, case-by-case precisification, resulting from the adjudication of borderline cases aimed at furthering their rationale. Thus, one of the main functions of vagueness in the law, according to Soames, is to appropriately delegate a limited kind of law-making power to judges. For a significant set of cases, he says, the PD/CS theory entails this function, given certain basic suppositions about the U.S. legal system and about legal practitioners, whereas its main competitor—the epistemic theory—does not. On the assumption that some version of hypothetico-deductive reasoning is appropriate in this case, legal practice therefore gives us good reason to favour the former theory over the latter, on Soames's view.

In the latter half of the chapter, I examine Soames's argument in considerable detail and elucidate—in particular—how the two theories of vagueness are supposed to make significantly different predictions about the value of vagueness in the law. For now, however, it suffices to point out that in order to establish these contrasting predictions, Soames, of course, has to move from claims about language to claims about law. To do so, he explicitly assumes the version of the communicative-content theory of law mentioned in the introduction: that the legal content of a statute or constitutional clause is identical with, or constituted by, its communicative content.[3]

---

[3] I should note that since there are several versions of the communicative-content theory, I am paraphrasing Soames's thesis to fit a more general form. For Soames's own formulation, see Soames 2012, pp. 99, 104.

Interestingly, this thesis is the only aspect of the argument that Soames seems to take to be uncontroversial, neither offering positive reasons for it nor addressing possible objections to it. However, as recent work by Mark Greenberg, Lawrence Solum, and Dale Smith demonstrates well, the communicative-content theory cannot be assumed without argument. Together, these critics draw attention to a wide range of cases—which I will discuss below—in which legal practice indicates a 'gap' between what the law is and what the relevant statute or constitutional clause says, which puts serious pressure on the theory. We can call this the *Gappiness Problem* for the communicative-content theory of law.[4]

Before I go on to discuss the problems raised by Greenberg, Solum, and Smith, I should note that it is not always clear exactly what relation proponents of the communicative-content theory take to obtain between the communicative content of a statute or constitutional clause and its legal content. It might be a metaphysically 'tight' relation like identity or constitution, or it might a slightly 'looser' relation like supervenience or 'direct correspondence'. As I have indicated, Soames's thesis is most straightforwardly taken to be either an identity claim or a constitution claim, and this—as we will see—makes it susceptible to the Gappiness Problem.

It is also not always clear what people mean when they talk about the legal content of a statute or constitutional clause. Sometimes, it seems to refer simply to the legally relevant propositional content of the authoritative utterance in question, which makes sense if the relation between communicative content and legal content is taken to be one of identity or constitution. Legally authoritative utterances, however, do more than simply represent what legal obligations, powers, permissions, etc. we have in virtue of the law being what it is; they also create them, which is why we can speak about the 'effect' that the enactment of a statute or constitutional clause has on the law. It seems appropriate, therefore, to identify the legal content of a statute or constitutional clause with the contribution that it makes to our legal obligations, powers, permissions, etc.

---

[4] I should note that there are two main theories/notions of communicative content in the contemporary literature in philosophy of language and linguistics—we can call them the *objective theory* and the *subjective theory*. According to the objective theory, the content that a speaker counts as having communicated is determined by the inferences that a rational hearer, knowing the context and conversational background, is warranted in making about the speaker's communicative intentions. See e.g. Goldsworthy 2005, Soames 2011, and Marmor 2013. In contrast, on the subjective theory, the communicative content of a speaker's remark is simply the content that she intended to communicate. A speaker—in uttering a sentence—means, says, asserts, etc. what she intends to mean, say, assert, etc. See e.g. Schiffer 1972, Grice 1989, Neale 2005, and Bach 2006.

For the purposes of discussing the Gappiness Problem, we do not need to distinguish these two notions of communicative content, nor do we need to distinguish the two variants of the communicative-content theory of law with which these notions naturally—though not necessarily—correlate. The problem applies to both variants equally. As for Soames's argument for the PD/CS theory of vagueness, there will be other issues to discuss that I think are more pressing, but it seems possible to argue that his argument requires an objective notion of communicative content. I will not address this issue further on this occasion, but invite the reader to have this in mind when we get to the argument, in section 3.

Already, this presents a *prima facie* problem for Soames's version of the communicative-content theory. The communicative content of a statute or constitutional clause is—depending on your view about linguistic content—a set of possible worlds, an abstract information-carrying object (typically, an *n*-tuple of objects and properties, or—more recently—objects and properties bound together by some structure-providing relation), or a representational cognitive act-type. But the legal content of such a provision, I have said, is its contribution to the law—i.e. a legal obligation, power, permission, etc. (or set thereof). Metaphysically, therefore, these two types of content appear to be quite distinct. If that is correct, it cannot be the case that the legal content of such a provision is identical with, or constituted by, its communicative content. Soames's thesis thus appears to be false. Or so the worry goes.

This is an important worry, to be sure. But it is neither novel nor necessarily fatal. The most promising way to respond to this charge of 'category mistake', it seems to me, is to try to parallel replies to a similar objection in metaethics, to the effect that reasons can't be propositions because 'they are the wrong sort of beast'.[5] As many authors have pointed out, there are—contra critics' appeal to intuition—several refined ways to make fairly palatable the idea that reasons can be propositions.[6] We might therefore be able to make equally palatable the idea that legal obligations, powers, permissions, etc. are propositions, too. For one, it would be rather odd if propositions could constitute one type of normative phenomena but not another, unless we have some special, yet-to-be-identified reason to believe that reasons are somehow importantly different from obligations, powers, permissions, etc. or that specifically legal-normative phenomena are somehow importantly different from 'ordinary' normative phenomena.

We may, of course, not be persuaded by this response, and still be inclined to believe that, whatever they turn out to be, legal-normative phenomena definitely aren't propositions. For the purposes of this chapter, however, we do not need to settle this matter, since there are other, more decisive reasons to believe that legal content is not identical with, or constituted by, communicative content. As I argue below, all-in-all, the Gappiness Problem is persuasive against identity- and constitution-based versions of the communicative-content theory. My own response to the problem will be to propose a different version of the theory, on which the legal content of a statute or constitutional clause is neither identical with, constituted by, nor supervenes on its communicative content, but—rather—directly corresponds to it. If successful, the Pro Tanto view about legal content both avoids the category-mistake problem and allows us to provide a principled and unified response to the Gappiness Problem, while preserving a robust version of the communicative-content theory.

Before I go on to illustrate what kinds of apparent gaps Greenberg, Solum, and Smith take to present the most difficult problems for the communicative-content

---

[5] Dancy 2000, p. 115.

[6] See e.g. Schroeder 2007, Lord 2008, and Morganti and Tanyi ms; but see also Mantel 2015 for a recent critique of propositional accounts of reasons.

theory, I should note that Soames is far from alone in treating the theory as uncontroversial. Many authors seem to take some version of the communicative-content theory for granted, focusing their discussion on how we figure out what the communicative content of legally authoritative speech is. There are at least two reasons for this absence of argument, I believe. First, law-making appears—paradigmatically—to be a type of speech act: people make law by saying things. It is quite natural to think, therefore, that the content of the law is determined by what lawmakers communicate. This has significant implications for the proper interpretation of legal provisions: if correct, we figure out what the law is the same way we figure out what someone is trying to tell us in a conversation—by making reasonable inferences about what information the speaker is intending to convey, given the context and conversational background. This, therefore, is the task that we ought to concern ourselves with, insofar as our aim is to discover the content of the law. Or so it may seem natural to many to think.

Second, as Greenberg (2011a) has pointed out, the communicative-content theory is often taken to be a consequence of what he calls the *command paradigm of law*: roughly, if someone with legitimate authority issues a command, then the relevant subjects are obligated to comply simply because the person said so. If Greenberg is right that the command paradigm is the prevailing view in modern jurisprudence, it is thus clear that a lot hangs on whether or not the communicative-content theory holds up.[7]

1.1 Some apparent 'gaps' between communicative content and legal content

As I have indicated, what recent critics of the communicative-content theory have in common is that they direct our attention to run-of-the-mill examples in which legal practice indicates that there is some clear difference between the communicative content of the relevant legal provisions and their legal content. Insofar as the 'actual practice of skilled practitioners is good evidence of the relation between legal texts and the content of law', this means trouble for the communicative-content theory.[8]

Greenberg (2011a) points out, among other things, that in the United States, the requirement of *mens rea* is presumed to be part of any rule specifying a criminal offence, even if the language of the provision contains no such requirement. 'It would be a strain', he says, 'to argue that *mens rea* requirements are somehow part of the linguistic content of criminal statutes, whatever their wording and whatever the circumstances of their enactment.'[9] Rather, in Greenberg's view, the common law presumption modifies the legal content of statutes whose language do not contain the relevant requirement, and does so without thereby modifying their communicative content. Thus, if Greenberg is right, there is a gap between the communicative content of such criminal law statutes and their legal content.

---

[7] See Greenberg 2011a, pp. 43 ff.   [8] Ibid., p. 72.   [9] Ibid., p. 76.

At the constitutional level, Solum (2013a; 2013b) has pointed out that the legal content of the First Amendment of the U.S. Constitution appears to be considerably richer than its communicative content, due to the development of associated doctrines of constitutional law. For example, constitutional doctrine surrounding the First Amendment provides the legal landscape with rules concerning expression via billboards and notions such as *prior restraint*, neither of which can be said to part of the communicative content of the relevant constitutional text—i.e. that 'Congress shall make no law…abridging the freedom of speech'.[10] Nevertheless, both are typically taken to be part of the legal content of the First Amendment; the relevant doctrines, Solum says, 'provide the "legal content" of the First Amendment freedom of speech'.[11] According to Solum, it is therefore 'clear that [communicative content and legal content] are not identical', since the former 'does not contain the elaborate structure of free-speech doctrine.'[12]

Adding to the examples supplied by Greenberg and Solum, Smith (ms) delivers what is perhaps the most direct blow to identity- and constitution-based versions of the communicative-content theory. First, Smith—elaborating on a point made by Solum (2008)—points out that mistaken precedents seem to change the legal content of the relevant statutes in such a way that there is—necessarily and by definition—a difference between their communicative content and their legal content.[13] He invites us to consider, for example, an appellate decision resulting from a court's mistaken identification of a statute's communicative content. 'If the court's mistake is central to its decision', he says, 'that error becomes part of the law', by which he means that the decision modifies the legal content of the statute, without thereby modifying its communicative content.[14] Consequently, a gap has been created between the two types of content. Or so it seems.

Second, Smith argues, some statutes specify that other already enacted statutes should be interpreted in a particular way—perhaps in accordance with their remedial purpose or in accordance with human rights—and thereby seem to change the legal content of the relevant pre-existing statutes without any change in their communicative content. Victoria's Charter of Human Rights and Responsibilities Act, for example, specifies—among other things—that '[s]o far as it is possible to do so consistently with their purpose, all statutory provisions must be interpreted in a way that is compatible with human rights'.[15] In doing so, the Act modifies the contribution that some pre-existing provisions made to the content of the law, Smith argues.[16]

Note that it doesn't seem to make sense to argue that the Act also modified the communicative content of the statutes whose legal content was affected. How

---

[10] U.S. Const. am. 1.   [11] See Solum 2013b, p. 20; see also Solum 2013a.
[12] Solum 2013b, p. 20.   [13] See Solum 2008, p. 7.   [14] Smith ms, p. 21.
[15] *Charter of Human Rights and Responsibilities Act 2006* (Vic), sec. 32(1).
[16] Similar reasoning, I think, applies in the case of the Canadian federal Interpretation Act, which specifies that '[e]very enactment is deemed remedial, and shall be given such fair, large and liberal construction and interpretation as best ensures the attainment of its objects'. See the Canadian federal Interpretation Act, R.S., c. I-23, s. 11.

could it? As Smith points out, the Act cannot reasonably be taken to affect what the legislators intended to communicate by enacting the pre-existing, now modified, provisions. And the Act certainly does not constitute new evidence of their original communicative intentions. Thus, like mistaken precedents, interpretive provisions that affect pre-existing legal provisions appear to create a gap between communicative content and legal content, which—according to the communicative-content theory—should not exist.

The examples provided by Greenberg, Solum, and Smith all put serious pressure on the communicative-content theory of law. To be sure, one could argue that the communicative-content theorist might be able to account for the *mens rea* requirement as contextually implied, since criminal statutes are enacted in a context containing information about firmly established common law doctrines.[17] But this requires getting rather—and perhaps unjustifiably—creative with the resources available to the communicative-content theorist in order to get around the problem posed by Greenberg's example. Arguably, for example, a great deal of criminal law is addressed to ordinary citizens, who are by no means conversant with legal conventions, however firmly established. As a result, knowledge of substantive legal doctrines—such as *mens rea*—on behalf of the audience cannot always be assumed, which has significant consequences for this 'contextual enrichment' strategy.[18] Further, even if this could somehow be made to work, it is hard—if not impossible—to see how this approach could be used to tackle the examples provided by Solum and Smith.

In response to Solum's example, one could perhaps argue that it is a mistake to take at face value the apparent intuition of legal practitioners that doctrine

[17] See e.g. Manning 2003, p. 2467. See also Ekins and Goldsworthy 2014, p. 56.
[18] Consider e.g. the majority's reasoning in *Staples v. United States* (Scalia joining) (522 U.S. 398 (1998)). In *Staples*, the question was whether or not Mr Staples had—by possessing an unregistered machinegun—violated The National Firearms Act, 26 U.S.C. § 5861(d), which states that 'It shall be unlawful for any person...to receive or possess a firearm which is not registered to him in the National Firearms Registration and Transfer Record.' It was an undisputed fact that Mr Staples *did not know* that the firearm he possessed required registration, due to the fact that the weapon was a semiautomatic model inconspicuously modified to operate as an automatic one.

Now, the Act does not explicitly contain any requirements regarding the epistemic state of the 'possessor', and the district court therefore concluded that the Act *did* cover Staples's situation and he was sentenced to probation and a fine; the court of appeals affirmed. The Supreme Court majority, however, argued that the relevant part of the Act had to be construed 'in light of the background rules of the common law...in which the requirement of some *mens rea* for a crime is firmly embedded' (511 U.S. 600, 605 (1994)). For Justices Thomas and Scalia, this meant that the communicative content of the legislative utterance was something roughly equivalent to the following: it shall be unlawful for any person...to receive or possess a firearm which is not registered to him in the National Firearms Registration and Transfer Record, *unless the person does not know that the object in question belongs to a type of firearm that requires such registration.* In other words, due crucially to the background assumptions shared by the legislature and its intended audience, the actual communicative content of §5861(d) is a *pragmatic enrichment* of its literal content. Or so they argued.

The problem with this line of reasoning, however, is that if ordinary citizens are generally the intended audience of criminal law, then the doctrine of *mens rea* cannot reasonably be taken to form part of the actual common ground and, consequently, there is no linguistic basis for claiming that the communicative content of §5861(d) is a corresponding pragmatic enrichment of its literal content. Thus, if the Act's legal content includes a *mens rea* requirement, as legal practice says it does, then its legal content is different from its communicative content.

surrounding constitutional provisions *modifies* their legal content. Maybe doctrine just *adds* content to constitutional law, supplementary to the legal content contributed by the relevant provision. Supplementation is rather different from modification. Or so the response goes.

On this 'supplemental content' approach, the communicative content of the free speech clause would have to be some kind of general and abstract principle, which doctrine then 'implements' or adds more definite content to, rather than an unrestricted prohibition. Or else we are stuck with the appearance of modification—that is, of constitutional doctrine limiting the unrestricted scope of the free speech clause. This approach, then, requires the legal content added by constitutional doctrine to be *consistent* with the communicative content of the First Amendment.

I think we find the ingredients for something like the supplemental content approach in Solum's own work on originalism. As he points out, an originalist might say that while the Supreme Court does not have authority to change the legal content of the Constitution, it does—under certain conditions—have authority to adopt further rules of constitutional law, so long as they are consistent with that content.[19] I don't think we are forced, however, to say that these rules become part of the legal content of the First Amendment itself, as Solum's example assumes—it seems possible to hold instead that they constitute additional legal content, contributed by the development of constitutional doctrine. Such content is *associated* with the First Amendment, to be sure, but—on the view under consideration—doctrine does not actually contribute to the legal content of the Amendment itself.

As we will see, there is some kinship between this response and the Pro Tanto view introduced in section 2. However, in contrast to the Pro Tanto view, which aspires to offer a unified response to the Gappiness Problem, the scope of the originalist response under consideration is significantly limited. Due to the consistency constraint, for example, the supplemental approach cannot explain away Greenberg's *mens rea* example, since the doctrine is inconsistent with the communicative content of criminal statutes whose language does not contain such a requirement (functioning, as it does, to limit their scope). Nor does it offer a way to handle Smith's examples.

The Gappiness Problem, then, gives us good reason to reject identity- and constitution-based versions of the communicative-content theory. Granted, we might—with some creative effort—be able to explain away some of the apparent gaps in one way or another, but no unified or comprehensive strategy seems available to proponents of these versions of the theory. The 'contextual enrichment' strategy cannot explain away the apparent gap between the communicative content of the First Amendment and the legal content of free speech doctrine, just as the 'supplemental content' strategy cannot explain away the apparent gap between the communicative content of criminal statutes whose language does not contain a *mens rea*

---

[19] See e.g. Solum 2013b, p. 22.

requirement and their legal content. And, more importantly, neither strategy can at all explain away the apparent gaps created by mistaken precedent and interpretive statutes. If that is correct, Soames's version of the communicative-content theory is under very serious pressure, and with it his entire argument for the PD/CS theory of vagueness.

In addition to the problems these examples cause for Soames's argument, and—as we will see—indeed for any argument attempting to extract lessons about language from facts about legal practice, they also put the command paradigm of law—from which the communicative-content theory is often taken to follow—under serious pressure. The same goes for the prospect of resolving significant problems in legal interpretation with the application of advances in philosophy of language and linguistics. As of yet, these potentially devastating problems have either received less than adequate attention or they have not been responded to at all. In section 2, therefore, I will sketch my own account of legal content—the Pro Tanto view—and show how this account avoids the problems raised by Greenberg, Solum, and Smith in a principled and unified way.

2. The Pro Tanto View About Legal Content

The Pro Tanto view about legal content provides the ingredients for a principled and unified reply to the Gappiness Problem by allowing us to explain away the apparent gaps between the communicative content of the relevant statute or constitutional clause and its legal content. The key is to recognize that legal reasons—like 'ordinary' reasons—can be defeated by other reasons, either by rebutting or undercutting. A reason is subject to rebutting defeat if it is out-weighed by another conflicting reason—consider, for example, a scenario in which a person's reason not to damage her new shoes is outweighed by a reason to help someone in need. Undercutting defeat, on the other hand, occurs when a reason is affected by another reason in such a way that its weight is reduced, either partially or completely—such as, perhaps, when the weight of a reason to help is to some extent reduced by the fact that the person is herself responsible for being in trouble.[20]

I should note that the framework that forms the basis of the proposed account is far from novel. Rather, I take it to be a broadly Razian view that relies on an independently attractive framework for explaining the nature of reasons generally, inspired in part by recent work in epistemology, metaethics, and deontic logic.[21]

Although what follows is a preliminary sketch, the Pro Tanto view is ultimately intended as a contribution to the debate concerning the appropriate

---

[20] See Dancy 2004, p. 42.
[21] See e.g. Pollock and Cruz 1999, Dancy 2004, Schroeder 2011, Horty 2012, and Bader 2016; see also e.g. Prakken and Sartor 1996.

principles of individuation regarding legal content—that is, how legal obligations, powers, permissions, etc. are individuated. Broadly following Raz (1972),
the idea behind the proposed view is that it is theoretically beneficial to provide
what we can call an 'atomistic' account of legal content, an account that elucidates the contribution that individual laws make to people's legal obligations,
powers, permissions, etc. by 'carving small and manageable units out of the total
legal material in a way that will promote our understanding of the law by classifying laws into various types and by showing how these laws interrelate and
interact with one another'.[22]

Critics of the communicative-content theory tend to be sceptical about the
value of such accounts and often emphasize what we might call the 'holistic'
appearance of the law. Dworkin (1977), for example, plainly says that he pays
'no attention to [the general problem of the individuation of laws]', indicating
that what matters is the normative status of people subject to law (i.e. their obligations, permissions, powers, etc.), rather than the way in which their status is
'composed'—much like the significance of a book lies in the information it provides, rather than how the propositions it contains are individuated and how they
combine to form the content of the book.[23] In a similar vein, Greenberg (2004)
argues that the 'real' problem of legal content is how normative facts make certain
aspects of legal practice relevant to people's normative status, rather than how law
practices 'determine the content of the law by contributing propositions which
then get amalgamated'.[24] 'The content of the law', he says, 'is not determined by
any kind of summing procedure, however complicated'.[25] And it is a mistake, he
thinks, to assume that there are 'discrete issues of what considerations are relevant
to the content of the law and how the relevant considerations combine to determine the content of the law'.[26]

A full exposition of the Pro Tanto view is beyond the scope of the present chapter, but a proper defence of the view would have to include both a more thor-
ough examination of the problems raised by Greenberg, Solum, and Smith and
a response to a host of other worries, raised—in particular—by Greenberg in a
series of important papers.[27] For our purposes here, however, what matters is that
we get a grasp of the basic aspects of the Pro Tanto account, in order to see, first,
how this account avoids the Gappiness Problem and, second, that—despite being
a version of the communicative-content theory of law—the view does not suffice
to vindicate Soames's argument for the PD/CS theory of vagueness. If what I say
is correct, facts about legal practice do not, after all, seem to be able to adjudicate
between rival theories of vagueness—at least not in the way envisioned by Soames.
Moreover, due to the fairly complex relationship between language and law, we
should be quite cautious about drawing general conclusions about language on the
basis of facts about legal practice.

---

[22] Raz 1972, p. 831.   [23] Dworkin 1977, pp. 74, 75–6.
[24] Greenberg 2004, p. 176.   [25] Ibid., p. 177.   [26] Ibid., p. 192.
[27] See Greenberg 2004, 2010, 2011a, 2011b, and 2014.

2.1 The basic notions, and 'mechanics', of the Pro Tanto view

The basic idea of the Pro Tanto view is twofold and fundamentally fairly simple. (For ease of exposition, I will restrict the following explication to obligation-imposing statutes and constitutional clauses.) First, the legal content of an obligation-imposing statute or constitutional clause is neither identical with, constituted by, nor supervenes on its communicative content; rather, its enactment gives subjects a defeasible legal reason to take or refrain from a specified course of action (if certain circumstances obtain), a reason that *corresponds directly* to its communicative content.[28] Second, in much the same way as 'ordinary' *pro tanto* reasons interact with each other to determine what a person ought all-things-considered to do, the legal reasons provided by enactment often interact with other (antecedent or subsequent) legal content to determine the all-things-considered legal obligations that people subject to the relevant system have.[29]

On the Pro Tanto view, then—contrary to what most authors seem to assume, including critics of the communicative-content theory—it is not the case that the considerations appealed to (precedent, doctrine, presumption, interpretive provision, etc.) *modify* the content that the enactment of a legal provision contributes to the law (obligations, powers, permissions, etc.). Rather, they *interact* with that content in a certain way, by either undercutting or outweighing the reasons provided by it.[30]

To fix these ideas, let us contrast, for example, the Pro Tanto account with the view that, unlike excuses and other affirmative defences, decisions on justifying circumstances actually modify the 'affected' rule, by altering the conditions under which people count as having committed an offence.[31] On the 'modification view', the rule has changed and no longer gives subjects a reason to take or refrain from the specified course of action in the circumstances decided upon; the court's decision (that the defendant's actions were justified in the relevant circumstances)

---

[28] It is important to point out that direct correspondence, like supervenience, is not an explanatory relation, but rather a 'surface' relation reporting covariation in legal content and communicative content; see Kim 1993, pp. 167–8. A full defence of the Pro Tanto account, therefore, would have to say a great deal about what *grounds* this covariation, i.e. what 'deep' metaphysical dependence relation explains the pattern that the correspondence claim reports.

[29] In this chapter, I want to be as noncommittal as possible about the nature of legal reasons, but I do assume that law necessarily gives legal reasons and that this is not an 'empty' notion. On one such view, law at least gives reasons in the same way as chess gives chess-reasons, etiquette etiquette-reasons, and so forth. We can say that such reasons are 'real' reasons for people insofar as they have 'real' reasons to engage in the relevant practice (however we wish to define real reasons).

[30] For now, I leave it open how best to analyse particular cases. Some cases may be better analysed in terms of outweighing, but generally I think it is more promising to analyse the relevant cases in terms of undercutting defeat. It seems clearly odd, for example, to say that Virginia's Racial Integrity Act of 1924—which was deemed unconstitutional—gave white and non-white citizens a reason not to intermarry, while the constitution gave them a reason *against not*—i.e., *for*—intermarrying and that the constitutional reason outweighed the statutory reason. It seems clearly better to say that, in fact, the Equal Protection Clause *undercut* the reason provided by the statute, in such a way that, in fact, the Act carried no genuine weight at all (but that it *would have*, if it hadn't been for the 14th Amendment).

[31] See e.g. Fletcher 2000, p. 812.

has therefore altered the relevant statute's legal content, without affecting its communicative content. In contrast, on the Pro Tanto view the rule still provides the same reasons as before, but some of these reasons are now defeated by the court's decision.

We will get a better sense of the 'mechanics' of the Pro Tanto view when I explain how the view proposes to tackle the Gappiness Problem. As the example above illustrates, however, one of the core ideas behind this account is that a defeated reason is still a reason, which allows us to sensibly say that the (*pro tanto*) legal content of an 'affected' statute or constitutional clause remains intact.

The difference between modification and interaction is, of course, far from intuitive and it might be tempting to think that, say, decisions on justifying circumstances defeat some of the reasons provided by the relevant rule to such an extent that they no longer constitute any reasons at all.[32] In that case, the Pro Tanto view just collapses into a modification view. The usual way to counter this line of reasoning—due to Schroeder (2011)—involves a scenario in which someone's evidential reason is increasingly undermined by an iteration of the defeating condition, but we can illustrate the relevant point with an example that is closer to home.[33]

Let's stick with the criminal case in which a court decides on justifying circumstances and stipulate that the court in question is a trial court. By hypothesis, the decision of the trial court defeats some of the reasons provided by the statute (for subjects to take or refrain from the specified course of action, if certain circumstances obtain) to such an extent that they constitute no reasons at all. The set of reasons affected by the decision is determined by the scope of the justifying circumstances specified by the court. But let's then say that the decision is appealed and that the district court of appeal decides to uphold the trial court's judgment. As a result of the appellate court's decision, it seems that the statute in question now provides even *less* reason for subjects to take or refrain from the relevant course of action, vis-à-vis the specified circumstances. That is, the appellate court's decision adds some measure of practical 'oomph' to the trial court's decision on justifying circumstances, evidenced by the intuition that in deliberating about what to do, it is now appropriate for subjects to place more weight on the fact that any of the justifying circumstances obtain (if they do). This, however, makes sense only if, subsequent to the trial court's decision, the statute still provides reasons whose weight can be (further) reduced by the appellate court's decision, which contradicts the hypothesis.

We can iterate this scenario with increasing levels of judicial authority (e.g. state supreme court, federal district court, federal circuit court, and the U.S. Supreme Court). I want to be non-committal about what happens at the highest level, but at least until a decision has been made at that level, the statute in question still provides subjects with *some* reason to take or refrain from the specified action in

[32] See e.g. Pollock and Cruz 1999 (p. 37), Dancy 2004 (p. 74), and Horty 2012 (pp. 228–9).
[33] See Schroeder 2011, pp. 334–5.

the justifying circumstances specified by the trial court, although their weight may have been rendered 'inconsequential' already at that level.[34] And that is all we need to get the Pro Tanto view going.

The Pro Tanto view, then, relies crucially on the general idea that—just as with evidential reasons—many cases in which we are inclined to think that a practical reason has been completely defeated are actually cases of partial undercutting defeat. In these cases, the defeated reasons are still reasons, but their weight has been reduced below some threshold of relevance. Getting back to the Gappiness Problem, the strategy is to apply this line of reasoning to any alleged 'modification' of legal rules provided by the enactment of a statute or constitutional clause—unless this modification can reasonably be taken to have come about linguistically, by way of contextual enrichment. What is going on, according to the Pro Tanto view, when the contribution that a statute or constitutional clause makes to the body of law does not seem to completely mirror its communicative content is that there is some interaction between it and other legally relevant considerations which explains this apparent difference. Thus, despite appearances, there is—on this view—no real gap between the communicative content of the relevant provision and its legal content. It's just that its *all-things-considered* legal 'effect', if you will, depends on the legal content of other legal-normative considerations.

2.2 How the Pro Tanto view handles the Gappiness Problem

The Pro Tanto view, then, has a relatively straightforward way to handle the problems for the communicative-content theory of law raised by Greenberg, Solum, and Smith. Starting with Greenberg's *mens rea* example, and assuming we are talking about cases in which contextual enrichment is an unreasonable stretch, the Pro Tanto view takes criminal statutes whose language does not contain a *mens rea* requirement to actually give officials a reason to apply those statutes to cases in which a 'guilty mind' is absent; this reason, however, is defeated by common law doctrine. This analysis may seem to raise issues about the distribution of the burden of proof in criminal cases involving the relevant statutes, since the Pro Tanto view might seem to predict that the absence of *mens rea* should be treated as an affirmative defence, which does not reflect legal practice. Issues about the burden of proof, however, do not and—I think—should not depend on the metaphysics of legal rules. It does raise issues, though, regarding what weight we should give to the intuitions of skilled legal practitioners when we evaluate philosophical theories of law. I address this issue further at the end of this section.

---

[34] Another way to illustrate this point in the context of practical reasons is to imagine a scenario in which your boss, Al, tells you to ϕ, but then his boss, Burt, comes along and tells you to ignore Al's orders, only to be followed by Burt's boss, Cecil, who also tells you to ignore Al's orders. Assuming that authority is transitive in this case, it seems that although Burt's orders to ignore Al's orders undercut the reason you had to ϕ (in virtue of Al's having ordered you to), you have even less reason to ϕ now that Cecil has also ordered you to ignore Al's orders. If that is correct, then some reason must have remained after Burt's orders to ignore Al's orders, although its weight may have been reduced below some threshold of relevance.

Moving on to Solum's First Amendment example, the issue was that doctrine surrounding the First Amendment provides rules concerning prior restraint, expression via billboards, and other freedom-of-speech-related notions that cannot reasonably be said to be part of the communicative content of the constitutional text. This was considered a problem for the communicative-content theory because these rules are typically taken to modify the legal content of the First Amendment. Either the communicative content of the free speech clause is a general and abstract principle, the legal effect of which is made more definite by constitutional doctrine, or—compounding the problem—it is entirely unrestricted in character, but limited in its legal effect by the rules of implementation adopted by the Supreme Court. Either way, constitutional doctrine modifies the legal content of the First Amendment without modifying its communicative content and, hence, the former is neither identical with nor constituted by the latter.

The supplemental content approach, as we recall from the discussion in the previous section, requires the supplemented content to be consistent with the legal content provided by the free speech clause, which in turns requires us to take its communicative content to be a general and abstract principle, at least insofar as the aim is to save the communicative-content theory. (This consistency constraint was also the source of the limited scope of this approach.) On the Pro Tanto view, in contrast, there is no constraint of consistency, and so the communicative content of the First Amendment can readily be taken to be unrestricted, in which case its legal content is unrestricted, too. Absent other considerations, the First Amendment—on this view—gives officials a reason not to make *any* law abridging the freedom of speech, including, for example, law restricting expression via billboards, and to declare unconstitutional any law that does so.

The 'normative landscape' may change, however, once other relevant considerations are introduced. Consider, for example, the case of *Metromedia, Inc. v. City of San Diego*, in which the Supreme Court recognized that 'at times, First Amendment values must yield to other societal interests' and ruled that a San Diego ordinance substantially limiting the erection of billboards in the interest of traffic safety (and city appearance) was not wholly unconstitutional.[35] Once issued, the Court's ruling—on the Pro Tanto view—defeats some of the reasons that officials, in virtue of the First Amendment, previously had. What explains the appearance of restricted legal content in the case of the First Amendment—i.e. its *all-things-considered* legal 'effect'—is the interaction between reasons provided by the Constitution and reasons provided by constitutional doctrine. But the latter does not *modify* the legal content itself; a defeated reason is still a reason.

The Pro Tanto account offers a similar solution to the two problems raised by Smith. The first issue was that mistaken precedents seem to change the legal content of the relevant statutes in such a way that there is—necessarily and by definition—a difference between their communicative content and their legal content. On the Pro Tanto view, however, such precedents do not modify their content.

---

[35] *Metromedia, Inc. v. City of San Diego*, 453 U.S. 490 (1981).

An appellate decision, for example, may result from a court's mistaken identification of a statute's communicative content and the mistake may indeed become part of the law, broadly speaking, but—contra Smith—the error does not become part of the statute itself. Accordingly, there is no gap between communicative content and (*pro tanto*) legal content, although there is, of course, a gap between communicative content and *all-things-considered* legal effect. This gap, however, is explained by the interaction between reasons provided by the relevant provision and the reasons provided by the court's ruling.

The second issue raised by Smith was that some statutes specify that other already enacted statutes should be interpreted in a particular way and thereby seem to be able to change the legal content of the relevant pre-existing statutes without changing their communicative content (which remains fixed). On the Pro Tanto view, however, provisions like Victoria's Charter of Human Rights and Responsibilities Act do not actually modify the legal content of already enacted statutes whose pre-2006 legal contents were not fully consistent with human rights. Rather, their legal content remains the same, but some of the reasons they give rise to are defeated by reasons provided by the Act. The *all-things-considered* legal 'effect' of those statutes, then, is different post-2006, but there is no gap between their communicative content and their (*pro tanto*) legal content.[36]

This, then, is how the Pro Tanto view about legal content proposes to tackle the Gappiness Problem. Generally speaking, the problem comes from fact that the intuitions of skilled legal practitioners tell us that it is not uncommon for there to be some kind of gap between the communicative content of a statute or constitutional clause and its legal content, the most manifest of which are perhaps the gaps that seem to be created by subsequent modification of legal content. On the assumption that these intuitions are reliable indicators of the relationship between the two types of content, this gives us the ingredient for the following general argument against the communicative-content theory:

P1 If the legal content of a statute or constitutional clause is identical with, constituted by, supervenes on, or directly corresponds to its communicative content, then there cannot be a change in the legal content of a statute or constitutional clause without a change in its communicative content.

P2 There can be a change in the legal content of a statute or constitutional clause without a change in its communicative content.

[36] Note that the Pro Tanto view distinguishes between the legal content of a particular statute or constitutional clause—i.e. the legal obligations, permissions, powers, etc. that they give rise to—and the legal content of the law as a whole—i.e. the total set of legal obligations, permissions, powers, etc. Because the content that a particular statute or constitutional clause contributes to the (body of) law is *pro tanto*, it is going to look, first, as if the content of individual enactments differs systematically from its communicative content and, second, as if the content of the law as a whole is not just the set of legal obligations, permissions, powers, etc. contributed by individual legal norms. This apparent difference, however, is explained (away) by the interaction between *pro tanto* legal content contributed by individual enactments and other legally relevant considerations (precedent, doctrine, presumption, interpretive provision, etc.). In this way, the Pro Tanto view purports to explain the 'holistic' appearance of law, without giving up atomism. For a discussion, see Greenberg 2004, pp. 49 ff.

C It is not the case that the legal content of a statute or constitutional clause is identical with, constituted by, supervenes on, or directly corresponds to its communicative content.

The conclusion, of course, is that the communicative-content theory of law is false, in whatever version.

The Pro Tanto view allows us to resist P2 by holding that legal content provides (or consists in) *pro tanto* reasons for action, subject to possible defeat by other legal considerations, either by undercutting or outweighing. I say 'resist', because in order to demonstrate the falsity of P2, we would—depending on the modality involved—have to positively establish the impossibility of a change in the legal content of a statute or constitutional clause without a change in its communicative content either *tout court* or within the set of possible worlds 'like ours'. Both are tall orders, each with their own challenges. Addressing these further issues is beyond the scope of the present chapter, but what the Pro Tanto view does manage to show is that none of the problems described in section 1 suffice to establish P2.

The Pro Tanto view does require that we give up the claim that the actual practice of skilled practitioners is good evidence of the relation between the communicative content of an individual statute or constitutional clause and its legal content, which is arguably a significant cost. However, it does not require us to hold that the intuitions of skilled legal practitioners are wholly unreliable or irrelevant. Just as competent speakers of language have reliable intuitions about the content communicated via an utterance without having reliable intuitions about the exact semantic content of the words used and the details of how semantic content is affected by context to produce the content communicated,[37] skilled legal practitioners may well have reliable intuitions about the *all-things-considered* legal-normative 'status' of persons (i.e. their *all-things-considered* legal obligations, powers, permissions, etc.) without having reliable intuitions about the exact normative content of the relevant legal considerations and the details of how that content interacts to produce that status. As a result, I do not think it counts against the Pro Tanto account that it does not respect the intuition of skilled legal practitioners that the legal content of the relevant provision gets modified in the cases discussed.

Having explained the Gappiness Problem and sketched the Pro Tanto view as a response to it, it is time to show the implications that this version of the communicative-content theory has for Soames's argument for the PD/CS theory of vagueness. However, although the argument merits special attention, its role here is also to illustrate a certain general form of reasoning that we might be inclined to employ if our assumptions about the relationship between language and law are unduly strong. If successful, the Pro Tanto account has important implications for any attempt to draw general conclusions about language on the basis of facts about legal practice, of which Soames's argument, the PD/CS theory, is a prime example.

---

[37] See e.g. Bach 2002 (pp. 29–32), Neale 2005 (pp. 183–4), and Soames 2008 (pp. 460–2).

3. Explaining the Value of Vagueness in the Law

In outline, as we recall, Soames's argument for the PD/CS theory of vagueness runs as follows. His starting point is the observation that we seem to have good reason to believe that the value of vagueness in the law consists—in large part—in the fact that, under certain circumstances, it is a good idea for lawmakers to formulate laws in vague terms and thereby facilitate their incremental, case-by-case precisification, resulting from the adjudication of borderline cases aimed at furthering their rationale. Thus, one of the main functions of vagueness in the law, according to Soames, is to appropriately delegate a limited kind of law-making power to judges. For a significant set of cases, he says, PD/CS theory entails this function, given certain basic suppositions about the U.S. legal system and about legal practitioners, whereas its main competitor—the epistemic theory—does not. On the assumption that some version of hypothetico-deductive reasoning is appropriate in this case, legal practice therefore gives us good reason to favour the former theory over the latter, on Soames's view.

In the remainder of this section, I explain in brief the relevant features of the two rival theories of linguistic vagueness and the way in which they are supposed to generate different predictions about the value of vague language in the law—at least for a significant set of cases. I also explain how the predictions of the epistemic theory, but not the PD/CS theory, are supposed to conflict with our firm intuitions about that value.

3.1 Two rival theories of vagueness

It is standard to define vagueness with reference to borderline cases, in the sense that most writers on the topic hold that a term is vague either *only if* or *if, and only if*, it has possible borderline cases.[38] It is possible, for example, for someone to be borderline bald, for things to be borderline blue, for causes to be borderline probable, and so on. The nature of borderline cases is controversial, but most theorists would accept the characterization that these are cases in which there is inherent uncertainty regarding whether or not the relevant term applies. They will vary, however, in how they think this uncertainty ought to be understood.

As the name suggests, the PD/CS theory, espoused, for example, by Soames himself, holds that vague predicates—such as 'tall', 'bald', 'blue', 'cruel', 'unusual', 'excessive', 'reasonable', and the like—are both partially defined and context-sensitive.[39] Such predicates are partially defined because the semantic rules

---

[38] Sorensen 2001 e.g. accepts the stronger claim that a term is vague *if, and only if*, it has possible borderline cases, but several authors on vagueness take the existence of borderline cases alone to be insufficient for vagueness (see e.g. Soames 1999). It is also important to distinguish between *intensional* vagueness—the possibility of having borderline cases—and *extensional* vagueness—actual borderline cases. Vagueness is properly characterized in terms of the *possibility* of borderline cases.

[39] See e.g. Soames 1999, ch. 7.

governing them provide sufficient conditions for application and non-application that are mutually exclusive, but not disjunctively exhaustive. This is to say that in addition to the set of objects to which they apply—their *default extensions*—and the set of objects to which they do not apply—their *default anti-extensions*—there is also a set of objects to which they neither apply nor do not apply. For each vague predicate, then, there is a set of objects for which it is defined and a set of objects for which it is undefined.

Vague predicates are, on this view, also context-sensitive, because they have parameters that allow speakers to contextually adjust their extension and anti-extension, although their *default* extension and *default* anti-extension remain constant. Speakers have a certain amount of discretion, then, to adjust the extension or anti-extension so as to cover objects for which the predicate is undefined, to suit the needs of the relevant conversation. On this account, genuine borderline cases are cases in which the objects in question are neither in the default extension or default anti-extension of the relevant predicate, nor in the contextually adjusted extension or anti-extension. That is, borderline cases involve objects for which the predicate is undefined and which have not been 'contextually' included or excluded. For these objects, there is—on the PD/CS theory—*no fact of the matter* whether or not the relevant predicate applies to them.

On the PD/CS theory, genuine borderline cases can be included in the relevant predicate's extension or anti-extension further on in the conversation. If, for example, *o* is a borderline case of *P* and a speaker nevertheless predicates *P* of *o*, the audience may—instead of considering it an improper assertion—take this as an invitation to accommodate the speaker by adjusting the extension of the predicate to include *o*. Typically, such accommodation is successful only if the relevant adjustment suits the purpose of the conversation. But if accommodation is successful, *P* will then count as true of *o in that context* and *by stipulation*.

Unlike the PD/CS theory, the epistemic theory regards vague predicates as totally defined—they either (determinately) apply or do not apply to any given object. On this view, borderline cases arise when we cannot—in principle—know whether or not a predicate applies to an object.[40] The issue, according to the epistemic theory, is therefore not that vague predicates are undefined, but rather that for a range of objects we simply don't know—and cannot know—*how* they are defined. The reason we cannot know this, on this view, is that knowledge requires a 'margin for error'—in effect, this ensures that knowledge never depends on 'epistemic luck'. In non-borderline cases, this margin is satisfied—it is known that if *P* determinately applies to *o*, then *P* applies to all objects relevantly similar to *o*. We know, for example, that if three grains of sand are not a heap, then neither are two grains of sand, nor four. In other words, we know that for the purposes of applying *P*, two, three, and four grains of sand are relevantly similar, which is required in order to be justified in believing, on any given occasion, that three grains of sand are not a heap.

---

[40] See e.g. Williamson 1994. For Soames's account of this view, see Soames 2012.

According to the epistemic theory, this condition is—as a general matter—not satisfied in borderline cases. Vague predicates have sharp cut-off points the exact location of which we cannot know and so, for any object o in the borderline region of a predicate P, it is always possible that P does not apply to some objects relevantly similar to o. Thus, although P may in fact apply to o, we can never be justified in believing that it so applies, and so—as a principle—we cannot know that it does.

On the epistemic theory, speakers do not—semantically speaking—have discretion to contextually adjust the extensions and anti-extensions of vague predicates, since the relevant semantic rules provide sufficient conditions for application and non-application that are mutually exclusive *as well as* disjunctively exhaustive. Insofar as the primary concern in a given speech context is assertion—i.e. to state facts—there is thus no room, on this account, for scenarios in which a speaker predicates P of o in an attempt to stipulate that o is P (for the purposes of the conversation), unless the speaker's evidence is genuinely indifferent. Instead, every sincere utterance must be taken to presuppose that the speaker has sufficient evidence for believing that o is P. It follows from this that predicating P of a borderline object o is strictly speaking always improper, since borderline cases are cases in which we cannot possibly have sufficient evidence for believing that o is P, or that o is not P. It is important to note, however, that in some borderline cases, the evidence may slightly favour one over the other, in which case predicating P of o may be the right thing to do in scenarios in which a determinate verdict is for some reason required.

3.2 Inconsistent predictions regarding the value of vagueness in the law

Recall that, according to Soames, we have good reason to believe that the value of vagueness in the law consists—in large part—in the fact that, under certain circumstances, it is a good idea for lawmakers to formulate laws in vague terms and thereby facilitate their incremental, case-by-case precisification, resulting from adjudication of borderline cases aimed at furthering their rationale. The basic idea is that actual legislative practice gives us good reason to believe that lawmakers and other legal practitioners themselves think that 'legislation sometimes involves broad agreement about central objectives, combined with disagreement or ignorance at the margins, plus a confidence that those who implement the law and adjudicate disputes arising from it will, through acquaintance with the facts of particular cases and the benefit of an incremental procedure, be in a better position than the lawmakers to further the law's rationale'.[41] In this way, facts about legal practice are supposed to generate solid intuitions about the value of vagueness in the law.

For the purposes of this chapter, I have no problems with Soames's claim about legal practice. It might, of course, be objected that legal practitioners in general do not—and should not—expect those who implement the law and adjudicate borderline cases to be concerned with furthering the law's rationale. Legal practice may seem equally to give us reason to believe that the value of vagueness lies in the fact

---

[41] Soames 2012, p. 102.

that it allows legislators with conflicting intentions to reach a compromise and to fight for their interests on another front, i.e. in the courts. We can call this the *strategic-compromise function* of vagueness in the law. Soames is careful enough, however, to claim only that vagueness *sometimes* has the (more cooperative) power-delegating function he is concerned with. And this is all he needs to get the argument going.

According to Soames, the two theories of vagueness—the PD/CS theory and the epistemic theory—differ significantly in the extent to which they are able to explain our intuition about the power-delegating function of vagueness in the law. The difference, he says, lies in the fact that for a significant subset of borderline cases, the PD/CS theory allows judges and administrative officials—in line with our intuition about this function—to declare a borderline case o of P to be P for the purposes of one legal provision and not-P for the purposes of another, while the epistemic theory does not. On the PD/CS theory, it is perfectly permissible for speakers to adjust the extension of a predicate to include a borderline case in one context and to exclude it in another, depending on the purpose of the communication. If the purpose of a provision prohibiting vehicles in the park were to minimize noise pollution, for example, then it would make sense to count skateboards as vehicles. If, instead, the purpose were to reduce exhaust pollution and/or risk of serious accidents, then it would make sense not to do so. In this way, the PD/CS theory provides a 'smooth' and uniform explanation of how the judicial resolution of borderline cases is able to vary with the relevant provision's rationale and the theory thereby straightforwardly helps explain what facilitates the value of vagueness in the law, according to Soames.

On the epistemic theory, however, things are different, Soames says. For any borderline object o of P, o already is or is not P and, insofar as the primary concern of judges in such cases is to report legal facts, their task is to figure out whether o is more like those objects that are clearly P (in which case o is probably P) or more like those that are clearly not-P (in which case o is probably not-P). In many borderline cases, of course, the evidence may be genuinely indifferent, in which case the judges must base their verdict on other grounds. This is to be expected, for example, when the objects in question are well into the borderline region. However, Soames says, in a significant set of cases, the evidence will provide some pull in one direction rather than the other, in which case the judge is typically required to reach a verdict accordingly, unless she has very weighty reasons against doing so. This is one way, then, in which the epistemic theory is supposed to generate different predictions than the PD/CS theory and conflict with our intuitions about the value of vagueness in the law.

More importantly, however, once it has been settled whether the evidence favours counting o as P or as not-P, the legal system is in an important sense stuck with that verdict. Insofar as the primary concern of judges in the cases under discussion is to report legal facts and the evidence favours, say, counting o as P, it would not be permissible to count o as P in the case at hand and as not-P in another (a difference in evidence relating to o's being P notwithstanding). If, for example, a skateboard is judged to be more like things that clearly count as vehicles than things that don't, then—coupling Soames's account of the epistemic theory with his view of the role of judges—officials simply ought to consistently count skateboards as vehicles, no matter what the purpose of the relevant 'vehicle-related' provision is. According to Soames, then, the epistemic theory further predicts that there is a significant set of borderline cases the judicial resolution of which cannot vary with the relevant provision's rationale. This provides what is perhaps the strongest conflict with our firm intuitions about the power-delegating function of vagueness in the law, in Soames's view. As a result of all this, he concludes that we have a significant reason to favour the PD/CS theory over the epistemic theory. If Soames is right, then facts about legal practice can in an important sense adjudicate between rival theories of vagueness, which is an exciting conclusion, both from the point of view of philosophy of law and philosophy of language. It would also encourage investigation into further ways in which legal practice might be relevant to theorizing about language. A good deal, therefore, is at stake.

In section 4, we will take a closer look at the overall structure of Soames's argument, in order to see more clearly what work the communicative-content theory is doing. Before I go on, however, let me say that it seems to me that Soames significantly overstates the result of the argument. The reason is that—at least to a large extent—the weight of the reason in favour of the PD/CS theory is a function of the size of the set of cases for which the epistemic theory produces 'bad' predictions, vis-à-vis our intuitions about the value of vagueness in the law; and I think this set is significantly smaller than Soames suggests.

As we saw above, Soames does point out that the two theories make the same predictions with respect to borderline cases that are well into the borderline region. The set of cases with respect to which the theories make different predictions, however, is only a subset of the remaining set of borderline cases, definable—on the epistemic view—by the following four characteristics: (i) elements can be partially ordered along dimensions that determine the applicability of the relevant predicate; (ii) evidence for where an item falls on these dimensions is evidence for the claim that the predicate applies, or does not apply, to it; (iii) evidence that an item is closer to things that are known to be in the predicate's extension than to things known not to be in it provides justification for the claim that the item is in the predicate's extension; and (iv) the same holds for evidence that an item is closer to things known not to be in the predicate's extension than to things known to be in it.[42]

My concern about Soames's apparent conclusion regarding the weight of the resulting reason to favour the PD/CS theory is that very few legal provisions contain predicates that satisfy these conditions to a robust degree. The reason is twofold. First, it seems to me that the number of predicates that robustly satisfy these conditions is rather low—unidimensionally vague predicates (such as 'heavy', 'old', 'slow', and 'tall') are, of course, good cases in point, but once we move to multidimensional ones it quickly becomes very difficult to determine both where an item falls on the relevant dimensions and—perhaps more importantly—whether an item is closer to things that are known to be in the predicate's extension than

---

[42] Ibid., p. 104.

to things known not to be in it; the set of things known to be, or to not be, in the extension of such multidimensional terms is simply too heterogeneous. As Soames himself points out, using the term 'neglect' as an example, 'the variation in behavior exhibited by a range of obvious, non-borderline cases, is enormous'.[43] As a result, I think Soames is wrong to claim that '*surely* many [vague predicates satisfy the relevant conditions to a robust degree]'.[44]

Second, in addition to these purely linguistic considerations, the predicates that seem to most robustly satisfy Soames's conditions are typically avoided in law. And rather easily so: the easier it is for a predicate to satisfy these conditions, the easier it is to replace them with a cut-off point somewhere along a sufficiently relevant dimension. The easiest cases involve unidimensional predicates and multidimensional predicates that have—or are significantly correlated with—at least one totally ordered dimension; instead of using 'young' and 'child', for example, legislators will typically specify an age, and safe driving can be regulated using a precise speed limit (along with a host of other more or less precise rules). As the number of dimensions increases, the more difficult it tends to get to find an adequate, more precise replacement for the term in question. Consequently, we are more likely to see such predicates in legal provisions. However, it also becomes less likely that the relevant predicates robustly satisfy the conditions that define the set of 'test cases', the size of which determines the weight of the reason to favour the PD/CS theory. The likelihoods of a vague predicate satisfying Soames's 'test case' conditions and of it appearing in actual legal provisions seem to be inversely related.

As a result of all this, I think that even if we were to agree that the epistemic theory makes predictions that are not neatly in line with our intuitions about the value of vagueness in the law, those predictions concern a set the actual size of which is fairly limited. Thus, even if Soames's argument were unaffected by the problems facing his version of the communicative-content theory of law, the resulting reason to favour the PD/CS theory would be significantly less weighty than seems implied by his conclusion.

4. A Closer Look at Soames's Argument

Below, I provide what I hope is a reasonable breakdown of Soames's central argument. Basically, the idea is that the power-delegating function of vagueness in the law follows deductively from the PD/CS theory plus a few basic suppositions about the U.S. legal system and about legal practitioners (referred to below as 'S1', 'S2', and 'S3'). If these suppositions are true and we have good reason to believe that one of the main functions of vagueness in the law is to appropriately delegate a limited kind of law-making power to judges, then—assuming that some version of hypothetico-deductive reasoning is appropriate in this case—we have good reason to believe that the PD/CS theory is correct. Or, in any case, good reason to favour that

---

[43] Ibid., p. 103.   [44] Ibid., p. 104; my italics.

theory over those theories of vagueness that cannot explain this function—such as, and perhaps most notably, the epistemic theory.

We begin by assuming that the PD/CS theory of vagueness is correct. This is the hypothesis, then, which entails, among other things, that vagueness leaves borderline cases semantically undefined (assuming they have not been contextually included or excluded) and that the resolution of such cases modifies the linguistic content of the relevant statement (via the adjustment of the relevant predicate's extension). On the supposition that the legal content of a statute or constitutional clause is identical with, or constituted by, its communicative content—call this S1—this further entails that vagueness *in the law* leaves borderline cases *legally* unsettled and that the judicial resolution of such cases modifies the legal content of the relevant statute or constitutional clause. If, moreover, we suppose that legal practitioners more or less understand these facts about vagueness—call this S2—and that lawmakers can expect officials (on the basis of their obligations, qua officials) to maximize fidelity to legislative rationale in the resolution of borderline cases—call this S3—then vagueness can, at least under certain conditions, be valuable as a tool for appropriately delegating limited rule-making authority to officials.[45]

This, then, is how we are supposed to get from the PD/CS theory to the power-delegating value of vagueness in the law. Insofar as our choice stands between the PD/CS theory and the epistemic theory, we therefore have good reason to favour the former over the latter, according to Soames.

4.1 Soames's three suppositions

Soames's argument is deductively valid (when laid out completely), and the methodology seems sound enough to me, although it does require, of course, that our intuitions about the value of vagueness in the law properly count as evidence. This might, of course, be objected to, perhaps as a general matter or specifically on the grounds that this particular issue is too complex to allow for reliable intuitions. And even if we accept that intuitions count as evidence, a committed epistemicist might simply argue that if the epistemic theory of vagueness is not consistent with our intuitions about the value of vagueness in the law, then so much the worse for those intuitions. They may give us reasons to believe in their content, but these reasons are easily outweighed by good theory, she might say.

Obviously, then, there is already plenty to disagree about. Here, however, I will question neither the intuition-based methodology nor the claimed

---

[45] According to Soames, what is required is that 'all or most of the following conditions are fulfilled: (i) the vague formulation of the law assigns the clear, non-borderline cases of the term the legal status desired by most lawmakers; (ii) the variety of borderline cases of the term is wide, making them hard to exhaustively anticipate; (iii) the lawmaking body is either divided about the borderline cases or ignorant of the likely consequences of treating some such cases one way rather than another, and so is uncertain about what legal status they should have; and (iv) the lawmakers recognize the value of incremental, case-by-case precisification of the law resulting from adjudication of borderline cases aimed at furthering the law's rationale, in light of the full factual backgrounds uncovered in judicial proceedings', ibid., p. 102.

deliverance of our intuitions, vis-à-vis the value of vagueness in the law. This, then, leaves only Soames's three suppositions about the U.S. legal system and legal practitioners:[46]

S1 The legal content of a statute or constitutional clause is identical with, or constituted by, its communicative content.
S2 Legal practitioners more or less understand what vagueness is.
S3 Lawmakers can expect officials (on the basis of their obligations, qua officials) to maximize fidelity to legislative rationale in the resolution of borderline cases.

In his paper, Soames recognizes that S2 and S3 might be considered controversial. Even if the PD/CS theory of vagueness were true, legal practitioners might not recognize this. That is, they might fail to recognize that vagueness leaves border-line cases semantically undefined and that the resolution of such cases modifies the linguistic content of the relevant statement. Consequently, assuming S1, they might also fail to recognize that vagueness in the law leaves borderline cases legally unsettled and that the judicial resolution of such cases modifies the legal content of the relevant statute or constitutional clause. In that case, S2 would be false, which would undercut our reasons to believe the hypothesis. Soames, however, thinks that the way in which legal practitioners seem to think and behave gives us reason to believe that they more or less understand that vagueness is what the PD/CS theory says it is.[47]

It might also not be the case that lawmakers can expect officials to maximize fidelity to legislative rationale in the resolution of borderline cases. Perhaps officials have an obligation to do so, but do not reliably act in accordance with it. Or perhaps they have no such obligation. In this case, S3 would be false. It is Soames's contention, however, that actual legal practice indicates that officials do have such an obligation, and for good reason.[48]

On this occasion, we will not be further concerned with S2 and S3, although there is, of course, much to be discussed, as Soames himself points out. The remaining thesis, then, is S1—i.e. Soames's version of the communicative-content theory of law—which, I have argued, we have reason to give up in favour of the Pro Tanto view. The view, however, does not suffice to vindicate Soames's argument for the PD/CS theory, despite being a version of the same theory. The reason is that the explanation it provides for our intuitions about the value of vagueness in the law is rather different from the one favoured by Soames.

Recall that, on Soames's view, vagueness in the law leaves borderline cases legally unsettled and the judicial resolution of such cases—by precisification— modifies the legal content of the relevant statute or constitutional clause. Given S1, i.e. an identity- or constitution-based version of the communicative-content theory of law, this entails that such resolutions (thereby) also modify their com-municative content. In contrast, on the Pro Tanto account, adjudication modifies neither the legal content of vague provisions nor their communicative content.

---

[46] Ibid., p. 107.   [47] See ibid., p. 106.   [48] See ibid., p. 107.

Rather, adjudication provides (or constitutes) a reason to treat cases that are sufficiently similar to the resolved case in a certain way, a reason that the statute or constitutional clause itself does not furnish. Thus, although the law—broadly understood—has been precisified, perhaps in the aim of furthering the relevant provision's rationale, the provision itself remains just as vague.

This has significant implications for Soames's argument. Granted, facts about legal practice do seem to count against the epistemic theory to some degree, assuming that one agrees with Soames that the primary concern of judges is to report legal facts, but in order to explain the power-delegating role of vagueness in the law the Pro Tanto view only has to assume *some* theory on which vagueness leaves borderline cases semantically undefined. Nothing more is required of a theory of vagueness in that respect. Thus, although the view is consistent with the PD/CS theory, it is ultimately indifferent with respect to it. As a result, facts about legal practice do not, after all, seem to be able to adjudicate between rival theories of vagueness—at least not in the way envisioned by Soames.

5. Generalizing the Argument: Other Cautionary Tales

As I have indicated throughout the chapter, it is important to demonstrate that my point about Soames's argument is generalizable: since legal content is neither identical with nor constituted by communicative content, we should—as a general matter—be quite cautious about drawing general conclusions about language on the basis of facts about legal practice. I want to conclude the chapter, therefore, by illustrating this generality with a brief discussion of the cases of *Maurice v. Judd* and *Bronston v. United States*.[49]

5.1 *Maurice v. Judd*: Does legal practice show a need for 'carefully formulated metasemantic principles'?

As it is commonly presented, the main question in the curious case of *Maurice v. Judd* was whether whales were fish, for the purposes of an 1818 New York statute 'authorizing the appointment of guagers [sic] and inspectors of fish oils'.[50] James Maurice sued Samuel Judd for unpaid fees for 'gauging, inspecting, and branding' three casks of fish oil, but since the casks inspected contained whale oil, Judd's primary line of defence was that whales were not fish. Both parties presented a number of people from various professions (anatomists, merchants, seamen, etc.), testifying either that whales were indeed fish or that they were most certainly not. At the time, of course, people generally used the term 'fish' to include whales. The jury decided in favour of Maurice.

---

[49] Mayor's Court of New York (1818) and 409 U.S. 352 (1973), respectively.
[50] New York (State) Legislature 1819.

Sainsbury (2014) takes the jury's verdict in *Maurice v. Judd* to tell us something important about language: by generating a dilemma, he says, it teases out the need for 'carefully formulated metasemantic principles', at least regarding creature-kind terms like 'fish'.[51] The dilemma, according to Sainsbury, is that either we take the jury's verdict to have been wrong, which upsets the idea that 'the meaning of a word in a community is determined by how it is used in that community',[52] or we take it to have been correct, which makes the disagreement between the disputing parties a merely verbal one, rather than a substantive one.[53] He does not go on to tell us what these principles are, but it is clear that, by Sainsbury's lights, facts about legal practice allow us to draw significant general conclusions about language.

Now, on the assumption that legal content is identical with, or constituted by, communicative content, it makes sense—given some of the most prominent rhetoric in the case—to take the *Maurice* case to be about the meaning of the term 'fish', as used in the 1818 statute, and, thus, to view the jury's verdict from a linguistic perspective. However, once we give up this assumption in favour of the Pro Tanto view and remind ourselves that various kinds of legal content interact to determine the proper all-things-considered legal result of a case, both prongs of Sainsbury's dilemma go away. As we will see below, taking the jury's verdict to be incorrect does not require giving up the idea that the meaning of a word in a community is determined by how it is used in that community, and we can take it to be correct without reducing the dispute to a merely verbal one.[54]

To see this, consider Judge Riker's instructions to the jury. As he made clear, there were several ways to think about the case and it was the jury's job to decide on which of them to base the verdict.[55] And not all of them concerned the meaning of the term 'fish' (or 'fish oil'). One way to go, for example, was to take into consideration the fact that the common law treated whales as fish. If this was the controlling factor in the jury's decision, then taking the decision to have been incorrect is not inconsistent with the idea that the meaning of a word in a community is determined by how it is used in that community. Rather, the problem—on this analysis—is that the jury incorrectly gave controlling weight to what it thought was legal content provided by common law. And taking the decision to have been correct does not render the disagreement between the parties insubstantial, let alone merely verbal. As we see from the records, there was plenty of disagreement about what weight should be given to the common law in deciding the matter.[56]

Another way to reason about the case was to take into consideration not the actual meaning of the term 'fish' but the expected or intended application of the

---

[51] Sainsbury 2014, p. 5. I avoid using the term 'zoological kind term', since that seems to beg the question against outdated 'ordinary' understandings of the term.
[52] Ibid., p. 4.   [53] Ibid.
[54] In addition, recent work on the semantics and pragmatics of disagreement shows that we have significant reason to doubt the idea that 'substantive disagreement requires agreement in meaning'. See e.g. Plunkett and Sundell 2013.
[55] See Sampson 1819.   [56] Ibid.

term 'fish oil'. That is, to place controlling weight on the fact that (most likely) the term was intended to include whale oil, not by virtue of this intention being a determinant, or evidence, of the actual meaning of the term 'fish', but rather by virtue of it being such an intention. If this was the controlling factor in the jury's decision, then taking the decision to have been incorrect does not conflict with the idea that meaning is determined by use. Rather, the error would have involved a misidentification of the legal content of the statute, or that unwarranted weight was given to the expected application of the term 'fish' (or 'fish oil'). And—as Philips (2014) draws our attention to in his reply to Sainsbury—taking the decision to have been correct does not conflict with our intuition that the debate was substantive.[57] There was plenty of disagreement both about whether to give weight to the application intentions of the lawmakers and about the extent to which such intentions could be established.[58]

Maurice v. Judd is an interesting case, to be sure, but, as the preceding discussion shows, Sainsbury is too optimistic about what we can learn about language by looking at the law. In order to generate the dilemma that motivates his conclusion that carefully formulated metasemantic principles are needed in order to account for creature-kind terms like 'fish', Sainsbury has to assume that the jury's verdict is to be evaluated exclusively from a linguistic perspective, which is correct only if the matter turns solely on whether or not the meaning of the term 'fish' includes whales. This makes sense on an identity- or constitution-based version of the communicative-content theory, but the dilemma goes away once we adopt an account on which the relationship between legal content and communicative content is more complex. Contra Sainsbury, legal practice does not show that there is anything 'paradoxical about fish'.[59]

5.2 *Bronston v. United States*: Does legal practice tell us anything about implicature in non-cooperative contexts?

So far, we have been concerned with cases involving the legal (and communicative) content of statutes and constitutional clauses, but I think the cautionary lesson extends even further. Consider, for example, the case of *Bronston v. United States*, in which the question was whether Samuel Bronston had correctly been found guilty of perjury, by virtue of having provided an 'unresponsive' reply to a question that in ordinary conversation would be taken to trigger a relevance implicature (or quantity implicature, depending on the analysis), the content of which would be false.[60] Bronston, who for a five-year period had a personal bank account in Switzerland, was asked the following question: 'Have you ever [had a bank account in Switzerland]?' His reply was this: 'The company had an account there for about six months.'

Now, had the 'conversation' between Bronston and the examining lawyer been governed by the norms of ordinary conversation, i.e. the norms governing the

---

[57] See Philips 2014, p. 381. [58] See Sampson 1819.
[59] Sainsbury 2014, p. 5. [60] 409 U.S. 352 (1973).

cooperative exchange of information, Bronston would have counted as having—via implication—incurred commitment to the false proposition that he himself had not had an account in Switzerland. The Supreme Court, however, unanimously held that Bronston should not have been convicted of perjury.

Some authors are tempted to see this 'fact about legal practice' as evidence that in the context of cross-examination, the conversational maxim of relevance (or quantity) does not apply:[61] the thought is that absence of perjury means absence of implicature, which in turn means that the relevant maxim is suspended/in abeyance. If that is correct, then the law provides an important context within which we can empirically verify predictions made by different pragmatic theories: insofar, for example, as one theory of implicature predicts the existence of an implicature in *Bronston* while another does not, it seems that legal practice would give us a reason to favour the latter over the former.

Now, on the assumption that a witness is—vis-à-vis perjury liability—committed to p if, and only if, she communicates that p, it makes sense to take *Bronston* to be about the presence or absence of a false implicature, and, thus, to view the Supreme Court's verdict from a linguistic perspective. (The jury instructions provided at the District Court trial also do a lot to bolster this view.[62]) It may—on this perspective—also seem natural to take the Supreme Court's decisions as telling us something about the legal content of the perjury statute, namely whether or not it extends to false implicatures.

As before, however, the linguistic perspective is too simple. Most significantly, as the Court saw it, the issue in *Bronston* was not at all about the presence or absence of a false implicature, but—rather—the proper distribution of responsibility in an adversarial fact-finding process. 'If a witness evades', the Court said, 'it is the lawyer's responsibility to recognize the evasion and to . . . flush out the whole truth with the tools of adversary examination.'[63] Their verdict was that the perjury statute did not apply to literally true, but unresponsive answers, even on the assumption that such responses were 'false by negative implication'.[64] It is entirely consistent, then, with the Court's decision to reverse Bronston's conviction that an implicature was in fact present in the context of his cross-examination. As a result, facts about legal practice regarding the treatment of perjury cases do not seem able to adjudicate between rival pragmatic theories—at least not in the way envisaged. It is simply not the case that a witness is—vis-à-vis perjury liability—committed to p if, and only if, she communicates that p.

Further, once we give up the assumption that legal content is identical with, or constituted by, communicative content in favour of the Pro Tanto view, the Court's decision also no longer tells us anything about whether the perjury statute extends to false implicatures. As we have seen, on the Pro Tanto view, the fact that a statute provides a jury/court with a *pro tanto* reason to convict does not necessarily make for the end of the matter—it still has to be determined whether any other

---

[61] See e.g. Levinson 1983 (pp. 121–2), Martinich 1984 (p. 33), and Sinclair 1985 (p. 384).
[62] 409 U.S. 352 (1973), 355.   [63] Ibid., 358–9.   [64] Ibid., 352.

legally relevant considerations defeat that reason. The trial court held that none did, while the Supreme Court found otherwise. So, on the Pro Tanto view, it is not inconsistent with the Court's decision that the perjury statute applies to false implicatures.

Now, whether this is the best analysis of the case is up for debate, of course, but that is not the issue here; rather, the point is simply that once we recognize the fairly complex relationship between language and law, it becomes clear that the decision in *Bronston* does not tell us very much about the presence or absence of implicatures in the context of cross-examination or about the legal content of the perjury statute.[65]

References

Bach, Kent. 2002. 'Seemingly Semantic Intuitions'. In *Meaning and Truth*, edited by J. Keim Campbell, M. O'Rourke, and D. Shier, 21–33. New York: Seven Bridges Press.

Bach, Kent. 2006. 'The Top 10 Misconceptions About Implicature'. In *Drawing the Boundaries of Meaning*, edited by B.J. Birner and G. Ward, 21–30. Amsterdam: John Benjamins.

Bader, Ralf. 2016. 'Conditions, Modifiers and Holism'. In E. Lord and B. Maguire (eds), *Weighing Reasons*, edited by Errol. Lord and B. Maguire, 27–55. Oxford: Oxford University Press.

Dancy, Jonathan. 2000. *Practical Reality*. New York: Oxford University Press.

Dancy, Jonathan. 2004. *Ethics Without Principles*. Oxford: Oxford University Press.

Dworkin, Ronald. 1977. 'The Model of Rules II'. In *Taking Rights Seriously*, 46–80. Cambridge (MA): Harvard University Press.

Ekins, Richard. and Jeffery. Goldsworth. 2014. 'The Reality and Indispensability of Legislative Intention'. *Sydney Law Review* 36: 39–68.

Fletcher, George. 2000. *Rethinking Criminal Law*. Oxford: Oxford University Press.

Goldsworthy, Jeffery. 2005. 'Moderate and Strong Intentionalism: Knapp and Michaels Revisited'. *San Diego Law Review* 42: 669.

Greenberg, Mark. 2004. 'How Facts Make Law'. *Legal Theory* 10: 157–98.

Greenberg, Mark. 2010. 'The Communication Theory of Legal Interpretation and Objective Notions of Communicative Content'. *UCLA School of Law Working Paper Series, Public Law & Legal Theory Working Paper* 10–35.

Greenberg, Mark. 2011a. 'The Standard Picture and Its Discontents'. In *Oxford Studies in Philosophy of Law*, Vol. 1, edited by Leslie Green and Brian Leiter, 39–106. Oxford: Oxford University Press.

[65] This research was supported in part by the Icelandic Research Fund and an H.L.A. Hart Visiting Fellowship at the Oxford Centre for Ethics and Philosophy of Law. I am grateful to audiences and participants at the University of Chicago Workshop in Semantics and Philosophy of Language, the Oxford Jurisprudence Discussion Group, the University of Edinburgh Legal Philosophy Seminar, and the Reykjavik Summer Philosophy Workshop. Special thanks goes to Ryan Doerfler, Luís Duarte d'Almeida, Erik Encarnacion, Guðmundur Andri Hjálmarsson, Chris Kennedy, Gregory Klass, Brian Leiter, Eliot Michaelson, John Mikhail, Robert Mullins, David Plunkett, Alex Sarch, Dale Smith, Lawrence Solum, Matt Teichman, Elmar Unnsteinsson, and Malte Willer.

Greenberg, Mark. 2011b. 'Legislation as Communication? Legal Interpretation and the Study of Linguistic Communication'. In *The Philosophical Foundations of Language in the Law*, edited by Andrei. Marmor and Scott. Soames, 217–56. New York: Oxford University Press.

Greenberg, Mark. 2014. 'The Moral Impact Theory of Law', *Yale Law Journal* 123: 1288–342.

Grice, H. Paul. 1989. *Studies in the Way of Words*. Cambridge (MA): Harvard University Press.

Horty, John. 2012. *Reasons as Defaults*. New York: Oxford University Press.

Kim, Jaegwon. 1993. *Supervenience and Mind: Selected Philosophical Essays*. Cambridge: Cambridge University Press.

Levinson, Stephen. 1983. *Pragmatics*. Cambridge: Cambridge University Press.

Lord, Errol. 2008. 'Dancy on Action for the Right Reason'. *Journal of Ethics and Social Philosophy* 2(3): 1–6.

Manning, John F. 2003. 'The Absurdity Doctrine'. *Harvard Law Review* 116(8): 2387–2486.

Mantel, Susanne. 2015. 'Wordly Reasons: An Ontological Inquiry Into Motivating Considerations and Normative Reasons'. *Pacific Philosophical Quarterly*.

Marmor, Andrei. 2013. 'Truth in Law'. In *Current Legal Issues: Law and Language*, edited by M. Freeman and F. Smith, 45–61. Oxford: Oxford University Press.

Martinich, Aloysius. 1984. *Communication and Reference*. New York: De Gruyter.

Morganti, Matteo and A. Tanyi. Ms. 'Can Reasons Be Propositions?' Manuscript on file with author.

Neale, Stephen. 2005. 'Pragmatism and Binding'. In *Semantics versus Pragmatics*, edited by Z. Szabó, 165–285. Oxford: Oxford University Press.

New York State Legislature. 1819. *Journal of the Assembly of the State of New-York: At Their 42nd Session*. Albany: J. Buel.

Philips, Ian. 2014. 'Cetacean Semantics'. *Analysis* 74: 379–82.

Plunkett, David and T. Sundell. 2013. 'Disagreement and the Semantics of Normative and Evaluative Terms'. *Philosopher's Imprint* 13(23): 1–37.

Pollock, John L. and J. Cruz. 1999. *Contemporary Theories of Knowledge*. New York: Rowman and Littlefield.

Prakken, Henry and G. Sartor. 1996. 'A Dialectical Model of Assessing Conflicting Arguments in Legal Reasoning'. *Artificial Intelligence and Law* 4: 331–68.

Raz, Joseph. 1972. 'Legal Principles and the Limits of Law'. *Yale Law Journal* 81: 831.

Sainsbury, Mark. 2014. 'Fishy Business'. *Analysis* 74: 3–5.

Sampson, William. 1819. *Is a Whale a Fish? An Accurate Report of the Case of James Maurice Against Samuel Judd*. New York: Van Winkle.

Schiffer, Stephan. 1972. *Meaning*. Oxford: Oxford University Press.

Schroeder, Mark. 2007. *Slaves of the Passions*. New York: Oxford University Press.

Schroeder, Mark. 2011. 'Holism, Weight, and Undercutting'. *Noûs* 45: 328–44.

Sinclair, M.B.W. 1985. 'Law and Language: The Role of Pragmatics in Statutory Interpretation'. *University of Pittsburg Law Review* 46: 373.

Smith, Dale. 'A Problem for the Equivalence Thesis'. Manuscript on file with author.

Soames, Scott. 1999. *Understanding Truth*. New York: Oxford University Press.

Soames, Scott. 2008. 'Drawing the Line Between Meaning and Implicature—and Relating both to Assertion'. *Noûs* 42(3): 440–65.

Soames, Scott. 2011. 'What Vagueness and Inconsistency Tell Us About Interpretation'. In *Philosophical Foundations of Language in the Law*, edited by Andrei. Marmor and Scott. Soames, 31–57. Oxford: Oxford University Press.

Soames, Scott. 2012. 'Vagueness and the Law'. In *The Routledge Companion to Philosophy of Law*, edited by Andrei. Marmor, 95–108. New York: Routledge.

Solum, Lawrence. 2008. 'Semantic Originalism'. *Illinois Public Law Research Paper No. 07-24*. Available at: <http://ssrn.com/abstract=1120244>.

Solum, Lawrence. 2013a. 'Communicative Content and Legal Content'. *Notre Dame L. Rev.* 89: 479–520.

Solum, Lawrence. 2013b. 'Construction and Constraint'. *Jerusalem Review of Legal Studies* 7(1): 17–34.

Sorensen, Roy. 2001. 'Vagueness Has No Function in Law'. *Legal Theory* 7: 385.

Williamson, Timothy. 1994. *Vagueness*. London: Routledge.

5

Semantics, Metaphysics, and Objectivity in the Law

*Michael S. Moore**

1. Introduction: What is Objectivity in Law?

By 'objectivity' in this chapter I shall mean determinacy. More specifically, law is *objective* in the sense which interests me if and only if singular propositions of law have determinative, mind-independent truth values and if some of those propositions have the truth value 'true'. Let me unpack this a bit.

A singular proposition of law is the kind of proposition of law that can decide particular cases.[1] Such propositions can be decisive in this way because they refer to the particular legal relation between specific people. For example, 'The contract between Jones and Smith is valid.' Such propositions are proposition of law because they predicate a legal quality (e.g. validity) to a particular, and they are authoritative for particular case decisions. They form what lawyers call the 'law of the case'. Such propositions may well be derived from *general* propositions of law, propositions like 'all contracts require offer, acceptance, and consideration to be valid'. Even so, singular propositions of law are distinct from such general propositions of law.

Singular propositions of law are the focus here because they are decisive of particular cases. Asking whether singular propositions of law have determinate truth-values is thus to ask whether particular cases have answers judges are obligated to reach in their decisions of such cases (Moore 2003a). Judges are, of course, obligated

* Much of sections 3, 5, and 6 were presented at the International Congress on Contemporary Problems in the Philosophy of Law, National Autonomous University of Mexico, Mexico City, 2003, and then as the keynote address for the 2003 annual meeting of the Argentinean Association for Legal Philosophy, Cordoba University, Cordoba, Argentina. This partial version was published as part of Moore 2007. Much of sections 7 and 8 were presented at the meeting of the Jurisprudence Section, 'The Relevance of Metaphysics to Law', American Association of Law Schools Annual Meeting, Washington, D.C., 2006. The entire chapter was presented to the Philosophy Department, Australian National University, Canberra, 2008, then to the Conference on Objectivity in Law, University of Texas, Austin, 2008, then to the Conference on Vagueness, Ontology, and Natural Kinds in Law and Philosophy, Humboldt Universität, Berlin, 2010.

[1] See Moore 2003a, pp. 25–6 and 29–30.

to *base* their decisions on general propositions of law, but their decisions themselves are expressed in the form of singular propositions of law.

For law to be objective, singular propositions of law have to have determinate truth-values independently of how a judge has decided (or will decide) a case. Law would not be objective if truth-values were borne by such propositions only by virtue of past or future facts about judicial decisions. Then, while judges could *make* such propositions true by their (actual or predicted) decisions, such propositions' pre-existing truth could not ground a judge's obligation to decide a case one way rather than another.

There is one last ambiguity that requires clarification here. Sometimes those who worry about law's objectivity want more than determinate truth-values to the propositions of law decisive of particular cases. They also want a *causal* thesis to be true, *viz*, that sitting judges are by and large caused to decide as they do by the legal materials giving singular propositions of law their truth-values.[2] For such theorists, objectivity demands more than logical relations to hold between general propositions of law and the singular propositions of law decisive of particular decisions; they want judges' beliefs about those general propositions to cause such judges to decide consistently with the logical outcome the law demands.

It would in truth be a disturbing fact if judges were incapable of reaching objectively correct decisions. Indeed, if this were a systematic incapacity of judges, one might care little whether there were objectively correct decisions judges were obligated to reach.[3] I shall assume here the contrary, confining myself only to the question of whether there are objectively correct decisions in law cases, decisions that it is the obligation of every judge to reach.

2. Objectivity and the Semantics of Natural Languages

For it to be even plausible that a legal system is capable of assigning determinant, pre-existing truth-values to singular propositions of law, a number of things must be true of it. To begin with, there must be laws, i.e. general propositions of law. To be sure, it is conceivable that there could be determinate truths of law at the case decision level but no (general) laws from which such truths followed. This would be a kind of particularism or nominalism, much like the 'situation ethics' of the 1950s. Yet almost always such particularism degenerates into the sceptical view that particular decisions have no determinate truth-value until a decision maker *gives* them one by making her decision.

---

[2] See e.g. West 1990.

[3] Brian Leiter has long construed The American Legal Realists as being as much concerned about how judicial decisions are caused, as they were concerned with the indeterminacy of the legal materials on the basis of which judges could make objective decisions. See Leiter 1998. Mark Greenberg takes a hard look at Leiter's endorsement of the Realists' supposed substitution of the causal question for the normative (correctness) question, in Greenberg 2011a, pp. 419–51, and Greenberg 2011b, pp. 453–75 (erratum subsequently published).

So for objectivity we need general laws. We also, of course, need logic—that truth-preserving engine of valid inference—to be objective. That surely is not a problem. Yet laws plus logic do not yield up determinacy, even when we add truthful descriptions of the facts of individual cases. As Herbert Hart noted many years ago (Hart 1958), logic is blind to the classification of particular facts under legal rubrics. Needed is something else, a fourth kind of objective truth, namely, an interpretive premise, connecting authoritative, general law to true descriptions of the facts of particular cases. For singular propositions of law to be objective, we do not need only authoritative general laws, logic, and true facts; we also need interpretation of the general, connecting it to the particular, to be objective.

It is this last need that gets us to semantics. Any even remotely plausible theory of legal interpretation gives some weight to the meanings of the words and phrases that appear in the general laws being interpreted. To be sure, sensible theories of interpretation never give the last word to semantics; but they surely do give such semantics the first word, in the sense that what words mean generally should have some bearing on what those words mean in legal texts. The semantics of the word, 'vehicle' for example, has some bearing on the legal meaning to be found for an ordinance prohibiting there being any *vehicles* in the city park.[4] Without such a connection, it would be difficult to give credence to the genuine values of legislative supremacy and citizen notice, values that should motivate and shape any theory of legal interpretation.[5]

It might be tempting to think that although interpretation in law depends on semantics, it does not depend on the meanings of ordinary words in natural languages. Legal terms like 'contract', 'malice', and 'intention' can have distinctively legal meanings, meanings at some remove from the meanings of such words in the natural language of English. While this is, of course, true for some words such as these, ultimately such words themselves are understood in terms of other words that are derived from ordinary, non-legal English. Ultimately, the semantics of natural languages governs even here (Moore 1985, pp. 328–38).

3. Kinds of Semantics and Degrees of Objectivity

3.1 Strong and weak versions of objectivity

The thesis that law is objective (in the sense that its singular propositions have determinate truth-values) has a weak as well as a strong version. The weak version consists of the common-sense view that only some singular propositions of law have pre-existing truth-values; as for the others, they are *given* a truth-value by the judge who decides the case of which they are decisive but before such decision they are neither true nor false. This translates into the idea that there are two kinds of cases,

---

[4] Hart's famous example in Hart 1958.   [5] Argued for in Moore 1985, pp. 313–21.

easy cases where the meaning of the terms in the laws have obvious application, and hard cases where such meaning is indeterminate.[6]

The strong version of the objectivity thesis regards the hard cases/easy cases distinction as epistemic only: easy cases are easy to decide because the answer is obvious, whereas hard cases are more difficult to decide because the answer is not obvious. Nonetheless, the strong version of the thesis holds that there is an answer to even the hardest of hard cases, difficult as it may be to ascertain what that answer is. The strong version holds that *all* singular propositions of law have a determinate truth-value, not just some.[7]

Whether the strong or the weak version of the objectivity thesis is true depends in part on one's view of semantics. The weak version is plausible on what I have called conventionalist semantic theories. The strong version is plausible on what I have called realist semantic theories. Before exploring these connections we should first describe these two kinds of semantic theories.

3.2 Two kinds of semantic theories

3.2.1 Conventionalist semantics

On the traditional view of semantics, the meaning of words is a matter of convention. The conventions of our linguistic community have assigned certain properties as fixing the extension of a word like 'gold', or they have assigned the word 'gold' to name certain particular hunks of metal (whatever their properties might be). In either case, there are certain analytically necessary truths, statements that are true by convention: 'gold is a yellow, ductile metal', or 'the stuff in storage at Ft Knox is gold', are commonly thought to be examples of such truths.

Conventionalist semantics comes in quite a few varieties. A useful way of organizing those varieties for present purposes is by the resources available to answer the critique of the other kind of semantics we shall consider, realist semantics. Let us accordingly group conventionalist semantics into three levels, the levels organized by the degree of reconstruction contemplated for the facts of raw, linguistic usage. At the first and most shallow level, there is what might be called the behavioural semantics of ordinary language philosophy. On this view of semantics, the conventions that give a word its meaning are those conventions accurately generalizing how most native speakers use the word. What it would be odd and not odd to say is used as the touchstone of the meaning of words. Consider the word 'voluntary'. Gilbert Ryle urged that it would be odd to call an action voluntary if it were not up for some kind of appraisal; from this usage fact Ryle concluded that 'voluntary' could not mean a willed bodily movement—for many of such movements are not up for appraisal (Ryle 1949, p. 69).

I call this a behavioural semantics because it does no reconstructive work on the raw data of linguistic usage. (It does not even divide conventions of usage between

---

[6] Hart's view in his 1958.   [7] I examine this thesis in detail in Moore 1987a.

the semantic conventions related to truth, and the pragmatic conventions related only to appropriate utterance.) The second level of conventionalist semantics does some reconstruction of raw usage facts. It distinguishes semantic conventions from merely pragmatic conventions, regarding the semantic conventions as extension-determiners. (An extension in semantic theory is the class of things of which a predicate is true.)

At this level one parses usage into one of two kinds of extension-determiners. One such kind is in terms of definitions, which are lists of properties anything within the extension of some predicate must—analytically must—possess. The other is in terms of paradigmatic exemplars, particulars that analytically must be within the extension of the predicate for which they are paradigms.[8] I shall describe each briefly in turn.

The criterial theory is one kind of definitional theory of semantics. It holds that the meaning of a term like 'bachelor' is given by a crisp definition: anything that is unmarried, male, and a person is a bachelor. Such a definition gives three properties, possession of each of which is individually necessary and possession of all of which is jointly sufficient for the correct usage of the word 'bachelor'. Another definitional theory is the criteriological theory, according to which there is a list of properties analytically connected to each meaningful word; only the properties are not individually necessary, and no subset of the properties is jointly sufficient, for correct application of the word.[9] Rather, there is simply an overlapping of properties, some determining the extension on some occasions while other properties determine the extension on other occasions. Still, even on this less crisp definitional theory, the entire list of properties is jointly necessary and jointly sufficient for correct use of the word.

The paradigm version of this second level of conventionalist semantics is known as the Paradigm Case Argument, or PCA semantics.[10] Here it is not words but things that are linked by convention to the word whose meaning is in question. On this view, the meaning of a word like 'gold' is given by the things (pieces of gold, presumably) early speakers noticed and baptized with the label 'gold'. 'Gold' necessarily applies to those things; if one didn't apply the word to those items, he would be said not to know the meaning of the word—because it is those items that give the word its meaning.

The extension of 'gold' includes more than these paradigmatic exemplars. It also includes those items that are similar to the paradigm cases of gold. Such similarity is not to be cashed out in terms of certain properties that the similar items share. For if this were possible, then one could frame a definition out of such properties.[11] Rather, the analogies between paradigmatic and penumbral instances within the

---

[8] I explore these in greater depth in Moore 1981, pp. 281–92, and Moore 1985, pp. 291–2 n. 25 and 295–6.

[9] A view often attributed to Wittgenstein in his PI 67 (Wittgenstein 1958). See Wellman 1962, Lycan 1971, and Rorty 1973.

[10] See the citations in Moore 1981, p. 286.

[11] A point much stressed by legal theorists who adopted PCA semantics. See Hart 1958 and Borgo 1979, p. 437.

extension of 'gold' are based on a primitive similarity relation, a relation not limited to a few properties in respect of which two things might be similar.

The third level of conventionalist semantics is what I have called 'deep conventionalism'.[12] Here one iterates the reconstructions of usage done at level two, so that a term's usage yields two layers of semantic conventions. There are conceptions (or interpretations) of the meaning of some words given either in terms of definitional properties or in terms of paradigmatic exemplars; and there are concepts giving the meaning of words, again conceived either in terms of properties or exemplars.[13] The definitions or exemplars giving the meaning of concepts are more general, deeper, more agreed-upon, than are the definitions/exemplars making up the conceptions of such concepts. The idea is to accommodate considerable disagreement between the conventions that constitute distinct conceptions while preserving the idea that there is still a convention-based meaning for every word in terms of that word's concept.[14]

3.2.2 The reaction of realist semantics

There are two shoals on which all forms of conventionalist semantics founder. One has to do with when a word should be said to change its meaning. Both disagreements within a culture at a time, and disagreements between cultures over time, are hard to make sense of on conventionalist accounts of meaning. If you (or the ancient Greeks) mean by 'whale' a big fish, and I mean something mammalian, how can we disagree? After all, you and the Greeks have fixed the meaning of 'whale' one way, and I have fixed it another, so we will just talk past each other even though both sides use the same word, 'whale'. Or you (and Norman Malcolm in Malcolm 1959) mean by 'dreaming' the only criterion we had for dreaming prior to 1950, viz, a waking remembrance of occurrences during sleep known not to be real. Certain scientists discover REM and EEG patterns usually accompanying dreaming, and hypothesize that we do not remember all that we dream. If you fixed the meaning of 'dreaming' by the criterion of waking remembrance, then the idea of an unremembered (and certainly an unrememberable) dream is literally senseless (Putnam 1962).

As Kripke and Putnam originally pointed out, this inability to capture our sense that these disagreements are meaningful (because the words in terms of which such disagreements are carried on do not change their meaning when used by the opponents in such disagreements), and that one side of such disagreements is or at least can be right (so that science is capable of progress), is a damning indictment of conventionalist semantics. Equally damning is another implication of conventionalist semantics, this one having to do with the idea, not of changing meaning, but of running out of meaning. Suppose one comes across a piece of metal that is white and ductile; on the criteriological and PCA versions of meaning, there is no

---

[12] See Moore 1985, pp. 298–300.
[13] See generally Gallie 1956; see also Dworkin 1985, pp. 128–31.
[14] The use to which Dworkin puts such deep conventionalism in Dworkin 1986.

answer as to whether or not this piece is or is not gold, for it shares only some of the properties definitive of gold (on the criteriological view) and it is only somewhat analogous to paradigmatic instances of gold (on the PCA view). The word is vague, meaning we have run out of conventions sufficient to place the item definitely in or definitely out of the extension of 'gold'.

Yet most of us sense that there is an answer as to whether the thing is or is not gold. 'Gold', that is, seems to have a meaning sufficient to determine whether or not these items are within its extension; since we have run out of conventions, meaning must be constituted by something other than these conventions.

These two theoretical considerations militate strongly against any form of conventionalist semantics, at least for any discourse where: (1) meaningful, theoretical disagreement about the extension of some predicate exists in the face of there being differing definitions, paradigms, or other supposedly extension-fixing conventions; and (2) meaningful questions about the extensions of some predicate exist in the face of there being no relevant or non-vague definitions, paradigms, or other supposedly extension-fixing conventions. Such considerations point to an alternative semantics, what I shall call realist semantics. One can divide this semantic theory into semantic and metasemantic theses. The semantic thesis is that the meaning of a word is given by (or at least heavily influenced by) its extension. The metasemantic thesis explains how this could be so: speakers discover certain exemplars they provisionally think might be instances of a kind; they baptize the kind with a word (e.g. 'gold'); there is a causal chain of usage with each succeeding speaker intending to refer to the kind first baptized with the label 'gold'; expertise develops about what that nature is and what are its exemplars; paradoxically, it may turn out that the initial items people took to be exemplars of the kind are in fact not such exemplars, but merely lucky heuristics to the discovery of the kind.

The main pay-off of such a semantics is its ability to handle the two theoretical concerns that bedevil all forms of conventionalist semantics: (1) people can meaningfully disagree because the terms they employ have the same meaning, i.e. the same thing to which their words refer; and (2) people do not run out of meaning as fast as they run out of conventions because meaning is a function of the world and its nature, which may only be partially known and thus only partially reflected in conventions.

3.3 The link of the two versions of the objectivity thesis to the two kinds of semantics

The strong version of the objectivity thesis holds that all cases have right answers; that is, that all singular propositions of law are determinatively true or false. This strong version can be held only by those who adopt a realist semantics for their interpretation of legal texts. This is because it is only plausible that one doesn't run out of meaning in hard cases on the realist semantics.[15] Rather, meaning for the

---

[15] Argued for in Moore 1985, pp. 322–38, and Moore 2000, pp. 273–7.

realist can be seen as being as rich as the nature of the things referred to; whereas conventions exist only because of recurring situations that have occurred, or situations one can anticipate occurring. Conventions are thus necessarily indeterminate in the face of novel cases, cases that have neither happened before nor have they even occurred in anyone's imagination.

A mode of legal interpretation that includes a realist semantics is, of course, not all one needs in order to make the strong version of the objectivity thesis plausible. One also needs non-contradictory legal norms, for example. And one needs the things (to which words in legal texts refer) to have a nature rich enough to make bivalence plausible. Still, one at least needs a realist versus a conventionalist semantics, in order for the strong version of the objectivity thesis to have a chance.

Many conventionalists in semantics, perhaps most, accept the fact that conventions run out and that novel cases are thus indeterminate in their resolution under such conventions.[16] Three groups of conventionalists dispute these conclusions, however. One, call them 'shallow conventionalists', believe that there can be closure rules to give answers in precisely those cases where conventions otherwise run out. The rule of lenity in criminal law is often paraded as an example of such a closure rule: the rule of lenity (sometimes called the rule of 'strict construction') provides that if something is not *clearly* prohibited by the criminal code, then that act is permitted.[17] In novel cases, the idea is, conventions will not *clearly* either cover or not cover the facts in issue. Therefore, the closure rule kicks in to provide an answer otherwise not available. So, if a motorized skateboarder is apprehended in the park of a city with an ordinance prohibiting vehicles in the park, since a motorized skateboard is not clearly a vehicle, the activity is permitted.[18]

There are two problems for the shallow conventionalist's resolution of indeterminacy in terms of closure rules. One is that such rules rarely exist in mature legal systems, and for good reason: they uniformly provide a mechanical answer, one divorced from the purpose a rule may serve, when what is wanted is an intelligent extension of that purpose onto novel cases. Second, even where such rules exist, they do not eliminate indeterminacy due to vagueness. Notice that for rules like that prohibiting vehicles, two vague lines are created by the rule of lenity: the line between what is *clearly* prohibited (versus only arguable prohibited), and the line between what is *clearly* not prohibited (versus only arguably permitted), are vague—indeed, as vague as the line between what is prohibited versus not prohibited that exists without a closure rule. Closure rules thus move vagueness around a bit, but do not eliminate it.[19]

The second group of conventionalists—let us call them the 'rich conventionalists'—hope that if one has enough rules in the corpus of the legal text, all cases will be covered one way or another. Bentham was such an optimist, hoping that one could write a code sufficiently rich that 'one could but open the great book of laws

---

[16] See e.g. Hart 1958.   [17] Hans Kelsen's example in Kelsen 1934, pp. 474–82.
[18] Ronald Dworkin also clutches at this straw in his attempt to show that the vagueness of all natural languages is not defeating of a right answer thesis in law. See Dworkin 1985, p. 129.
[19] Joseph Raz' answer to Dworkin on this point. See Raz 1979, pp. 73–4.

and find therein the answer to every question that could meaningfully be asked' (Bentham 1782/1970, ch. 19, par. 10). In our own time Ronald Dworkin has shared Bentham's optimism here, thinking that sheer numbers of standards could eliminate indeterminacy in all but a handful of 'ties'.[20]

Such optimism rarely takes the trouble to spell out how increasing the number of vague rules works to eliminate the indeterminacy due to vagueness. Here is my own suggestion:[21] Quine once thought that an overlapping of vague terms could reduce vagueness (Quine 1960, p. 127). His attractive analogy was to a painter whose use of shaded watercolours in overlapping patterns could approach the precision of a worker working with mosaic tiles. Yet as I have shown elsewhere (Moore 1981, p. 198), such overlapping of vague terms only moves vagueness around, so that for every case where vagueness is eliminated there is another case where new vagueness is created.

Moreover, increasing the number of rules using vague terms is extremely likely to increase conflict between rules (Moore 1981, pp. 198–9). The more rules there are, the more chance of overlap between terms that have conflicting legal remedies attached to them. The result of numerous rules can thus be a decrease in determinacy, not an increase.

The third kind of conventionalist response to indeterminacy—what I call the 'deep conventionalist'—I described in section 2. This is the view that substitutes deep conventions (the ones that form a 'concept' as opposed to a 'conception') for the nature of something referred to, as the means by which indeterminacy can be reduced and theoretical disagreement made meaningful.[22] This idea is that people can meaningfully disagree in their *conceptions* so long as there exists that 'plateau of agreement that makes disagreement possible' —i.e. an agreed upon *concept*. Such depth cannot of course eliminate indeterminacy, because the *concept* itself will be vague so that the deepest disagreements about its meaning will not be resolvable as a matter of convention (Moore 1985, pp. 298–301 and 309 n. 64).

The upshot is that conventionalist semantics makes possible only the weak version of the objectivity thesis for law. For the strong version to be true, a realist semantics is needed in legal interpretation.

4. The Desirability of Using Realist Semantics in the Interpretation of Legal Texts

There are three reasons generally favouring the use of a realist semantics in legal interpretation rather than one of its conventionalist alternatives.[23] The first of these reasons stems from the general correctness of the realist theory as a theory of meaning in natural (i.e. non-legal) discourse. One of the items that makes a semantic

---

[20] See e.g. Dworkin 1978.   [21] Laid out in Moore 1981, pp. 197–9.

[22] See Dworkin's use of this Rawlsian distinction in Dworkin 1986.

[23] Explored by me in greater detail in Moore 1985, pp. 322–38.

theory correct is its conformity to the intentions with which ordinary speakers of the language speak. While I shall attend to these intentions in more detail in section 5, for the contrast with conventionalist theories we can paint with a broader brush.

When ordinary people use words like 'gold', 'whales', 'polio', 'dreams', and 'death', do they intend either certain examples or certain definitions to fix the extension of these words? Do they intend by 'gold' to mean anything resembling some paradigm example of gold, even if that example turns out to be 'fool's gold' (i.e. iron pyrites)? Do they intend by 'gold' to mean anything that matches the definition they have in mind (such as yellow, valuable, metal), even if it turns out gold becomes less valuable and comes in a white variety? I call these 'rich' semantic intentions, and they are the kind people should have if conventionalist semantics were correct (Moore 1985, p. 340).

Contrast these with spare semantic intentions (Moore 1985, p. 340). These are intentions to refer to a kind with words like 'gold', but the speaker does not intend his exemplars or his definitions to fix what is in the extension of the word. This is not his business and he knows it. He knows that it is up to science to discover what gold really is; it is not up to him or his fellow native speakers to stipulate what something must be to be gold.

The psychological fact supporting a realist over a conventionalist semantics is that most people speak most of the time with spare semantic intentions and most audiences so understand such speakers to be so speaking. If this is so generally, then it is very likely so for legal speakers and legal audiences; that is, those who lay down general propositions of law and those who must understand these propositions in order to obey them. Insofar as such lawmakers' authority extends to what they *mean* (and not just to what they *say*), and insofar as citizens' understanding of what is meant is relevant to what words used in legal texts should be held by judges to mean, then the fact that spare semantic intentions are present (and are understood to be present) supports the use of the realist semantics in law.

The second and third reasons for using a realist semantics in legal interpretation both stem from the two systematic advantages realist semantics generally holds over its conventionalist competitors. These were that on a realist semantics: (1) overriding conventional wisdom about what properties are distinctive of a kind need not betoken a change in meaning, only a better theory about what that meaning really is (in light of a better theory about the nature of the kind referred to); and (2) one doesn't run out of meaning just because one has reached the outer limit of conventional understanding about some kind.

Take (1) first. In limiting the judicial function, it is desirable that judges be limited in their authority to change the law. It is not that they should never overrule a common law precedent or change a statute's 'plain meaning', but changing the law in these ways requires a special showing, a showing more compelling than simply that a new rule would have been the better one to have been selected initially. But realist semantics allows a judge to change the prevailing theory about the nature of some kind without changing the law in this way. For on the realist semantics she is not changing the meaning of the legal text; only discovering (via a *better* theory) what that meaning always was. To the extent that such activist judging is a good thing, a realist semantics licenses it in a way smoothly consistent with the law's own depiction of judging.

Now consider the second systematic advantage of realist semantics generally. In keeping with the desirability of a limited judicial function, it is also desirable that there be enough law to decide even the hardest of hard cases. Then judges are never free to stipulate some new law to resolve novel situations. They are merely discovering law that was pre-existing their decisions, however difficult it may have been to see. This allows judges a uniform role (following the law), rather than a bifurcated role (following the law in easy cases, and legislating by their own lights in hard cases). This is not only theoretically advantageous, but such uniformity of role also encourages judges to try harder to find such answers (since there are no 'hard cases' in which they have license to legislate). As we saw in section 3, only a realist semantics makes it possible to have enough law to justify the univocal view of the judicial role. The desirability of such a role thus supports the use of realist semantics in legal interpretation.

5. Some Varieties of Realist Semantics Within Contemporary Legal Theory

When I first urged the use of a realist semantics in legal interpretation in Moore 1981, it was a novel idea with few other adherents. Such a semantic theory has pretty much swept the field in linguistics/philosophy of language since then, however, and this general dominance has resulted in the theory's more widespread usage within legal theory. In what follows I shall distinguish three versions of such a semantics within legal theory. Of particular interest in this context is how the realism gets left out of a 'realist semantics' on two of the more recent versions of such a theory.

5.1 The standard model

Those of us who were Hilary Putnam's students in the early 1970s when he was writing 'The Meaning of "Meaning" ' took away the following interpretation, what I shall call the 'standard model' of realist semantics.[24] On this model realist semantics is appropriate when but only when two sorts of facts are true. First, there is an environmental fact: the world must contain the item to which apparent reference is being made in the use of the word in question. In the case of singular terms, these items will be particulars; in the case of general predicates, these items will be universals, namely, kinds.[25] For such kinds to be apprehended there must in addition

---

[24] See Moore 1981 and Moore 1985. See also Platts 1979.

[25] Thus Putnam carefully separated the question of whether speakers intend to refer to a kind from the question whether there is in fact a kind, using the example of jade. See Putnam 1975. For a more detailed discussion of a variety of ways in which reference to an apparent kind can fail, see Soames 2002, pp. 281–4.

be particulars whose similarities *inter se* suggest that there is a kind of which they are instances. Such kinds, on the standard model, must not be mere aggregation of individuals; rather the kind must have a nature sufficiently robust and unitary that it can be referred to without mention of its instances. Second, there must be what I have elsewhere called 'facts of usage' (Moore 1998), and what others call 'social facts' (Simchen 2007). On the standard model there are three such usage facts:

(i) Speakers must use the predicate in question with indexical intentions, that is, an intention to name whatever local stuff happens to be around them. In Putnam's famous example (Putnam 1975), we on Earth use 'water' to refer to the local stuff around here (H_2O, as it turns out), but the speakers of English on Twin-Earth use 'water' to refer to their clear, colourless, life-giving, etc., local stuff (XYZ, as it turns out). 'Water' is thus indexical in the same way as 'I' (Bar-Hillel's original example of indexicals in Bar-Hillel 1954), depending for its reference on whatever is in the environment of the original speakers.

(ii) Speakers must use the predicate in question with referential (versus attributive) intentions.[26] The distinction is most easily grasped with singular terms, so to use one of Leo Katz's examples (Katz 1987, p. 85): your wife directs you to meet 'the man in the Brooks Brother suit, the Yves St Laurent tie, and the Gucci shoes'. If her intention is to refer to some one particular person, no matter what he is in fact wearing, then her intention is referential; if her intention is to refer to whoever is wearing these three items, then her intention is attributive. For predicates like 'gold' analogously, if we speak intending to name a kind whatever its properties turn out to be, our intentions are referential; if we speak intending to name whatever class of individuals turns out to possess the properties we take to be definitive of gold, then our intentions are attributive.

(iii) Speakers must be willing to defer to any well-evidenced expertise others may possess about the true nature of the kind to which all refer. Putnam calls this the 'division of linguistic labor' (Putnam 1975), while others call it 'linguistic deference' (Simchen 2007).[27] It is this deference that makes it plausible how any individual speaker can 'mean more than he knows' because he can rely on and incorporate the knowledge of others in his referential intentions.

One might well call the standard model of realist semantics *the* realist model for that semantics' applicability. For the environmental fact required is a realism about kinds, and the social facts required are facts true only of speakers who are themselves some kind of realists in their metaphysics. My own early application of realist semantics to legal and moral theory,[28] together with like applications by David

---

[26] Keith Donellan's distinction. See Donellan 1966.

[27] Simchen pays greater attention to linguistic deference in Coleman and Simchen 2003.

[28] Moore 1981 and Moore 1985; see also Moore 1982, Moore 1992a, and Moore 2003b. For realist semantics applied to constitutional law, see Moore 1989a and Moore 2001.

Brink,[29] Mark Platts,[30] and others,[31] illustrate this metaphysical understanding of realist semantics.

5.2 The pedestal model

A less robustly metaphysical view of 'realist' semantics has been developed by Nicos Stavropoulos (in his 1996 volume) and Ronald Dworkin.[32] On this model, the environmental fact needed to ground realist semantics is quite modest: only that there be certain particulars that can be classed together, and a concept so grouping these particulars together that is accepted by the speakers who use the word for this purpose.[33] The usage facts are also comparatively modest: speakers need to have indexical intentions, making their words' reference hostage to the accidents of the portion of the environment that they happen to encounter; and speakers must be willing to defer to expertise when it is possessed by those with theories about the concepts that group the particulars in question. (This latter feature is what leads Ori Simchen to accuse Dworkin and Stavropoulos of placing theorists on a pedestal; thus my name for this model; Coleman and Simchen 2003, pp. 10–11). On the 'pedestal' view, there is no need for speakers to have referential intentions with respect to a kind; it is enough that they are willing to defer to experts about a concept of the kind.

5.3 Simchen's version of realist semantics

Like Stavropoulos, Simchen dispenses with any metaphysics of kinds as a presupposition of 'realist' semantics. The only environmental fact needed is that there be some particulars susceptible to grouping into a class by speakers. (There apparently need not even be a shared concept of how such grouping should be defined.) Simchen retains referential intentions, but to what they refer appears to be the conventional groupings accepted by the linguistic community. Unlike Stavropoulos, Simchen rids realist semantics of any need for linguistic deference; speakers need not be willing to defer to anyone, even in principle, because they rightly think themselves to be in possession of the correct classificatory scheme grouping certain particulars together. Such classificatory scheme is 'correct' only

---

[29] Brink 1988 and Brink 1989a. Brink is more guarded in the metaphysical commitments of such semantics in Brink 1989b. See also Brink 2001.

[30] Platts 1979.

[31] See Katz 1987, pp. 85–7, and Soames 2009. For a variety of views relating K-P semantics to realist metaphysics, see the collection of essays in Beebee and Sabbarton-Leary 2010.

[32] Stavropoulos, Dworkin's former student, so interpreted Dworkin's early interpretivism. See Stavropoulos 1996, pp. 129–36 and 160; on this force fitting of Dworkin's interpretivist views into such a semantics, compare Moore 1998, p. 102 n. 7. Dworkin eventually changed his views so as to accept Stavropoulos' pedestal model of such semantics. See Dworkin 2004.

[33] On Stavropoulos' version of 'realist' semantics, 'key concept-words are intended to pick out the concepts they stand for, whatever their content may be', and 'the content of the relevant concepts is determined by substantive theory, which is constrained by paradigmatic applications and abstract characterizations of the relevant practice of application' (Stavropoulos 1996, p. 160).

in the sense that correctness is here a matter of convention: if some scheme is in accord with the classificatory abilities possessed by most native speakers, then it is 'correct'.[34]

6. No Objectivity on the Cheap: The Need for a Metaphysics of Kinds to Justify a Realist Semantics

Simchen and I are in agreement in rejecting the 'Dworkin/Stavropoulos' version of realist semantics, although our reasons for doing so are somewhat different. We both think that Dworkin/Stavropoulos have failed to justify any deference to theorists by ordinary users of English predicates. I think this, however, because I link the justifiability of such linguistic deference to there being something, a kind, with a deep nature amenable to theoretical treatment; Stavropoulos' requirement that there be a concept justifies only a theory of the nature of that concept, a kind of deep conventionalist semantics at best. Whereas Simchen rejects Stavropoulos' theorizing on the ground that no such theorizing or deference is required (nor is there any in fact for many words) for realist semantics to be applicable; all that is needed are the ordinary classificatory abilities of native speakers, which abilities require and in fact generate no deference to experts.

Turning then to Simchen's version of realist semantics, my first query is whether his version can garner for itself the two theoretical advantages that realist semantics possesses vis-à-vis all forms of conventionalist semantics. Consider first the constancy of meaning that makes possible radical disagreement. Without the

---

[34] See Coleman and Simchen 2003, p. 20:

> Schematically, to be a chair is to be taken by the average speaker as having the same intended function, general appearance, and so on, as paradigmatic chairs. Determining whether or not some item bears the sameness relation to a paradigmatic chair is something which an average speaker can be expected to do... the 'essence' of chairs depends on ordinary speakers' everyday classificatory capacities.

See also Coleman and Simchen 2003, p. 22 ('the equivalence relation itself was determined by speakers' ordinary stuff-involving classificatory capacities'), p. 28 ('Whether or not sameness obtains between a given item and a paradigmatic instance of law is determined by the average speaker's ordinary classificatory capacities'), p. 28 n. 39 ('whether or not the relevant similarity relation obtains... is determined by the average speaker's ordinary classificatory capacities'), p. 30 ('Something belongs to the extension of "law" just in case it would be deemed by the average speaker as relevantly similar to paradigm cases'), and p. 33 ('the extension... is fixed by the average speaker's classificatory tendencies').

It is an understatement to say that I am at a loss to reconcile this straightforward conventionalism with the seemingly *objective* (i.e. non-conventional) similarity relations that determine extension in Simchen's later paper (Simchen 2007). Simchen in private correspondence seeks to reconcile the two by characterizing his earlier statements as only 'metasemantic' but not semantic. Three points: first, this doesn't seem to be the status stated in the quotes above (e.g.: 'the "essence" of chairs depends on ordinary speakers' everyday classificatory capacities'). Second, even if these are merely metasemantic theses about how people come to adopt and use a realist semantics, what then is Simchen's *semantic* thesis about what unifies the kind? Objective similarity relations must be similar in some respect(s), respect(s) presumably determined by the nature of some kind, natural or social. Third, even if only metasemantic, Simchen's explanation (in terms of ordinary speaker's classificatory capacities) ill suits one with a more realist(ic) explanation: people have such capacities because these are natural kinds.

environmental fact that reference to a genuine kind has succeeded, and without the usage fact that speakers typically intend to refer to such kinds in their usage of the relevant words, I don't see how meaning remains constant across very divergent beliefs. All Simchen's version of realist semantics has to work with is the environmental fact that there are certain particulars picked out by a term, grouped into the extension of that word by the normal classificatory abilities of native speakers, and the usage fact that speaker's intentions are indexical, i.e. the word is intended to pick out whatever particulars are in the vicinity of native speakers.

These two facts are perhaps sufficient to reject criterial semantics, for the actual and intended indexicality of a term makes the ordinary criteria for use inadequate to determine reference; 'water' as used on Earth has the same criteria of use as on Twin-Earth, and yet the reference is different in the two different environments. Yet these two facts are not sufficient to show how there can be the converse situation, namely, where the reference is the same but the criteria are different, as in the 'whale' and 'dreaming' examples earlier. And it is this latter kind of example that is needed to show constancy of meaning despite very different criteria for use. Even if we and the Greeks both happened to stumble across genuine instances of gold, our differing beliefs about the stuff could generate sufficiently different classificatory schemes by the two groups of speakers that there was little overlap—in which case (on Simchen's semantics) the extension of 'chrysos' and of 'gold' would differ and we and the Greeks would be talking past each other when we disagreed about the nature of gold.

Now consider the second theoretical advantage of realist semantics, that of successful reference despite vague, non-existent, or conflicting conventions guiding usage. Only the intent to refer to a kind whose nature outstrips current convention, together with the existence in fact of such a kind, together generate the needed implication about successful reference despite indeterminate conventions. Simchen's classificatory abilities shared by native speakers is just a convention, and like other conventions it is no more comprehensive than the behaviour from which it is constructed. Where ordinary speakers' classificatory tendencies are confused, fragmented, or conflicted, there will be no answer to the question of whether some item is within the extension of some predicate. Realist semantics on Simchen's version fares no better here than any other form of conventionalist semantics.

Which introduces my second query: isn't Simchen's version of realist semantics just a reversion to some form of conventionalist semantics? Not the definitional form of such semantics, for the reason mentioned earlier (indexicality prevents sameness of definition from guaranteeing sameness of extension). Yet how does Simchen's semantics differ from either PCA semantics or the shallow, behavioural semantics of ordinary language philosophy? Consider each in turn.

Whether Simchen's semantics collapses back into the old PCA semantics depends on how Simchen regards the paradigms that speakers baptize with the name of a class. Many years ago I distinguished strong from weak paradigms (Moore 1981, pp. 287–8). A strong paradigm is a particular that is (analytically) necessarily within the extension of the predicate for which it is a paradigm. Such paradigms are tied by convention to words, so that anything that is a paradigmatic exemplar of blue, or is relevantly similar to such exemplars, is necessarily blue. Weak paradigms, by contrast, are no more than heuristics: they indicate to speakers that they are instances of a kind. But however much such paradigms were the original evidence for the existence of a kind, however much they are the standard learning tools by which a culture teaches the use of the kind-word, weak paradigms may turn out not to be instances of the kind at all. The original exemplar of flat may have been the ocean; the way 'flat' is taught may be by pointing at the ocean, yet the ocean is not in fact within the extension of 'flat'. It just looks flat.

I am unclear how Simchen's semantics permits any but strong paradigms. After all, if there need be no kind referred to by some predicate, only some particulars sharing whatever properties as happen to be picked out by the ordinary classificatory abilities of native speakers, then what would make any paradigm only provisionally within the extension of some predicate? To what deeper insight is its status hostage, in the absence of any but the most conventional nature?

If Simchen's semantics does rely on there being strong paradigms, similarity to which determines the extension of each predicate, then Simchen's semantics are indistinguishable from the conventionalist PCA semantics of fifty years ago, a semantics to which realist semantics was supposed to be the antidote.

Perhaps, however, Simchen wishes to regard paradigms as weak, which is to say, provisional and defeasible. Perhaps the linguistic dispositions of native speakers are held to trump the paradigmatic status of any given particular (although it is hard to see how such classificatory dispositions could dispense with *all* such paradigms, as it should in principle be able to do if the paradigms are truly weak paradigms). Yet then, what distinguishes Simchen's semantics from the behavioural approach of ordinary language philosophy? Common to both is ultimate reliance on what people are disposed to say, such shared, classificatory sayings determining what they are talking about.

My third query has to do with why Simchen is attracted to a version of realist semantics that is stripped of the metaphysics of kinds, stripped of intentions to refer to such kinds in the typical uses of words, and stripped of any deference by ordinary speakers to the expertise others may possess about the nature of such kinds. One temptation for this stripped-down version of realist semantics could be ontological: one could doubt the realist (i.e. anti-nominalist) metaphysics of kinds, either across the board or at least for many of the predicates making up a language. Simchen's motives, however, do not seem to stem from ontological parsimony. Rather, his doubts are rooted in the usage facts depended upon by the standard version of realist semantics. He doubts whether ordinary speakers have the metaphysical views he thinks they would have to have in order to intend to refer to kinds with a nature others may know better than do they.

It is worth quoting Simchen here, since he seeks to load the dice a bit. Simchen thinks that any attribution 'to ordinary speakers of the metaphysical realist intention to employ "water" to refer to anything relevantly similar to paradigmatic instances of water from the standpoint of the world as it is in itself, beyond whatever we might come to believe about the matter', is highly implausible (Simchen 2007, p. 227). Or again: 'such a view attributes to speakers, when using a kind term N, the intention to refer to everything having the same underlying nature as some paradigmatic sample of N quite apart from what any expert doctrine about the nature of N does or would reveal' (Coleman and Simchen 2003, p. 36 n. 43).

There are several things to untangle in these rather exaggerated characterizations of the referential intentions needed by the standard version of realist semantics. To begin with, in this context the distinction between Peircean (or Putnam's 'internal') realism, on the one hand, and metaphysical (or 'external') realism, on the other, is a red herring. I doubt (as does Simchen) that ordinary speakers' referential intentions are sufficiently fine-grained so as to pick out one or the other of these metaphysical views. Fortunately, however, this does not matter to the issues at hand, which are (1) whether such speakers presuppose that there is a kind to which they intend to refer and about the nature of which they intend to defer when confronted with a better theory (the usage fact); and (2) whether there is in fact such a kind (the environmental fact). As I have argued elsewhere (Moore 2003b, p. 694), the internal realist can match the metaphysical realist stride for stride in these commitments, so a presupposition of either form of realism (or the undifferentiated combination of both) is sufficient to support the referential intentions and metaphysical presuppositions I argue are needed to use realist semantics.

The second clarification has to do with the place of paradigmatic examples and similarity functions in ordinary speakers' referential intentions. We should distinguish the referential intentions of the original baptizers of a kind, from those far down the causal chain of reference. Only the baptizers need have before them puzzlingly similar particulars from which they self-consciously hypothesize a kind;[35] later users need not think about (or even believe in the existence of) any paradigmatic exemplars.[36] Their intentions can be simpler: to refer to a kind with their general predicates in the same way they refer to a particular with their singular terms. Such later users need have in mind no complex function of similarity relations over certain particulars.

Notice that both of these points simplify considerably the content of the referential intentions the standard version of realist semantics would attribute to contemporary language users. The first rids that content of any total independence 'from what any expert doctrine about the nature of N does or would reveal'. The second rids that content of any isolation of paradigmatic samples and universal quantification over particulars sharing the nature of such samples. The content of the relevant referential intention is easier: it is to refer to a kind that exists independently of whether the speaker or her community thinks it exists (a realism about universals); and such intention is accompanied by the belief that the nature of the kind may only be partially revealed (to either the individual speaker or to her linguistic community). That these simpler psychological states are required on the standard

---

[35] Scott Soames nicely describes the limited precision and limited explicitness of baptizing intentions and dispositions needed for K-P semantics to be appropriate in Soames 2002, pp. 284–6, and Soames 2010, pp. 88–9.

[36] Other than for the word, 'meter', can one identify plausible paradigms? Surely any original bits of metal, e.g., have been lost to us even if they were our linguistic community's initial samples of gold.

version of realist semantics makes the latter version more plausible because these states are more easily ascribed to ordinary speakers.

Having clarified the content of the requisite referential intentions, it remains to clarify the nature of the claim made when it is claimed that a speaker *has* the requisite referential intention and accompanying belief. As Simchen recognizes, this is of a piece with one's general views on what is required to ascribe intentional attitudes to another. One thing that is not required is that there be some Joycean phenomenology explicitly containing the content of the intention and the belief. We do not require such conscious recitations to ascribe intentions and beliefs generally, so there is no warrant for requiring such here.

What is required to ascribe intentions and belief is that there be certain dispositions, which is to say that certain counterfactuals are true of the individual whose mental states they are. In the case of referential intentions, the most pertinent dispositions are verbal dispositions, specifically: what would the speaker think and say on learning certain surprising facts about some subject of his discourse? To enlist an old intuition pump of mine (Moore 1985, pp. 293–4, 297–300, and 322–8), suppose the speaker has pronounced as *dead* a person who has lost consciousness and whose heart and lungs have ceased spontaneous functioning because he has been immersed under very cold water for thirty minutes. What would such a speaker think if presented with the conclusion that the drowning victim 'is not really dead' and if presented with the medical evidence supporting that conclusion (intact brain function, revivability, etc.)? If the speaker's intentions had been attributive in using the word 'dead'—so that anything that possesses the properties definitive of 'death' for the speaker is necessarily dead—then he should refuse the conclusion as senseless. Such a victim may not be *smead* (a new state defined by brain function), but that victim is necessarily *dead*. Whereas if the speaker's intentions were referential, then he would readily accede to the meaningfulness of the conclusion and to the relevance of the evidence for sustaining it; he would thus regard his own conclusions about death as fallible and recognize that experts' views about death might well be better than his, even though theirs too are fallible. These are the beliefs of a realist about the kind of event that is death, even though such a speaker is wholly ignorant of the realism/ anti-realism debate in philosophy.

My own empirical intuition is that such referential intentions are quite widespread, both as to people holding them and as to words with respect to which they are held. Reverting to the death example, surely few native speakers of English will cut the organs out of a drowning victim who meets the prevailing definition of 'death' but who is not really dead.

7. The Correct Metaphysics as the Truth-Maker of Propositions of Law

As we saw in section 3, strong objectivity requires use of a realist semantics in the interpretation of legal texts. As we just saw in section 6, realist semantics in turn requires both that certain usage (or social) facts be true, and that certain ontological facts be true. In this and section 8 I want to examine the ontological facts needed for law to be strongly objective.

My concern in this section is with the truth-makers for propositions of law. These include general propositions of law (such as 'contracts require consideration or reliance in order to be valid') and singular propositions of law (such as 'this contract is valid'). In section 8 I will deal with the truth-makers of propositions *about* law; that is, propositions of legal theory.

Focusing on the truth-makers for propositions of law, it may seem as though all legal terms must refer to natural kinds in order for law to be strongly objective. For it is with natural kinds that the nature of the kind holds out the promise of a richness sufficient to answer all meaningful questions about the kind. If one is a moral realist, one might extend this to moral kinds as well.[37] Then the thought would be: so long as the law uses words referring to natural or moral kinds, then it can be strongly objective.

In the analysis that follows I shall first pursue this natural thought, examining cases where the law does use words referring to natural or moral kinds. I shall then examine cases where the best interpretation of legal texts is to construe their words as *not* referring to natural or moral kinds. In such cases the law creates an artificial kind, what I call a functional kind. We shall want to see if in these cases too the law could be strongly objective. In the last subpart of this section, I shall examine more complicated cases. These are cases where the best interpretation of a legal text partly relies on the correct metaphysics of a natural kind and partly relies on a more instrumental analysis.

7.1 Natural and moral kinds as truth-makers for propositions of law

Over the past quarter-century I have used many examples of legal texts where the best interpretation took the words in them to refer to natural or moral kinds. For example: statutes that regulate the mining of *gold*, that make inheritance rights, estate taxes, organ transfers, homicide prosecutions, and other things depend on when someone is *dead*, that deal with *water* rights, that regulate the taking of *whales, fish*, or *birds*, that deal with *diseases*, etc.; or statutes that award custody to whichever parent in a divorce proceeding as will maximize the *best interest* of a child, or that grant citizenship to those possessed of *good moral character*, or that deport non-citizens convicted of a crime of *moral turpitude*, or that read into all contracts a covenant of *good faith* and *fair dealing*, or that ban *unfair* trade practices or *unfair* and *deceptive* advertising, etc.; or constitutional texts requiring protection of the law that is *equal*, process that is *due*, searches that are *reasonable*, and punishments that are not *cruel*.[38] In each case the argument was not just that certain natural or moral kinds existed so that they could be referred to by the words in legal texts, nor

---

[37] See Moore 1982, Moore 1992a, Brink 1988, and Brink 1989a.
[38] See the citations in n. 28.

even that the authors of such texts intended to so refer in the choice of their words. Rather, the complete argument included a moral premise, *viz*, that the value behind the rule was best served by construing such words as referring to a kind whose nature was to guide legal meaning.

Rather than rehashing these old examples, consider a more recent one, the meaning of 'cause' as that word is used in tort and criminal law liability rules. In a recent book (Moore 2009), I argue that the purpose served by the causal requirements of both tort and criminal law is an aspect of justice, corrective justice in the case of tort and retributive justice in the case of criminal law. In a nutshell, corrective justice is served only when culpable *causers* of a harm have to compensate the victims suffering such harm; retributive justice is served only when the more severe punishments are meted out to those who culpably *cause* some harm (more severe in comparison to the punishment appropriate to intenders or riskers of a harm that is not caused).

The justice-oriented purposes of such cause-based liability rules demand the application of the correct metaphysics of that natural kind of relation we call causation. There is no room here for an artificially constructed notion of causation, one peculiar to the law, if these justice values are to be served. Duties of compensation and more severe punishments turn on when someone really causes some harm; not on when someone 'causes' that harm in some constructed, artificial sense of the term (Moore 2009). The very policies behind these liability rules demand that judges *not* look to policies in deciding on tort and criminal liability. Rather, they must apply the best metaphysics of the causal relation, as best they can ascertain it. That, of course, is a formidable task. Fortunately there are good books to help them.

7.2 Functional kinds as truth-makers of propositions of law

Many rules of law are not like the liability rules of tort and criminal law just discussed. Rather, in many cases the best interpretation of legal texts is *not* to fix the meaning of the words within such texts by the correct metaphysics of natural or moral kinds. In such cases the problem is not that such kinds do not exist; rather, even when such kinds do exist the legal rule is sometimes best construed (in light of its purpose) so as not to refer to those kinds.

My earlier examples of such words has included: 'malice' (in homicide law), 'contract', 'insanity', 'vehicle', and the like (Moore 1985). Now consider an old example, the spatial location where a crime or a tort took place.[39] Rules governing the choice of which state's law applies, which forum has jurisdiction to legislate, which forum has jurisdiction to adjudicate, where venue (place of trial) is properly laid, traditionally make such questions turn, at least in part, on *where* the crime or tort took place.[40] Some examples: first, the defendant on a river bank on the South Carolina side of the river shoots at his victim on the other side of the river in

---

[39] Oliver Wendell Holmes' example of the courts' use of metaphysics gone awry. See Holmes 1881.
[40] Explored by me in Moore 1993, pp. 293–301.

Georgia.[41] Two variations: the bullet strikes and kills the victim, or the bullet misses but lands on Georgia soil. Which state can apply its law to this situation? Which state can try the accused? Does it matter if the charge is murder (when the death occurred in Georgia), or attempted murder (where no death need occur)?

Second, the defendant lives in New Jersey and wishes to kill the victim who lives in California.[42] Defendant sends poisoned candy through the mail from New Jersey to California, where the victim eats the candy and dies. Again, whose law applies here? Who can try the defendant?

Third, the defendant shoots and wounds the victim in one county of Indiana, but the victim escapes, only to die later (of the bullet wound) in another county of the same state.[43] Which is the proper county in which venue may be laid for trial?

Fourth, the defendant shot two deer while he was on his own land.[44] One of the deer was also on the defendant's land when it was shot, although it managed to walk off that land onto the land belonging to another before it died. The second deer was already on the land of another when it was shot by the defendant from his own land; the deer died on the land of another too. The defendant is privileged to kill deer on his own land; it is tortious to kill deer on land not his own.

Each of these legal rules are traditionally framed in terms of *where* the defendant's wrongful act took place. The correct metaphysics of events is not silent about this question. On the Davidsonian theory of events, defended elsewhere (Moore 1993), the deaths of the human and animal victims are no proper parts of the wrongful acts of killing them. To be sure, such deaths *are* part of what makes acts of this *type*—the type, killing—wrongful. But the deaths are not part of the particular acts done by these defendants. Those act-tokens ended where the bodily motions of the defendants ended, however much we refer to those bodily motions through phrases using causal properties like 'killed the deer' (Moore 1993).

One might dispute this metaphysics but doing so, or defending against such disputation, does not serve the present purpose. Suppose Davidson's theory captures the correct metaphysics of events—should lawyers take the location language in the various rules as referring to such metaphysical nature? I think plainly not (Moore 1993, pp. 295–8). The purposes of the rules of choice of law, jurisdiction to legislate, jurisdiction to adjudicate, venue, and landowners' privileges, are poorly served by giving these rules this metaphysical reading. California, for example, surely has as much interest as New Jersey in prosecuting (under its law) a killer of a California citizen while that citizen was residing in California. That the *act* of killing was wholly done in New Jersey is metaphysically true, but it is a legally idle metaphysical truth. The purposes of the locational rules demand that such metaphysical truths be put aside in favour of a legally constructed (i.e. fictional) location of actions.

This conclusion about such examples may seem to preclude strong objectivity being possible for laws consisting of rules such as these. But that need not

[41] *Simpson v. State*, 92 Ga. 41, 17 S.E. 984 (1893).
[42] *People v. Botkin*, 132 Cal. 231, 64 Pac. 286 (1901).
[43] *Peats v. State*, 213 Ind. 560, 12 N.E. 2d 270 (1938).
[44] *Jemmison v. Priddle*, [1972] 1 All Eng.Rep. 539, [1972] Q.B. 489.

be so. There may be kinds referred to by the words used in such rules, even though they are not natural or moral kinds. I call the kinds referred to here, whose nature determines meaning, *functional kinds*.[45] A functional kind is an instrumental good, a good that is good only because it serves some other value. *Legal location*—the place of a killing as determined by maximizing the policies behind the location-dependent rules above—is an instrumental good whose nature is given by maximally serving the values behind the rules in which it appears. If one is a moral realist, this is a nature rich enough to justify the realist theory of meaning and strong objectivity—even though the nature is not a natural or even an (intrinsic) moral kind.

7.3 Truth-makers for legal propositions that are about neither wholly natural nor wholly functional kinds

Sometimes the policies behind legal rules require an even more complicated answer as to the nature of what it is that makes the legal propositions expressed in such rules true. Consider but one example, the much litigated question of contract interpretation at the heart of the insurance controversy following the 2001 destruction of the World Trade Center in New York.[46] The casualty policy insured the Center against all risks with a limit of approximately 3.6 billion dollars 'per occurrence'. The extensively litigated question was whether the coordinated attack by two jet planes crashing into two separate towers, each plane bringing down one tower, was one occurrence or two occurrences. Under New York insurance law, this question turned on New York's 'single event' test. A 3.6 billion dollar question of event-individuation!

My own conclusion about this case was that the correct answer was that there were two occurrences here, not one (Moore 2003c). For present purposes the content of that answer doesn't matter. What matters is what could make such an answer true. The truth-makers for the singular proposition of law at issue here is a blend. Partly a blend of the correct metaphysics of events, partly a blend of certain conventions of the common sense individuation of objects in daily life, partly a blend of prior New York insurance cases, and partly a blend of any actual intentions the contracting parties may have had in their choice of their use of this long standard phraseology.

I suppose we could call this blend a 'mongrel kind'. But what the truth-maker here actually is is a functional kind whose nature is partly given by the true metaphysics of events and partly given by conventions and intentions. What justifies the blending of these disparate items are the values that guide a good contract interpretation. These policies prominently include the desirability of contract obligations being self-imposed obligations, particularly in non-consumer contexts where there is equality of information, bargaining position, and deliberative capacity, such as

---

[45] Moore 1985; see generally Moore 1992b.
[46] An example I consider in detail in Moore 2003c.

here. That blend that maximally serves such policies is the correct truth-maker for the 'one-event' or 'two-event' answer here, which is why this is another functional kind. As such, its nature is again sufficiently rich so as to guide meaning, even in (epistemically) hard cases such as the Twin Towers litigation.

7.4 Truth of general propositions of law

In the Introduction I urged that law is strongly objective if each singular proposition of law (decisive of some disputed law case) has a determinate truth-value that is independent of how the judge deciding that case has or will decide it. Relatedly, I urged that law is weakly objective if this is true of *some* singular propositions of law even though not of all.

I assumed that some intimate relation must exist between general and singular propositions of law, such that the latter is in some sense derived from the former. (The details of such derivation are given by one's theory of interpretation.) Now we should ask: for law to be (strongly or weakly) objective, must the general propositions of law (from which singular propositions of law are in some sense derived) themselves be true?

Seemingly the answer to that question must be in the affirmative. Singular propositions of law are to be derived by judges from general propositions of law. This process of derivation involves: (1) statements of general law, such as, 'all killings with malice aforethought are murders'; (2) statements of the facts of each particular case, for example, 'this killing was done intentionally and without provocation'; (3) statements of interpretive facts, here, 'all killings done intentionally and without provocation are done with malice aforethought'; and (4) application of standard deductive logic. Standard logic is a truth-preserving engine, meaning that if one logically derives a true conclusion (here, the singular proposition of law), every premise to the derivation must itself be true. Bismarck once opined that if you would make people conservative you must first give them something to conserve (he was speaking in favour of Germany's then novel social security system). So here: if we are to be in the business of logic—to preserve truth—one first must have truth (in the premises) to preserve.

Heretofore in my talk of propositions of law as truth-bearers and states of affairs (like the existence of kinds) as truth-makers, I have presupposed some kind of correspondence theory of truth. Some might be tempted to think that this must change for general propositions of law. Such a thought might be based on the doubt whether there can be plausible truth-makers for general propositions of law. What, one might worry, makes true that all contracts require offer acceptance, and consideration in order to be legally valid?

In truth this difficulty is illusory. The worry is based on a confusion of *propositions* (of law) with *sentences* laid down by legal authorities such as courts or legislatures. If one thinks in terms of canonically formulated sentences issued by legislatures, then it may well seem like the only 'truth-maker' for such sentences could be the historical fact that such a pronouncement was made. On this view, the sentence, 'All non-holographic wills require two witnesses in order to be legally valid', is made true by a legal authority (such as a legislature) uttering such a sentence on some appropriate occasion. The sentence is 'true', on this view, not because it corresponds with anything, mind-independent or not; rather, such a sentence is 'true' on this view only in the anaemic sense that it was authoritatively pronounced, i.e. it was 'made true' as a performative utterance.

Yet general propositions of law are not to be confused with the authoritatively laid down sentences that may be used to *express* them.[47] A legislature may utter the sentence, 'No one shall obstruct the passage of the U.S. mail', or 'No one shall engage in practices in restraint of trade'; the general propositions of law which such sentences express are more accurately rendered, respectively: 'No one shall obstruct the passage of the U.S. mail unless for good reason', and, 'No one shall engage in practices that unreasonably restrain trade.'

General propositions of law are no more and no different than the singular propositions (of all conceivable law case) that make them up. Natural, moral, and functional kinds will play their same roles as truth-makers for such general propositions no less than for their singular constituents. Thus, the extensions of gold, water, tigers, property, liberty, equality, wills, malice aforethought, and death will be referred to by the predicates in such general propositions of law no less than in the singular propositions of law derived from them via interpretation. The central insight of realist semantics—that kind terms refer to kinds just as proper names and definite descriptions refer to individuals—makes the truth-maker for general propositions of law no more mysterious and no different than the truth-makers for singular propositions of law. At least this will be so for anyone whose realism opposes nominalism as well as idealism.

8. The Correct Metaphysics as the Truth-Maker for Propositions about Law

Propositions of law are propositions internal to a legal system. In that sense their truth is a truth relative to a legal system. Thus, 'malice aforethought is required for murder', asserted by an Anglo-American lawyer, judge, or citizen, implicitly qualifies itself as, 'In Anglo-American criminal law, malice aforethought is required for murder.' Propositions about law, by contrast, are not internal to particular legal systems in this way. Such propositions are in this sense part of an external jurisprudence. Such propositions are 'meta-', or external, just in that they say something about law as such, not law in France, law in Italy, etc. Such propositions are thus aptly called part of a *general* jurisprudence.[48]

---

[47] I use the 'may' advisedly, because for general propositions of common law, as opposed to statutory law, there are no canonically formulated sentences authoritatively issued by courts in precedent cases. On this, see Moore 1987b. For such non-canonical legal rules, the source-based temptation of the legal positivist discussed in the text does not even arise.

[48] I explore the differences between an internal particular jurisprudence and an external general jurisprudence in Moore 1998.

The most general question asked in an external general jurisprudence is the question, 'What is law?' What is wanted in answer to such question is some list of essential features a thing must have to be law. Call a list of such features a theory of law. We can ask of such theory, and of each of its propositions about law, whether it and they are or can be *objective*.

When we ask after the objectivity of propositions of legal theory, we are using 'objectivity' in the same sense(s) as we used in asking after the objectivity of propositions of law. That is, we are asking whether such propositions are capable of having a truth-value independently of what some group believes, and whether some of such propositions are true in this mind-independent sense. And, as before, we can distinguish two versions of this objectivity, a strong and a weak version. On the weak version, only some propositions about law have determinate truth-values; others are indeterminate in their truth. On the strong version, all meaningful propositions about law are either true or false (even if epistemically it can be difficult to know sometimes which is the correct truth-value).

Also, as before, the strong version of objectivity will be plausible for propositions of legal theory only if a realist semantics is appropriate for the words used in expressing such propositions. Consider cases like that of international law, primitive law, U.S. constitutional law, or common law.[49] It may well be (as some legal theorists have held) that our conventions, linguistic and otherwise, that give meaning to our concept of law on any non-realist account, run out or conflict about such cases. These are then the 'hard cases' of legal theory, indeterminate under any conventionalist semantics for propositions about law. But under a realist semantics, the nature of the beast (law) may provide a determinate answer to the question whether these are law, even though it may take considerable theoretical argument about the nature of law to see these answers.[50]

With all this happy repetition and sameness, it might seem as though settling the question of objectivity of propositions of law settles the question as well for propositions about law. This would be a mistake. It is like thinking that propositions about vagueness have to be themselves vague, or that propositions about interpretation have to be themselves interpretive.[51] It is a crude mistake. Meta-languages need share none of the features of the (object) languages they are about.

So the question of the objectivity of propositions of legal theory is a live one, despite what we have said before about the strong objectivity of propositions of law. Not only is the answer to the question not determined by our answer to the like question about propositions of law; also, our interest in these two questions of objectivity differs.

Our interest in the objectivity (determinacy) of propositions of law was partly practical. We were motivated by two such practical interests: (1) Strong objectivity meant that judges did not run out of law in hard cases, and this was important to

---

[49] The borderline cases of law for legal positivists like Bentham and Hart. See e.g. Hart 1961.

[50] I explore the differences between a conventionalist search for a *concept* of law with the realist search for the *nature* of law in Moore 1992b.

[51] I separate interpretivism about law from interpretivism about legal theory in Moore 1989b.

how judges should judge in such cases; and (2) strong objectivity meant that change in conventions did not necessarily betoken a change in law, so that judges were more at liberty to change such conventions in their judging than they would be if such conventions constituted the law. These practical pay-offs for deciding between strong versus weak objectivity are lacking for propositions about law in legal theory. If legal theory is or is not strongly objective, that will not impact on the obligations of judges.

Still, the objectivity of legal theory has theoretical implications that should command our interest. These correspond to the two practical interests we have in the objectivity of propositions of law. These parallel theoretical interests are: (1) we do not run out of answers in supposed borderline cases of law, such as international law, if strong objectivity is true for propositions about law. And (2) radical disagreements between legal theorists become meaningful because they are disagreeing about the nature of the same thing (*viz*, law). These are theoretical pay-offs, making the question of objectivity of propositions about law not without interest.

So—are propositions about law strongly objective? Is there a right answer to questions about whether common law is really law, or whether law is a union of primary and secondary rules?[52] On what I earlier termed the standard model of realist semantics, two sorts of facts must be true for realist semantics to be appropriate (and thus strong objectivity possible): certain social facts of usage, and certain ontological facts about reality.

The usage facts we need are indexical and referential intentions of speakers when they discuss law, together with intentions of deference by non-experts about law. Consider first the indexical intentions of natural users of the word 'law'. As we have seen, there are plausibly thought to be such indexical intentions: (1) when the speakers in question have access to local samples of the stuff; and (2) they have an ostensive intention to refer to anything else that is 'the same' (i.e. similar in relevant respects) as the local samples they have seen. The word 'law' is plausibly so used. Everyone thinks they know clear cases of laws and of law (i.e. legal system), because they all have had some contact with the stuff in their daily lives. Moreover, their referential intention is plausibly indexical: 'anything else just like the stuff I know to be law, must be law too'. Even legal theorists have such indexical intentions in using 'law'; witness Hart's beginning with 'mature municipal legal systems' like that in England as his starting point in generalizing about law (Hart 1961).

Second, the intentions of users of 'law' are also plausibly referential and not attributive. This is evidenced in part by the defeasibility with which users of 'law' regard their own definitions or theories of law. As Stavropoulos too notes, 'lawyers treat legal properties as genuine properties over which ... [they and others] may be in substantive error. In terms of intentions, legislators (crucially) intend that the *property* a concept stands for rather than their own attempt at capturing its nature, be respected in the law' (Stavropoulos 1996, p. 46). Law has a nature that ordinary speakers take as fixing the meaning of 'law'; they do not think they are in possession

---

[52] Bentham and Hart's questions, respectively.

of extension-determining definitions that can't be wrong because such definitions fix the meaning of 'law'.

Coleman and Simchen dispute that most users of 'law' can have such referential intentions; this, because they think such intentions not only have to be intentions 'to refer to everything having the same underlying nature as some paradigmatic sample' (Coleman and Simchen 2003, p. 36 n. 43). They also demand that such intentions have to recognize that such nature can outstrip any actual theory about it, including any possible theory in the future, and yet the intention is to refer to such unknown and unknowable nature (Coleman and Simchen 2003, p. 36 n. 43). Yet as I urged before, this is to stick the referential intentions needed here with far more than is in truth essential. Ordinary speakers do not have to distinguish Peircean (or 'internal') realism from metaphysical realism in order to have the referential intentions sufficient for the application of a realist semantics.

Third, typically there is an intention to defer to experts when a realist semantics is appropriate. Coleman and Simchen do a nice job of detailing when such deferential intentions exist as a matter of social fact (Coleman and Simchen 2003, *passim*). Past successes by experts, importance to daily life of their insights, lack of disagreements between them, convergence over time of such disagreement as does exist, or simple trust in the expertise for some other reason, may suffice to generate widespread intentions to defer to experts about the nature of gold, dreams, fish, etc. Coleman and Simchen's rejection of the 'pedestal' view of Dworkin/Stavropoulos lies precisely in their scepticism that there is any deference to the expertise of legal theorists about the nature of law. There are experts about propositions *of* law, and ordinary people do intend to defer to them; we call such experts 'lawyers'. But there is a comparatively limited deference to legal theorists on propositions *about* law.

Yet there is a kind of deference being overlooked here. It is the kind of deference involved in moral discourse, where people also commonly (although not universally) think that there are no experts.[53] Because of the intent to refer to the nature of some moral or legal kind, and because of the modesty of most people in thinking that they are not infallible in their own beliefs about those natures, they must intend to defer to the expertise that would be necessary to grasp the nature of such kinds. Such expertise may reside in their own future insights as well as those of others; they may attribute it to God, to theologians,[54] to the wisest of their friends, to an epistemically idealized observer, or to no one in particular. But by intending to *refer* (to some such nature), they do intend to *defer*.

Leaving the social facts needed to make realist semantics (and strong objectivity) plausible for propositions about law, I turn to the ontological facts needed. As we have seen, the classificatory abilities common to native speakers (Coleman/ Simchen), the existence of a concept under which particulars can be grouped (Dworkin/Stavropoulos), etc., will not do. These are too conventional. Needed is

---

[53] See e.g. Waldron 1992.

[54] See e.g. Judge Jerome Frank, who in his concurring opinion in *Repouille v. United States*, F.2d 152 (2d Cir. 1947), urged remand for a finding on what our 'ethical leaders' (by which he seemed to mean religious leaders) thought on the moral question at issue in the case.

the existence of a kind whose nature is rich enough to guide meaning even when conventions run out or conflict.

Everyone who has approached the application of realist semantics to law has observed, correctly, that law is not a natural kind like gold, water, dreams, etc. Law is a human creation, an artefact.[55] From this truism one might make the inference that there can be no nature to such artefacts to be referred to by the word 'law', or at least no nature richer than that explicitly given such artefacts by their human creators. The worry is that such nature, being constituted by intentions and conventions, will run out far too often to support a realist semantics and strong objectivity.

Illustrative of this worry is a (true) anecdote about 'the pucker'. (A pucker is a certain stitch taken by seamstresses from time immemorial). A Professor of Home Economics at a mid-western college approached her Dean one day with a new course proposal. She had taken to heart the high prestige of theory in today's academy, and therefore wished to devote a new course to studying 'the theory of the pucker'. Needless to say, the Dean (who happens to be my father in law) could not see a nature to the pucker rich enough to sustain a semester's course.

It is true that not all kinds have a nature invitive of a deep theory. A deep theory of the pucker—or of chairs, ponds, pebbles, or tables—is not likely forthcoming. One can, of course, imagine very surprising facts coming to light about such items, such as Hilary Putnam's imagined discovery that pencils are alive (Putnam 1975, p. 243). Speakers can thus have both indexical and referential intentions in their use of such words. But the likelihood is that many kinds are not theoretically interesting.

Yet the line between kinds with deep versus shallow natures is not congruent with the natural/artificial line.[56] Not only are some kinds in nature (like pebbles, ponds, and pigs)[57] not at the deep end of this spectrum, but also some human creations are. Co-ordination solutions, Nash equilibriums, democracy, judicial function, liberty from coercion by others, artificial intelligence, depth grammar, legal insanity all come to mind. Law too seems to be a kind with this kind of theory-inviting depth.

Ordinary people are readily familiar with law because we all have contact with law in our daily lives. This leads some to regard the question of what is law as about as obvious as the question, 'What is a chair?'[58] Yet legal theorists know that this ordinary familiarity is deceptive. Law is intriguingly complex in its nature, sustaining centuries of theoretical speculation by sophisticated theorists. Its distinctive structures (general rules? sanctions?) and its distinctive function (rule of law values? co-ordination? moral gap-filling? integrity?) and its distinctive place within the objective reasons that bind actors are individually complex, and their combination into law even more so. In very general terms, law is a functional kind (Moore 1992b), similar to the functional kinds that are the referents of words used

---

[55] See e.g. Bix 2003.   [56] A point also noted by Coleman and Simchen 2003, p. 18.

[57] A hog may be a natural kind, but a pig is just a small hog.

[58] A personal example: my co-teacher of a course in psychology years ago had strong anti-natural law views on the nature of law. Upon enquiry, it turned out he had received an extremely unfavourable judgment in his recent divorce case. (Thus, he was certain that law bore no relation to justice.)

to express both general and singular propositions of law ('malice,' 'contract,' etc.). As such, the values it serves, and the structures that maximally serve those values, and its obligatory capacities, are far from simple or obvious.

Indeed, the very complexity of law, and the resulting disagreements about its nature, inclines some to scepticism that it has any nature at all. Yet even from a naturalist world-view, such scepticism about law is unwarranted.[59] Its nature is there to be referred to, with a richness inviting theoretical development.

References

Bar-Hillel, Yehoshua. 1954. 'Indexical Expressions'. *Mind* 63(251): 359–79.

Beebee, Helen and Nigel Sabbarton-Leary (eds). 2010. *The Semantics and Metaphysics of Natural Kinds*. New York: Routledge.

Bentham, Jeremy. 1782/1970. *Of Laws in General*. London: Athlone Press.

Bix, Brian H. 2003. 'Can Theories of Meaning and Reference Solve the Problem of Legal Determinacy?' *Ratio Juris* 16(3): 281–95.

Borgo, John. 1979. 'Causal Paradigms in Tort Law'. *Journal of Legal Studies* 8(3): 419–55.

Brink, David. 1988. 'Legal Theory, Legal Interpretation, and Judicial Review'. *Philosophy and Public Affairs* 17(2): 105–48.

Brink, David. 1989a. *Moral Realism and the Foundations of Ethics*. Cambridge: Cambridge University Press.

Brink, David. 1989b. 'Semantics and Legal Interpretation (Further Thoughts)'. *Canadian Journal of Law and Jurisprudence* 2(2): 181–91.

Brink, David. 2001. 'Realism, Naturalism, and Moral Semantics'. *Social Philosophy and Policy* 18(2): 154–76.

Coleman, Jules L. and Ori Simchen. 2003. 'Law'. *Legal Theory* 9(1): 1–41.

Donellan, Keith. 1966. 'Reference and Definite Descriptions'. *The Philosophical Review* 75(3): 281–304.

Dworkin, Ronald. 1978. *Taking Rights Seriously*. Cambridge (MA): Harvard University Press.

Dworkin, Ronald. 1985. 'Is There Really No Right Answer in Hard Cases?' In *A Matter of Principle*, 119–45. Cambridge (MA): Harvard University Press.

Dworkin, Ronald. 1986. *Law's Empire*. Cambridge (MA): Harvard University Press.

Dworkin, Ronald. 2004. 'Hart's Postscript and the Character of Political Philosophy'. *Oxford Journal of Legal Studies* 24(1): 1–37.

Gallie, Walter B. 1956. 'Essentially Contested Concepts'. *Proceedings of the Aristotelian Society* 56: 167–98.

Greenberg, Mark. 2011a. 'Naturalism in Epistemology and the Philosophy of Law'. *Law and Philosophy* 30(4): 419–51.

Greenberg, Mark. 2011b. 'Implications of Indeterminacy: Naturalism in Epistemology and the Philosophy of Law II'. *Law and Philosophy* 30(4): 453–75.

Hart, H.L.A. 1958. 'Positivism and the Separation of Law and Morality'. *Harvard Law Review* 71(4): 593–629.

---

[59] The ontology of law is explored by me in Moore 2003b.

Hart, H.L.A. 1961. *The Concept of Law*. Oxford: Clarendon Press.

Holmes, Oliver Wendell. 1881. *The Common Law*. Boston: Little, Brown.

Katz, Leo. 1987. *Bad Acts and Guilty Minds*. Chicago (IL): University of Chicago Press.

Kelsen, Hans. 1934. 'The Pure Theory of Law'. *Law Quarterly Review* 50: 474–82.

Leiter, Brian. 1998. 'Naturalism and Naturalized Jurisprudence'. In *Analyzing Law: New Essays in Legal Theory*, edited by Brian Bix, 79–104. Oxford: Clarendon Press.

Lycan, Bill. 1971. 'Non-Inductive Evidence: Recent Work on Wittgenstein's "Criteria"'. *American Philosophical Quarterly* 8(2): 109–25.

Malcom, Norman. 1959. *Dreaming*. London: Routledge.

Moore, Michael. 1981. 'The Semantics of Judging'. *Southern California Law Review* 54(2): 151–294.

Moore, Michael. 1982. 'Moral Reality'. *Wisconsin Law Review* 1982(6): 1061–156. Reprinted in Michael Moore. 2004. *Objectivity in Ethics and Law*, 3–98. Aldershot: Ashgate Publishing.

Moore, Michael. 1985. 'A Natural Law Theory of Interpretation'. *Southern California Law Review* 58(1, 2): 277–398.

Moore, Michael. 1987a. 'Metaphysics, Epistemology, and Legal Theory'. *Southern California Law Review* 60(2): 453–506. Reprinted in Michael Moore. 2000. *Educating Oneself in Public: Critical Essays in Jurisprudence*, 247–93. Oxford: Oxford University Press.

Moore, Michael. 1987b. 'Precedent, Induction, and Ethical Generalization'. In *Precedent in Law*, edited by Laurence Goldstein, 183–213. Oxford: Oxford University Press.

Moore, Michael. 1989a. 'Do We Have an Unwritten Constitution?' *Southern California Law Review* 63(1): 107–39.

Moore, Michael. 1989b. 'The Interpretive Turn: A Turn for the Worse?' *Stanford Law Review* 41(4): 871–957. Reprinted in Michael Moore. 2000. *Educating Oneself in Public: Critical Essays in Jurisprudence*, 335–423. Oxford: Oxford University Press.

Moore, Michael. 1992a. 'Moral Reality Revisited'. *Michigan Law Review* 90(8): 2424–533. Reprinted in Michael Moore. 2004. *Objectivity in Ethics and Law*, 99–208. Aldershot: Ashgate Publishing.

Moore, Michael. 1992b. 'Law as a Functional Kind'. In *Natural Law Theories*, edited by Robert George, 188–242. Oxford: Oxford University Press. Reprinted in Michael Moore. 2000. *Educating Oneself in Public: Critical Essays in Jurisprudence*, 294–332. Oxford: Oxford University Press.

Moore, Michael. 1993. *Act and Crime: The Philosophy of Action and its Implications for Criminal Law*. Oxford: Clarendon Press.

Moore, Michael. 1998. 'Hart's Concluding Scientific Postscript'. *Legal Theory* 4(3): 301–27. Reprinted in and cited from Michael Moore. 2000. *Educating Oneself in Public: Critical Essays in Jurisprudence*, 79–107. Oxford: Oxford University Press.

Moore, Michael. 2000. *Educating Oneself in Public: Critical Essays in Jurisprudence*. Oxford: Oxford University Press.

Moore, Michael. 2001. 'Justifying the Natural Law Theory of Constitutional Interpretation'. *Fordham Law Review* 69(5): 2087–117.

Moore, Michael. 2003a. 'The Plain Truth About Legal Truth'. *Harvard Journal of Law and Public Policy* 26(1): 23–47. Reprinted in Michael Moore. 2004. *Objectivity in Ethics and Law*, 293–317. Aldershot: Ashgate Publishing.

Moore, Michael. 2003b. 'Legal Reality: A Naturalist Approach to Legal Ontology'. *Law and Philosophy* 21(6): 619–705. Reprinted in Michael Moore. 2004. *Objectivity in Ethics and Law*, 319–405. Aldershot: Ashgate Publishing.

Moore, Michael. 2003c. 'The Destruction of the Twin Towers and the Law on Event-Identity'. In *Agency and Action,* edited by John Hyland and Helen Steward, 259–342. Cambridge: Cambridge University Press.

Michael Moore. 2004. *Objectivity in Ethics and Law*. Aldershot: Ashgate Publishing.

Moore, Michael. 2009. *Causation and Responsibility*. Oxford: Oxford University Press.

Platts, Mark. 1979. *Ways of Meaning*. London: Routledge.

Putnam, Hilary. 1962. 'Dreaming and "Depth Grammar"'. In *Analytic Philosophy: First Series,* edited by Ronald J. Butler, 211–35. Oxford: Oxford University Press.

Putnam, Hilary. 1975. 'The Meaning of "Meaning"'. In *Language, Mind, and Knowing,* edited by Keith Gunderson, 131–93. Minneapolis: University of Minnesota Press.

Quine, Willard Van Orman. 1960. *Word and Object*. Cambridge (MA): MIT Press.

Raz, Joseph. 1979. '"Legal Reasons, Sources, and Gaps'. In *The Authority of Law*, 53–77. Oxford: Oxford University Press.

Rorty, Richard. 1973. 'Criteria and Necessity'. *Noûs* 7(4): 313–29.

Ryle, Gilbert. 1949. *The Concept of Mind*. London: Hutcheson.

Simchen, Ori. 2007. 'Metasemantics and Objectivity'. In *Law: Metaphysics, Meaning, and Objectivity*, edited by Enrique Villanueva, 215–34. Amsterdam: Rodopi.

Soames, Scott. 2002. *Beyond Rigidity: The Unfinished Semantic Agenda of Naming and Necessity*. Oxford: Oxford University Press.

Soames, Scott. 2009. 'Interpreting Legal Texts: What Is, and What Is Not, Special about the Law'. In *Philosophical Essays, Vol. I*, 401–24. Princeton: Princeton University Press.

Soames, Scott. 2010. *Philosophy of Language*. Princeton: Princeton University Press.

Stavropoulos, Nicos. 1996. *Objectivity in Law*. Oxford: Clarendon Press.

Waldron, Jeremy. 1992. 'The Irrelevance of Moral Objectivity'. In *Natural Law Theories*, edited by Robert George, 158–87. Oxford: Oxford University Press.

Wellmann, Carl. 1962. 'Wittgenstein's Conception of the Criterion'. *The Philosophical Review* 71(4): 433–47.

West, Robin. 1990. 'The Supreme Court 1989 Term. Foreword: Taking Freedom Seriously'. *Harvard Law Review* 104(1), 43–106.

Wittgenstein, Ludwig. 1958. *Philosophical Investigations*. Translated by G.E.M. Anscombe. Oxford: Blackwell.

PART II

VAGUENESS
PHENOMENA IN LAW

6

Pragmatic Vagueness in Statutory Law

Andrei Marmor

There has been a growing awareness among philosophers of language and linguists that the content communicated by a speaker on an occasion of speech is often, perhaps most often in ordinary conversations, under-determined by the semantic content of the expression uttered. What a speaker communicates is often the pragmatically enriched content that the speaker intended to convey and hearers can recognize as such. Thus, quite normally, when the hearer grasps the content communicated by an utterance, the uptake is a result of a defeasible inference drawn by the hearer from the meaning of the sentence uttered (semantics and syntax), some contextual background that is common knowledge between speaker and hearers, and some normative framework that governs the conversational situation.[1] In this chapter, however, I want to focus on the opposite type of cases, where contextual background actually muddles the communicated content, making things less, rather than more, clear. There are some interesting cases, I will argue, in which an expression uttered by a speaker, that would normally be clear or specific enough, becomes less clear due to a certain pragmatic factor that obtains in the particular context of the conversation. And I will argue that this happens in law, quite frequently, and in ways that make the interpretation of statutory law difficult, in fact, sometimes intractable from a linguistic perspective. I will label such cases as instances of *pragmatic vagueness*. By the label, however, I do not mean to suggest that pragmatic vagueness mirrors standard semantic vagueness, or even that the two types of vagueness are very similar; they are similar in some respects but not others.

1.

There are two main kinds of factors that together constitute the pragmatic or contextual background of a speech act: certain relevant facts that are common

---

[1] For various purposes, it has proved convenient to distinguish between what is said by an utterance in a given occasion of speech, and what might also be implicated (or presupposed) by it. It is widely accepted, however, that asserted content, what the speaker says on an occasion of speech, is also frequently pragmatically enriched content. I elaborated on this issue, and its applications to the legal context, in Marmor 2014, ch. 1. For the purposes of this chapter, the distinction between what is said and what is implicated is not going to be important.

Pragmatic Vagueness in Statutory Law. First Edition. Andrei Marmor. © Andrei Marmor 2016. Published 2016 by Oxford University Press.

knowledge between speaker and hearer, and a normative framework that determines what kind of linguistic behaviour we can expect from speakers (and hearers) in the context of the speech act in question. The contextual facts that are relevant to pragmatic enrichment can be specific to the conversation in question, sometimes gathered from previous stages of the conversation, or they can be facts of a general nature, presumed to be widely known. Either way, the idea of context has to be understood epistemically. The context of an utterance consists of elements that the speaker assumes to be known or taken for granted by the hearer and known by the hearer to be known or assumed by the speaker. In addition to the factual context, however, there is also some normative framework in place, depending on the kind of conversation in play. If the conversation is essentially cooperative, like a truthful exchange of information, then the familiar Gricean maxims of conversation apply, such as the maxims of relevance and quantity. If the conversational context is different, other maxims may be in play.[2] Either way, the contextual background must include some normative assumptions about ways in which speakers and hearers are expected to behave, and common knowledge of certain facts that are relevant to the conversation. Together, these factors constitute the contextual or pragmatic background of the conversation in question.

There are probably two main types of cases that generate pragmatic vagueness. One type of case where contextual knowledge generates pragmatic vagueness concerns situations in which an utterance's presumed or implicated content is muddled or contradicted by a salient fact that obtains in the context of the utterance. The tragic incident of the charge of the Light Brigade during the Crimean War is probably the most famous case of this kind in history. On 25 October 1854, during one of the battles in the Crimean War, the British army commander, Lord Raglan, sought his light cavalry unit, the Light Brigade, to chase down a Russian force retreating with some captured British guns. His order was 'Advance rapidly to the front, follow the enemy, and try to prevent the enemy carrying away the guns . . .'. Clearly Raglan meant to refer to the British guns captured earlier in the battle. However, the commander of the cavalry, Lt General Lucan, positioned elsewhere in the battlefield, could see several different Russian forces carrying guns; and he had no idea that one of them, an easy target of attack for his forces, carried away British guns. Tragically, Lucan assumed that the order referred to the Russian forces just about a mile ahead of him,[3] down the causeway, and charged ahead into the valley, where his forces suffered very heavy casualties. Historians never accused Lucan of a silly mistake; from his vantage point, and without the knowledge of the earlier incident of the

---

[2] In Marmor 2014, ch. 2, I explained this point in greater detail, arguing that the strategic nature of legal conversation makes the Gricean maxims much less secure, particularly in the context of statutory interpretation. The strategic nature of legal conversation will not be brought to bear on the discussion in this chapter.

[3] In fact, Lucan sought some clarification from the messenger, Captain Nolan, but Nolan only raised his hands in a vague gesture, leaving it to the commander of the Light Brigade to figure out what Lord Raglan meant.

British guns, Lucan was right to assume that his orders were to charge down into the valley; it was the most salient option. (Why he decided to follow that order is less clear.) In the popular press at the time, and in many historical accounts, Lord Raglan comes out of this tragic incident as the commander accused of giving inadequately worded orders.[4] But, at least from a linguistic perspective, there was nothing wrong with Raglan's order. From his vantage point on the battlefield, it would have seemed obvious which Russian forces he wanted the Light Brigade to attack. Unfortunately, it happened to be the reverse from the vantage point of Lucan; the salient option for him looked very different. The vagueness here was pragmatic, entirely due to the discrepancy in the factual circumstances presumed between speaker and hearer.

Needless to say, most instances of pragmatic vagueness are much less dramatic. Thus, consider the following examples:

1. 'It was Jane who broke the vase.'
Presupposition: the vase spoken about is broken and somebody has broken it.
Context: there is only one vase in the vicinity and it is not broken.
2. 'All the Republicans and Senator McCain voted against the bill.'
Presupposition/implication: Senator McCain is not a Republican.
Context: Senator McCain is a Republican.
3. 'John and Mary went to Paris last summer.'
Implication: they went to Paris together.
Context: John and Mary are divorced and have not spoken to each other in years.

What clearly happens in such cases is that context makes it actually more difficult for the hearer to infer the content that the speaker intended to convey. When somebody utters (1), pointing to a vase that seems to be in perfect shape, the hearer is likely to be confused; and not because there is some semantic indeterminacy in the expression uttered. The sentence is clear enough, and so is the presupposition of its utterance; the problem is that the presupposition is contradicted by what seems to be the relevant fact. And the same goes for (2) and (3). Now, of course, it is possible to imagine a completion of the contextual background in such cases in ways that would make it easy for the hearer to grasp the communication intention of the speaker. We can imagine a conversation, for example, in which (3) is uttered as part of a conversation suggesting that perhaps after years of separation John and Mary are getting together again; and we can imagine a context in which the utterance of (2) makes perfect sense, given the common knowledge that Senator McCain was expected to break rank with his Republican fellows and vote for the bill. Absent such completions, however, when no such additional facts are

---

[4] There are countless historical accounts of this tragic blunder, partly made famous by Tennyson's poem. Many of these accounts, contemporaneous and later, were coloured by the widely held perception that Raglan was an utterly incompetent military commander. Indeed he was, and there is little doubt that he was utterly negligent in this case as well. But the facts were more complicated; nobody knows, e.g., why Nolan was so evasive in his response to Lucan (he died in the battle) or why Lucan decided to follow Raglan's order; such orders were frequently ignored during the Crimean war. For a recent account, see e.g. Figes 2010.

known to the hearer, the fact that contradicts some content that is clearly implicated or presupposed by the expression uttered is going to generate some doubt or confusion. The hearer will be left wondering what is it that the speaker really wanted to convey. Notice, however, that in such cases there is nothing semantically amiss, indeterminate, or vague; the vagueness, if we can call it that, is generated by context.

The second type of cases in which we get pragmatic vagueness concerns borderline applications of maxims of conversation. In ordinary conversations we assume that parties are essentially cooperative; as Grice famously showed, a cooperative framework of conversation, particularly when parties are supposed to be engaged in a truthful exchange of information, entails certain norms or maxims that speakers and hearers are presumed to follow, such as the maxims or relevance, truthfulness and quantity (Grice 1989, p. 28). Generally speaking, the hearer's ability to infer the communicated content of an utterance in a given occasion of speech crucially depends on the maxims that are presumed to apply. The problem that generates pragmatic vagueness stems from cases in which it is not entirely clear, from the context of the conversation that is common knowledge between speaker and hearer, whether the relevant maxim has been adhered to or not. Consider the following examples:

   4. 'It is not raining.'
   Context: it is a beautiful sunny day outside (relevance).
   5. 'The meal was delicious.'
   Context: uttered by a guest to the host of a dinner party (truthfulness).
   6. 'All men who are mortal end up paying taxes.'
   Context: all men are mortal (quantity).

The utterance of a sentence like (4), under normal conditions, would typically aim to convey the information that it is not raining here now, where and when we speak. Of course we can think of various contexts of conversation where (4) is not meant to be about the here and now. But let us assume that there is nothing in the background of the conversation in our example that would indicate such an option. The speaker just looks outside the window and utters (4), although it is a beautiful sunny day, in midsummer, with not a cloud in the horizon. The result is that the hearer will be left wondering about the relevance of the utterance; how does it contribute some relevant information to the conversational background, when the fact is that nobody would have thought otherwise? There is some content here left hanging in the air, in need of completion or clarification.

The situation is somewhat different in a context like (5). What hangs in the air here is the question of whether the speaker adheres to the maxim of quality (don't say something that you know to be false). Waiters often come to your table in the middle of the dinner asking whether you like the food; they are not really interested in the truth, presumably. Mostly, they just want to be polite. But, of course, by asking they give you the option of telling the truth, and therefore it is generally not entirely clear whether you do so or not. When you tell the host of your dinner party that the food was delicious, you may just be polite, as you should be, but you may also mean what you say. It is not always clear, and often for a good reason. It is the nature of such conversations that the commitment to the truth of what you say is somewhat unclear, and purposefully so. If the hearer is totally uninterested in your opinion, she would not have bothered to ask, or so we often assume. On the other hand, given the context of the conversation, you are not necessarily expected to be entirely truthful either. The application of the maxim of quantity in such context is deliberately left hanging in the air, not clearly applying and not clearly flouted either.[5]

The expression of (6) relates to the maxim of quantity. If somebody asserts something like 'All X's that are F...', the implication is that, at least for all the speaker knows, there might be an X that is not F. If the speaker knows, and assumes his hearers to know, that all Xs are necessarily or inevitably F, he would have expressed too weak a proposition; he would have said too little, as it were. Now, since we all know that men are mortal, the expression of something like (6) is likely to make the hearer assume that there is some point in stating the obvious, some content that the speaker intended to convey, beyond the content actually asserted by the expression. But it would be somewhat unclear what that content is. Once again, such expressions leave some content hanging in the air, that the hearer may or may not be able to figure out, depending on many other factors.

These two types of cases in which pragmatic vagueness is generated by contextual factors are not meant to be exhaustive, of course. But they will do for our purposes. It is important to see, however, how they relate to, and how they differ from, ordinary semantic vagueness. The ordinary, semantic, sense of vagueness concerns the relation between the meaning of a word in a natural language and the objects that the word designates or picks out. The simple idea is that with most words we use in a natural language, there is a set of objects the word clearly designates, objects about which there is no doubt that the word applies (definite extension); there are innumerable objects to which the word clearly does not apply (definite non-extension); and then there are borderline cases in between, objects about which there is no saying, as it were, whether the word applies or not. In other words, between the definite extension of the word and its definite non-extension, there is a range of borderline cases that, at least from a semantic perspective, can be classified either way; if an object, O_i, is in this borderline zone of a word W, it would not be a semantic error to say that O_i is W, nor would it be a mistake to say that it is not. Furthermore, and this is what generates the famous sorites paradox, there is no saying where exactly the borderline cases begin and where they end. The border between the definite extension of a word and its borderline applications is

---

[5] An alternative explanation here might be that what is not clear is the nature of the utterance: is it a statement, aiming to convey some propositional content, or a conventional performative, like, e.g., saying 'Good morning'; the speaker is not stating that the morning is good. The expression of 'Good morning' is meant as a linguistic move in a conventional practice, expressing recognition of the convention and compliance with it. It is not truth-apt. So perhaps saying 'The food was delicious', in some contexts, is just a conventional performative, like 'Good morning' (see Marmor 2009, pp. 118–30).

inherently fuzzy.[6] Take, for example, a colour word, like 'blue'. Now suppose that you pick a can of blue paint, clearly and undeniably blue, if anything is, and then start adding tiny drops of white to the colour. At some point the blue will become so light-blue that it may no longer be clear that the colour is blue at all; you will reach some borderline cases of blue. But the problem is that we cannot tell where exactly that borderline colour begins; between the definite extension of the word and its range of borderline cases, there is no clear cut-off point. And this, of course, is what generates the sorites paradox.

All this characterization of semantic vagueness is superficial; it is how vagueness of words in a natural language appears to us. Philosophers have different views about the underlying explanation of this linguistic phenomenon, arguing for different views about the deeper aspects of vagueness and its underlying logic. The pressure for deep theories comes from the sorites paradox; if there is a way to avoid a logical paradox, we should look for it. But this is not what I aim to explore here. My point is to emphasize two ways in which pragmatic vagueness would seem to differ from semantic vagueness, at least on the surface. First, in the pragmatic sense, we don't necessarily get anything like a sorites sequence. If an expression is pragmatically vague about the content it conveys in a context of its utterance, it just means that some content is up in the air, perhaps neither here nor there, but it does not mean that we have some possible sequence of moving from clearer to less clear specifications of the communicated content. Sometimes we might; if the pragmatic vagueness is generated by some doubts about the maxim of relevance, for instance, then we may get some sequence, from interpretations that are more to less relevant to the conversational context. But this is not the usual type of case, as the examples of (1)–(6) above demonstrate.

The second possible difference between the pragmatic and the semantic sense of vagueness concerns the relevance of truth: with the exception of epistemic theories of vagueness, most conceptions of the semantic phenomenon admit that there is no truth of the matter about the question of whether a borderline case of a vague term is within the extension of the word or not. Semantically, it can go either way, and we have no sense of what could possibly make one answer true and another false. There are two familiar versions of this. According to the first one, it is widely conceded that borderline cases are inquiry resistant: if there is a question about whether W applies to a borderline case, there is nothing we can come to know that would possibly settle the question. Even if there is a truth of the matter about it, as epistemic theories maintain, they admit that this truth is not knowable. The second, and more common view is that there is nothing to know here because there is no truth of the matter about it.[7]

---

[6] In the literature this is sometimes called second-order vagueness (*viz.*, vagueness about where borderline cases begin and end). Since I doubt that there is any genuine issue of hierarchy here, I think it's better to avoid this expression.

[7] The main argument for an epistemic theory of vagueness is in Williamson 1994; for a non-epistemic account applied to law, see e.g. Soames 2012.

The phenomenon of pragmatic vagueness might seem to be very different in this respect. Since it is a pragmatic issue to begin with, we do have a clear criterion of success, and therefore a pretty clear sense of what would make one precisification true and others false. If you think about communicated content as the kind of content that the speaker intended to convey, and the hearer is supposed to grasp, then we do seem to have a clear answer to the question of what would be the truth of the matter in cases of doubt: the truth would entirely depend on what the speaker actually intended to communicate. Perhaps we may have doubts about what that content is, given the pragmatic uncertainty that is generated by the contextual factors in play, but at least we know what would count as true and what would count as false. Anything that the speaker actually intended to say or to implicate is the truth about what the utterance says or implicates in the context of its expression, and otherwise, if it is not what the speaker intended, it is false that the content forms part of what is said or implicated. This, at least, is how Griceans would have it. But I think that they would be wrong.

It is very important not to conflate two distinct questions here: 'What are the *criteria of success* for an act of communication?' and 'What is *the content that has actually been communicated* on an occasion of speech?' It is very plausible to assume that an act of communication (fully) succeeds when, and only when, the hearer has fully grasped the content that the speaker intended to convey by his or her utterance. In this sense, it is clearly true that the criteria of success for an act of communication are reducible to the relation between the content that the speaker intended to convey and the hearer's actual uptake. Therefore, even in case of doubt, we can say that there is a truth of the matter about success or failure, determined by facts about communication intentions and hearer's uptake. But things look differently when you focus on the question of what is it that the speaker has actually managed to communicate. Here, the question itself presupposes some objective standpoint. We are simply not asking what it is that the speaker intended to convey, but what it is that he actually did; what was it that was said and/or implicated by the speaker's utterance in a given context of speech? In answer to this question, we cannot rely exclusively on the intentions of the speaker, because speakers may fail to communicate what they had intended to; and we cannot rely on the actual uptake of the hearer for the same reason: that hearers may fail, on particular occasions, to register what they should have inferred from the utterance in the relevant context. In other words, the question itself presupposes that we have in mind some objectified sense of uptake. What is actually said and/or implicated by an utterance in a given context of speech is determined by reasonable uptake: what is the content that a reasonable hearer, knowing all the relevant contextual background of the utterance, would have inferred from what was uttered in that context? Under normal circumstances, if the communication was successful, then a reasonable hearer would have inferred exactly what the speaker intended to convey. But this is only the limiting case; things might turn out differently on actual occasions.[8]

Now, the relevant point is that if the question we ask is about the communicated content, understood objectively, then we might have cases in which there is no truth of the matter about it. Consider a case like (5), where the speaker tells the waiter in the restaurant that 'the meal is delicious', in response to the waiter's question; it is possible, of course, that the speaker intended to convey exactly what she said, namely, that she finds the meal delicious. But it is also possible that she just wanted to sound polite, or was busy in her conversation with her partner and couldn't be bothered to think about it, or such. Whatever her communication intentions were, we can come up with an answer to the question of success or failure; whatever she intended to convey she would have succeeded to convey iff the waiter fully grasped her intentions. But now suppose that the question is different: we want to know what is it that the patron actually communicated, objectively speaking, by her utterance? What did she really say and/or implicate? I submit that under the circumstances, there may not be a truth of the matter about it; we don't quite know, because there is nothing to know here. The expression was pragmatically vague, it could be understood as a sincere expression of appreciation, or mostly as a polite hand waving, or anything in between, and there is just no saying, as it were, which one of these is true. And that is so, simply because there is no truth of the matter about it. And notice that this might be the case regardless of the speaker's actual communication intentions, or the hearer's uptake.

Similarly, consider cases in which the content of an utterance, explicit or implied, is obviously contradicted by a salient contextual factor. Consider, for example, the utterance of (2), where there is no previous background suggesting that Senator McCain was widely expected to break rank with his Republican fellows on the particular vote in question. So, somebody just says, 'All the Republicans and Senator McCain voted against the bill.' Clearly, a reasonable hearer would be left wondering: 'Does the speaker not know that McCain is also a Republican? Was there something in the context that he missed? Was the utterance expressed ironically?' Now, of course, it is quite possible that there is an answer to the question of which one of these options (or some other) the speaker intended; he may have assumed that the context would make it clear, or he may have thought that there is enough information here for the hearer to grasp that he meant what he said ironically, or any other such option. But the fact is that there just might not be enough information for any reasonable hearer to conclude which one it is. Thus, from an objective standpoint, there might not be a truth of the matter about what exactly is said or implicated by the utterance in the particular context of the conversation. Let me call such cases *genuinely indeterminate*.

---

[8] I defended an objective conception of asserted content in Marmor 2014, chs 1 and 5. It may be worth mentioning that implicatures are usually described in terms of a speaker's *commitment* to some communicated content, and commitment also indicates an objective standpoint.

Practically speaking, in ordinary conversations, such problems rarely persist. Hearers can ask, and speakers can clarify, what is it that they had meant to say. And then we would have a new utterance with newly communicated content that takes over the previous one. But we aim to get to the legal context, and one of the main problems there is that legislation is not an ordinary conversation; judges don't get to ask, and legislatures don't get to clarify, what it is that they really wanted to convey in cases of doubt. In fact, as I will show with some examples, the legislature may actually not know how to answer such a question; there is no fact of the matter about it even from its own intentional perspective. More on this a little later.

2.

As we noted in section 1, we have a pretty good sense of what constitutes success or failure of an act of communication: an act of communication fully succeeds when the hearer has fully grasped the communication intentions of the speaker. There is no reason to assume that the criteria of success would be different in law. Legislatures aim to communicate certain contents that they intend to be grasped by the relevant hearers; and if hearers fully grasp the relevant legal content, the act of communication succeeds. It is equally clear, however, that legal cases don't tend to make it to the courts, especially appellate courts, when legislative communication succeeded. Cases come before the courts, in need of interpretation, in cases of some failure. Generally speaking, the need for statutory interpretation arises in two main types of cases: sometimes the law itself, the legal content of an act, is clear enough, but it does not quite answer the legal question the court faces; we know exactly what the law says, but what the law says (and implicates, etc.) doesn't quite settle the particular case at hand. I will largely ignore such cases, focusing on the second main type of cases, probably much more prevalent anyway, where there is some doubt about what exactly the law says or implicates. My point is to show that just as there are cases in which legislative content is semantically genuinely indeterminate, there are also cases in which statutory interpretation faces cases in which the statutory content is pragmatically genuinely indeterminate.

Let me emphasize, however, that genuine linguistic indeterminacy, whether semantic or pragmatic, does not necessarily entail that courts have no good reason to decide the case one way rather than another. Courts need to make reasoned decisions, and the reasons in play are not exclusively linguistic. There are many kinds of reasons bearing on the resolution of a legal dispute, and sometimes those reasons are determinate enough, even if the relevant statute in play is linguistically genuinely indeterminate. A nice case in point is *Garner v. Burr*: the British Road Traffic Act of 1930 stipulated that any 'vehicle' traveling on a public highway must be fitted with pneumatic tyres. Mr Burr fitted a poultry shed with iron wheels and pulled it with his tractor on a stretch of a highway. The court of appeals reasoned, quite sensibly, that even if a poultry shed fitted on wheels is a borderline case of 'vehicle', it counts as a vehicle for the purposes of the law, because the manifest purpose of the law requiring pneumatic tyres is simply to prevent damage to the asphalt roads.[9] The *Burr* case is about semantic vagueness, of course; from a semantic perspective, the question of whether a poultry shed fitted on wheels is a 'vehicle' or not is genuinely indeterminate; there is no truth of the matter about it (or, if you insist, there is a truth about it which is unknowable). However, as the *Burr* case shows, linguistic indeterminacy does not entail indeterminacy all things considered. And the kind of things that can and should be considered by courts in deciding such cases are numerous, though admittedly, often contentious. In this case, the court reasoned from presumed legislative purposes; it reasoned that the purpose of the legislation is clear enough, and it determines the case one way rather than another. This strikes me as a very sensible approach, but it is not part of my argument in this chapter to have any views about the kind of considerations that should be brought to bear on decisions of this kind; I am not going to suggest any particular interpretive method to deal with cases of linguistic indeterminacy. My aim is only to show that there are cases that exhibit pragmatic vagueness and thus are genuinely indeterminate from a pragmatic perspective.

Another clarification might be helpful before we proceed. In ordinary conversations, particularly when parties to the conversation aim at a truthful exchange of information, hearers are typically more interested in what the speaker intended to convey than what the speaker actually said or implicated, objectively speaking. Think about cases in which a hearer can reasonably say to the speaker: 'You may have intended to say that X, but what you actually said is Y.' This happens, sometimes; but in ordinary conversations we let it pass. We would normally register what the speaker intended to convey, even if it is not exactly what the speaker asserted (or implicated or such). If my wife tells me 'Shut that window please', but I know that she actually meant the door, not the window, I would go and shut the door. But in the legal case, this might be quite different. There is a normative question here about the relations between courts and legislatures: on one possible view, the courts should be interested in what the legislature intended to convey, even if what the legislature actually asserted (and implicated) is not quite what it wanted to assert. According to an opposite view, the only relevant content enacted by a piece of legislation, legally speaking, is the content that the legislature actually asserted or implicated, even if it failed to say exactly what it intended. Textualists are famous for holding this latter view, and not implausibly, I must say (Marmor 2014, ch. 5). At least from a linguistic perspective, and that's the only one I want to focus on here, it is very plausible to hold the view that the legal content of an act is the content actually asserted by it, objectively speaking, that is. Now again, this is a view about legal content, not about the all things considered reasons that judges need to exercise in their decisions. Let me give an example to clarify this point. In the case of *Whiteley v. Chappell*, the relevant statute made it an offence to fraudulently 'personate any

---

[9] *Garner v. Burr* [1951] 1 KB 31. The case is discussed in Endicott 2014 and in Carston 2013, pp. 20–1.

person entitled to vote'.[10] The defendant had fraudulently voted in the name of his neighbour, whose name was on the voter rolls, but who also happened to be dead by then. There is little doubt that the purpose of the law was to make it an offence to vote fraudulently by impersonating anyone else, and the defendant's conduct is precisely the kind that should have been covered by the definition of this offence. Alas, the law was badly formulated, making it an offence to impersonate only those who are 'entitled to vote'. Dead people do not fall into this category; they are not 'entitled to vote'. The court therefore concluded that the defendant's conduct did not fall within the bounds of the criminal offence. From a linguistic perspective, this seems quite right. Whether the court should have chosen to ignore what the law actually *says* in favour of deferring to what the lawmakers may have intended to say, or perhaps what it is that they should have said given their purposes in enacting this law, is a separate, normative question I will not purport to answer here.

3.

It is, at long last, time to consider some examples of what I take to be instances of pragmatic vagueness in statutory law.[11] Consider the famous case of *FDA v. Brown & Williamson Tobacco Corp*, decided by the U.S. Supreme Court in 2000.[12] The litigation concerned the question of whether the Federal Drug Administration (FDA) has the legal authority to regulate tobacco products. The background of this case is rather complex. The FDA was reshaped by Congress in 1965 in the amendment to the Food, Drug and Cosmetic Act of 1938 (FDCA), giving the federal agency the authority to regulate, in the relevant section, any 'articles (other than food) intended to affect the structure or any function of the body'. Needless to say, in the 1930s (or even the 1960s, for that matter), nobody thought that tobacco products would fall within the ambit of the FDA's regulatory authority. And indeed, for decades, the FDA has explicitly declined to assert any authority to regulate tobacco products. This changed in 1996, when the newly appointed director of the FDA, backed by the Clinton administration, changed course and declared that the FDA does have such authority granted to it by the original FDCA.[13] However, the FDA faced a serious problem here. Other sections of the FDCA made it clear that if tobacco products fall within the ambit of its regulatory authority, the FDA may have no choice but to prohibit the sale of tobacco products entirely. That is so because the FDCA created two separate regulatory schemes for products (other than foods and cosmetics) that purport to have some medicinal benefits and those that do not. If a product is claimed by its manufacturer to have some medicinal

[10] L.R. 4 Q.B. 147 (1868).
[11] The cases discussed here are also analysed, in a separate paper, in the context of defeasibility in law (see Capone and Poggi 2016).
[12] 529 U.S. 120 (2000).
[13] For an historical account of the facts and circumstances that brought about this litigation, see Ruger 2011.

benefit, the FDA needs to conduct a series of hearings, based on scientific research, to determine whether to approve the product or not. However, if the manufacturer does not claim any medicinal benefit with respect to a given product, which is clearly the case with tobacco products, and the product proves to be harmful, the FDA must prohibit its sale. Obviously, the FDA wanted to avoid this legal result, and argued in its briefs that it has legal ways to avoid banning the sale of tobacco entirely, even if regulation of tobacco products falls within its jurisdiction and it is found to be harmful. The argument about this particular point was rather ingenious, but a bit too much so; the courts did not buy it, and proceeded to examine the legal question here with the assumption that if they find the FDA to have the authority to regulate tobacco products, the FDA may have little choice but to prohibit their sale altogether.

So far, so good; it seems to be an easy case, at least from a linguistic perspective. The relevant section of the law gives the FDA a very wide authority to regulate any product that is 'intended to affect the structure or any function of the body'. Surely cigarettes and other tobacco products fall within the extension of this expression. Tobacco products certainly intend to 'affect the function of the body'; it's what they are made to do. But keep in mind that the complete legislative content here is more complex, as it goes something like this: if a product has quality X, the FDA has the authority to regulate it; and if the product has qualities X and Y (Y = harmful) but not Z (Z = intended for medicinal use), then the FDA must prohibit its sale to the public. Since it is not disputed here that tobacco products have the quality Y and not Z, the conclusion is that the FDA must prohibit their sale; that is, if it is found that tobacco products fall within the definition of X.

Now here is an additional fact about the context: over the years, between 1965 and 1996, Congress enacted six pieces of legislation explicitly regulating the sale and particularly the advertisement of tobacco products. These laws imposed various restrictions on the ways in which cigarettes and other tobacco products can be sold, prohibiting their sale to minors, restricting advertisement, and imposing various labelling requirements. Now evidently, all these laws implicate that the sale of tobacco products, albeit restricted, is not illegal. If Congress says that you can only sell a product X if it is labelled as Y, it clearly implicates that if the product is labelled as Y you may go ahead and sell it. Or if Congress says that you may not sell X to minors, it clearly implicates that you are allowed to sell X to adults. So here is what we get here, at least if we are willing to regard the various acts of Congress an 'overall statutory scheme', to use the court's expression: we get implications of one set of laws contradicted by explicit denials of another set.

Now, you may worry that I make the mistake of ignoring the time sequence of the various pieces of legislation here. On the contrary, the time sequence only makes the problem of pragmatic vagueness more evident. Suppose, for the sake of the argument, that there is no doubt that the original FDCA, from 1965, actually asserts—regardless of what Congress may or may not have intended—that tobacco products fall within the jurisdiction of the FDA; and consequently, due to other parts of the statute, and the fact that tobacco products are undeniably harmful, it follows that the FDA must ban their sale. So far, so good, at least until subsequent

legislation comes along. Now it is a widely accepted principle of democratic legislation that Congress has the authority to amend its previous laws. Therefore, the
real question here is whether the later pieces of legislation, regulating the sale of
tobacco products, actually withdrew the putative authority of the FDA to ban
tobacco products or not. Remember that these later pieces of legislation, six of
them, clearly implicate, even if they don't quite say so, that the sale of tobacco
products is legal. In my view, there is no answer to this question; it is pragmatically
genuinely indeterminate. Why is that? Mostly because the contextual background
of these later pieces of legislation is muddled; when they were enacted, the FDA
did not claim authority to regulate tobacco products and nobody really assumed
that the FDCA grants the FDA the authority to regulate tobacco, and therefore to
ban their sale. The authority is claimed here *ex post facto*, as it were; which means
that the legislature cannot be said to have altered the original authority of the FDA
by subsequent legislation because they could not have been taken to assume that
there was such an authority to begin with (although, at some points, some legislators may well have suspected that to be the case).[14] In other words, we do not have
clear criteria of relevance here. Whether the subsequent legislation, implicating the
legality of tobacco sales, is relevant to the FDA authority is neither here nor there;
pragmatically speaking, the relevance of the implicated content of the later pieces
of legislation is indeterminate. And hence it is indeterminate whether the authority
of the FDA to regulate tobacco products has been withdrawn or not, which is the
relevant legal question here.

A linguistically similar, though factually much simpler case is *West Virginia
University Hospitals v. Casey*.[15] This is one of the textbook cases for textualism in
action, where Justice Scalia, writing for the court's majority opinion, reasoned to
the decision on linguistic grounds. *Casey* stems from a civil suit filed by the Hospital
of West Virginia University against the Medicaid system adopted by the state of
Pennsylvania, concerning remuneration of Medicaid costs for out-of-state services,
which, the Hospital claimed, was in violation of Federal and Constitutional law.
The Hospital prevailed at the trial court and pursuant to the provision of a federal statute was awarded the cost of its attorney's fees, which included the cost of
expert fees paid by the attorneys to their non-legal experts. The case went to the
Supreme Court only on this last point: the defendant argued that expert fees are not
included within the expression of the federal statute allowing the court to award 'a
reasonable attorney's fee'. The experts are not attorneys. Justice Scalia agreed, but
not because the ordinary meaning of the expression under consideration would
naturally exclude the cost of experts to the attorney's in question. It is pretty clear
from the decision that none of the justices on the Supreme Court thought that
the matter can be settled by simply looking at the semantic content of the relevant

---

[14] In fact, we know that the situation was very unclear because over the years there were several
attempts to amend the FDCA by both camps; there were attempts to grant the FDA explicit authority
to regulate tobacco and attempts to deny such authority, and both types of amendments failed to gain
the requisite majority in Congress.
[15] 499 U.S. 83 (1991).

expression here. Interestingly, Scalia's argument was based on pragmatics: it was based on the fact that in many other acts of congress (though not all of them) awarding attorney's fees to a prevailing party in a civil litigation, the act explicitly mentions attorney's fees *and* expert witness fees. *Ergo*, if Congress chose to use only the expression 'attorney's fees' without the addition of expert fees, the latter were meant to be excluded.

So far, so good; the pragmatic inference sounds very reasonable. But, as the dissenting opinion made clear, this pragmatic inference ignores the fact that Congress clearly 'intended to make prevailing plaintiffs whole'. There is, indeed, a great deal in the context of such legislation to suggest that the simple purpose of the legislative provision was to make sure that a plaintiff in a civil law suit who prevails in trial could recover its reasonable litigation costs from the losing party. And of course, it is widely known that litigation costs often include much more than the fees paid to the attorneys; attorneys often employ various experts in the service of the litigation. Evidently, there are two possible interpretations of the circumstances of the legislation here: one possible scenario is that the statutory provision was poorly drafted; Congress probably intended to shift attorney's fees broadly understood and the drafters just forgot, or were not aware of the fact, that in other pieces of legislation the expression included an explicit reference to expert fees as well. The second scenario is the one Scalia attributed to the legislature, namely the communication intention to exclude expert fees in this case.

Now, *ex post facto*, there is evidence to suggest that it is the first scenario that was closer to the truth, because Congress swiftly enacted an amendment to the act, overruling the decision in *Casey*. It is this possibility that I want to focus on. Suppose, therefore, that the facts were as suggested by the dissent, namely, that Congress simply erred, and forgot, as it were, that other pieces of legislation mention expert fees explicitly. Does it necessarily follow that the act, in this case, actually says or implicates that expert fees are included? I don't think so. If we ask this question from the objective standpoint, of what is it that a reasonable hearer, knowing all the relevant overt circumstances of the enactment, including the previous relevant legislative language, would have inferred about the content of the law, my sense is that there is no determinate answer; it is an instance of pragmatic vagueness. From a linguistic perspective, concerning the question of what it is that the speaker says or implicates by an utterance in this context, it can go either way.

Some readers may resist this last conclusion; people may think that if we just knew enough about the circumstances of the legislation and the intentions of those involved in its production, we should be able to know what is the right answer. But this is wrong on two accounts: First, remember that it is an objectified sense of uptake that we must consider here. The question is not directly about the intentions or purposes of various agents involved in the process of legislation, it is a question about reasonable uptake. Knowing all the relevant contextual background, what would a reasonable hearer infer? The simple point is that, even if all the relevant background is known, the inference to communicated content of some particular aspects of the communicated content might remain genuinely indeterminate. Suppose, for example, that the truth of the matter about the legislation of the Act in

Casey is that the drafters just made a mistake, they forgot that other pieces of similar legislation refer explicitly to expert fees. But suppose that they actually intended to include them. Still, this would not necessarily settle the issue. There is no contradiction in saying that by saying that P, X indented to communicate that Y, but failed to do so. Speakers may assume all sorts of things about the context of their utterance that happen to be false, and may be known to be false by the hearer, in which case the content that was actually communicated and the content that the speaker intended to communicate may come apart. (Remember Lord Raglan and his orders to the Light Brigade.) If we are, legally speaking, interested in the former, not the latter, the pragmatic vagueness of the utterance remains even if we know everything about the subjective intentions of the speaker. So we know what the speaker, Congress in this case, *wanted* to say, but it's not necessarily what they said (or implicated).

Second, we should bear in mind that speakers don't always have a very clear idea in mind about all that they wanted to convey by their utterance in a given occasion. Even individual speakers, in ordinary conversations, may not have actually formed a very precise idea of what they intended to communicate. We often say something that has some clearly communicated content in some respects, and indeterminate content in others, without having any particular intentions with respect to the indeterminate content. Perhaps we just haven't thought about it, or if we did, we decided to leave that kind of content hanging in the air, indeterminate as it seems. There is no reason to assume that legislation is different in this respect; on the contrary, for obvious reasons having to do with the complex legislative procedures, we can safely assume that it happens with legislation much more frequently than in ordinary conversations.

Either way, I hope that we can see how the examples discussed above generalize to many other cases. The legal landscape in which legislatures act is very complex, saturated with countless previous legal arrangements; there is a huge amount of law out there, and every piece of a newly enacted legislation is like an addition of a tiny new piece to a giant puzzle. There should be little surprise if it turns out that the pieces do not fit neatly together. Factual assumptions underlying or presupposed by acts of legislation may turn out to be false, legally or otherwise; and then various forms of pragmatic vagueness may ensue, even if the statutory expression is not otherwise vague or particularly indeterminate. What I have tried to argue here is that at least in some of these cases, pragmatic vagueness is, from a linguistic perspective, genuinely indeterminate; there is no truth of the matter about the content, asserted or implicated, that the act of legislation can be taken to have actually communicated.

References

Capone, Alessandro and Francesca Poggi. 2016. 'Defeasibility and Pragmatic Indeterminacy in Law'. In *Pragmatics and Law*, edited by Alessandro Capone and Francesca Poggi, 15. Cham: Springer.

Carston, Robyn. 2013. 'Legal Texts and Canons of Construction'. *Law and Language: Current Legal Issues* 15: 8–33.

Endicott, Timothy. 2014. 'Law and Language'. In *The Stanford Encyclopedia of Philosophy* (Spring 2014 edn), edited by Edward N. Zalta. Available at <http://plato.stanford.edu/archives/spr2014/entries/law-language/>.

Figes, Orlando. 2010. *The Crimean War: A History*. New York: Metropolitan Books.

Grice, Paul. 1989. *Studies in the Way of Words*. Cambridge (MA): Harvard University Press.

Marmor, Andrei. 2009. *Social Conventions: From Language to Law*. Princeton: Princeton University Press.

Marmor, Andrei. 2014. *The Language of Law*. Oxford: Oxford University Press.

Ruger, Theodore W. 2011. 'The Story of FDA v Brown and Williamson (2000): The Norm of Agency Continuity'. In *Statutory Interpretation Stories*, edited by William Eskridge, Philip Frickey, and Elizabeth Garrett, 334–65. New York: Foundation Press.

Soames, Scott. 2012. 'Vagueness and the Law'. In *The Routledge Companion to Philosophy of Law*, edited by Andrei Marmor, 95–108. New York: Routledge.

Williamson, Timothy. 1994. *Vagueness*. London: Routledge.

7

Second-Order Vagueness in the Law

*Frederick Schauer**

Most of the philosophical literature on vagueness starts with the identification of the term whose vagueness is at issue—'tall', 'short', 'night', 'day', 'bald', 'tadpole', etc. But in legal interpretation an additional problem arises, because it is not always obvious which term in a legal text, or even which legal text, is the operative one. H.L.A. Hart's idea of a rule of recognition conceptualizes the way in which some second-order rule is necessary to identify which first-order rule is applicable to some form of conduct, but it is often the case that the second-order rule itself exhibits various forms of vagueness. When that is so, vagueness appears as a distinct problem, with important but often unrecognized implications.

1.

An intriguing feature of the philosophical literature on vagueness is the typical lack of vagueness in identifying the term whose vagueness is at issue. When Bertrand Russell discussed *sorites* vagueness in the context of the word 'bald', for example (Russell 1923), he expressed no doubts about the fact that it was the word 'bald' whose vagueness was at issue. And if in response to this example some critic had responded that the word 'rabbit' was not vague in the same way, or not vague at all,[1] Russell would likely have been annoyed, for he was presupposing, at

* This chapter was first presented at the conference on Vagueness in Law: Philosophical and Legal Approaches, held at the Department of Philosophy, New York University, on 21–23 March 2013. I am grateful to the organizers—Paul Boghossian, Geert Keil, and Ralf Poscher—and also to the other conference participants for their challenging and helpful comments and questions. The initial version of this chapter was prepared while I was Visiting Professor of Law at the Columbia Law School, and I am pleased to acknowledge Columbia's tangible and intangible support.

[1] I put aside as not relevant here the fact that Russell used the example as a precursor to an argument that *all* language is vague. And thus I bracket for now the question whether 'rabbit' is vague in the same way that 'bald' is vague and until section 5 below the question of open texture—whether the potential vagueness of 'rabbit' in the face of hitherto unknown creatures might make that word, and all others, potentially vague. On the latter, the seminal work is Waismann 1951. On open texture in law, an idea first put forth, but murkily, in Hart 1961/2012, pp. 124–36, see Schauer 2013.

least in the most immediate context, that it was the word 'bald' and not the word 'rabbit' that was under discussion and analysis.

But now suppose that it is 1923, and that we are listening to Russell deliver the lecture on which his paper was based. And suppose further that we are not native speakers of English, that there is a loud electric fan whirring in the room, that we are sitting in the back of the room, and that Russell had a tendency to look down and to mumble when speaking. Under these conditions, imagine that at an early point in the lecture, after saying—clearly—that the topic to be discussed was vagueness, and that he wanted to start with an example, Russell says that the example he will use is the word 'bald'. But at the moment he makes that statement we, the just described listener, thinks that he might have said 'bald', but we are not sure. Maybe he said 'old'. Or was it 'ball'? Or perhaps 'doll'? At that moment there is vagueness—perhaps we can label it *aural vagueness*—about just which word it is whose vagueness is or will be under discussion. And because we are vague about the word whose vagueness Russell might be discussing, it seems useful to think of this kind of vagueness—the aural vagueness in the example—as a variety of *second-order vagueness*.[2]

The fact that the second-order vagueness in the example is aural is fortuitous. We can imagine a similar example in which we discover an ancient and partly obliterated manuscript containing the word 'b##d,' and we are unsure whether the word is 'bald', or perhaps 'bend', or maybe 'bard'. Or suppose we are attending a series of lectures, and miss the third lecture. At the fourth lecture the lecturer says she will pick up with the example from the previous lecture, but at the moment we are unsure as to just which example she is talking about. Maybe it is the 'bald' example from the first lecture, but perhaps it is the 'game' example from the second. We simply are not sure.

These fictional anecdotes are designed to illustrate a larger point, *viz.*, that most philosophical discussions of vagueness, and they are legion, start with a particular word or predicate (or, sometimes, a phrase, or even a sentence, or, for some, a concept) that exhibits the property of vagueness to some greater or lesser extent—not only 'bald', but also 'red', 'tall', 'heap', 'tadpole', 'religion', 'art', 'democracy', and so forth. Philosophers seeking to understand the phenomenon of linguistic vagueness start with the fact that we cannot definitely say with respect to some people that those people are or are not bald, just as with respect to some creatures on the borderline we are in doubt as to whether they are frogs or tadpoles. But whatever might be the correct philosophical account of the vagueness of words like 'bald' or 'tadpole', the starting point for the discussion is ordinarily an uncontroversially identified linguistic unit, of which 'bald' and 'tadpole' are clear examples.

But, again, what if we were uncertain about whether to begin the analysis with the word 'bald', or instead with the word 'tadpole', and that something of consequence turned on whether we chose to start with 'bald' instead of 'tadpole', or 'tadpole' instead of 'bald'. Or what if there were consequences attached to being

---

[2] I say 'a variety of' second-order vagueness because the phenomenon I describe here has at most an attenuated relationship to the higher-order or second-order vagueness frequently discussed in the philosophical literature. See e.g. Keefe 2000, pp. 33–4, Hampton 2007, and Williamson 1999.

bald, but that the specification of those consequences was itself vague, as with the possibility that bald people were entitled to 'special consideration', but with no further specification of what did or did not count as 'special consideration'. Or perhaps being bald 'sometimes' entailed those consequences, but with no further specification of 'sometimes'.

In circumstances such as these, we appear to have added an additional layer on top of the vagueness of the word 'bald'. And although this additional layer of vagueness may not be of much—or any, for that matter—philosophical interest, it turns out to be of central importance in law. And thus, in law but not always elsewhere, the question of the vagueness of a word or phrase is often contingent upon the second-order (or preliminary, if you will) determination of whether this is the word or phrase with which we are concerned, and also often implicates the different second-order question of what consequences might follow from that word or phrase rather than some other word or phrase being the appropriate locus of analysis. And, importantly, these second-order questions might themselves be subject to vagueness problems. This form of second-order vagueness is different from, albeit related to, the phenomenon of second-order or higher-order vagueness often discussed in the philosophical literature, and it is this form of second-order vagueness that is central to thinking about the issue of vagueness in law.

2.

The reason that the examples and anecdotes just noted are not pointless when we are thinking about law is because law, being a fundamentally source-based and authoritative practice, often presents difficulties quite analogous to these very instances. In law we often do not know whether some source is or is not a valid *legal* source, and thus we do not know whether or not it is usable in legal argument and decision making. In the positivist tradition, the distinction between usable and non-usable authorities is ordinarily, since H.L.A. Hart (1961/2012, pp. 94–110), designated as and by the *rule of recognition*, the rule (or practice) by which a society recognizes some sources as valid sources of law and others as outside the law. The rule of recognition is the secondary rule (in contrast to primary rules of conduct) that picks out the subset of valid legal rules (or sources of law) from the set of all rules or sources or factors that might be used in making some sort of decision or rendering some sort of judgment. A rule of recognition is what tells us, typically but not inevitably, contingently but not necessarily, that 'It is prohibited to drive an automobile on public roads without a driver's licence' is a rule of law but that 'It is necessary to write a thank-you note after receiving a gift' is not.

Hart may have been somewhat misleading in describing the rule of recognition as a *rule*, and it is perhaps better understood as a more fluid practice with no canonical linguistic form.[3] But whether it be a rule or a practice, the rule of recognition

---

[3] See Schauer 2012a and Simpson 1973.

may still turn out to be vague with respect to some source, thus producing uncertainty as to whether the source is valid law or not. In English courts, for example, it was for generations clearly understood that a book or article (a so-called *secondary source*, in contrast to primary sources such as constitutions, statutes, and reported court decisions) written by a still-living author was not a valid legal source.[4] Around 1945, the practice began to change,[5] and thus there was a period of time when it was uncertain whether some secondary source could be used in legal argument, a form of vagueness antecedent to the potential vagueness surrounding what that source actually said.

Hart does discuss the possibility of 'uncertainty in the rule of recognition' (Hart 1961/2012, pp. 123, 147–54, 251), but does so primarily in the context of arguing that the rule of recognition is ultimately a matter of social fact. The content of the rule of recognition may be this or that, but identifying the ultimate[6] rule of recognition is an empirical matter and not a question of legal validity.

So consider the 1889 New York Court of Appeals decision in *Riggs v. Palmer*,[7] the case first made famous by Benjamin Cardozo in *The Nature of the Judicial Process* (Cardozo 1921, pp. 40–1), and then by Henry Hart and Albert Sacks in their materials on the legal process (Hart and Sacks 1958/1994, pp. 80–94), and thereafter by Ronald Dworkin, both in *Taking Rights Seriously* (Dworkin 1977, p. 23) and in *Law's Empire* (Dworkin 1986, pp. 15–23). The facts of the case are simple: Elmer Palmer's grandfather wrote a will designating Elmer as the beneficiary of all, or at least most, of his considerable wealth. At some point Elmer feared that his grandfather, possibly because of disapproval of Elmer's behaviour, was on the verge of changing his will. In order to prevent this from happening, and also to accelerate his inheritance, Elmer killed his grandfather with poison. Elmer was duly apprehended, tried, convicted, and imprisoned, but the question of the inheritance remained. Elmer, relying on the clear language of a law called The Statute of Wills, claimed that the law contained no exception for murderers, and thus that Elmer was entitled to the inheritance. But the alternative beneficiaries, the ones who would inherit if Elmer did not, argued that the venerable principle of 'no man shall profit from his own wrong' prevented Elmer from inheriting, the clear language of the Statute of Wills notwithstanding.

Initially, we might ask what made the New York Statute of Wills even relevant. And the answer would be that a rule of recognition made it relevant. The rule of recognition implicitly established that statutes enacted according to appropriate procedures by the New York legislature were to be considered as law, and treated

---

[4] The reasons for this are complex, and somewhat beside the point here. But at least one reason was that living expert authors might change their minds, rendering reliance on their pre-change writings less authoritative. But once they are no longer living, such reversals are impossible.

[5] See Schauer and Wise 2000.

[6] There may be subsidiary or subordinate rules of recognition, but their status as law is dependent on being recognized by higher rules of recognition, and the highest rule of recognition, what Hart called the 'ultimate rule of recognition', is antecedent to the question of *legal* validity because it is the foundation on which all legal validity ultimately rests.

[7] 22 N.E. 188 (1889).

by courts (and citizens) as such. And the New York Statute of Wills, being such a statute, was thus the law for purposes of the dispute between Elmer Palmer and the alternative beneficiaries. Moreover, nothing about the implicit rule that made the Statute of Wills applicable was vague. Nor was the Statute of Wills itself vague, at least as applied to this dispute.[8]

Although the determinacy and relevance of the Statute of Wills is thus clear, the relevance of the 'No man may profit from his own wrong' principle is much less so. That is, the principle, expressly relied upon by the *Riggs* majority, might be considered to be part of the governing law, and it might not be. Assuming that judges are obliged to apply the governing law, or at least assuming that judges are empowered, even if not required, to apply the governing law, then if the 'No man...' principle *is* part of the governing law, its status vis-à-vis the Statute of Wills is itself indeterminate. A rule of recognition might contain priority rules, for example that a clear statute like the Statute of Wills would have priority over a less clear principle, or vice versa. But in U.S. legal reality no such second-order priority rule exists, nor did it at the time that *Riggs* was being decided, at least in the United States. And thus it appears that the rule of recognition is, or was at the time of *Riggs*, vague, both as to what it recognizes (was the 'No man...' principle valid law or not?) and as to the priority among the sources of law that it does recognize.

3.

As with most other examples of vagueness, the vagueness of the rule of recognition arises principally in the context of borderline cases.[9] It is clear, at least in the United States, that statutes enacted by Congress in proper constitutional fashion are to count as law. And it is just as clear that, again in the United States, the prescriptions or advice given to a judge by his father or mother are not to count as law. So, like night and day, bald and thatched, frogs and tadpoles, and much else, we have non-borderline applications of the term, which here is the rule of recognition in all of its complexity. But we also have borderline applications, and it is unclear and debated whether, for example, moral principles, foreign law, and empirical data not determined at trial are to count as law.[10] With respect to such items, therefore, the

---

[8] Strong support for this conclusion is provided by the fact that both the majority opinion *and* the dissenting opinion in the New York Court of Appeals agreed that the Statute of Wills, by itself, clearly provided that Elmer should inherit. Thus, although Dworkin characterizes *Riggs* as a 'hard case', its hardness is decidedly *not* a function of the vagueness (or other indeterminacy) of the Statute of Wills. Dworkin's characterization of this as a hard case is thus non-standardly dependent on Dworkin's entire theory of law, a theory that makes a host of legal and moral principles legally relevant. Under a more standard understanding of what makes a hard case hard, this was an easy and not a hard case, although it being a legally easy case need not be dispositive as to what a judge should do when the legally easy result would produce a morally defective outcome.

[9] Or perhaps *only* in the context of borderline cases, although terms will vary with respect to the proportion of their extensions that are borderline cases. Almost all extensions of 'insect' are not borderline, even though there are lots and lots of insects. But a much higher percentage of applications of 'nice', 'pretty', 'fair', and 'unreasonable' are debatable, and thus, in a sense, borderline.

[10] See Schauer 2008a.

rule of recognition is vague, just as the distinction between night and day is vague with respect to dusk, and as the distinction between bald and not-bald is vague with respect to many of the actual heads on actual men.

As Hart notes, judges, when faced with decisions raising this kind of vagueness, will proceed to make decisions about whether some item is or is not within the rule of recognition. And thus, as it would be put in the vagueness literature,[11] judges are typically empowered and authorized, at least in common law jurisdictions, to engage in the task of precisification—sharpening—of the rule of recognition, and their precisifications will then authoritatively place within the non-borderline region some instances that were previously on the borderline. Thus, if the rule of recognition had been vague prior to *Riggs v. Palmer* with respect to whether principles were part of the law, or with respect to whether the 'No man shall profit from his own wrong' principle was part of the law, or whether that principle could prevail against the plain language of a duly-enacted statute, the decision in *Riggs* could be understood as having authoritatively removed that particular vagueness, at least in New York, and at least for the time being.

4.

But if judges are empowered to precisify the vague components of the rule of recognition when the exigencies of a particular controversy appear to demand (or indicate) it, then what does this say about the nature of a rule of recognition?

For Dworkin, such practices cast doubt on the very idea of a rule of recognition (Dworkin 1977, p. 23), or at least one that demarcates the domain of the legal from the domain of the non-legal. His view has some affinity with epistemic accounts of vagueness, because Dworkin maintains that the principle was part of the law all along, even if not explicitly acknowledged as such, in much the same way that epistemic accounts of vagueness insist that there is a fact of the matter even if we do not recognize it and cannot identify it. For Dworkin, the precisification of the rule of recognition in cases like *Riggs* is an act of law-discovery and not of law-creation, and this is what lies behind his famous and controversial claim that there is always a right answer to any question of law (Dworkin 1985, pp. 119–45).

More importantly, Dworkin believes that the process exemplified by *Riggs* and the other cases in his stable of examples shows that there is no such thing as a rule of recognition apart from the fact of judicial practice, and that actual judicial practice shows that there is no source of norms,[12] at least in the United States, that cannot be used by a judge to decide a case. And because all norms, or at least all moral, political, and legal norms, are always available, the rule of recognition, for Dworkin,

---

[11] See e.g. Båve 2011.

[12] This is an over-simplification, because Dworkin does draw a distinction between policy and principle, believing that judges are and should be in the business of doing the latter but not the former (Dworkin 1986, pp. 221–4, 243–4).

collapses, in much the same way that the very concept of bald would collapse if all actual and possible men were bald, or if all actual and possible men were not.

5.

But it is now time to bring open texture[13] back into the picture. We start with the idea, following Waismann, that open texture is not vagueness, but rather is the ineliminable *possibility* of vagueness. I have argued elsewhere that law is not necessarily open-textured, apart from the necessary open texture (assuming, for present purposes, that Waismann is correct) of the language in which law is written (Schauer 1998 and 2012b). But that does not mean that some legal system might not *choose*, contingently, to treat its rule of recognition as open-textured. In other words, some legal system might be structured or understood such that even the clearest rule of recognition is understood to be defeasible in the face of unforeseen circumstances. And if New York in the late nineteenth century were such a system, and if *Riggs* were such a case, then the previously unforeseen possibility that an heir would murder the testator in order to claim the inheritance might occupy the same position that Waismann's gigantic cat or J.L. Austin's exploding goldfinch occupy for language (Waismann 1951, p. 119; Austin 1979, p. 88). Something we had not anticipated arises, and we just do not know what to say. That we do not know what to say does suggest a non-epistemic account of vagueness in the rule of recognition, but, more importantly, it also provides a different way of understanding Dworkin's challenge to the idea of a rule of recognition. If the potential grounds of law are unlimited, then the idea of a rule of recognition becomes pointless, precisely because everything is potentially recognizable. And if everything—every source—is potentially recognizable, then the rule of recognition becomes like a concept of baldness that allows all men to be bald or a concept of red that encompasses all the colours of the spectrum.

6.

It is important, however, that we understand the lesson of open texture carefully and properly. Let us assume that Waismann is correct about the ineliminable open texture of language, although I acknowledge that this is a matter of serious and legitimate debate. But even if it is true that all of the terms of a language are open-textured in that they always contain the *possibility* of vagueness, this does not entail the conclusion that those terms do not operate in a predictable way before their open-texture is manifested. Although I recognize that a goldfinch might explode or quote Virginia Wolff, to use Austin's example, or that a cat, to use Waismann's,

---

[13] See above, n. 1.

might grow to gigantic size or come back from the dead, I still do not hesitate in identifying certain birds as goldfinches, and I know of no professor of English literature who brings a goldfinch to class in the expectation that it will quote Virginia Wolff. That which is possible, and ineliminably possible, is not that which is probable, or even likely enough to worry about.

So too with uncertainty in the rule of recognition. Dworkin is correct that our existing rules or practices of recognition remain open to addition and subtraction from an unlimited and thus unrecognizable—in the rule of recognition sense of 'recognizable'—array of sources. And he is also correct, as *Riggs* demonstrates, that drawing on previously unrecognized sources[14] is more common than goldfinches exploding or deceased cats coming back to life. But probabilities matter. And so do presumptions. Consequently, to the extent that a rule of recognition recognized all and only the statutes of New York (putting aside federal law and constitutional law) and the reported cases of the New York Court of Appeals as legitimate sources of law, the possible judicial outcome of adding to or derogating from that law would be understood as having to overcome a strong presumption against it.

Indeed, the history of *Riggs*-type cases bears this out. Elmer Palmer did not inherit, but most unworthy beneficiaries in fact do inherit, including some who have been responsible for the death of the testator.[15] Moreover, some of these outcomes have occurred in jurisdictions that recognize the 'No man may profit from his own wrong' principle as part of the law. But these jurisdictions have a rule of recognition that gives non-absolute and non-lexical priority, but priority nonetheless, to clearly worded statutes. This priority treats the clear words of a clear statute like we ordinarily treat the idea and the reality of a fully grown frog. Yes, such a creature might suddenly grow a long tail and lose its legs, thus moving it from the category of clearly a frog into the category of possibly a frog and possibly a tadpole. But barring such an occurrence, even without denying its possibility, we treat such a creature as clearly a frog and as different from the younger exemplars that might present borderline cases. Those younger exemplars, however, do not make the normal mature frog any less clearly and non-vaguely a frog. Similarly, existing rules of recognition might generate clear cases, even as there are unclear cases, and even as the clear cases might become unclear in potentially but currently unforeseen and even unforeseeable circumstances.

7.

If we return from the possibility of vagueness to its actuality, we can see that, at least in the United States, and perhaps in most of the United States, issues arising from

---

[14] That the principle that determined the outcome in *Riggs* was previously unrecognized is not so clear, but this is a defect only in the example. Another of Dworkin's examples—*Henningsen v. Bloomfield Motors, Inc.*, 161 A.2d 69 (N.J. 1960), in which a loose sense of unfairness or unconscionability prevailed against a clear rule—may be a better example.

[15] The cases are collected in Schauer 2004.

vagueness in the rule of recognition are a real and frequent occurrence. And thus it might be useful to offer a brief and incomplete catalog of the ways in which such issues arise.

First, it might be unclear whether a law really is a law. It will rarely be unclear whether a word really is a word, but on many occasions, including some discussed by Hart, there will be doubts concerning whether what looks like a law actually is a law. Perhaps it is a statute enacted by some unusual procedure. Perhaps it is a judicial decision that may or may not have been overruled. Or maybe it is a constitutional amendment that may or may not have been ratified according to the requisite procedures. In all of these instances, and more, some application of the rule of recognition will produce borderline cases of what is a law.

Second, the rules or practices of recognition may recognize multiple sources of law as law, but be vague or silent about their priority ranking. Even if it is abundantly clear that the principle that no man may profit from his own wrong is law, the lack of a designated priority between this as statutes such as the Statute of Wills presents another example of vagueness in application of the rule of recognition.

Third, there may be sources that are or are not law, but in a different sense from questions about the formalities of enactment and the like. For example, sources such as foreign law, empirical data from published social science sources, and moral principles might be law, and might not be, and such sources often present genuine issues on the borderline of a hypothesized law/non-law distinction and thus on the borderline of the rule of recognition.

Fourth, there may exist second-order or secondary rules or principles for the interpretation of the first-order or primary rules. Some of these second-order rules might make some primary rules non-vague, as when a recognized principle of interpretation directs us mandatorily to the intentions of those who wrote or enacted the primary rule and when there is clear evidence of what those intentions were. But other secondary rules might make some non-vague primary rules vague, as when a rule of interpretation mandates that all rules—even non-vague ones—be interpreted and applied according to their purposes, and where the purpose is unclear. Moreover, some of secondary rules of interpretation might themselves be vague, or the conditions for their application might be vague, providing still another example of second-order vagueness.

There may be still other forms of second-order vagueness, and analysing them, as well as the ones mentioned, may well be assisted by drawing on the existing philosophical wisdom about linguistic vagueness. Linguistic vagueness is in part about language, but it is also an instantiation of the uncertainties that pervade our entire existence. Law's second-order vagueness—vagueness about what is law and what is not—is partly linguistic, partly epistemic, and partly deontic, this last in the sense of law being part of the logic of norms in a multi-norm legal normative world. But no analysis of vagueness in law will be complete unless it includes consideration of the initial question whether the term we are considering is or is not law. And when we confront this question, we may discover still more vagueness, making the questions of vagueness in law especially, even if not uniquely, difficult.

8.

In a previous paper, Professor Poscher has argued, correctly, that the kinds of cases I am discussing here belong to the pragmatics and not the semantics of legal language (Poscher 2012). Fire engines are non-vaguely vehicles, for example, but whether to think of them as vehicles for purposes of a 'no vehicles in the park' rule[16] is a matter of legal pragmatics.

So far so good. But one way of understanding the argument I present here is as saying that the pragmatic issues may be vague even when the semantic ones are not. Moreover, the relationship between the semantics and the pragmatics may also be vague. So noting that there are pragmatic issues as well as semantic ones is a good start, but it is only a start, and one of the things that make law special, even if not uniquely so, is that the pragmatics may play an especially important role. And thus without understanding the possibility of vagueness in the pragmatics, we may not fully understand the way in which vagueness operates in the law.

Indeed, the problem is even greater. When we draw a distinction between interpretation and construction, as so many theorists do these days,[17] we often presuppose a second-order principle according to which the words of the law are first to be interpreted, even if not constructed, as ordinary and non-technical language. But law is also replete with technical terms, such as 'equal protection', 'due process', 'will', 'trust', 'covenant running with the land', and so on. In interpreting such terms, we cannot rely on ordinary language, and must understand the role that technical language plays in the law, and what role the goals and purposes of law play in interpreting legal technical language.[18] Even if we are sceptical of Lon Fuller's tentative suggestion that *all* of the terms of law are technical ones to be interpreted in light of the purposes of a legal system (Fuller 1967, pp. 11–23), we cannot avoid admitting that at least some of the terms in law, and often the most important ones, are technical and thus draw at least part of their meaning—semantic meaning—from law's goals, purposes, history, and distinctive methods. Recognizing this may weaken the importance of the distinction between interpretation and construction, but even if it does not, it brings to the fore a new set of second-order considerations about whether we should interpret the words in the law as ordinary or technical.[19] And these considerations, like the other second-order considerations in legal interpretation and application, may themselves be vague.

References

Austin, John L. 1979. 'Other Minds'. In *Philosophical Papers*, 2nd edn, 76–116. Oxford: Oxford University Press.

---

[16] For exploration of this well-known Hartian example, see Schauer 2008b.
[17] See e.g. Solum 2013 and Chian and Solum 2013.
[18] See Schauer 2015a.   [19] See Schauer 2015b.

Båve, Arvid. 2011. 'How to Precisify Quantifiers'. *Journal of Philosophical Logic* 40(1): 103–11.

Cardozo, Benjamin N. 1921. *The Nature of the Judicial Process*. New Haven (CT): Yale University Press.

Chian, Tun-Jen and Lawrence B. Solum. 2013. 'The Interpretation–Construction Distinction in Patent Law'. *Yale Law Journal* 123(3): 530–614.

Dworkin, Ronald. 1977. *Taking Rights Seriously*. London: Duckworth.

Dworkin, Ronald. 1985. 'Is There Really No Right Answer in Hard Cases?' In *A Matter of Principle,* 119–45. Cambridge (MA): Harvard University Press.

Dworkin, Ronald. 1986. *Law's Empire*. Cambridge (MA): Harvard University Press.

Fuller, Lon L. 1967. *Legal Fictions*. Stanford (CA): Stanford University Press.

Hampton, James A. 2007. 'Typicality, Graded Membership, and Vagueness'. *Cognitive Science* 31(3): 355–84.

Hart, Henry M., Jr and Albert M. Sacks. 1958/1994. *The Legal Process: Basic Problems in the Making and Application of Law*. Westbury (NY): Foundation Press.

Hart, H.L.A. 1961/2012. *The Concept of Law*, 3rd edn. Oxford: Oxford University Press.

Keefe, Rosanna. 2000. *Theories of Vagueness*. Cambridge: Cambridge University Press.

Poscher, Ralf. 2012. 'Ambiguity and Vagueness in Legal Interpretation'. In *The Oxford Handbook of Language and Law*, edited by Lawrence Solan and Peter Tiersma, 128–44. Oxford: Oxford University Press.

Russell, Bertrand. 1923. 'Vagueness'. *Australasian Journal of Psychology & Philosophy* 1(2): 84–92.

Schauer, Frederick. 1998. 'On the Supposed Defeasibility of Legal Rules'. In *Current Legal Problems 1998*, edited by Michael Freeman, 223–40. Oxford: Oxford University Press.

Schauer, Frederick. 2004. 'The Limited Domain of the Law'. *Virginia Law Review* 90(7): 1909–56.

Schauer, Frederick. 2008a. 'Authority and Authorities'. *Virginia Law Review* 94(8): 1931–61.

Schauer, Frederick. 2008b. 'A Critical Guide to Vehicles in the Park'. *New York University Law Review* 83(4): 1109–34.

Schauer, Frederick. 2012a. 'Is the Rule of Recognition a Rule?' *Transnational Legal Theory* 3(2): 173–9.

Schauer, Frederick. 2012b. 'Is Defeasibility an Essential Property of Law?' In *The Logic of Legal Requirements: Essays on Defeasibility*, edited by Jordi Ferrer Beltrán and Giovanni Battista Ratti, 77–88. Oxford: Oxford University Press.

Schauer, Frederick. 2013. 'On the Open Texture of Law'. *Grazer Philosophische Studien* 87: 195–213.

Schauer, Frederick. 2015a. 'Is Law a Technical Language?' *San Diego Law Review* 52: 501–13.

Schauer, Frederick. 2015b. 'On the Relationship Between Legal and Ordinary Language'. In *Speaking of Language and Law*, edited by Lawrence M. Solan, Janet Ainsworth, and Roger W. Shuy, 35–8. New York: Oxford University Press.

Schauer, Frederick and Virginia J. Wise. 2000. 'Non-Legal Information and the Delegalization of Law'. *Journal of Legal Studies* 29(S1): 495–515.

Simpson, A.W. Brian. 1973. 'The Common Law and Legal Theory'. In *Oxford Essays in Jurisprudence (2nd series)*, edited by A.W. Brian Simpson, 77–99. Oxford: Oxford University Press.

Solum, Lawrence B. 2013. 'Communicative Content and Legal Content'. *Notre Dame Law Review* 89(2): 479–519.

Waismann, Friedrich. 1951. 'Verifiability'. In *Logic and Language (First Series)*, edited by Antony Flew, 117–44. Oxford: Basil Blackwell.

Williamson, Timothy. 1999. 'On the Structure of Higher-Order Vagueness'. *Mind* 108(429): 127–44.

8

The Non-Conservativeness
of Legal Definitions

Marc Andree Weber

Briefly and abstractly, the outline of this chapter is as follows: I start by dividing vague terms into two categories, those having the 'normal' kind of vagueness
that we associate with sorites cases, and those exhibiting cluster vagueness, which
depends on a certain similarity to paradigm cases that cannot be analysed further
(section 1). I then argue that the vagueness of natural language expressions is always
of the second kind, and that only scientific or artificial expressions can be soritically vague (section 2). After explaining what conservative extensions are (section
3), I observe that, unlike scientific terms, those legal definitions that posit precisifications of natural language terms constitute non-conservative extensions of our
everyday language; that is they not only add aspects of meaning to existing expressions but also effectively change the meanings of these expressions (section 4). The
reason for this lies in the fact that unprecisified natural language expressions are
cluster-vague, whereas their precisifications are soritically vague (if at all vague). I
conclude (in section 5) that *we should avoid precisifying ordinary expressions with the
help of legal definitions to the extent that we wish legal language to be in line with natural language.* Moreover, I point out that an advantage of being in line with natural
language is that we can deal with gaps in our laws at the very moment we become
aware of them, and not just afterwards.

1. Two Categories of Vagueness

Before we can distinguish the relevant kinds of vagueness, we need an auxiliary
definition:

>**Definition 1.** *A **gradable characteristic** is a characteristic that comes in one of
>infinitely many degrees.*

The definition is not meant to have any ontological implications; whether or not
there really are properties or characteristics is not supposed to matter. Besides, I do
not want to elaborate on the expression 'comes in a certain number of degrees'.
I will simple cite some examples to clarify what I have in mind.

The Non-Conservativeness of Legal Definitions. First Edition. Marc Andree Weber. © Marc Andree Weber.
Published 2016 by Oxford University Press.

Examples for gradable characteristics are size, brightness, and aliveness. As for size, there obviously are not only two or three different sizes such that every possible object has one of them, but rather very many different sizes. Similarly for brightness: there are many degrees of it, not only bright and dark. And even such a property as aliveness comes in degrees because dying takes time, at least some milliseconds. So if we regard the process of dying with a sufficiently high temporal resolution, there are points of time at which a given creature is neither still alive nor already dead. For that reason, merely using the two categories *dead* and *alive* to describe a creature's state of aliveness is at times rather simplistic.

Note that, in order to be gradable, it does not matter whether a characteristic comes in uncountably many degrees, as in the case of size, brightness, and aliveness, or whether there are only countably infinitely many of them, as in the number of grains in a heap of sand. (Of course, given a specific heap of sand, the number of grains in it is finite; there are, however, infinitely many numbers that can, in principle, be the number of grains in a heap.) In both cases, the gradable characteristic gives rise to a sorites series, in which the adjoining objects differ only to a small degree. This is more easily seen in the case of countably many degrees: a million grains of sand clearly form a heap; then, according to the plausible principle that one single grain cannot make all the difference between a heap of sand and something too small to be dubbed a heap, a million minus one grains of sand clearly also form a heap; then, according to the same principle, a million minus two grains clearly form a heap as well; and so on, until, after one million applications of that principle, we are forced to conclude that zero grains of sand form a heap too, which clearly is absurd. Similar though less paradigmatic versions of this paradox can be obtained in the case of uncountably many degrees if we presuppose, for instance, that a tiny difference in size, brightness, or time cannot make all the difference between large and small, bright and dark, or dead and alive.

Examples of characteristics that are *not* gradable include the primeness of natural numbers, which comes in only two degrees, since each natural number is either prime or not, as well as being a certain day of the week, which comes in only seven degrees. These characteristics do not give rise to sorites series.[1]

The kind of vagueness that we associate with sorites cases I call *soritical* (short for sorites-susceptible) *vagueness*:

> **Definition 2.** *A term* t *is **soritically vague** if and only if there is a fixed number* $n > 0$ *of gradable characteristics such that whether or not an object is a borderline case of* t *depends solely on the degrees to which that object has these characteristics.*

Borderline cases of a term are those objects to which the term can be neither clearly applied nor clearly withheld. A man who is 180 cm in height, for example, is a borderline case of 'tall'. The definition of soritical vagueness entails that soritically vague terms have borderline cases in this sense. For if there are (actual or merely

---

[1] There are also gradable characteristics that do not induce sorites cases, for example being a natural number. In what follows, these gradable characteristics play no role.

possible) objects for which being borderline cases of *t* depends solely on the degrees to which they have certain gradable characteristics, then there are (not necessarily the same, and not necessarily actual) objects which have these characteristics to such degrees that they are indeed borderline cases of *t*. Since terms are commonly regarded as vague if they admit of (actual or merely possible) borderline cases, it follows that soritically vague terms are vague. The converse is generally not the case.

Examples of soritically vague terms for which the number *n* of gradable characteristics is equal to 1 are 'bald' and 'heap'. In the case of 'bald', the gradable characteristic is the number of hairs; in case of 'heap', it is the number of grains. 'Chair' may be regarded as an example of a soritically vague term with *n* = 2, the gradable characteristics being the length of the back and the length of the seat.[2] If the back is too short, then a certain piece of furniture is a stool rather than a chair; and if the seat is too long, then it becomes a chaise longue. So we can imagine two kinds of sorites series concerning chairs, one that turns a chair into a stool and one that turns it into a chaise longue.

Terms for abstract objects can be soritically vague as well. If we forget everything we know about Gettier cases and define knowledge as justified true belief, then knowledge has two gradable characteristics because a proposition can be more or less justified, and it can be more or less believed. Since it cannot be more or less true, the third characteristic of pre-Gettier knowledge is not a gradable one, and the vagueness of 'knowledge' does not depend on it. Nonetheless, the term 'knowledge', if understood in the pre-Gettier sense, falls under definition 2.

The kind of vagueness I want to distinguish from soritical vagueness can be named *cluster-vagueness*:

Definition 3. *A term* t *is **cluster-vague** if and only if*

1. *whether or not an object is a borderline case of* t *depends at least partly on how similar (in the right way) that object is to paradigm cases of* t, *i.e. objects to which* t *clearly applies or clearly does not apply; and*

2. *this similarity cannot be analysed into a fixed number of characteristics.*

Examples of cluster-vague terms are 'game', 'religion', and 'cat'. In all these cases, there is no fixed number of gradable characteristics and respective degrees thereof on which the applications of these terms solely depend; we have to rely instead on an unanalysable similarity to paradigm cases of games, religions, or cats. (Note that it is not required that an object's being or not being a borderline case depends on its similarity to *all* relevant paradigm cases. The reason is that paradigm cases of the same kinds of things can be very dissimilar to each other. Football and Scrabble, for instance, are both perfect examples for games.)

---

[2] This example is taken from Burks 1946, p. 482. The vagueness of terms for which there is not exactly one gradable characteristic on which an object's being a borderline case of that term solely depends is called *non-linear* by Burks, *multi-dimensional* by others (see e.g. Hyde 2008, p. 17). Since non-linear vagueness does not require that there is a fixed number of gradable characteristics, it need not be sorital.

A further example is again 'knowledge', this time understood in the post-Gettier sense according to which knowledge is justified true belief *plus X*, where *X* is some component that we have not yet identified or, more likely, that is principally unidentifiable. In this last case there would be nothing more specific to discover, so that knowledge could not be analysed into a fixed number of characteristics. If this is true, post-Gettier knowledge would not be soritically vague but cluster-vague.

In the definition of cluster vagueness, the first condition has a twofold function: it ensures that cluster-vague terms are at all vague, for if an object's being a borderline case of *t* depends on its similarity to other objects, there must be (not necessarily the same, and not necessarily actual) objects that have exactly the right degree of similarity to other objects in order for them indeed to be borderline cases of *t*; and, more importantly, it identifies the source of this vagueness, namely a certain similarity of which nothing more particular is said except that it has to be 'of the right kind'. What exactly the right kind of similarity is depends on what (bundles of) properties we are about to compare: if we speak about colours, a vermilion flower might be similar in the right way to a fire engine. The function of the second condition is to specify the similarity mentioned in the first one, albeit in a negative way, stressing its unanalysability in terms of a fixed number of gradable characteristics. It is thereby guaranteed that cluster-vague terms cannot be soritically vague.

What is more, the following theorem holds:

Theorem 1. *A vague term is either soritically vague or cluster-vague.*

According to the last paragraph, a vague term that is cluster-vague cannot be soritically vague. It remains to show that a vague term that is not cluster-vague has to be soritically vague. To see this, assume that the similarity which borderline cases of vague terms bear to paradigm cases can be analysed into a finite number of characteristics that together determine the degree of similarity. At least some of these characteristics must be such that they are not either satisfied or dissatisfied but instead satisfied to a certain degree, for otherwise there would only be a (small) finite number of degrees of similarity and no need to speak of borderline cases at all. In other words, some of these characteristics have to be gradable. Hence, the reason a term admits borderline cases has to do with either a fixed number of gradable characteristics or a similarity to paradigm cases that cannot be analysed into a fixed number of (gradable or non-gradable) characteristics.

Since a similarity that cannot be analysed into a fixed number of characteristics precludes the existence of necessary and sufficient conditions, we have the following corollary stating a connection between soritically vague terms and those for whose application we can give necessary and sufficient conditions:

Corollary. *Let t be a vague term. Then if there are necessary and sufficient conditions for being t, t is soritically vague.*

As a result of theorem 1, an equivalent definition of cluster vagueness would be that a term is cluster-vague if and only if it is vague but not soritically vague. Although this definition is agreeably simple and elucidates why soritical and cluster vagueness are not only two kinds of vagueness but two *categories* of it, I prefer our original definition because it sheds more light on the peculiar nature of the vagueness under consideration. The crucial point here is not the categoricalness of the distinction but the discrepancy of its underlying sources.

Be that as it may, the fact that a cluster-vague term is not soritically vague does not mean that it cannot play the decisive part in a sorites case. To see that it can, imagine a series of creatures. Start with a cat. Then exchange one of its molecules, then another, and so on until you end up with a mouse. Two adjoining creatures in this series differ only by one molecule. Surely, if something is cat, then it is still a cat after you have exchanged one molecule (for it is still sufficiently similar to one). But surely a mouse is not a cat.

However, there is something special about sorites cases for cluster-vague terms such as 'cat': as a consequence of the unanalysability into a fixed number of characteristics, at least one dimension of change has to be characterized with the help of the elusive notion of resemblance (or a similar one). For instance, our molecule-for-molecule exchange results in a sorites series only because, normally, a tiny change on the microphysical level does not result in a huge change on the macrophysical level; two animals differing by only one molecule resemble each other to a very high degree. Otherwise, we would not regard such a tiny change as insufficient for making all the difference between a cat and a non-cat, and our sorites case would break down. In other words, it is not the gradable characteristic of the number of molecules that makes our sorites series from cat to mouse work but rather the overwhelming macrophysical resemblance of animals with almost identical molecular structures, which just holds contingently.

In the philosophical literature, many distinctions between kinds of vagueness can be found. Why do I propose another one? There are two reasons: first, I find the existing differentiations unclear in relevant respects. Take the one closest to mine, namely Alston's distinction between what he calls *degree-vagueness* and *combinatory vagueness* (Alston 1967, p. 219). Alston does not give definitions of these concepts; he merely explicates them in an indefinite way. For him, combinatory vagueness is the 'source of indeterminacy of application [that] is to be found in the way in which a word may have a number of logically independent conditions of application'. As an example, he cites the word 'religion', which is combinatorily vague because paradigm cases of religions exhibit a plurality of characteristics such as requiring belief in supernatural beings or involving ritual acts, none of which is necessary for being a religion; in fact, it is even indefinite what combinations of these features suffice. Yet 'religion' is an easy example of a term with 'logically independent conditions of application'. What about soritically vague terms that have borderline cases which may have many gradable characteristics? From what Alston writes, it is unclear whether the combinatory vagueness of a term precludes that its correct application depends *on a fixed number* of characteristics, or whether it just rules out that we can specify what combinations of (degrees of) possibly finitely many characteristics are necessary for its correct application. It is unclear, in other words, whether Alston draws the same distinction that I do.

Similarly, it is unclear whether cluster-vagueness is precisely the vagueness that family resemblance concepts display. Wittgenstein describes what he calls *family resemblance* as 'a complicated network of similarities overlapping and criss-crossing' like 'the various resemblances between members of a family' (Wittgenstein 1953/ 2001, §§ 66, 67). Concepts such as *game* display family resemblance because we use them to talk about such dissimilar things as badminton matches, computer games, or jigsaw puzzles, which do not share a specific feature that all non-games do not have. Every game, however, shares some features with at least some other games and so is similar to them in this respect, while these other games may resemble still other games for different reasons. Although 'game', like 'religion', is cluster-vague, it is hard to tell whether the vagueness such family resemblance concepts display is generally of that sort. Wittgenstein at least does not take any pains to relate it to paradigmatic soritical cases—an omission, by the way, for which I think he has a good reason (see section 3).

The second reason for proposing a new distinction between kinds of vagueness is that this one enables us to work out the differences between vagueness in everyday discourses and vagueness in scientific contexts. Let me explain what I mean.

2. Vagueness in Everyday Contexts

I used 'chair' as an example of a soritically vague term, saying that chairs have two gradable characteristics: the length of the back and the length of the seat. Now this seems somewhat idealized because there are obviously other gradable characteristics that play a role—although perhaps a less prominent one—for the proper application of 'chair', for example the length of the legs or the width of the seat. The problem here is not that we overlooked some gradable characteristics, and that there are actually not two but four or six features on which the proper application of the term depends. There rather seems to be no point in trying to come up with an exhaustive list of characteristics. Idealization aside, there is no fixed number of gradable characteristics by reference to which we can, without further ado, decide whether any given object is a chair. In everyday discourse, where there is neither room nor need for idealizations, 'chair' is not soritically vague but cluster-vague. The reason why we so readily accepted the word as an example for soritical vagueness is that we do not usually expect any harm from ignoring seemingly peripheral features that are difficult to accommodate within a scientific analysis, especially if the idealization is so close at hand.

What holds for 'chair' also holds for other prime examples of soritical vagueness. Whether we would call someone 'bald' depends not only on the number of his hairs, but also on their length, thickness, distribution, and so on; and whether we would call something a 'heap' depends not only on the number of grains of which it consists but also on their size, colour, and distribution, to name but a few features. Things are different with 'knowledge', understood in the pre-Gettier sense as justified true belief. Here, we have a concise definition that limits the number of characteristics that play a role in determining whether something is knowledge to three in total, or two if we count only gradable ones. No further idealization is needed; the idealization is already built into the definition, which renders the concept of pre-Gettier knowledge artificial.

It seems to be true generally that only idealized and artificial concepts display soritical vagueness, whereas natural language concepts do not. The reason for this is that, in analysing vagueness, even slight idealizations can be crucial because aspects of vagueness tend to be exactly what is idealized away by slight idealizations. Therefore our expectation that we can safely ignore what is difficult to accommodate and seems to be secondary, though more often than not true, leads us astray in this case.

Besides, if natural language terms are normally not soritically vague, it follows from the corollary that there are normally no necessary and sufficient conditions for their application. This fits nicely with the observation that many terms in our natural languages resist proper definition. Things are different in scientific contexts, in which we define terms by giving necessary and sufficient conditions. When we define a disease using particular symptoms, or a biological species using certain biological characteristics, then we state such conditions; as a result, our *definienda* are soritically vague. (Insofar as we regard properly defined artificial and scientific expressions as part of our natural languages, these languages include soritically vague terms. That is why I said that natural language terms are not *normally* soritically vague. Understood narrowly, they are *never* soritically vague.)

Moreover, my claim that ordinary expressions are cluster-vague has no direct semantic or logical consequences. According to what can be called the classical picture, the meaning of a term fixes its extension, i.e. the set of objects to which it clearly applies. In this view, a vague term not only has an extension and an anti-extension, i.e. a set of objects to which it clearly does not apply, but also a penumbral extension in between that contains all those objects to which the term neither clearly applies nor clearly does not apply. This classical framework is the basis of virtually all prominent logical approaches to vagueness (i.e. supervaluationism, many-valued theories, the epistemic view), which differ from each other only in how they integrate (or, in the case of the epistemic view, rule out) the penumbral extension. According to a non-classical semantic picture such as the one put forward in Sainsbury 1990, the whole idea that the meanings of terms fix certain sets of objects is misguided because sets have sharp boundaries: for any set and any object, the object either belongs to the set or does not belong to it. In contrast, for most natural language expressions, there are objects to which they cannot be either clearly applied or not clearly applied; they come without sharp boundaries. Ordinary terms may rather be compared to magnetic poles that attract different iron filings to different degrees, depending on their size and position: there is no non-arbitrary way to categorize these filings according to the pull exerted on them. Although this non-classical picture bears some similarities to my thesis that ordinary expressions are cluster-vague—both views criticize the fixation on the sorites as well as the predominant tendency to idealize away crucial features of vague terms—the definition of cluster vagueness is also compatible with the classical framework in that it merely states that an unanalysable similarity plays an essential role in identifying borderline cases; whether there can be a fixed set of objects that are clearly non-borderline is left open (as is the question of how to model vagueness logically).

In short, the vagueness of many artificial and scientific expressions is soritical, whereas the vagueness of natural language expressions usually is not. To put it differently, the definitions of soritical and cluster vagueness are tailor-made to distinguish between the vaguenesses of these kinds of expressions. In addition, these definitions do not preclude any semantic or logical approaches to vagueness. For these reasons, I think that the distinction between soritical and cluster vagueness is valuable in its own right. In this chapter, however, I will go further and use it to reveal an interesting feature of legal definitions of natural language terms: their non-conservativeness.

3. Conservative Extensions

We usually demand of a sensible definition that it be conservative, in the sense that it should not enable us to draw any essentially new conclusions. A definition should fix the meaning of the *definiendum* without doing any damage to the meanings of terms that are not synonymous with it. One way to make this loosely formulated criterion more strict is implemented in the following definitions:

> **Definition 4.** *An **extension of a language** is the addition of a new term (together with its application conditions).*

> **Definition 5.** *Let E be an extension and Σ the set of statements that do not contain the new term. Then E is **conservative** if and only if exactly those S ∈ Σ are deducible from other statements in Σ that were deducible previously to the extension.*

In other words, for conservative extensions the following is true: if some statement formulated in the old, unextended language follows from other statements, also formulated in the old, unextended language, *after the extension*, then it already followed *prior to the extension*; and if some statement formulated in the old, unextended language does not follow from other statements, also formulated in the old, unextended language, *after the extension*, then it already did not follow *prior to the extension*.

Examples of conservative language extensions are the definitions of a foot and of gold. When we define a foot as a certain unit of measure equal to 30.48 cm, we introduce the new term 'foot' into English. It does not matter that there already exists a word 'foot' in the language. Depending on how one would prefer to individuate words, one can either say that 'foot', denoting a certain part of the body, and 'foot', denoting the unit of measure, are two different (although phonetically and graphically identical) words in English, or that now the word 'foot' can be used to refer to two different things. In both cases, the meaning of the old usage of 'foot' does not change, and no formerly invalid deductions concerning statements in which 'foot' is used in the old way become valid (and no formerly valid deductions become invalid). Nor, of course, is there any change of validness or invalidness in deductions that do not contain the word 'foot' in whatever sense. For that reason, our definition adds a new term, together with its application conditions, and leaves the rest of the language as it was. Hence it is conservative.

The scientific definition of gold—an element with the atomic number 79—is a clarification of the English term 'gold', with the help of which we talk about some bright yellow, malleable, and inert metal without caring about its inner structure. So when we talk of gold in the scientific sense, we are more exact than when we talk of gold in the everyday sense. Nevertheless, even if we keep in mind how to use 'gold' in scientific contexts, its use in non-scientific contexts remains the same; no new inferences arise. As in the case of 'foot', it does not matter that the scientific expression and the non-scientific one are (at least phonetically and graphically) identical; we could easily imagine that, whenever exactness matters, we would say and write 'sci-gold' instead of 'gold' to signal that now we are talking about gold in the scientific sense. And in the unlikely case that we come to know that the extensions of 'sci-gold' and 'gold' differ considerably, we could stop talking about gold altogether without becoming aware of it, for we would still say 'gold' but mean sci-gold.

The next example—this time one involving a non-conservative language extension—is more artificial. It may therefore help to introduce a phonetically and graphically new term into English in order to make matters more transparent (note, however, that nothing hinges on choosing that term instead of a well-known one). The example concerns *precisifications* of cluster-vague terms. Assume, for instance, that we attempt to sharpen the meaning of 'child' by introducing the term 'child*' into our language and defining that *a person is a child* if and only if he or she is younger than fourteen*. We have then missed our point because this definition of 'child*' violates a highly plausibly necessary condition for precisifications of general terms such as 'child', namely that, in all clear cases of application, the imprecise general term applies to an object if and only if the precisified general term applies to that object. More formally:

(Equiv) $\forall x \big(x \text{ is not a borderline case of 'child'} \big) : x \text{ is a child} \leftrightarrow x \text{ is a child}^{*}.$

In the case of 'child*', this condition is violated because there may be, for example, thirteen-year-olds who are, by maturity and appearance, clearly not children. According to our definition of 'child*', however, they clearly are children*. So there are people to which the natural language expression definitely does not apply, whereas its alleged precisification definitely does apply. We can find such people because of the cluster vagueness of 'child', which simply precludes that we can precisify this term by setting an age limit, for the vagueness of the word does not depend solely on the gradable characteristic age and hence cannot be ironed out by sharpening only this dimension. As cluster-vague terms are imprecise in potentially infinitely many dimensions, and as any precisification, being a finite string of letters, can specify only finitely many dimensions, cluster-vague terms generally do not admit the kind of precisification that we tentatively proposed for 'child'.

In order to give a proper precisification of 'child' we must instead add *consequences of application* to our definition of 'child*': *if someone is a child, he or she must* *be younger than fourteen; and if someone is not a child, he or she cannot be younger than fourteen.* (Note that this addition to the definition of 'child*' explicitly concerns non-borderline cases of *children*, not of *children**.) These consequences of application guarantee that (Equiv) is satisfied by changing our use of 'child': some thirteen-year-old, whom we definitely would not have called a child because of maturity and appearance, now has to be regarded at least as a borderline case of a child. It is thus part of the refined definition of 'child*' that we use our old term 'child' in a slightly new way so as to make it properly specifiable at all. In looking for a suitable precisification, we ended up with a fastidious rectification of the use of a term for which no rectification was originally asked for. In short, the definition of 'child*'—and, more generally, any precisification of a cluster-vague term—is non-conservative.

Now imagine that, instead of introducing the word 'child*' into English, we would have used 'child' to refer to both children and children*, in the same way that we use 'gold' to refer to both gold and sci-gold. In most contexts, no difficulties would arise; and regarding the few problematic scenarios where confusion can be imagined, it could easily be resolved by making explicit what exactly the word is supposed to mean. So, as already anticipated, nothing depends on using a new word such as 'child*' for the precisification.

The view of precisifications as non-conservative extensions of natural language expression is foreshadowed in Wittgenstein's *Philosophical Grammar*:

> About the problem of the 'heap': Here, as in similar cases, one might think that there is an official concept like the official length of a pace; say 'A heap is anything that is bigger than half a cubic metre.' But this would still not be the concept we normally use. For that there exists no delimitation (and if we fix one, we are altering the concept); it is just that there are cases that we count as within the extension of the concept, and cases that we no longer count as within the extension of the concept.
>
> (Wittgenstein 1974, p. 240)

Wittgenstein's idea here is that a precisification does not result in sharpening the concept, or extending it to new areas of application, but in altering it: *if we fix a delimitation, we are altering the concept*. I think this is also the reason why Wittgenstein does not relate his discussion of family resemblance concepts to soritical vagueness: at the very moment at which we focus on one gradable characteristic and alter it by slight degrees, we are not using our ordinary concepts any more. Therefore sorites cases are something artificial, which can only occur when we do not use our natural language (in the strictest sense of the term) but instead some slightly idealized version of it in which terms are presupposed to admit of conservative precisifications.[3] If this is true, then my distinction between the

---

[3] How could one deal with the sorites paradox, given such an account of vagueness? Here is a suggestion of a solution, or at least a resolution, of the paradox in a way that agrees with Wittgenstein's thinking:

> The idea of the radically pragmatic solution to the sorites paradox is that it only makes sense to use a predicate P in a context—i.e. with respect to a comparison class—, if it helps to clearly demarcate the set of individuals within that comparison class that have property P from those that do not.... [U]sing predicate P when *explicitly* confronted with a set of objects that form a sorites series is *inappropriate*. (de Jaegher and van Rooij 2011, pp. 53–4)

vaguenesses of scientific and artificial expressions and of natural language terms is indeed Wittgensteinian.

4. The Artificiality of Legal Precisifications

The term 'legal definition' can be taken to refer to the definition of a legal term or to the legal definition of a natural language term. In the first sense, legal definitions establish the use of technical legal vocabulary, which is not normally used outside legal contexts. They state, for instance, what terms such as 'tort law' or 'national sovereignty' mean or what the difference between a barrister and a solicitor is. In the second sense, their *definienda* already have a specific, albeit indeterminate meaning in our everyday language, a meaning that should be made more exact by the definition in order to make it appropriate for legal purposes. Terms which are specified by this kind of legal definition often denote offences against certain laws and need to be defined to ensure more unequivocal subsumption. Examples are 'rape', 'theft', 'stalking', or 'hate crime'. Other common terms in need of legal specification include 'death', 'religion', and 'disability'. It might even transpire that the same natural language term is subject to various legal definitions, depending on its different applications. Which people count as children, for instance, may be viewed differently when talking about juvenile crime as opposed to child labour or child pornography.

Legal definitions in the first sense are stipulative definitions used for introducing technical terms; they are obviously conservative and of limited theoretical interest from a linguistic and philosophical point of view since their *definienda* can, at least in principle, be eliminated from our language without loss by substituting their *definientia* for them. So the second meaning of 'legal definition', which is also more widespread, is the more interesting; and it is this understanding that I will adopt in the rest of this chapter (unless otherwise noted).

Like scientific definitions, legal definitions state necessary and sufficient conditions (otherwise there would be no good reason to call them proper definitions). It follows, by our corollary, that the terms thus defined are soritically vague (if at all vague), whereas vague ordinary language expressions are cluster-vague. However, unlike many scientific definitions, legal precisifications are not based on empirical or conceptual findings about concrete or abstract objects. They rather draw more or less arbitrary boundaries. In doing that, they neither elucidate the meanings of natural language expressions nor establish new ones. Instead, legal precisifications alter the meanings of the terms they should define. In short, they are non-conservative. Viewed in this light, the expressions defined by legal precisifications are usually even further away from natural language than those defined by scientific definitions.

One could object as follows: according to what I have said in the preceding section, the scientific definition of 'gold' is conservative because it does not change the meaning of 'gold' in the non-scientific sense. So in a way, we distinguish two languages that are mostly parallel to each other, the ordinary language and the scientific one, and only when they intersect do we have to decide whether a certain token of 'gold' belongs to one or the other. Why could we not make the same claim for legal definitions? For instance, if there were a legal definition of 'child' stating that for legal purposes a child is someone younger than fourteen (a child in this legal sense is what I called a child*), why could we not then say that in all legal contexts 'child' means someone younger than fourteen, while in all non-legal contexts the meaning of 'child' remains the same? We could, it seems, simply distinguish legal language from normal language and claim that we can use 'child' in the latter as we are accustomed to using it, and in the former as defined, in the same fashion that we allow our traditional use of 'gold' to coexist with the new one. We could, in other words, abstain from adding consequences of application. Our definitions would then not be proper precisifications in the sense of section 3. However, they would be conservative.

There are two remarks to make here. First, an important difference between scientific definitions and such conservative legal definitions consists in authority. Technical language and natural language may exist parallel to each other most of the time, but if they meet, a decision has to be made concerning whether a term is better to be understood in the one sense or in the other. Making such a decision, however, does not pose much of a problem in the case of scientific definitions. Imagine a scenario in which someone claims that some yellowish substance is gold because of its density, malleability, and ductility, and in which this substance turns out not to have atomic number 79. Is this substance gold? Of course not; if the traditional criterion clashes with the scientific one, the latter trumps the former because it is grounded in comprehensive empirical findings and our best theories about the nature of reality, whereas the traditional criterion is little more than an uninformed guess at a feasible, yet unreliable criterion of classification. In stark contrast to this, if the legal sense of a word is established by a conservative definition, it is regarded as being not superior but rather inferior to the ordinary one when both senses lead to different results. Confronted with a very grown-up looking thirteen-year-old, we do not consider him or her to be a child, even if we are well aware that legally he or she counts as one. Our knowledge of the legal point of view does then not hinder us in abstaining from applying the legal expression, except in distinctly legal contexts. The underlying reason for this is that a legal definition is not commonly taken to reveal, in any sense, some hidden structure or essence of what it purports to define. It has no natural authority over our pre-theoretic understanding.

Of course, we could leave it at that. Instead of precisifying natural language terms by non-conservative legal definitions, we could give conservative ones for the very limited range of cases that are of explicit legal interest. Then—and this is my second remark—it is somewhat misleading to use phonetically and graphically identical words for both everyday contexts and legal ones because this gives the impression that the words essentially have the same meaning, and that the legal word is only more exact, as carefully defined terms usually are. Yet, instead of refining our usage of an ordinary term, we actually introduce a new term with a different usage. The result is that, whereas the technical vocabularies of the sciences are widely and beneficially applicable, the technical vocabulary of the legal language is neither of any help outside courtrooms, nor can it be properly understood there. In fact, the definition we have given is merely stipulative, like the definitions of expressions such as 'tort law'. The question is whether we can do better.

Non-conservative precisifications are more ambitious. Like scientific definitions, they aim at making our common use of a term more systematic and efficient by carefully carving out what seems most essential. Consequently, they can claim a similar authority. Were it not for their easily overlooked non-conservativeness, which exposes the foundation of this authority, they would clearly be the better choice. By contrast, the idea of stipulative legal definitions as a substitute for proper specifications is likely to become more attractive only in the light of the artificiality of precisifications in general—an understanding of which is, in turn, based on the insight that natural language terms are normally cluster-vague, if at all vague.

So our dilemma is this: we may either want our legal definitions to be real precisifications of natural language terms. Then they need to have a certain authority over our ordinary usage. We can provide them with that authority only by making our definitions non-conservative. This move may appear artificial to some extent since we are thereby attempting to change something naturally evolving, namely our language, by decree. Or else we could be content to define terms for legal usage alone. Although we could use words that are phonetically and graphically identical to ordinary language terms for this purpose, the newly defined terms are not in the least specifications or explications of ordinary ones. Hence this move is even more artificial, as it deepens the gap between natural and legal language.

In both cases, legal definitions neither state natural additions to nor intuitive explications of commonly used terms. As a consequence, their meanings cannot be extrapolated by laymen. This violates an important maxim in legislation, namely that legal texts ought to be understandable, at least as far as possible, in layman's terms.[4]

5. Consequences

What I have said so far can be summed up as follows:

Theorem 2. *To the extent that we wish legal language to be in line with natural language, we should avoid precisifying ordinary expressions with the help of legal definitions.*

This holds for legal precisifications of ordinary expressions, for precisifications are generally non-conservative, as reflections on their vagueness reveal. As we have

---

[4] Cf., for instance, § 42 Art. 5 of the *Joint Rules of Procedure of the Federal Ministries*: 'The language used in bills must be correct and understandable to everyone as far as possible' (published by the German Federal Ministry of the Interior, 6 March 2002, adopted by the German Federal Government on 1 Dec. 2006. Available at <http://www.bmi.bund.de/cae/servlet/contentblob/150474/publication File/13399/Moderner_Staat_-_Moderne_Id_23340_de.pdf>).

seen, conservative legal definitions do not present a way out, for these can only be used to define expressions for distinctly legal purposes.

It is important to note that this theorem, though normative with regard to respecting a particular causal relation, is not normative with regard to the question of whether legal precisifications should constitute a substantial part of legal language. It only states a condition: *if* we wish our legal language to have certain characteristics, *then* we should develop it in certain ways. Whether it is good for legal language to have these characteristics is left open. Although being understandable to everyone as far as possible is certainly a significant advantage, one could also argue that the non-conservativeness of legal definitions is a price well worth paying for the benefit of achieving proper precisifications. To be in line with natural language is not per se valuable; it is valuable only under the premise that natural language is an appropriate and efficient means of talking about all sorts of things. Once we reject this premise, for instance because we are convinced that a more exact and systematic usage of certain natural language terms would be preferable in general (and not only in legal contexts), our problems with legal precisifications disappear.

There are two further points to be made. First, a psychological one: when we decide whether a certain term is to apply in a specific case, we usually compare the case to paradigmatic scenarios of application. We do not ask whether some definition we have in mind is satisfied. In legal contexts, the same procedure would result not in checking legal definitions of the relevant expressions but in using our sense of language. Referring to legal definitions is thus less natural than referring to paradigm cases. In the same fashion, a more natural way to decide a case is not to determine whether a certain law applies to it but to determine to which paradigm cases it is sufficiently similar. So, compared to the psychological processes underlying statutory law those underlying case law are more similar to the psychological processes that govern our ordinary way of speaking. This means that it is not only the avoidance of legal precisifications but also the psychology of speaking that makes case law more attractive for those who wish legal language to be as close as possible to our natural one. Again, this is not a normative claim: my point is merely that there is an interesting connection between case law and closeness to ordinary language.

Second, assume that we like legal language to be as close to natural language as possible. What then are the consequences of theorem 2 for legal practice?

We should, for instance, refrain from defining a child as a person who is, say, younger than fourteen. We should rather decide whether someone is a child on a case-by-case basis, against the backdrop of the particular context, of similar cases, and of our sense of language.

Another example more relevant for legal purposes is a well-known case of electricity theft:[5] a mechanic manipulated a power line so that he could use electric power he had not paid for to light his room. A court had to decide whether this was a case of theft. However, according to the relevant definitions, something could be stolen only if it was *movable*. So the court had in effect to decide whether electric

---

[5] RGSt 32, 165 (Decision of the Supreme Court of the German Reich, May 1899).

power is a movable thing. It decided that it is not; as a result, the mechanic was acquitted on the charge of theft.

Things would have come out differently if the relevant legal definition had not played such a central role. The mechanic obviously committed an act of theft by manipulating the power line because what he did is more similar to paradigmatic cases of theft than to cases in which clearly no theft is involved; therefore, he is obviously guilty of a crime. This, by the way, was generally acknowledged by all parties; as a consequence, a new law was established that prohibited stealing electricity. Yet a new law would not have been necessary had the old one not relied on legal definitions according to which, counter-intuitively and unbeknownst to the law's drafters, the theft of electricity was impossible for purely conceptual reasons. What is more, had the old law not relied on such detailed legal definitions, the court could have dealt differently with the unprecedented and unanticipated phenomenon of electricity stealing when it first occurred, and could have decided that, according to the common legal understanding of theft, the mechanic had committed an act of theft. In general, discovering loopholes and slipping through them, whether intentionally or not, would be much harder. In short, one advantage of not clinging too tightly to legal definitions is that we can deal with loopholes at the very moment we become aware of them, and not just afterwards. As is well known, this could be of increasing importance nowadays given the rapid technological progress in areas that need to be regulated by, for example, copyright law or internet legislation.

References

Alston, William P. 1967. 'Vagueness'. In *The Encyclopedia of Philosophy Vol. 8*, edited by Paul Edwards, 218–21. New York: Macmillan.

Burks, Arthur W. 1946. 'Empiricism and Vagueness'. *Journal of Philosophy* 43(18): 477–86.

de Jaegher, Kris and Robert van Rooij. 2011. 'Strategic Vagueness, and Appropriate Contexts'. In *Language, Games, and Evolution*, edited by Anton Benz, Christian Ebert, Gerhard Jäger, and Robert van Rooij, 40–59. Springer: Berlin.

Hyde, Dominic. 2008. *Vagueness, Logic and Ontology*. Aldershot: Ashgate.

Sainsbury, Mark. 1990. 'Concepts without Boundaries'. Inaugural Lecture, given at King's College London, 6 November 1990. In *Vagueness: A Reader*, edited by Rosanna Keefe and Peter Smith, 251–64. Cambridge (MA): MIT Press, 1997.

Wittgenstein, Ludwig. 1953/2001. *Philosophical Investigations*. Oxford: Blackwell.

Wittgenstein, Ludwig. 1974. *Philosophical Grammar*. Oxford: Blackwell.

9

The Role of Vagueness and Context Sensitivity in Legal Interpretation

*Nikola Kompa**

1. Introduction

Most (if not all) general terms of natural languages are vague. Vague terms are commonly characterized by their failure to draw (sharp) boundaries; at least they draw 'no known boundary' (Åkerman and Greenough 2009, p. 280). The term 'rich', for example, doesn't draw a sharp boundary between those who are wealthy and those who are 'only' relatively well off; the term 'tall' doesn't draw a sharp boundary between those who are considerably above average and those only slightly above average; and similarly for other terms. Consequently, any boundary drawn nonetheless is bound to be arbitrary (from a semantic point of view). Yet legal practice ought to comply with a principle of non-arbitrariness. At the same time, '(l)egal interpretation is all about deciding cases' (Poscher 2012, p. 137). Taken together, these assumptions seem to land us in trouble. In everyday contexts, suspension of judgement might be the way to go when one encounters an unclear case. Alternatively, one might say something like 'He is neither rich nor not-rich' or employ certain hedging techniques by saying something like 'He is sort of bald'. But as Ralf Poscher aptly puts it: '"neither" is not an option in legal interpretation' (Poscher 2012, p. 134). Presumably, 'sort of' is not an option either.[1]

In what follows, I will argue that although 'vagueness is ineliminable arbitrariness' (Raffman 2014, p. 108), it does not pose a problem for legal interpretation. What proves to be challenging (but may also be of value) is the context sensitivity of linguistic interpretation in general. But the problems posed by context sensitivity

* I am very grateful to Geert Keil and Ralf Poscher who invited me to a conference and two workshops on the topic of vagueness and law and who gave me the opportunity to present earlier versions of this chapter (or parts thereof). I would also like to thank the other participants of the conference and the workshops for their valuable comments and critique; I am especially grateful to Diana Raffman, Stephen Schiffer, and Jason Stanley for very helpful discussions. I would also like to thank the participants of the colloquium at the Institute of Philosophy at the University of Osnabrueck for reading and commenting on earlier drafts of the chapter. Finally, I would like to thank Eric J. Engstrom, Rudi Owen Müllan, and Marc Andree Weber for proofreading the manuscript.

[1] Hedging techniques, just as ambiguity or ellipsis, ought to be (and commonly are) avoided in legal language; cf. e.g. Endicott 2005, p. 18.

The Role of Vagueness and Context Sensitivity in Legal Interpretation. First Edition. Nikola Kompa:.
© Nikola Kompa 2016. Published 2016 by Oxford University Press.

differ from those allegedly posed by vagueness, as they have nothing to do with arbitrariness, or so I will try to show.

I will begin by inquiring into the semantics of vague terms and then put forward a set of necessary conditions for vagueness (section 2). In section 3, two problems will be diagnosed that vagueness might be thought to raise in the context of legal interpretation. And since what is at issue here is the vagueness and context sensitivity of general terms, I will ask how terms become general, how generality is related to vagueness and context sensitivity, and how the latter two features are to be distinguished (section 4). The context sensitivity of linguistic interpretation will be discussed in more detail in section 5. The question of how and to what extent context sensitivity affects legal interpretation will be addressed in section 6, while section 7 will be devoted to the problem of how to legitimately draw a boundary in light of vagueness. I will close by summarizing the main points (section 8).

2. Borderline Cases and Tolerance

It is a simple observation that normal and competent speakers sometimes hesitate to apply a predicate p to an object o, although it wouldn't be a category mistake or in any other obvious way mistaken to apply p to o. And they hesitate not because they take themselves to be inadequately positioned to pronounce on o's being p; they don't feel they lack any relevant knowledge.[2] They hesitate even when all the relevant information is in. Object o is a *borderline case* of application of predicate p, one might say. As Max Black already noted, '[t]he vagueness of a term is shown by producing "borderline cases", i.e. individuals to which it seems impossible either to apply or not to apply the term' (Black 1937, p. 71). And according to a more recent characterization, 'vagueness just is the possibility of borderline cases' (Schiffer 1998, p. 199). The characterization of vagueness in terms of borderline cases is prevalent in recent debates on vagueness.

There is no unanimity, however, when it comes to the question of what makes something a borderline case. Suppose Joe is a borderline case of a bald man. Is it because normal and competent speakers are torn between two possible classifications; is vagueness a form of unwillingness or uneasiness and thus a psychological phenomenon? Or does the meaning of the term fail to provide a rule of application for all cases; is vagueness a semantic phenomenon? Or is it actually either a fact that Joe is bald or a fact that he is not bald? We just don't know which fact obtains; is vagueness a type of ignorance and therefore an epistemic phenomenon?[3]

In what follows, vagueness will be treated as a semantic phenomenon. The notion of a borderline case will have to be spelled out accordingly, yet not all cases left

---

[2] Appearances may be deceptive, or at least that is what the epistemic view of vagueness claims. According to the epistemicist, vagueness is a form of ignorance (cf. e.g. Williamson 1992, 1994, 1996, and 1997). Crispin Wright also defends the idea that a kind of ignorance is involved in cases of vagueness: he has it that people who encounter borderline cases are in a quandary as to what to say, although he is not subscribing to the epistemic view (Wright 2001).

[3] Still others blame vagueness on the world. For an overview of problems and questions regarding ontic vagueness cf. Keil 2013.

semantically open give rise to vagueness-related problems. Some cases that remain semantically open may be justifiably settled in context. They are borderline cases only at first glance (more on this below). Also—and this is a well-rehearsed point in the literature by now—admitting borderline cases provides at best a necessary condition for vagueness. A predicate with a sharply delineated set of positive cases, a sharply delineated set of negative cases, and a sharply delineated set of borderline cases would not be vague. A vague term doesn't yield a three-fold sharp division of this sort (Wright 1976). Higher-order vagueness, i.e. the possibility of borderline cases at any boundary one might be tempted to draw, seems to be what gets us into trouble.

But then, isn't the whole idea of attempting to resolve vagueness by drawing increasingly fine boundaries misguided from the start? Is not the application of vague terms bound by a *principle of tolerance*? According to Crispin Wright, a predicate

F is tolerant with respect to φ if there is also some positive degree of change in respect of φ insufficient ever to affect the justice with which F applies to a particular case.

(Wright 1976, pp. 156–7)

Tolerance, in turn, can be (partly) held accountable for vague predicates' sorites-susceptibility, as the major premise of the sorites paradox seems to implement a principle of tolerance. Take the following example (Fine 1975, p. 138):

A man with no hairs on his head is bald.

If a man with n hairs on his head is bald then a man with $(n+1)$ hairs on his head is bald.

∴ A man with a million hairs on his head is bald.

The second premise exploits the idea of tolerance: there are changes too small to make a difference to the application of the predicate 'bald'.[4] Note that tolerance does not require that adjacent objects o_i and o_{i+1} be phenomenally indistinguishable; all that is required is that the degree of change be so small as not to justify unequal treatment. Moreover, for the paradox to get off the ground, the predicate in question also has to have clear cases of its application. A man with no hair on his head is clearly bald, just as a man with a million hairs on his head is clearly not bald. Consequently, one might say that a predicate is vague only if

(i)   it admits borderline cases with respect to all boundaries one might be tempted to draw;

(ii) its application is governed by a principle of tolerance;

(iii) it has a clear case of its application.

---

[4] Different versions of the Principle of Tolerance ought to be distinguished (cf. e.g. Åkermann and Greenough 2009 or Raffman 2014). Some (such as Crispin Wright) prefer to couch it in more justificatory terms, as is also commonly done in forced-march-versions of the sorites paradox. The degree of change between objects o_i and o_{i+1} is said to be too small to *justify* a differential classification: if a speaker classifies o_i as *F* she ought (in order to be epistemically justified, semantically competent, or psychologically coherent—different senses of 'ought' make for different versions of the Tolerance Principle) to also classify o_{i+1} as *F*.

The latter two conditions combine to yield sorites-susceptibility (as they seem to issue inconsistent instructions; cf. Wright 1976, p. 153).

3. Partial Definition, Discretion, and Arbitrariness

The seeming impossibility of drawing boundaries (due to vagueness) has led some people to think that the 'essence [of vagueness] is to be found in the idea that vague concepts are concepts without boundaries' (Sainsbury 1990, p. 251). But then again, not anything goes. What is right is that no particular boundary is semantically mandated. The rules of language governing vague predicates are silent when it comes to certain cases. These predicates seem to be partially defined, as suggested by Scott Soames:

> [V]ague predicates are partially defined, in the sense of being governed by rules that provide sufficient conditions for them to apply, and sufficient conditions for them not to apply, but no conditions that are both individually sufficient and disjunctively necessary for them to apply, or not to apply, to an object.
>
> (Soames 2010, p. 46; cf. also Soames 2012, pp. 96–7, and Wright 1976)

The term 'red,' for example, might be governed by a rule that says that if something is a typical, ripe tomato then it is red. Yet if that is so, the rule provides guidance only for clear, paradigmatic cases. To those cases a speaker will apply the predicate (or its negation) lest he be disqualified from the group of competent speakers. This is occasionally put by saying that vague terms are subject to a clear-case constraint (e.g. by Graff Fara 2000, p. 57).[5] Yet if that is so, semantic rules fail to provide guidance in those cases where we need guidance the most (as they settle only clear cases).

But then, if semantic rules fail to guide us as soon as we turn away from clear cases, aren't we free to extrapolate as we like? Stewart Shapiro puts it thus:

> The rules of language use, as they are fixed by what we say and do, allow someone to go either way.
>
> (Shapiro 2006, p. 10)

And according to David Lewis, if nothing is at stake, speakers happily go along with their conversational partners:

> When in a state of semantic indecision, we are often glad to go either way, and accommodate our own usage temporarily to the whims of our conversational partners.
>
> (Lewis 1994, p. 313; cf. also Lewis 1979)[6]

---

[5] There are also logical constraints or what Kit Fine called penumbral connections:

> [L]ogical relations may hold among predicates with borderline cases or, more generally, among indefinite sentences. Given the predicate 'is red,' one can understand the predicate 'is non-red' to be its contradictory: the boundary of the one shifts, as it were, with the boundary of the other. [...] Let us refer to the possibility that logical relations hold among indefinite sentences as penumbral connections [...].
>
> (Fine 1975, p. 124)

[6] In Lewis 1986, he explains that he regards 'vagueness as semantic indecision: where we speak vaguely, we have not troubled to settle which of some range of precise meanings our words are meant to express' (p. 244).

Shapiro draws on Lewis' notion of a conversational score in his account of vagueness, the conversational score or record being 'a sort of running database' (Shapiro 2006, pp. 12–13) that tends to evolve in such a way that whatever has been asserted is—*ceteris paribus* and if no one objects—construed (if possible) as to count as correct.[7] So if someone asserts of a hitherto unsettled borderline case that it is *F*, then this will go on the record, or so Shapiro claims. Soames makes a similar point:

[...] speakers have the discretion of adjusting the extension and antiextension to include initially undefined cases. When one does this by predicating P of o, or by denying such a predication, and one's hearers go along, the extension (or antiextension) of P is contextually adjusted to include *o*, plus all objects that bear a certain relation of similarity to it.

(Soames 2010, p. 46)

Yet although speakers, occasionally, may go either way, there are limits to what they are allowed to do. First, while speakers may arbitrarily adjust a term's extension as they see fit, they are not in a position to insist on their judgment being true. Truth seems to give out here. In the legal case, a binding stipulation may be made; but in ordinary conversations the participants usually lack the required authority to do so. Second, speakers are free to go either way in the face of unsettled cases only if nothing turns on it. Put otherwise: audiences are accommodating only to the extent that they don't care (more on this below). Third, what counts as a clear case may be subject to contextual variation. In the context of a Yul Brynner look-alike contest Joe might be a borderline case of a bald man; in other contexts he may count as a clear case of baldness. Accordingly, the margin of discretion varies contextually. Fourth, and although not everyone would agree, there might also be something like a borderline-case constraint. According to Diana Raffman, for example, classification as borderline is always optional: 'Intuitively, one is never required to classify something as borderline; a judgment of "borderline" is always optional' (Raffman 2014, p. 67). But then, don't we have to classify certain cases as borderline? Think of a series of fifty coloured patches smoothly changing from red to orange with a clearly red patch at the beginning and a clearly orange one at the end. When it comes to patch #25, a speaker might say something like 'Patch 25 is a borderline case of red'. He could also hedge his utterance by saying something like 'The patch is sort of red' or 'The patch is reddish-orange', or something to that effect. Yet if he asserted flat-out that patch #25 was red, without the slightest sign of uneasiness, or if he even insisted on the patch being red when challenged, wouldn't he be disqualified from the group of competent speakers? Don't we have to recognize borderline cases as such? If nothing depends on it, a speaker might innocuously classify patch #25 as (sort of) red; but he ought not to insist on his classification. Consequently, although one might

---

[7] How does it help solve the paradox? According to Shapiro, the inductive premise (for each $i<n$, if Pa_i then Pa_{i+1}) is false. It is not true that for all i, if a speaker judges i to be P, then he will also judge $i+1$ to be P, for at some i in the series he will jump. For all that, there are no strong counterexamples to the inductive premise: 'That is, there is never a number i, such that "man i is bald" and "man $i+1$ is not bald" are both on the record at the same time' (Shapiro 2006, p. 23).

not have to explicitly classify a borderline case as such, one ought to recognize its precarious status. Moreover, just as the clear-case constraint has to be 'contextualized' because what might reasonably count as a clear case will depend on the context, so a borderline-case constraint has to be contextualized as well. What counts as borderline cases may vary with the context accordingly.

For all that, speakers occasionally use their discretion to draw boundaries, for example by counting Tom but not Tim among the bald men, although Tim's hair situation is only marginally different from Tom's. And sometimes speakers just have to draw a boundary, for instance for legal purposes. Even everyday purposes sometimes require that a boundary be drawn. Think of the owner of an arts supply store who has to put the red paint on one shelf, the orange paint on another, and the yellow paint on a third one (cf. Sainsbury 1990, p. 259). While it may be true that vague terms don't draw boundaries, speakers nonetheless sometimes draw boundaries. Yet any boundary thus drawn seems to be drawn arbitrarily.

Where does the arbitrariness stem from? Vagueness, some say, is due to the continuous character of nature and reality. But continuity is not the problem; if the world were discrete there would still be vagueness as long as the differences between adjacent items were too small to justify any language-driven classificatory distinction. That, again, is what tolerance requires. More specifically then, the discrepancy between the 'fine-grained' character of reality and the 'tolerant' character of linguistic classification is to be held accountable. Classification, in turn, is achieved by means of general terms. They are general in that they are equally applicable to, and so true of a whole bunch of entities (cf. Quine 1960, pp. 90–1). They are tailor-made to sort things into classes: the class of chairs, the class of red things, and so on. Consequently, they are a means of drawing boundaries if ever there was one. That would not be a problem if the entities in the world came neatly sorted into perfectly distinct, clearly bounded classes.[8] But they don't (many of them have evolved, for instance). And if they don't come thus sorted, any partitioning by means of language will be somewhat arbitrary from a semantic point of view in that there might have been other, albeit equally admissible ways of drawing the line. As Diana Raffman puts it, 'at a certain point, the rules give out and competent linguistic practice must become arbitrary' (Raffman 2014, p. 22). That is what gets the sorites paradox going:

In the broadest terms, vagueness is a form of arbitrariness—ineliminable arbitrariness. No rule dictates a particular stopping place in a sorites series. Thus the application of a vague

---

[8] Those who want to stick with the traditional model of classification by means of individually necessary and jointly sufficient conditions are called upon to provide an error theory that explains why we fail to come up with any such set of conditions. The traditional model came under attack as many as forty years ago with the advent of Prototype Theory in the 1970s. But vagueness also poses a problem for other models of classification such as prototype theory because there are (or may be) cases for which it may be unclear whether they are similar enough to the prototype for *F*-ness, say, to merit classification as an *F*.

word is, in this sense, unruly. If there is a rule in the vicinity, it dictates that speakers must stop *at no particular place.*

(Raffman 2014, p. 108)

Raffman also emphasizes that variation is permissible: if you and I classify a particular borderline case differently, we will not think the other one mistaken. We will not take ourselves to be genuinely disagreeing with one another.[9] And if tomorrow I classify the object differently than I do today, I would not see myself as retracting or correcting my earlier classification. I did not make a mistake back then. Any rule that obliged us to draw a sharp line—and always the same line at that—would require that we be sensitive to ever so slight differences between any two objects. Given that our discriminatory abilities are limited, compliance would not be possible. Yet even if our discriminatory abilities were up to the task, we should want the terms of our language to be vague (to not draw perfectly sharp boundaries). It is not that we're simply missing a linguistic convention that tells us which way to go, i.e. whether to apply the word 'bald' only to people with less than, say, 432 hairs on their scalp. Any such convention would be extremely tedious to the point of not being practicable any more. We would have to count grains before we could apply the predicate 'is a heap', or hairs before we could apply the predicate 'is bald', or shillings before we could apply the predicate 'is rich'. As Crispin Wright emphasizes:

'Heap' is essentially a coarse predicate, whose application is a matter of rough and ready judgement. We should have no use for a precisely demarcated analogue in contexts in which the word is typically used.

(Wright 1976, p. 157)

Consequently, the following line of reasoning may seem convincing:

1. Vague predicates are 'essentially coarse' and 'partially defined'; facts about meaning do not settle all cases.

2. Yet, in hitherto unsettled cases, speakers are free to go either way, as long as they can get away with it.

3. Consequently, the extension of vague terms varies in a rather whimsical fashion; any boundary drawn is drawn arbitrarily.

We are now in a position to diagnose two problems that vagueness raises in the context of legal interpretation. Vague terms force us to arbitrarily draw boundaries;

---

[9] Or to the extent that we take ourselves to be in disagreement, we take the disagreement to be faultless. As Crispin Wright points out:

[E]ven in the most robustly objective area of inquiry, vagueness—whether in the content of a statement at issue, or in the standards for appraising it, or in what one might style permissible thresholds of evidence—may set up the possibility of disagreement in which nothing worth regarding as a cognitive shortcoming is involved. It's tempting to say, indeed, that a statement's possessing (one kind of) vagueness just *consists* in the fact that, under certain circumstances, cognitively lucid, fully informed and properly functioning subjects may faultlessly differ about it.

(Wright 1992, p. 144)

and they are given to capriciously changing their extension. These are not exactly appealing features from a legal point of view.

Yet in what follows, I will argue that neither arbitrariness nor capriciousness pose a problem for legal interpretation. In the following sections, it will be argued that capriciousness is not a problem. Although it is true that the extension of general terms happens to vary according to the context, it does so—to a great extent at least—in a much more systematic fashion than vagueness would predict. And in section 7, I will argue that arbitrariness poses no problem either, as the arbitrariness forced on us by vagueness is of an innocuous kind.

4. General Terms

Legal rules, just as semantic rules, are supposed to provide guidance for all possible cases. But they, too, are bound to fail on that score. Semantic rules governing the use of general terms provide only partial guidance. And legal rules, being formulated by means of general terms, seem to inherit their 'gappy' character. It might therefore be worth our while to inquire into the workings of general terms in more detail.

General terms are a means of classification as they are supposed to be equally applicable to different, albeit similar entities. How similar (and similar in what respect) these entities have to be depends on the context. Moreover, new cases that we haven't provided for may turn up. In semantics, just as in law, we may come across hitherto unsettled cases and then have to decide how to classify them. As Dirk Geeraerts puts it:

Meanings change, and there is good reason for that: meaning has to do with shaping our world, but we have to deal with a changing world. New experiences and changes in our environment require that we adapt our semantic categories to transformations of the circumstances, and that we leave room for nuances and slightly deviant cases.

(Geeraerts 2006, p. 4)

The meaning of natural-language expressions seems to be a function of the ways people can reasonably and purposefully interact with the world, as Julius Moravcsik (1998) points out.[10] Yet we may conjure up fancy cases. Friedrich Waismann emphasizes the open texture of our concepts ('die Porosität der Begriffe'):

Suppose I have to verify a statement such as 'There is a cat next door'; suppose I go over to the next room, open the door, look into it and actually see a cat. Is that enough to prove

---

[10] He claims, e.g.:

There is one everyday meaning for 'snow.' But it generates an indefinite variety of denotational uses (how dry? how light? How much of it in flakes?). These are the function of human interactions with nature. We cannot predict or give a qualitative exact specification of all past and future human interactions with nature that have or will affect our use of 'snow.'

(Moravcsik 1998, p. 43)

my statement? Or must I, in addition to it, touch the cat, pat him and induce him to purr? And supposing that I had done all these things, can I then be absolutely certain that my statement was true? (…) What, for instance, should I say when that creature later on grew to a gigantic size? Or if it showed some queer behavior usually not to be found with cats. (…) The fact that in many cases, there is no such thing as a conclusive verification is connected with the fact that most of our empirical concepts are not delimited in all possible directions.

(Waismann 1945, pp. 37–8; cf. also Wittgenstein 1984 PU §80
and Bix 2012, pp. 149–52)

Yet due to technical innovation, genetic engineering, and so on, fancy new entities might actually turn up, entities that could not have been anticipated. General terms have to be malleable and not 'delimited in all possible directions', so that they can be adapted to new cases. If we subsume entities under a given term that we haven't subsumed before, the term's extension thereby changes. Does that also effect a change in meaning? No factory-new car ought, it seems, to change the meaning of 'car'. But what if an engineer skilfully contrived a new 'kind' of vehicle? On the partial-definition model one might say that those new and not-yet-settled cases will be contextually settled at first; there may be good reasons (in context) to classify them one way or the other. Yet as time goes by, they may turn into clear cases, thereby changing the meaning of the term.

But how do general terms become general in the first place? They become general by abstraction, i.e. by the omission of distinguishing, yet irrelevant detail. We want not only to classify phenomenally *indistinguishable* items in the same manner, but also, as pointed out before, to group *distinguishable* (yet similar) items together. Say, for example, we want to classify different objects as chairs and that they may differ in size, form, material, whether they have arms rests, back rests, etc. This requires that we omit distinguishing details that are irrelevant to the purpose of the classification and focus on the respects in which the things to be arranged in classes are (relevantly) alike.

One might say that the more general a term is, the larger its extension will be. The term 'animal' is more general (in that sense of the term) than the term 'tiger' (cf. Endicott 2005; Waldron 1994, p. 522). Similarly, one might say that the more general a term is, the more varied the items in its extension will be. Some general terms can be used to sort together a wide variety of otherwise differing entities (or behaviours). Therefore, they may prove particularly useful for legislative purposes, as

(…) the law must predominantly, but by no means exclusively, refer to classes of persons, and to classes of acts, things, and circumstances; and its successful operation over vast areas of social life depends on a widely diffused capacity to recognize particular acts, things, and circumstances as instances of the general classification which law makes.

(Hart 1961, p. 121)

Yet Timothy Endicott holds that '(p)recise standards are impossible when the law needs to regulate widely varying conduct with a general standard' (2005, p. 24).

One of his examples is the term 'neglect' as used in the *Children and Young Persons Act* from 1933:

By statute, it is an offence to cause a child or young person to be 'neglected, abandoned, or exposed, in a manner likely to cause him unnecessary suffering or injury to health.'

(Endicott 2005, p. 16)

Very different types of behaviour can constitute cases of neglect, depending on the particularities of the situation. The term 'neglect' requires a multidimensional evaluation 'with (at least some) incommensurable constitutive elements' (Marmor 2014, p. 89; cf. also Soames 2011, p. 39). Other general terms such as 'reasonable', 'proper', or 'avoidable' are also applicable to a wide variety of cases. Yet this seems to be due to the fact that they are highly abstract and pick out a feature that a wide variety of entities may exhibit; and they specify one feature of a situation or action without specifying any other. More specifically, they are mainly used to evaluate, rather than describe. General terms often express thick concepts (cf. Williams 1985, p. 129; cf. also Waldron 2011, pp. 72–3) that involve descriptive as well as *evaluative* components.[11] They require that a particular kind of evaluative assessment of the situation be made (cf. Väyrynen 2013, p. 170). As Jeremy Waldron puts it: 'it is part of the meaning of these words to indicate that a value judgment is required...' (Waldron 1994, p. 527). Again, terms like 'proper' or 'reasonable' don't seem to provide much descriptive content, but they are still a means of evaluating actions in light of certain purposes, interests, norms, etc.

The multidimensionality as well as the abstract and evaluative character of general terms makes them highly *context-sensitive*. What may count as reasonable or proper behaviour, what may count as an avoidable risk or as constituting neglect, depends on the context. Using those terms is a way of increasing context sensitivity. So while Endicott calls them 'extravagantly vague' (Endicott 2005, p. 17; cf. also Soames 2012, p. 103), I suggest that we call them 'extravagantly context-sensitive'.[12]

This is not to deny that they too are vague. Yet context sensitivity ought to be distinguished from vagueness (Kompa 2015a). Vagueness has to do with the fact that the class of cases falling under a term will be fuzzy at the edges. (Is a certain prehistoric animal already a tiger or yet another species?) Context sensitivity has to do with the fact that the delineation of the class might vary with contextually differing interests and purposes. (Are toy tigers tigers?)[13] Vagueness, as pointed out above, is *arbitrary* variation. Due to their vagueness, the extension of general terms

---

[11] For a detailed investigation into the semantics and pragmatics of thick concepts, cf. e.g. Väyrynen 2013.

[12] Endicott is well aware of the distinction between vagueness (or indeterminacy) and context sensitivity, drawing the distinction himself in Endicott 2000, pp. 19–21. For more comprehensive attempts at distinguishing different forms of incompleteness, indeterminacy, ambiguity, generality, and vagueness, cf. e.g. Endicott 2000, Poscher 2012, or Solan 2012.

[13] Quite a few philosophers and legal scholars emphasize the value of vagueness in the law (cf. e.g. Endicott 2005, Poscher 2012, or Waldron 2011). Yet given the distinction between vagueness and context sensitivity suggested here, one might wonder whether many of the virtues ascribed to vague terms aren't due to their context sensitivity or generality rather than their vagueness (cf. Soames 2011, p. 39).

varies in a haphazard fashion, as speakers are free to go either way (if nothing turns on it) and their interlocutors are likely to accommodate their usage to the speakers. What is thereby overlooked, though, is that a general term's extension also varies with the context—at least to a considerable degree—in a systematic fashion and not just in the haphazard, random fashion that vagueness would predict. Context sensitivity, as opposed to vagueness, is *systematic* variation in the extension of a term with features of the context of utterance. Failing to distinguish the two phenomena has an untoward consequence, as one will miss the fact that while vagueness can never fully be resolved, context sensitivity can be resolved, and justifiably so. Vagueness makes any boundary drawing slightly arbitrary. Context sensitivity, on the other hand, may require extra interpretive effort and a contextually salient standard to which to appeal. Consequently, context-sensitive terms are *valuable* in communication to the extent that they are amenable to consensual interpretation (within context). To this I now turn.

5. Context Sensitivity

Linguistic interpretation is sensitive to contextual variation.[14] Speakers usually say what they say for a reason and with a particular purpose in mind. And audiences interpret what others say in light of (presumed) shared interests, purposes, concerns, and against a backdrop of certain assumptions (cf. Searle 1980). Most natural language expressions are context-sensitive.

CS: An expression type is context-sensitive only if different tokens of it can have different extensions relative to different contexts of its use.[15]

Context sensitivity is a form of under-determination (the price to be paid for the generalness) and context has to fill in the missing information. Using and interpreting the same expression differently in the different contexts of its use allows us to employ a finite vocabulary in order to talk about or describe an—in principle—infinite array of situations. It makes natural language extremely efficient (cf. Goodman 1976, p. 8, Barwise and Perry 1983, p. 5, Cohen 1985, p. 132, Moravcsik 1998, p. 44).

Whom we call rich, tall, interesting, or bald and what we call red, good, important, or evident varies in accordance with our changing interests, concerns, and

[14] There is, unsurprisingly, a huge debate about the extent to which and the ways in which natural language is context-sensitive (cf., among many others, Carston 2002, Borg 2004 and 2012, Récanati 2004, Cappelen and Lepore 2005, Predelli 2005, and Preyer and Peter 2007). I tend to side with pragmatically oriented philosophers and linguists such as Robyn Carston or François Récanati, but will not go into that here (cf. Kompa 2010 and Kompa and Meggle 2011).
[15] How to semantically model context sensitivity is a topic of heated debate that, for the time being, I will leave to one side. It is often construed either as a form of subtle incompleteness or of polysemy. I prefer a different semantic model, one that draws on Kaplan's distinction between contexts of utterance and circumstances of evaluation; it is a version of what came to be called—following John MacFarlane—'Nonindexical Contextualism'. The Nonindexicalist will locate the context sensitivity at issue not at the level of content but at the level of circumstances of evaluation (cf. MacFarlane 2009, Kompa 2014 and 2015b).

purposes. Someone might be said to be tall when we are talking about a sixth-grader, yet not tall when we are talking about NBA players; a wine might be said to be good when compared to ordinary table wines, yet not good when compared to Premier Crus, etc. If we call someone rich, for example, the purpose or point of the conversation, the participants' interests and concerns, their shared background assumptions, and so on determine something like a 'standard' for richness, i.e. the standard someone has to meet in order to count as rich in the context at hand. And the extension of the term 'rich' varies *systematically* with changes in the context of utterance. Similar contexts will determine similar standards (and thereby similar extensions). Given certain interests, purposes, concerns, and background assumptions, Joe will reasonably count as being tall; given other interests, etc. he will not.[16] A particular interpretation can be justified if it is shown to be the most reasonable one in light of all relevant contextual features. Suppose a speaker, call her Mira, says 'Mary is rich', once in the course of a conversation about middle-class people and their income and assets, and again in the course of a conversation about Bill Gates and people of that ilk. What did Mira mean to communicate? In the first conversation it was, presumably, something to the effect that Mary is rich compared to middle-class people. In the second conversation it was, presumably, something to the effect that Mary is rich compared to Bill Gates and his peers. Someone privy to the second conversation might reason as follows:[17]

Mira said 'Mary is rich'. I take it that she tried to say something true. Given that we have been talking about people such as Bill Gates, her utterance would be true only if Mary were rich compared to these people. Accordingly, that is what she meant to get across.

If a standard has not yet been mutually established, a speaker, by saying something like 'Mary is rich', may be *suggesting* to her audience that 'rich' ought to be understood in such a way that Mary falls under the term in the context at hand (that is, again, a case of accommodation; Lewis 1979; cf. also Richard 2004, p. 226). But others may disagree. And so the standard need not be shared from the start and may have to be negotiated. In case a shared standard cannot be established, speakers will fall back on subjective uses of the terms in question. (Instead of saying 'Joe is tall', for example, they might say something like 'I find him tall'; cf. Kennedy 2013.)

In all other cases, the speaker tries to say something that comes out true *in context*, i.e. relative to a standard of richness operative in the context at hand. And in all these cases, interpretation requires that the purpose or point of the conversation,

---

[16] For more on the semantics of gradable adjectives, cf. e.g. Kennedy 2007.

[17] The interpreter is thereby performing a pragmatic (or abductive) inference, an *inference to the best interpretation* (cf. also Dworkin 1986, p. 52). It is a defeasible (non-monotonic) inference in which the interpreter will draw on all kinds of contextually relevant information (about the speaker, the world, the purpose of the conversation, etc.). She will also rely on certain communicative principles along the lines sketched by Paul Grice (cf. Grice 1989). As Robyn Carston puts it: 'These interpretative inferences are taken to be guided by certain pragmatic principles concerning standards of communicative behavior that we are entitled to expect from rational agents' (Carston 2013, p. 13). While traditionally it was thought that to interpret an utterance was to semantically interpret its syntactic structure, the result being a truth-apt content, contextual interpretation is a semantic-pragmatic joint venture. Pragmatic inferences seem to encroach upon formerly semantic terrain (cf. e.g. Kompa 2010).

the participants' interests and concerns, be taken into account (as these factors help determine the standard in question). Achieving communicative understanding is a multi-level process. Syntactic-semantic interpretation requires competence regarding the lexical meaning of the words and the rules of grammar. Pragmatic interpretation is successful to the extent that the interpreter grasps what the speaker meant to get across, including implicatures, presuppositions, etc. But in order to fully secure uptake, the interpreter has to also grasp the point or purpose of the utterance. She has to understand what further moves (beliefs, utterances, and actions) it would be appropriate to make, what inferences would be sanctioned, etc. Only then has full *contextual understanding* been achieved. Contextual interpretation is a kind of practical, means–end reasoning; it is intimately tied to purposes, goals, and interests.

This is all the more obvious when it comes to interpreting orders, rules, norms, etc. Here is an example cited by John Searle to illustrate the point. As Searle argues, the verb 'cut' is polysemous. It can be used to describe slightly different actions, as one can (i) cut the grass; (ii) cut someone's hair, (iii) cut the cake; (iv) cut one's skin, etc. (cf. Searle 1980, p. 221). And as he remarks, if 'someone tells me to cut the grass and I rush out and stab it with a knife (…) I will have failed to obey the order' (Searle 1980, p. 223). Yet a listener will usually be able to correctly interpret the order and to appropriately act on it because he knows that what one does when one cuts the grass is different from what one does when one cuts the cake or one's hair or one's skin. In each case, different purposes are being pursued. The reason why we hardly ever get mixed up is that we know a lot of things about grass and cakes, etc.: we know what people have lawns for, what they have cakes for, what purposes it commonly serves to cut the grass or to cut the cake, and so on and so forth (Searle 1980, pp. 226–7). There are many different uses to which we may put the words of our language—as many as there are different goals that might be pursued in interacting with the world (cf. Moravcsik 1998, p. 37).

6. Legal Interpretation

Do these considerations carry over to the case of legal interpretation? What is required in order to interpret the law is a hotly contested issue, and the role of the lawmaker's original intention is especially controversial. In German legal hermeneutics, the canon of interpretation requires, first, that the interpretation be true to the literal meaning of the rule (a somewhat problematic conception in light of language change, context sensitivity, and vagueness). Second, the interpretation ought to take into account the purpose the lawmaker was originally pursuing by promulgating the rule, i.e. the problem the rule was initially meant to resolve. Moreover, it ought to be systematic in that it has to fit into a reconstruction of the whole system of statutes or rules that are thought of as implementing a coherent set of values. And it ought to comply with the values manifest in the constitution. Finally, the purpose that the rule can be taken to serve today is also relevant to interpretation (cf. Hassemer 2011 and Schroth 2011).

But one might wonder whether interpretation is always called for in order to understand what the law says in the first place. Ronald Dworkin famously argued that interpretation is always required (Dworkin 1986). Moreover, purposes play an important role:

> Interpretation of works of art or social practices, I shall argue, is essentially concerned with purposes not causes. But the purposes in play are not (fundamentally) those of some author but of the interpreter. Roughly, constructive interpretation is a matter of imposing purpose on an object or practice in order to make of it the best possible example of the form or genre to which it is taken to belong.

> (Dworkin 1986, p. 52)

Andrei Marmor, on the other hand, is among those who think that interpretation is the *exception*. He claims that it is called for only if some aspect of context is not clear enough or in cases of indeterminacy of content.[18] He acknowledges the context sensitivity of natural language, but still has it that

> ... context sensitivity of communicated content does not entail that in understanding such expressions the hearer is necessarily engaged in anything we can call interpretation. In most ordinary cases, the context of conversation is *common ground*, shared by speaker and hearer, and thus enables the hearer to grasp the relevant content without any particular difficulty or need for interpretation.

> (Marmor 2011, pp. 139–40)

Obviously, it all depends on how demanding a conception of interpretation one favours. The above conception of contextual interpretation is less demanding than Dworkin's notion of interpretation; and it is compatible with Marmor's claim that speakers may often effortlessly understand context-sensitive utterances. Nonetheless, in all cases of context-sensitive utterances I prefer to speak of interpretation (although in the end, this is a terminological point), as there is room for misinterpretation and different speakers may interpret a given utterance differently. Still, what I'm arguing here is only that contextual interpretation, in the sense outlined above, is required in legal interpretation to the extent that legislative language employs context-sensitive terms.[19] Moreover, the account of contextual interpretation draws attention to an important question, to wit the question of whose context (and so also of whose purpose and interests) counts.

For the law must be interpreted by different groups of people, such as those applying it and those subject to it. Do those applying the law engage in contextual interpretation at all? To see that they do, consider the following slightly overworked example that was once the subject of a fierce controversy between Lon L. Fuller and H.L.A. Hart. At the entrance to a park there is a sign that reads: 'No vehicles in the park'. What counts as a vehicle depends, presumably, on the context. Suppose the question comes up whether skateboards, roller skates, wheelchairs, and strollers

---

[18] Timothy Endicott makes a similar point: 'Interpretation comes into play when there is a possibility of argument as to the meaning of the law' (Endicott 2012, p. 112).

[19] For a discussion of further parallels between legal canons of construction and pragmatic, neo-Gricean principles of interpretation, cf. Carston 2013.

should count as vehicles. These are actual borderline cases, i.e. cases so far not settled. Those who have to apply the law may specify what ought to count as a vehicle by trying to make explicit what the interests, purposes, desires, and so on were when the rule was made and what reasons those promulgating it had for doing so. If those interests have changed in relevant respects so that the context they find themselves in significantly differs from the original context, they may also (have to) take those new interests into account and so let their actual context count. That would accord well with the canon of interpretation sketched above. (Yet on Dworkin's account, the purposes that ought to be taken into account are those of the interpreters. Whether that is a viable procedure is a topic that will be taken up below.)

Suppose that the guiding interest was (and still is) to ban noisy, air-polluting objects from the park because the park is meant to be a recreational area. Consequently, interpreters may come to agree that wheelchairs and strollers are not to count as vehicles: because they do not make much noise and do not pollute the air, they ought to be permitted access to the park. Skateboards, on the other hand, make too much noise and so ought to count as vehicles, while roller skates, making less noise than skateboards, may again be permitted access to the park. Interpreters thus manage to justify setting a boundary.[20] It is not a sorites-resolving boundary. Yet it is contextually admissible in that all relevant contextual factors have been taken into account (or so we may suppose). As Timothy Endicott put it: '[T]he context can and characteristically does answer questions of (i.e. determine) the application of words' (Endicott 2000, p. 20).

That seems to be a case of contextual interpretation. It is essentially concerned with purposes. Context sensitivity is resolved in context by appealing to salient purposes and a common understanding of what means (banning certain kinds of vehicles form the park) it would be proper to apply in order to achieve a particular end (less noise in the park). Making explicit how the context sensitivity has been resolved, i.e. how the ordinance ought to be interpreted in the case at hand, amounts to justifying that a particular entity ought or ought not to be included in the extension of the context-sensitive term 'vehicle' as it was employed in the formulation of the ordinance. Interpretation and justification are two sides of the same coin.

To sum up, context sensitivity can be successfully resolved in context only by appeal to a shared standard for what counts, for example, as a vehicle or as reasonable or as non-aggressive driving. Those standards may change over time. By employing context-sensitive terms in legislative language, those applying the law are put in position to take new interests and purposes into account. Context sensitivity therefore seems to guarantee continuity and adaptability of the law, as well as its material adequacy to each particular case (cf. Middelschulte 2007, p. 92). Moreover, context-sensitive legislative language is of value to those applying the law because it is a means of delegating power: '. . . the legislature in effect delegates the

---

[20] Commonly, things will not be that simple. There may be conflicting interests so that we have to balance reasons: is the no-exposure-to-noise-aspect or the recreational aspect more important? And maybe only slow-moving objects should be allowed into the park in order to avoid accidents. Also, sometimes it may be less clear what the relevant interests, etc. are in the first place.

decision of how to make the standard more precise to the courts or to administrative agencies' (Marmor 2014, p. 94; cf. also Endicott 2005, § 8).

What about those subject to the law? Do they have to engage in contextual interpretation? And do they also benefit from context-sensitive legislative language? For one might think that the above considerations gloss over a huge problem. Some statutes or provisions may not be readily interpretable to those subject to the law. According to American constitutional law, a statute is void for vagueness if its meaning can only be guessed at and if people will differ in its application.[21] Also, a term's meaning and application may be fairly clear at one time, but due to technical, medical, or other innovations borderline cases of its application may suddenly arise. Those subject to the law may be at a loss as to the correct interpretation of a particular rule (Hassemer 2011).

But then how much guidance has to be provided by a legal rule? Think of a moral principle that says that one ought not to harm other people. Is it void for vagueness? And yet isn't it exactly what we want people to do: not to harm other people? Consider the following example cited by Jeremy Waldron. He tells us that in 1917 the Ohio General Code contained the following provision:

§ 12603: Whoever operates a motor vehicle or motorcycle on the public roads or highways at a speed greater than is reasonable or proper, having regard for width, traffic, use and the general and usual rules of such road or highway, or so as to endanger the property, life or limb of any person, shall be fined not more than twenty-five dollars.

(Waldron 2011, p. 59)

Waldron is interested in the question of whether a provision like this one is at odds with the idea that law ought to be able to guide people's actions or behaviour. For he thinks that norms or rules are a means for guiding action or conduct (cf. Waldron 2011). He claims that even in cases such as §12603, in which it is left to the driver to figure out for himself which specific action is required of him, the provision offers some guidance by 'directing his practical reason to a problem to which the law draws attention, and requiring him to come up with and implement a solution' (Waldron 2011, p. 65). Waldron distinguishes between standards and rules:

And when we distinguish rules from standards, we sometimes say that the difference is that a standard is a norm that requires some evaluative judgement of the person who applies it, whereas a rule is a norm presented as the end product of evaluative judgements already made by the law-maker.

(Waldron 2011, p. 65)

Interpreting standards involves practical reasoning skills—just as interpreting other highly context-sensitive utterances does. And as Waldron rightly points

[21] As Poscher has pointed out, there is a similar doctrine in German criminal law (Poscher 2012, p. 130). And again, this is commonly not due to vagueness in the philosopher's sense of the term discussed in section 2 but is, again, rather due to the highly general and context-sensitive character of the terms employed. Also, people may disagree over whether a particular rule is void-for-vagueness or not (Waldron 2011).

out, the driver may still be cited for driving at an unreasonable speed (Waldron 2011, p. 64). Even in cases of extravagant context sensitivity as exhibited by words such as 'reasonable', the context sensitivity may be resolved, given the circumstances at hand, by issuing a justified verdict. Moreover, isn't 'driving at a reasonable speed', again, exactly what we want people to do? There is no better way of putting it, it seems. So it better be interpretable. We don't want them to go 10 mph or 20 mph—we want them to drive at a reasonable speed, presumably because we think that someone who drives at a reasonable speed will be less liable to cause accidents and so be no risk to the life and health of others. Those highly abstract and extravagantly context-sensitive terms allow us to pick out a particular feature that we want a vast variety of actions to have in widely differing circumstances—being reasonable, for example. One might even claim that those terms invoke a certain ideal—the ideal driver, for example, or the ideal parent. And as C.A.J. Coady points out,

it is often more functionally efficient to direct people to the ideal than to something more concrete and achievable well short of it. The very vagueness and 'unreality' of the ideal paradoxically may make compliance with it and guidance by it more manageable than the focus on specific reality. (...) [T]he relative vagueness or incompleteness of the ideal allows considerable scope for the work of practical intelligence and imagination in implementing it.

(Coady 2008, pp. 61–2)

But there is a catch. If someone is driving at an unreasonable speed, it may well be that he fails to share 'our' standard of reasonableness. This may be due to ignorance and so be an epistemic problem; he may simply not know what the standard requires (he ought not to be punished but needs to be educated, one might think). Yet there may be others who share our standard, but who violate it on purpose—they just do not want to be reasonable. It seems they fail to value what we value. We are left with the following problem: contextual interpretation is successful in context only if the relevant standards and values are shared; and while it is not implausible to assume that they will (mostly) be shared among those applying the law, those subject to the law may fail to share them. They are, presumably, not privy to the discussions in which the standard is fixed (thus raising a question of power and authority that I am not considering here). Their purposes play a role only to the extent that those who set the standard happen to take them into account. That is not to deny that, in justifying a particular verdict, common sense and public weal are often appealed to (Dworkin 1986, p. 23). Yet it may explain why they came into conflict with the law in the first place (at least in the case of ignorance). Moreover, those who fail to share the standard (of what might count as proper behaviour, for example) are exactly those whose behaviour needs to be governed by the rule. Those who have the most problems in correctly interpreting the norm are those whose behaviour needs regulating the most. Consequently, while highly context-sensitive legislative language may prove beneficial to those making or applying the law, it is not beneficial to those mainly affected by it.

But then, whose behaviour is the law meant to govern anyway? Not many people will be familiar with the details and exact formulations of most codified laws. On the assumption that the law is to guide the behaviour of those applying the law, the use of context-sensitive legislative language is easily justified as it proves beneficial to those applying the law—it allows them to accommodate changes in interests and purposes and makes the law highly adaptive. Yet on the assumption that the law is meant to guide people's behaviour, context-sensitive language ought to be avoided, given that those who need guidance the most fail to acknowledge the relevant standards. Consequently, precisely formulated rules—for example ones that specify precise speed limits—would be more effective and desirable. Yet is it admissible to decide on a precise speed limit (or voting age, etc.) given the threat of arbitrariness discussed above?

7. ...Vagueness Still Remains

Suppose we managed to resolve all context sensitivity in a particular case. We would still not be able to settle all cases. As Timothy Williamson rightly emphasizes: 'Vagueness and context dependence are separate phenomena (...) vagueness remains even when the context is fixed' (Williamson 1994, p. 215). Semantic rules together with contextually relevant interests, purposes, etc. do not decide all cases; they may justify settling certain hitherto unsettled cases, but they don't justify drawing a sorites-resolving boundary.

Take the Hart example again. Suppose we also try to set a speed limit for those moving objects that are granted access to the park. Given our overall purposes, we would like to ban fast-moving objects; only slow-moving objects ought to be allowed. But when asked whether the limit is to be set at 4.9 mph or 5.0 or 5.1 mph, we are undecided. Each limit would equally serve our purpose of banning fast-moving objects. And again, any dividing up of a continuum is arbitrary to some extent—there would have been alternative ways of drawing the line. Nothing of concern to us turns on where exactly the line will be drawn. Our interests and purposes seem to be themselves vague, a point emphasized by Delia Graff Fara:

So when I say (...) that our purposes and desires can be vague, I mean that we may have purposes and desires with achievement or satisfaction conditions that may seem tolerant in the requisite sense, and hence boundaryless. When I desire some coffee, as I do every morning, how could it be that the desire I have could go from being satisfied to being unsatisfied—or even from being definitely satisfied to being borderline satisfied—just by removing one little drop of coffee from the cup I have in front of me?

(Graff Fara 2000, p. 49)

Yet while Graff-Fara seems to think that appearance is deceptive here, I am inclined to think that interests, purposes, and desires may well be vague. Yet their vagueness cannot be traced back to any context sensitivity. Instead, it results from the fact that nothing in our interests, etc. justifies the drawing of a sorites-resolving boundary.

But then again, in the speed-limit case we simply have to draw a boundary. Not a particular boundary, but a boundary nonetheless. At least it would dramatically increase process value as well as guidance value:

Precision (…) is valuable in two ways: it has *guidance value* in offering a precise proposal for action to persons subject to a standard, and it has *process value* in controlling the system's techniques for applying the standard.

(Endicott 2005, p. 15)

This may be enough to justify the drawing of *a* boundary (cf. Marmor 2014, p. 90). Consequently, in the speed-limit case, practical considerations will come into play. Presumably, we want the boundary to be manageable, in order to increase process value, and easy to keep in mind and to implement, in order to increase guidance value. We will prefer to draw the boundary at 5 mph instead of at 4.999 mph or at 5.107882 mph. Practicability will thereby become another (contextually determined) interest of ours. It is subordinate to the other interests we had in enacting the ordinance, though. For there is no reason we could cite for why we set the limit at 5 mph and not somewhere else other than that this is just somehow easier to manage and to keep in mind; and that we just have to draw it somewhere. (Note that even this boundary is not a sorites-resolving boundary as there are still borderline cases; it may be indeterminate exactly when a moving object travels at the speed of 5 mph. Still, the boundary may serve all practical purposes.)

However, in other (non-legal) cases, practicality may impose no particular constraints. Suppose we are employees in an arts supply store and our task is to distribute sixty-five oil colours on two shelves. Ought we put thirty-three on the upper or on the lower shelf? That seems arbitrary. Any boundary to be drawn has to respect semantic and contextual constraints. Yet within the remaining area of borderline cases, any boundary seems to be just as good as any other. No single particular boundary suggests itself. The semantic and contextual constraints are silent on the question of where exactly the boundary ought to be drawn. But if we have to draw a boundary, then given that there is still leeway, can't we draw it anywhere we like as long as we are meeting all relevant constraints? Drawing a boundary in an arbitrary way seems to be semantically and contextually admissible if all semantic and contextual constraints have been taken into account. According to Timothy Endicott, '[a]rbitrariness is resistance to or absence of reason' (Endicott 2005, p. 20). Yet that is a problem only if reasons that are absent are required; but they are required only if relevant interests are affected without having been taken into account. But if context sensitivity has been successfully resolved, all contextually relevant interests have been accounted for (as in the Hart example discussed above)—and that is what it means to resolve context sensitivity. The problem of drawing a boundary for practical purposes is not the problem of drawing a sorites-resolving boundary. For all practical purposes, context sensitivity (and the resolution thereof) is more of an issue than vagueness.

8. Summary

My main concern was to show that vagueness—contrary to received opinion—does not challenge legal interpretation. To that end, I first inquired into the semantics of vague language. I tried to distinguish vagueness from context sensitivity. I characterized the former as an arbitrary variation and the latter as a systematic variation of a term's extension with contextual features such as the participants' interests, purposes, and concerns. I then argued that ordinary discourse is thoroughly context sensitive and that contextual interpretation is called for. And it is called for in legal interpretation as well. The context sensitivity of legal language guarantees the continuity and adaptability of the law (as is further witnessed by the fact that judges' verdicts often change over time even when the law remains the same).

Yet in order to successfully resolve any context sensitivity, we must appeal to contextually salient standards, values, etc. But not everyone subject to the law will share those standards (or values) and, unfortunately, those who fail to share them are the ones whose behaviour needs regulating the most. Highly context-sensitive language is therefore beneficial only to those applying the law.

Finally, even in cases where context sensitivity has been successfully resolved, there will still be vagueness. But within the remaining borderline area we are free to draw a boundary wherever we like as long as it is semantically admissible and all contextually relevant interests, etc. have been accommodated. Arbitrariness is not a problem as long as no one's legitimate interests are thereby affected. This is not to say that there is no problem, but simply that the problem hasn't much to do with vagueness and that it is instead one of deciding whose context counts and which interests are legitimate. (And that problem is huge.)

References

Åkerman, Jonas and Patrick Greenough. 2009. 'Vagueness and Non-Indexical Contextualism'. In *New Waves in Philosophy of Language*, edited by S. Sawyer, 8–23. Basingstoke: Palgrave Macmillan.

Barwise, Jon and John Perry. 1983. *Situations and Attitudes*. Cambridge (MA): MIT Press.

Bix, Brian. 2012. 'Legal Interpretation and the Philosophy of Language'. In *The Oxford Handbook of Language and Law*, edited by Lawrence Solan and Peter Tiersma, 145–145. Oxford: Oxford University Press.

Black, Max. 1937. 'Vagueness: An Exercise in Logical Analysis'. *Philosophy of Science* 4(4): 427–55. Reprinted in and quoted from Rosanna Keefe and Peter Smith (eds). 1997. *Vagueness: A Reader*, 69–81. Cambridge (MA): MIT Press.

Borg, Emma. 2004. *Minimal Semantics*. Oxford: Oxford University Press.

Borg, Emma. 2012. *Pursuing Meaning*. Oxford: Oxford University Press.

Cappelen, Herman and Ernie Lepore. 2005. *Insensitive Semantics: A Defense of Semantic Minimalism and Speech Act Pluralism*. Oxford: Blackwell Publishing.

Carston, Robyn. 2002. *Thoughts and Utterances: The Pragmatics of Explicit Communication*. Oxford: Blackwell.

Carston, Robyn. 2013. 'Legal Texts and Canons of Construction: A View from Current Pragmatic Theory'. In *Law and Language. Current Legal Issues Vol. 15*, edited by Michael Freeman and Fiona Smith, 8–33. Oxford: Oxford University Press.

Coady, C.A.J. 2008. *Messy Morality. The Challenge of Politics.* Oxford: Oxford University Press.

Cohen, Jonathan L. 1985. 'A Problem about Ambiguity in Truth-Theoretical Semantics'. *Analysis* 45(3): 129–34.

Dworkin, Ronald. 1986. *Law's Empire.* Oxford: Hart Publishing.

Endicott, Timothy. 2000. *Vagueness in Law.* Oxford: Oxford University Press.

Endicott, Timothy. 2005. 'The Value of Vagueness'. In *Vagueness in Normative Texts*, edited by Vijay K. Bhatia, Jan Engberg, Maurizio Gotti, and Dorothee Heller, 27–48. Bern: Peter Lang. Reprinted in and quoted from Andrei Marmor and Scott Soames (eds). 2011. *Philosophical Foundations of Language in the Law*, 14–30. Oxford: Oxford University Press.

Endicott, Timothy. 2012. 'Legal Interpretation'. In *The Routledge Companion to Philosophy of Law*, edited by Andrei Marmor, 109–22. New York: Routledge.

Fine, Kit. 1975. 'Vagueness, Truth and Logic'. *Synthese* 30(3): 265–300. Reprinted in and quoted from Rosanna Keefe and Peter Smith (eds). 1997. *Vagueness: A Reader,* 119–50. Cambridge (MA): MIT Press.

Geeraerts, Dirk. 2006. 'Introduction: A Rough Guide to Cognitive Linguistics'. In *Cognitive Linguistics: Basic Readings*, edited by Dirk Geeraerts, 1–28. Berlin/New York: de Gruyter.

Goodman, Nelson. 1976. *Languages of Art. An Approach to a Theory of Symbols,* 2nd edn. Indianapolis: Hackett Publishing.

Graff Fara, Delia. 2000. 'Shifting Sands: An Interest-Relative Theory of Vagueness'. *Philosophical Topics* 28(1): 45–81.

Grice, H.P. 1989. 'Logic and Conversation'. In *Studies in the Way of Words*, 22–40. Cambridge (MA): Harvard University Press.

Hart, H.L.A. 1961. *The Concept of Law.* Oxford: Clarendon Press.

Hassemer, Winfried. 2011. 'Rechtssystem und Kodifikation: Die Bindung des Richters an das Gesetz'. In *Einführung in die Rechtsphilosophie und Rechtstheorie der Gegenwart*, edited by Arthur Kaufmann, Winfried Hassemer, and Ulfrid Neumann, 8th edn, 251–69. Heidelberg: C.F. Müller.

Keil, Geert. 2013. 'Introduction: Vagueness and Ontology'. *Metaphysica* 14(2): 149–64.

Kennedy, Christopher. 2007. 'Vagueness and Grammar: The Semantics of Relative and Absolute Gradable Adjectives'. *Linguistics and Philosophy* 30(1): 1–45.

Kennedy, Christopher. 2013. 'Two Sources of Subjectivity: Qualitative Assessment and Dimensional Uncertainty'. *Inquiry* 56(2–3): 258–77.

Kompa, Nikola. 2010. 'Contextualism in the Philosophy of Language'. In *Meaning and Analysis: New Essays on H. P. Grice*, edited by Klaus Petrus, 288–309. Basingstoke: Palgrave Macmillan.

Kompa, Nikola. 2014. 'Knowledge in Context'. *Rivista Internazionale di Filosofia e Psicologia* 5(1): 58–71. Reprinted in Hans Jörg Sandkühler (ed.). 2014. *Wissen: Wissenskulturen und die Kontextualität des Wissens*, 181–98. Frankfurt/Main: Peter Lang.

Kompa, Nikola. 2015a. 'Vagheit'. In *Handbuch Sprachphilosophie*, edited by Nikola Kompa. Stuttgart: Metzler.

Kompa, Nikola. 2015b. 'Contextualism and Disagreement'. *Erkenntnis* 80(1): 137–52.

Kompa, Nikola and Georg Meggle. 2011. 'Pragmatics in Modern Philosophy of Language'. In *Foundations of Pragmatics. Handbook of Pragmatics Vol. 1*, edited by Wolfram Bublitz and Neal R. Norrick, 203–28. Berlin/Boston: de Gruyter Mouton.

Lewis, David. 1979. 'Scorekeeping in a Language Game'. *Journal of Philosophical Logic* 8(1): 339–59. Reprinted in and quoted from David Lewis. 1983. *Philosophical Papers, Vol. 1*, 233–49. Oxford: Oxford University Press.

Lewis, David. 1986. *On the Plurality of Worlds*. Oxford: Blackwell Publishers.

Lewis, David. 1994. 'Reduction of Mind'. In *A Companion to Philosophy of Mind*, edited by Samuel Guttenplan, 412–31. Oxford: Blackwell.

MacFarlane, John. 2009. 'Nonindexical Contextualism'. *Synthese* 166(2): 231–50.

Marmor, Andrei. 2011. *Philosophy of Law*. Princeton: Princeton University Press.

Marmor, Andrei. 2014. *The Language of the Law*. Oxford: Oxford University Press.

Middelschulte, Christiane. 2007. *Unbestimmte Rechtsbegriffe und das Bestimmtheitsgebot. Eine Untersuchung der verfassungsrechtlichen Grenzen der Verwendung sprachlich offener Gesetzesformulierungen*. Hamburg: Verlag Dr. Kovac.

Moravcsik, Julius M. 1998. *Meaning, Creativity, and the Partial Inscrutabilty of the Human Mind*. Stanford: CSLI Publications.

Poscher, Ralf. 2012. 'Ambiguity and Vagueness in Legal Interpretation'. In *The Oxford Handbook of Language and Law*, edited by Lawrence Solan and Peter Tiersma, 128–44. Oxford: Oxford University Press.

Predelli, Stefano. 2005. *Contexts: Meaning, Truth, and the Use of Language*. Oxford: Oxford University Press.

Preyer, Gerhard and Georg Peter (eds). 2007. *Context-Sensitivity and Semantic Minimalism: New Essays on Semantics and Pragmatics*. Oxford: Oxford University Press.

Quine, Willard Van Orman. 1960. *Word and Object*. Cambridge (MA): MIT Press.

Raffman, Diana. 2014. *Unruly Words: A Study of Vague Language*. Oxford: Oxford University Press.

Récanati, François. 2004. *Literal Meaning*. Cambridge: Cambridge University Press.

Richard, Mark. 2004. 'Contextualism and Relativism'. *Philosophical Studies* 119(1): 215–42.

Sainsbury, Mark. 1990. 'Concepts without Boundaries'. Inaugural Lecture, given at King's College London, 6 November 1990. Printed in and quoted from Rosanna Keefe and Peter Smith (eds). 1997. *Vagueness: A Reader*, 251–64. Cambridge (MA): MIT Press.

Schiffer, Stephen. 1998. 'Two Issues of Vagueness'. *The Monist* 81(2): 193–214.

Schroth, Ulrich. 2011. 'Hermeneutik, Norminterpretation und richterliche Norman-wendung'. In *Einführung in die Rechtsphilosophie und Rechtstheorie der Gegenwart*, edited by Arthur Kaufmann, Winfried Hassemer, and Ulfrid Neumann, 8th edn, 270–97. Heidelberg: C.F. Müller.

Searle, John. 1980. 'Background of Meaning'. In *Speech Act Theory and Pragmatics*, edited by John Searle, Ferenc Kiefer, and Manfred Bierwisch, 221–32. Dordrecht: Reidel.

Shapiro, Stewart. 2006. *Vagueness in Context*. Oxford: Clarendon Press.

Soames, Scott. 2010. 'The Possibility of Partial Definition'. In *Cuts and Clouds. Vagueness, Its Nature, and Its Logic*, edited by Richard Dietz and Sebastiano Moruzzi, 46–62. Oxford: Oxford University Press.

Soames, Scott. 2011. 'What Vagueness and Inconsistency Tell Us About Interpretation'. In *Philosophical Foundations of Language in the Law*, edited by Andrei Marmor and Scott Soames, 31–57. Oxford: Oxford University Press.

Soames, Scott. 2012. 'Vagueness and the Law'. In *The Routledge Companion to Philosophy of Law*, edited by Andrei Marmor, 95–108. New York: Routledge.

Solan, Lawrence. 2012. 'Linguistic Issues in Statutory Interpretation'. In *The Oxford Handbook of Language and Law*, edited by Peter M. Tiersma and Lawrence Solan, 87–99. Oxford: Oxford University Press.

Väyrynen, Pekka. 2013. *The Lewd, the Shrewd, and the Nasty*. Oxford: Oxford University Press.

Waismann, Friedrich. 1945. 'Verifiability'. *Proceedings of the Aristotelian Society, Suppl. Vol.* 19: 119–50. Reprinted in and quoted from G.H.R. Parkinson (ed.). *The Theory of Meaning*, 35–60. Oxford: Oxford University Press.

Waldron, Jeremy. 1994. 'Vagueness in Law and Language: Some Philosophical Issues'. *California Law Review* 82(3): 509–40.

Waldron, Jeremy. 2011. 'Vagueness and the Guidance of Action'. In *Philosophical Foundations of Language in the Law,* edited by Andrei Marmor and Scott Soames, 58–82. Oxford: Oxford University Press.

Williams, Bernard. 1985. *Ethics and the Limits of Philosophy*. London: Fontana Press.

Williamson, Timothy. 1992. 'Vagueness and Ignorance'. *Proceedings of the Aristotelian Society, Supp. Vol.* 66: 145–62. Reprinted in and quoted from Rosanna Keefe and Peter Smith (eds). 1997. *Vagueness: A Reader,* 265–80. Cambridge (MA): MIT Press.

Williamson, Timothy. 1994. *Vagueness*. London/New York: Routledge.

Williamson, Timothy. 1996. 'What Makes It a Heap?' *Erkenntnis* 44(3): 327–39.

Williamson, Timothy. 1997. 'Précis of Vagueness'. *Philosophy and Phenomenological Research* 57(4): 921–8.

Wittgenstein, Ludwig. 1984. *Tractatus logico-philosophicus, Tagebücher 1914–1916, Philosophische Untersuchungen*. Frankfurt/Main: Suhrkamp.

Wright, Crispin. 1976. 'Language-Mastery and the Sorites Paradox'. In *Truth and Meaning: Essays in Semantics*, edited by Gareth Evans and John McDowell, 223–47. Oxford: Clarendon Press. Reprinted in and quoted from Rosanna Keefe and Peter Smith (eds). 1997. *Vagueness: A Reader,* 151–73. Cambridge (MA): MIT Press.

Wright, Crispin. 1992. *Truth and Objectivity*. Cambridge (MA): Harvard University Press.

Wright, Crispin. 2001. 'On Being in a Quandary'. *Mind* 110(1): 45–98.

PART III

DEALING WITH
VAGUENESS IN LAW

10

Why It Is So Difficult to Resolve Vagueness in Legal Interpretation

Lawrence M. Solan

We use language to communicate, but our language faculties are imperfect communication systems. We misspeak; we think we heard someone say one thing when the speaker actually said another; we use words that have broader or narrower application than we wish; in spoken language our capacity to generate coherent and grammatical utterances exceeds our capacity to remember what was said; we produce ambiguous utterances that can mean one thing or another, which we can sometimes resolve from context, but at other times we cannot; and we use terms that are vague and can be understood in ways that are closely related, but conceptually distinct. This chapter first situates vagueness in this universe of misunderstanding as residing at the interface between language and conceptualization. It then describes three distinct, inconsistent ways in which the U.S. legal system resolves vagueness. All three are taken from opinions by the late Justice Antonin Scalia of the U.S. Supreme Court. Together, they demonstrate how situational statutory interpretation is, especially when it comes to dealing with vague terms. The chapter then briefly discusses purposive interpretation as an alternative and shows that this approach works only in limited circumstances as well, and is better suited to resolving linguistic ambiguity, as distinguished from vagueness. Finally, the chapter turns to the question of whether vagueness is good or bad for a legal system. It concludes that the answer to that question is also situational.

1. Where Vagueness Comes From

Vagueness is about borderline cases (see Endicott 2000, Sorensen 2002, and Poscher 2012). How wide does a chair have to be before we would rather call it a love seat? How wide does a love seat have to be before we stop wanting to call it a love seat and would rather call it a sofa? How long do you have to sit quietly in a doctor's office waiting for your appointment before you can start stirring and still keep your sense of yourself as a patient patient?

Things and events in the world match our concepts only in degree. Language contains some terms whose meanings incorporate this fact directly. Some adjectives,

Why It Is So Difficult to Resolve Vagueness in Legal Interpretation. First Edition. Lawrence M. Solan.
© Lawrence M. Solan 2016. Published 2016 by Oxford University Press.

for example, are both graded and contextualized (Kennedy 2007). Saying that a basketball player is tall does not imply that he is the same height as a tall eight-year-old child, even though we also say that the child is tall. And some can be 'very' tall or 'a bit tall for his age'. Even there, borderline cases sneak in. If a coach decides that she wants only tall players on the team, what should she do about someone whose height is just on the borderline between what she would call tall and what she would not call tall in that context? As Poscher (2012) notes, a word may be both ambiguous and vague at the same time. 'Bring me some tall ones' makes no sense if we do not know what 'ones' refers to, and once we do know, we may not be able to separate the tall ones from those that are not tall, at least at the margins.

Vagueness lies at the interface between language and conceptualization. In recent years, linguists have proposed an architecture to the language faculty that includes a computational system from which both syntax and aspects of meaning that derive from the formal properties of language arise; and a series of interfaces between the computational system on the one hand, and other linguistic and non-linguistic cognitive faculties on the other (see Jackendoff 2003, Chomsky 2005, and Wechsler 2015). To take a classic example, our computational system can generate infinitely long and complex sentences, but human memory, with which the language faculty must interact, is not sufficient to process and remember them once they reach a certain length and complexity ('The man from Argentina whose brother moved from Germany to Paraguay about seven years ago after their cousins from Chile decided that it might be better to stay in Europe even though the people there are not getting along well in part because the EU…'). Memory limitation is the most prominent example of the difference between linguistic competence and linguistic performance, as spelled out in Chomsky's early work (see Chomsky 1965).

Our linguistic systems must also interface with our capacity to draw inferences from context. The field of linguistic pragmatics is about this interface (see e.g. Bach 2005). To take a well-known legal example, when the police stopped a car driven by a young Latino driver, what did the officer mean when he asked the driver, 'Does the trunk open?'[1] Surely he was not making a concerned inquiry about the spring mechanism in the car. Rather he meant indirectly either to ask the driver to open the trunk or to order the driver to open the trunk. The difference is legally important because the officer had no right to give such an order, if an order it was. Yet the language of commanding and of requesting is the same. How the words are construed depends crucially on the power relationships between the parties in the interaction. In this case, the Supreme Court decided that the fact that the utterance was phrased as a question made it a request, and that the driver had voluntarily agreed to open the trunk of his car. Therefore, the contraband that was seized was permitted to stand, and the driver was convicted (see Solan and Tiersma 2005 for further discussion of the linguistic aspects of this case).

As for word meaning, we have all had the experience of feeling that we have used a word that does not best reflect what we were actually thinking. This suggests that

---

[1] *Schneckloth v. Bustamonte*, 412 U.S. 218 (1973).

at least some thought occurs prior to putting it into words, for one cannot be wrong about expressing a thought unless there is a thought to express (see Jackendoff 2012 for recent discussion of this perspective). Vagueness most often comes from a related problem. We use words primarily in their ordinary sense without regard to whether they may be vague at the margins. When I say that I recently read Timothy Endicott's book on vagueness, it makes no difference that a short paperbound volume may be on the borderline between being a book and a pamphlet. Endicott's book is really a book, so I had no need to obsess about the fact that the word 'book' can become vague in certain contexts. Yet many legal cases involving the interpretation of statutes, including classic cases, are exactly about events occurring at the margins of a legally relevant concept that can be, and typically is, applied to clear cases. As we will see below, the 'ordinary meaning' approach to word meaning that courts apply (see Slocum 2015) closely mimics the 'prototype' approach to word meaning espoused by psychologists during the past quarter-century or more (see Rosch 1975).

Legislators cannot possibly predict all of the unusual situations to which government lawyers or private lawyers will later attempt to apply laws of general application in order to gain a litigation advantage. Thus, it should not surprise us that cases of vagueness predominate over cases of other kinds of linguistic indeterminacy, such as ambiguity (Waldron 1994, Scalia and Garner 2012, Solan 2012). A case of vagueness is by definition a hard case. It requires the judge to decide between two closely related interpretations of a law that can be construed either way.

This closeness in meaning does not generally hold for cases of linguistic ambiguity. In most instances of ambiguity, in contrast to vagueness, the potential meanings are quite remote from each other. In the classic case of syntactic ambiguity, 'visiting relatives can be annoying' (Chomsky 1965), whether one is annoyed at an aunt who stayed too long or at having stayed too long at the aunt's house is not likely to be a matter of great confusion. Similarly for lexical ambiguity. When a word has two senses remote from each other in meaning (such as 'bank' and 'bank' in English), no one will confuse the two senses. For that reason, there are very few—if any— legal cases in which that sort of ambiguity is in issue. Simply put, people are good contextualizers, able to determine which sense of a word was intended by a speaker or writer (Miller 1996, p. 2).

Yet there are times when ambiguity does yield more than one meaning that makes sense in context. To illustrate, in English it is not always possible to determine the intended scope of an adverb, and laws have many state-of-mind adverbs. Thus, if a statute says, 'Whoever knowingly sells food stamps in violation of this statute and the regulations promulgated under it shall be punished', we cannot determine from the syntax whether the perpetrator must know only that he is selling food stamps, or whether the perpetrator must also know that selling food stamps is illegal. Since ignorance of the law is generally not an excuse for disobeying it, one can imagine a legislature intending either of these interpretations. In *Liparota v. United States*,[2]

---

[2] See *Liparota v. United States*, 471 U.S. 419 (1985). I have taken the liberty of editing the statute discussed in the case to make the linguistic ambiguity more salient.

the case on which this example is based, the Court recognized the unresolved ambiguity and held that the statute does not apply, using the rule of lenity, which resolves uncertainty in favour of the defendant in criminal cases.

Other sorts of ambiguity also show themselves in legal cases. Consider a woman who states in her will, 'I leave $100,000 to my grandchildren, to be divided among them equally.' Did she mean 'my grandchildren' to be understood as a shorthand for the four grandchildren she had and loved at the time she made out her will, or did she mean the five she had when she died six years later, never having met the fifth, and having become too demented to know about her most recent grandchild? Assuming that most people would intend such a bequest to include all of the grandchildren at the time of death, U.S. law has a rebuttable interpretive presumption to that effect. The same ambiguity occurs in other contexts. When you 'agree to abide by the terms of the user agreement' in purchasing internet service, do you agree to individual terms, or simply to be bound by whatever the terms are, whether you have read them or not? The answer may matter in determining how much scrutiny a court will give to the fairness of the provisions. (See Anderson 2014 for broader discussion of this ambiguity in legal contexts.)

Despite the occasional case of syntactic or semantic ambiguity, it really is vagueness that dominates the landscape of legal cases resolving linguistic uncertainty. And at least in the United States, the courts do not have any single approach for resolving it. In fact, there are at least four distinct approaches to the problem. All of them make some degree of sense in particular cases. Yet there is no metatheory that tells the courts when to apply one approach, when to apply another. The result is that while each case looks principled, the larger picture is one of the exercise of broad discretion.

Below I will discuss each of these approaches, illustrating them with cases decided by the Supreme Court of the United States. The problem of vagueness is highly situational, so that the lack of consistency should not be surprising. In fact, we will see that Justice Antonin Scalia had endorsed three of them in different cases. In pointing this out, by no means do I mean that Scalia was being a hypocrite. Rather, the problem lies in the fact that there really is no single approach to vagueness that transcends the situation, so even the most committed formalist will be forced to shift from one approach to another. The four approaches to be discussed are:

1. Choose the meaning that best reflects the way the word in dispute is ordinarily used because the legislature most likely intended the words in a statute to be understood in their ordinary sense.

2. Choose the meaning that would make the statute most coherent with the surrounding body of law because the legislature most likely intended that body of law to be coherent.

3. Choose the meaning that would make the statute most coherent with the surrounding body of law because it is the courts' obligation to make sense out of the body of law, read as a whole.

4. Choose the meaning that would best advance the purpose of the statute.

Some of these approaches may assign different interpretations to the same vague language. For example, an interpretation that coheres with other provisions in a code may not be the interpretation that best captures the ordinary meaning of the words of a statute. And while the result is the same, jurisprudentially there is a difference between building coherence in the code because the legislature intended it so, and building coherence in the code because the judiciary has an independent obligation to steer legislation in the direction of coherence regardless of what the legislature had in mind when it enacted the legislation originally.

Following that discussion, I will entertain the issue of whether vagueness actually does the legal system some good, or whether it is nothing more than a nuisance that arises from a gap between the design of our linguistic capacities and the rule-of-law values that we set out to use language to promote. Like Scalia in his use of legal principles to resolve vagueness, I will accept the fact that it plays several roles, some beneficial, some not.

2. Four Ways to Deal with Vagueness in Statutory Language

2.1 Legislative intent and ordinary meaning

One way to deal with vagueness is to avoid the issue by assuming that the legislature intends words to be construed in their prototypical sense, rather than in outlying senses. Justice Scalia put it this way in a 1992 decision that dealt with whether federal regulation of the airline industry pre-empts the states from issuing their own regulations: 'The question, at bottom, is one of statutory intent, and we accordingly "begin with the language employed by Congress and the assumption that the ordinary meaning of that language accurately expresses the legislative purpose".'[3]

This assumption is longstanding. The classic U.S. case of *Church of the Holy Trinity v. United States*,[4] decided exactly a century earlier, in 1892, employed the same presumption about legislative intent, as have many cases in between. In *Holy Trinity Church*, a law banned the payment of transportation for a person entering the United States 'to perform service or labor of any kind' (p. 458). The question was whether a New York church violated the law when it paid to bring its new minister from London to New York by ship. The Court said, in a famous quote, '[W]e cannot think Congress intended to denounce with penalties a transaction like that in the present case. It is a familiar rule, that a thing may be within the letter of the statute and yet not within the statute, because not within its spirit, nor within the intention of its makers' (p. 459). The Court did not speak of 'ordinary meaning', but that indeed was the rationale behind the decision, along with a controversial discussion of the law's legislative history (see Vermeule 2006).

---

[3] *Morales v. TWA*, 504 U.S. 375, 383 (1992).
[4] *Church of the Holy Trinity v. United States*, 143 U.S. 457 (1892).

The modern version of the argument is now commonplace. For example, does the word 'interpreter' include an individual who translates written documents, for purposes of a statute that allows the winning party in a lawsuit to recover certain costs, including 'compensation for interpreters'? In 2012, the Supreme Court said it does not, concluding that arguments to the contrary were not sufficient to demonstrate that 'Congress must have intended to dispense with the ordinary meaning of "interpreter".'[5]

Or consider Ms Dolan's plight.[6] The postal service had placed a package on her front porch in a place that they probably should not have left it. She tripped over it, hurt herself, and sued the postal service for negligence. The statute that permits government agencies to be sued has an exception for injuries 'arising out of the loss, miscarriage, or negligent transmission of letters or postal matter'. The question was whether that exception is limited to economic harm caused when the post office failed to deliver a package on time, or delivered it to the wrong address, or if something broke during delivery, or whether it included Ms Dolan's situation as well. The Court decided that the exception did not cover cases of this sort, the same way that it did not cover cases in which a mail truck injured someone because an employee of the postal service drove it negligently. Justice Thomas dissented, arguing:

There is no cause to conclude that Congress was unaware of the ordinary definition of the terms 'transmission' and 'transmit' when it enacted the [statute]. Nor is there textual indication that Congress intended to deviate from the ordinary meaning of these terms.

(*Dolan*, p. 494; Thomas, J., dissenting)

This form of argument is consistent with a 'prototype' approach to meaning, developed initially by Eleanor Rosch in the 1970s (see e.g. Rosch 1975). Although there is controversy about the actual role that prototypes play in word meaning (see e.g. Armstrong et al. 1983 and Prinz 2002), it is by now firmly established that part of our knowledge of words is a sense of how well the concepts they denote fit into a given category. A piano, for example, may be considered a piece of furniture, at least in a marginal sense, but it is not as good an example of furniture as is, say, a chair or a table. By the same token, returning to *Holy Trinity Church*, we can say that a minister indeed performs labour, although it is not the usual way we would think of 'labour' as a concept, which most often involves physical exertion. That was all the more true in the late nineteenth century when the case was decided. Because prototypical uses of a word are the more common ones, it stands to reason that when a court assumes that the legislature intended the words of a statute to be understood in their ordinary sense, the court has some likelihood of capturing the legislature's intended understanding of the statutory term.

But this chain of reasoning is by no means always justified in legal contexts. For one thing, it is not the case that we conceptualize *only* by virtue of prototypical instances of a category. We adjust our understanding of the breadth of a

---

[5] *Taniguchi v. Kan Pacific Saipan, Ltd*, 132 S.Ct. 1997, 2006 (2012).
[6] *Dolan v. United States Postal Service*, 546 U.S. 481 (2006).

communication by considering the context. Moreover, psychologists have demonstrated that defining features also play a role in how we conceptualize, even though definitions are difficult, if not impossible, for us to create so they are accurate. If I show you four cards, each of which has a very similar figure on it, but cut a round hole in the middle of one of them, you will say that the one with the hole is different because it has a specific, defining feature, even though all of them bear resemblance to each other, perhaps without regard to defining features (Medin et al. 1987).

In addition, sometimes there is good reason to believe that the legislature intended a broader meaning than the words of a statute taken in their ordinary sense. Consider the case of *Ledbetter v. Goodyear Tire and Rubber Company*.[7] The case became notorious during the 2008 presidential campaign as a symbol of the U.S. Supreme Court's disrespect for the civil rights laws. Lilly Ledbetter claimed that her employer, Goodyear, had been paying her less because she is a woman. She sued under the civil rights law, which has a six-month statute of limitations. Goodyear argued that because she had not discovered the discrimination and sued within six months of the time that the alleged discrimination had actually begun, her claim was time-barred.

The Supreme Court agreed with Goodyear. The majority argued that discrimination is an intentional act, and that the only intentional act occurred when the initial decision to discriminate was made. After that, there was no discrimination as that word is used in its ordinary sense. Rather there was only a series of ministerial acts by a payroll service, delivering Ledbetter's pay cheque to her as a matter of routine. Applying the language of the statute 'as written', the Court rejected Ledbetter's claim that the statute barred her only from recovering for any discriminatory payments occurring more than six months before she filed her lawsuit.

The majority was correct in saying that discrimination typically involves some kind of intentional act. If disproportionately many people of a single group are selected by a series of coin tosses (using a fair coin), the person flipping the coin cannot be said to have discriminated. But if someone performs an act intentionally and then periodically insures the success of that act through ministerial activity, are the ministerial acts unintentionally discriminatory? Even if one answers this question affirmatively, as the Court did, it is unlikely that the legislature meant to pass a law that gives employers a safe harbour to pay women and other protected groups less money until the end of time if the lower pay rate is not discovered in the first six months. If that were true, an employer could say with impunity, 'I want you to know that I pay you less because you are a woman. If you had discovered that fact within six months you would have been able to sue me. But we are now in month seven, so I can continue doing this with a smile.' That would amount to a pro-discrimination law for most employers, rather than an anti-discrimination law. The legislature recognized this and revised the law

---

[7] *Ledbetter v. Goodyear Tire and Rubber Company*, 550 U.S. 618 (2007).

to override the Supreme Court's decision.[8] What this suggests is that ordinary meaning may be evidence of communicative intent, but it is not dispositive of communicative intent.

Now consider *Chisom v. Roemer*, decided in 1990.[9] The Voting Rights Act was enacted in 1965 to ensure that states with long traditions of racial prejudice in their electoral schemes respected the rights of minority voters. Some U.S. states, including Louisiana, elect not only legislators, but also certain judges. The statute speaks of the election of 'representatives'. The issue in *Chisom* was whether the Voting Rights Act applies to the election of judges in Louisiana. A majority of the Court held that the statute includes judges, even though it is odd to think of elected judges as representatives. Looking at the purpose of the law and the legislative history, it did not seem plausible that the Congress would enact a civil rights law that left a safe harbour for racist election practices for judges.

Justice Scalia dissented, however, relying on a nuanced version of the ordinary meaning approach to legislative intent. Like a hydraulic jack that requires more liquid to be forced through a system to raise an automobile to a greater height, Scalia's interpretive approach required that the further a situation drifts from a category's prototypical usage, the stronger the extrinsic evidence must be that the legislature did not intend to limit the statute to prototypical cases:

I thought we had adopted a regular method for interpreting the meaning of language in a statute: first, find the ordinary meaning of the language in its textual context; and second, using established canons of construction, ask whether there is any clear indication that some permissible meaning other than the ordinary one applies. If not—and especially if a good reason for the ordinary meaning appears plain—we apply that ordinary meaning.[10]

Scalia used exactly this approach in his dissenting opinion in the 2015 case interpreting the Affordable Care Act, known as Obamacare.[11] The statute requires that financial assistance be given to individuals who buy health insurance through 'an exchange established by a state'. The plaintiffs in that case lived in states that did not establish their own health insurance exchanges. Rather, in keeping with a separate section of the law, the federal government established exchanges on behalf of those states. Scalia remarked:

Ordinary connotation does not always prevail, but the more unnatural the proposed interpretation of a law, the more compelling the contextual evidence must be to show that it is correct. Today's interpretation is not merely unnatural; it is unheard of.

(*King*, p. 39)

Exploring the arguments on both sides of the debate about the health care statute goes beyond the scope of this chapter. For our purposes, suffice it to say that a majority of the justices rejected the hydraulic approach, concluding instead that in the overall context of the law, the legislature must have intended the financial benefits

---

[8] The Lilly Ledbetter Fair Pay Act of 2009 (Pub.L. 111–12).
[9] *Chisom v. Roemer*, 501 U.S. 390 (1990).   [10] 501 U.S. at 404 (Scalia, J., dissenting).
[11] *King v. Burwell*, U.S. 2015 U.S. LEXIS 4248 (2015).

to cover all those who buy insurance through exchanges, whether the state establishes the exchange or the federal government establishes it on behalf of the state.

I can think of no justification for the hydraulic proposal, either linguistic or jurisprudential. As for language, to the extent that concepts are flexible at their boundaries, there is no reason to believe that we do anything other than to use context strategically to determine whether a particular thing or event is within those boundaries or outside of them (see Grice 1975). From this perspective, Scalia's evidentiary rule appears to be an arbitrary one, although perhaps a harmless one, since it does not seem to have gained acceptance by a majority of the justices on the Supreme Court.

Jurisprudentially, it is not at all clear how a legislature is to respond to such a rule. Legislatures expecting courts to give certain laws a broad interpretation cannot possibly anticipate the need to create more robust trails of evidence to accommodate the hydraulic approach. In short, Scalia's ordinary meaning approach finds good support, both linguistically and jurisprudentially in some cases, but not all cases. This leaves it up to the judges to decide when it is appropriate to apply it. The vigorous disagreements in some of the cases discussed above suggest that the approach leaves a great deal of discretion on the table.

2.2 Legislative intent and coherence

Legal systems in general accept coherence as a rule-of-law value. As Dworkin points out (Dworkin 1986), there is little more basic to the law than ensuring that like things are treated alike. Theorists writing in the civil law tradition similarly regard coherence as at the core of legal analysis (see e.g. Zippelius 2006, Perczenik 2008). One approach, then, in resolving vagueness, is to adopt an interpretation that is most likely to cohere with related provisions in the law. There are two rationales for doing this. The first is that the legislature enacting the law most likely intended the law to be consistent with other laws, and that therefore the court is merely enforcing the will of the legislature when it resolves a vague law to make it consistent with other laws. The alternative rationale is that regardless of what the legislature intended, the courts should make the body of law coherent because it is the job of the judiciary to make sense of the law and to promote rule-of-law values, regardless of estimating what the legislature intended for a particular situation. The first rational is the subject of this section, the second is the subject of section 2.3.

Consider this statement, again by Justice Scalia:

The meaning of terms on the statute books ought to be determined, not on the basis of which meaning can be shown to have been understood by a larger handful of the Members of Congress; but rather on the basis of which meaning is (1) most in accord with context and ordinary usage, and thus most likely to have been understood by the whole Congress which voted on the words of the statute (not to mention the citizens subject to it), and (2) most compatible with the surrounding body of law into which the provision must be integrated—a compatibility which, by a benign fiction, we assume Congress always has in mind.[12]

[12] *Green v. Bock Laundry Machine Co.*, 490 U.S. 504, 527 (1989).

In the quoted passage, Scalia proposes two approaches, both of which are designed to simulate the thought process of the legislature, and thus promote the legislative will. The first is the ordinary meaning approach discussed in section 2.1. The second is the presumption of coherence, 'which, by a benign fiction, we assume that Congress always has in mind'.

In U.S. law, this second rationale is realized in such doctrines as the 'whole act rule', the 'whole code rule', and the rule against surplusage, which assumes that the words in a statute all contribute meaning. The whole act rule has the strongest basis in fact. Courts assume that the legislature intends to use similar language to mean similar things from one part of a statute to another. This comports with common sense. The whole code rule, in contrast, has less empirical evidence to back it, and requires a stronger inference. Is it really likely that a legislature will intend that a word in some statute enacted eighty years ago as part of a fishing regulation should be given the same interpretation as a word in a totally unrelated law passed yesterday?

The same holds true for the presumption against construing language as surplusage. That rule presumes that a legislature will avoid non-identical, but similar language to amplify a point. Rather, different words are presumed to indicate an effort to say distinct things. Such presumptions about legislative intent as embodied in these canons of construction have received sharp criticism from those who study the legislative process. As for the avoidance of surplusage, Richard Posner noted: 'The conditions under which legislators work are not conducive to careful, farsighted, and parsimonious drafting. Nor does great care guarantee economy of language; a statute that is the product of compromise may contain redundant language as a by-product of the strains of the negotiating process' (Posner 1985, p. 281).

Recent empirical work supports Posner's perspective. Gluck and Bressman (2013) interviewed 137 Congressional staffers—committee counsels who are responsible for legislative drafting in the U.S. Congress. The results are radically inconsistent with the notion that the U.S. Congress drafts laws with the 'benign fiction' of coherence in mind, as reflected in grammatical canons of construction. For example, while a majority of staffers had heard of the rule against construing language as surplusage (called 'superfluities' in the Gluck and Bressman study), the staffers also said that the drafting process encourages surplusage, both to make sure that points are well covered, and to signal to relevant constituencies that they are being heard (Gluck and Bressman 2013, p. 934). After all, judges are not the only cohort for whom statutory language is important.

A similar story reveals itself with respect to the whole act and whole code rules, which specifically assume that legislatures attempt to use words uniformly both within the same statute, and across various unrelated statutes. As for coherence across unrelated statutes, the staffers said that they simply do not often strive to achieve that goal, although they are aware of it as a principle. Only nine per cent responded to the contrary (Gluck and Bressman 2013, p. 936). Within a single act, consistent word usage is valued, but not usually achievable, because different committees and subcommittees take separate responsibility for drafting, and there is inadequate communication among them. Moreover, many laws are now passed as parts of large 'omnibus bills', with all kinds of subject matter cobbled together. These too make even the whole act rule more an aspiration than a reality (see Eskridge 2016, pp. 102–18 for further discussion of these issues).

Gluck and Bressman's study was not the first. Rather, it expanded on an earlier study conducted by Nourse and Schacter (2002), who interviewed sixteen staff counsels of the Judiciary Committee of the U.S. Senate. Speaking generally about the canons of construction, one staffer commented:

> We do try to think of what a court will do with certain language, [giving, as an example, a consumer bill that would require *clear and conspicuous disclosure* of certain facts] but we don't have time for things like canons; it's not at that level.
>
> (Nourse and Schacter 2002, p. 601)

These findings are consistent with earlier work by William Buzbee (2000), criticizing what he called 'the one Congress fiction'. Studying the legislative history of a number of cases in which the Supreme Court evoked coherence as a goal of the legislature in enacting a particular law, Buzbee found that the legislature often has goals that are clearly articulated in which the language used in the law was not intended to be interpreted as consistent with the use of that language elsewhere in the United States Code.

Put simply, the benign fiction of legislative intent to create a coherent code is not so benign. This, of course, is not to say that drafters do not care about coherence, or even worse, that they strive toward *in*coherence. Rather, it means that the level of linguistic nuance that drives courts in resolving vagueness exceeds the attention that the drafters pay to the language they use. Thus, resolving vagueness by virtue of attributing to the legislature intentional decisions about wording across unrelated laws or even within the same body of related laws, or a desire to have small differences in meaning of very similar terms reflect different interpretive goals does not appear to be justified by the facts of the legislative process, at least in the U.S. Congress.

2.3 Coherence as a rule-of-law value

Now consider yet a third method for resolving vagueness, again proposed by Justice Antonin Scalia, this time in *West Virginia University Hospitals v. Casey*, a 1991 U.S. Supreme Court case.[13] Again, Justice Scalia writing for the majority:

> Where a statutory term presented to us for the first time is ambiguous, we construe it to contain that permissible meaning which fits most logically and comfortably into the body of both previously and subsequently enacted law. We do so not because that precise accommodative meaning is what the lawmakers must have had in mind (how could an earlier Congress know what a later Congress would enact?), but because it is our role to make sense rather than nonsense out of the *corpus juris*.
>
> (*West Virginia University Hospitals*, p. 101)

---

[13] *West Virginia University Hospitals v. Casey*, 499 U.S. 83 (1991).

The case is instructive. A civil rights law permits individuals (and entities) to sue a state that has violated the plaintiff's federal civil rights. If the aggrieved individual prevails, she is also awarded costs, 'including a reasonable attorney's fee'.[14] Under U.S. law, each party typically bears the cost of his own attorney. However, a number of statutes include fee-shifting provisions of this sort in order to encourage people to enforce their rights through private litigation. In *West Virginia University Hospitals*, a hospital in West Virginia had been treating indigent patients travelling there from Pennsylvania (the two states abut each other). Under federal law, Pennsylvania (Casey was its governor at the time) was required to reimburse the hospital for the cost of the medical care. The hospital claimed that it had been underpaid. It sued and won. Much of the cost of the litigation was for the payment of experts in medical economics that the lawyers hired to testify. Pennsylvania objected to paying these expert fees, since the statute calls only for the payment of 'a reasonable attorney's fee', not for the payment of expert fees incurred by the attorneys in the lawsuit.

A majority of the justices in the Supreme Court agreed with Pennsylvania. The most compelling argument for the majority view was that a number of statutes that shift fees to the losing party specifically mention that attorney's fees include the costs of experts. The law at issue in *West Virginia University Hospitals*, however, does not. It was with regard to this fact that Scalia spoke of the need to 'make sense rather than nonsense out of the *corpus juris*' in the passage quoted above.

But there is another narrative, the narrative on which the dissenting justices focused. Prior to the enactment of the law awarding attorney's fees in civil rights cases, courts often awarded such fees under their power to do equity. There was no clear practice as to whether the award of attorney's fees included the award of expert fees incurred by the attorneys. Then, the Supreme Court disallowed the practice. The result was the passage of the current law, which reinstated the practice, but did not say anything about expert costs.

Coherence is a basic rule-of-law value, but coherence requires an object. To cohere, an interpretation must cohere *with* something. And that's the problem, because coherence arguments require similarity judgments and things can be similar or dissimilar in all kinds of ways. As the philosopher Nelson Goodman pointed out, we make similarity judgments based upon the overall importance of those properties that are shared. He continues: 'But importance is a highly volatile matter, varying with every shift of context and interest, and quite incapable of supporting the fixed distinctions that philosophers so often seek to rest upon it' (Goodman 1972, p. 144).

It is not unusual for the parties, and often enough the justices in the Supreme Court, to disagree about what the decision should cohere with in an individual case. In *West Virginia University Hospitals*, for example, one narrative created a coherent story about the use of particular language to accomplish particular legislative goals. A competing narrative created a coherent narrative about a legislature's enacting a

---

[14] 42 U.S.C. § 1988.

statute with broad outer limits in order to override a court decision that the legislature found to have undermined its trying to achieve that same goal earlier.

2.4 A note on purposivism

Finally, in many of the cases discussed in this chapter, judges attempted to resolve vagueness by choosing the interpretive option that best furthered the purpose behind the statute. This strategy works when the two readings are sufficiently remote from each other that it is possible to make such a judgment. *Ledbetter* is such a case. The likelihood that the legislature would have created a civil rights statute whose principal effect would be to solidify employers' right to pay members of protected groups lower wages is remote, as the dissenting justices pointed out. Similarly, in *Holy Trinity Church*, a law designed to reduce competition with U.S. labourers would not be furthered by keeping a New York church from hiring a clergyman from London. Thus, resort to the purpose behind a statute—the standard consideration in civil law jurisdictions—can be helpful in cases of vague statutory terms.

Yet in other cases, reference to purpose suffers from the same difficulties as does reliance on coherence. The purpose of a law can be articulated in different ways, and how one states the purpose can affect the outcome. This is particularly true with respect to disputes over regulatory laws in which the issue is how much regulation towards a given goal the legislature has decided to impose. *West Virginia University Hospitals* is a good example. The law shifting attorney fees to the losing party when an individual sues a state for violation of federal rights was designed to make it more affordable for citizens to pursue claims against state governments, thereby acting as private attorneys general. If the law permits the shifting of expert witness fees as part of the attorney's fee, then it achieves that goal to a greater extent than if the law does not allow the shift of expert fees. In either case, however, the law achieves this goal to a much greater extent than if there had been no law at all. As Scalia accurately put it in *West Virginia University Hospitals*, 'the purpose of a statute includes not only what it sets out to change, but also what it resolves to leave alone' (*West Virginia University Hospitals,* p. 98). When leaving the status quo alone leads to a result that seriously contradicts any reasonable statement of the statute's goals (as, e.g., in *Ledbetter*), this statement has little force. When, however, the question is how much the law pushes the status quo after serious debate within the legislature, reference to purpose does not help a great deal.

3. Conclusion: There Is Little to Do

This chapter has focused on two points. First, because laws are written in language, language expresses concepts, and the concepts the language expresses become vague at the margins, it follows that laws are vague at the margins. Second, much of the effort to deal with vagueness in law consists of a search for uniform ways of resolving it, so that the law regains from legal methods the certainty it has lost from vagueness. However, there is no consistent way of resolving vagueness—at least none that I know of—from which it follows that laws necessarily carry some level of uncertainty.

All this means we are stuck with a level of uncertainty in legal interpretation. Some argue that this fact may have some benefits. Jeremy Waldron (1994 and chapter 15 this volume) argues that at least to some extent the contestability that follows from vagueness can be healthy for a society, by bringing significant issues to the fore. Endicott (2000, pp. 188–203) does not go quite that far, but argues that vagueness is not a deficit to rule-of-law values simply because it requires judges, on occasion, to exercise discretion. Discretion at the margins is a far cry from a society governed arbitrarily by despot.

Whatever valence one assigns vagueness, it is here to stay because it is a feature of our cognitive make-up. In some instances, vagueness appears to give judges the opportunity to take advantage of linguistic accident to undermine the results of the democratic process. In other instances, it provides both flexibility and an opportunity for society to debate important questions, such as the meaning and application of the ban on 'Cruel and Unusual Punishment', to take Waldron's example. Thus, I prefer to stay away from judging the overall value of vagueness. In that to resolve vagueness is to resolve close cases at the margins, it is fairly clear that societies, where most everyday activity is not at the margins, can survive with some level of legal uncertainty, regardless of whether one thinks this to be good or bad on balance. The best we can hope for is for judges to act both transparently and sincerely in choosing the tools to resolve uncertain language in each case they address.

References

Anderson, Jill C. 2014. 'Misleading Like a Lawyer: Cognitive Bias in Statutory Interpretation'. *Harvard Law Review* 127(6): 1521–92.

Armstrong, Sharon L., Lila R. Gleitman, and Henry Gleitman. 1983. 'What Some Concepts Might Not Be'. *Cognition* 13(3): 263–308.

Bach, Kent. 2005. 'Context *ex Machina*'. In *Semantics versus Pragmatics*, edited by Zoltán Gendler Szabó, 15–44. Oxford: Oxford University Press.

Buzbee, William. 2000. 'The One Congress Fiction in Statutory Interpretation'. *University of Pennsylvania Law Review* 149(1): 171–249.

Chomsky, Noam. 1965. *Aspects of the Theory of Syntax*. Cambridge (MA): MIT Press.

Chomsky, Noam. 2005. 'Three Factors in Language Design'. *Linguistic Inquiry* 36(1): 1–22.

Dworkin, Ronald. 1986. *Law's Empire*. Cambridge (MA): Harvard University Press.

Endicott, Timothy. 2000. *Vagueness in Law*. Oxford: Oxford University Press.

Eskridge, William N., Jr. 2016. *Interpreting Law: A Primer on How to Read Statutes and the Constitution*. St. Paul, Minnesota: Foundation Press.

Gluck, Abbe and Lisa Schultz Bressman. 2013. 'Statutory Interpretation from the Inside—An Empirical Study of Legislative Drafting, Delegation, and the Canons: Part I'. *Stanford Law Review* 65(5): 901–1024.

Goodman, Nelson. 1972. 'Seven Strictures on Similarity'. In *Problems and Projects* 23–32. Indianapolis: Bobbs-Merrill.

Grice, H.P. 1975. 'Logic and Conversation'. In *Syntax and Semantics 3: Speech Acts*, edited by Peter Cole and Jerry L. Morgan, 41–58. New York: Academic Press.

Jackendoff, Ray. 2003. *Foundations of Language: Brain, Meaning, Grammar, Evolution*. Oxford: Oxford University Press.

Jackendoff, Ray. 2012. *A User's Guide to Thought and Meaning*. Oxford: Oxford University Press.

Kennedy, Chris. 2007. 'Vagueness and Grammar: The Semantics of Relative and Absolute Gradable Adjectives'. *Linguistics and Philosophy* 30(1): 1–45.

Medin, Douglas L., William D. Wattenmaker, and Sarah E. Hampson. 1987. 'Family Resemblance, Conceptual Cohesiveness, and Category Construction'. *Cognitive Psychology* 19(2): 242–79.

Miller, George A. 1996. 'Contextuality'. In *Mental Models in Cognitive Science: Essays in Honour of Phil Johnson-Laird,* edited by Alan Garnham and Jane Oakhill, 1–18. East Sussex (England): Psychology Press.

Nourse, Victoria F. and Jane S. Schacter. 2002. 'The Politics of Legislative Drafting: A Congressional Case Study'. *New York University Law Review* 77(3): 575–624.

Peczenik, Aleksander. 2008. *On Law and Reason*. New York: Springer.

Poscher, Ralf. 2012. 'Ambiguity and Vagueness in Legal Interpretation'. In *The Oxford Handbook of Language and Law*, edited by Lawrence Solan and Peter Tiersma, 128–44. Oxford: Oxford University Press.

Posner, Richard A. 1985. *The Federal Courts: Crisis and Reform*. Cambridge (MA): Harvard University Press.

Prinz, Jesse J. 2002. *Furnishing the Mind: Concepts and Their Perceptual Basis*. Cambridge (MA): MIT Press.

Rosch, Eleanor. 1975. 'Cognitive Representations of Semantic Categories'. *Journal of Experimental Psychology: General* 104(3): 192–233.

Scalia, Antonin and Bryan Garner. 2012. *Reading Law: The Interpretation of Legal Texts*. St Paul (MN): Thomson/West.

Slocum, Brian G. 2015. *Ordinary Meaning: A Theory of the Most Fundamental Principle of Legal Interpretation*. Chicago (IL): University of Chicago Press.

Solan, Lawrence M. 2012. *The Language of Statutes: Laws and Their Interpretation*. Chicago (IL): University of Chicago Press.

Solan, Lawrence M. and Peter M. Tiersma. 2005. *Speaking of Crime: The Language of Criminal Justice*. Chicago (IL): University of Chicago Press.

Sorensen, Roy. 2002. *Vagueness and Contradiction*. Oxford: Oxford University Press.

Vermeule, Adrian. 2006. *Judging Under Uncertainty: An Institutional Theory of Legal Interpretation*. Cambridge (MA): Harvard University Press.

Waldron, Jeremy. 1994. 'Vagueness in Law and Language: Some Philosophical Issues'. *California Law Review* 82(3): 509–40.

Wechsler, Stephen. 2015. *Word Meaning and Syntax: Approaches to the Interface*. Oxford: Oxford University Press.

Zippelius, Reinhold. 2006. *Introduction to German Legal Methods*. Translated by Kirk W. Junker and P. Matthew Roy. Durham (NC): Carolina Academic Press.

11

Vagueness and Political Choice in Law

*Brian H. Bix**

1. Introduction

Vagueness has been a subject of on-going interest to legal practitioners and legal theorists. The interest is natural, given that law is a matter of interpreting and applying texts—whether statutes, constitutions, administrative regulations, contracts, wills, or trusts—and uncertainty in the meaning or application of language raises obvious issues about legal interpretation, legal reasoning, and the roles and limits of different legal actors. In many of the early papers on the topic of vagueness and the law, the focus had been, properly, on explicating to a legal audience the nature of vagueness and its many variations, the differences between vagueness and other forms of language-based uncertainty (like ambiguity), and some of the immediate implications of vagueness for legal decision making. This chapter will offer a somewhat different focus: looking at the role of vagueness and other forms of indeterminacy within a larger context of legal reasoning and decision making, emphasizing in particular the way that legal actors on occasion ignore or override semantic meaning in their interpretation and application of (vague and ambiguous, or semantically certain) terms in legal texts. It is a point that is, perhaps, ultimately obvious, but it is worth reiterating, because it sometimes gets lost when theorists focus too closely on theories of meaning and reference. There is a natural tendency for those of us who specialize in those topics to over-emphasize their importance, and the ability of better knowledge there to resolve all difficulties. We need to remember that in our legal system (and many other legal systems), judges have the authority, and perhaps also a (moral, political, or legal) duty to apply the law in ways that may diverge from the meaning, or meanings, of the legal texts considered on their own. Meaning and reference are important to law and legal reasoning, but so are political and moral choice.

* I am grateful for the comments and suggestions of Peter Hanks and the participants of the University of Minnesota Moral, Political, Legal and Social Theory Workshop, the Conference, 'Vagueness in Law: Philosophical and Legal Approaches', held at New York University, and the University of Edinburgh Law School Legal Theory Seminar.

2. Vagueness and the Law

When talking about uncertainty of meaning, what would be considered most interesting and most important to a philosopher of language may not be what is most interesting and most important to a legal theorist or legal practitioner. As this chapter will focus more on the relationship of uncertainty of meaning *within legal decision making*, I will not offer a full taxonomy of the different types of semantic uncertainty—for example, between ambiguity and vagueness, or the different levels of vagueness (e.g. Sainsbury 1991, Wright 1992), between vagueness and 'open texture' (Bix 2012), or between express and latent ambiguities.[1] This has already been very ably done by others (e.g. Poscher 2012, Marmor 2014, pp. 85–103).

Also, I agree with others that for present purposes there is no need to make any choice among different accounts of vagueness—for example, epistemic vs non-epistemic understandings (Williamson 1992, 1994, Poscher 2012, pp. 135–41; see generally Keefe and Smith 1997). It is sufficient to note that a word or text is vague, and little if anything in my analysis will turn on the precise meaning or grounding of vagueness (e.g. Raz 2001, p. 419, Greenawalt 2010, pp. 38–45).

What I wish to focus on is the role of vagueness *and other forms of semantic indeterminacy* in law and legal reasoning; in particular, I want to emphasize the residual institutional, moral, and political decisions still to be made, even after all semantic and other linguistic issues are resolved, and the way that institutional, moral, and political considerations may persuade legal officials to make decisions that override or ignore semantic/linguistic considerations, or falsely to portray a decision as required by semantic or linguistic concerns when that is in fact not the case.

As Lawrence Solan has pointed out (Solan 2013), uncertainty in the application of legal texts (statutes, etc.) is, in a sense, all but inevitable. For while the language of a particular statute or contractual provision may seem unambiguous on its face, there are always potential fact situations that could create uncertainty in application. Even where the terms may have boundaries as sharp as one could like (e.g. setting tax or child support obligations based on a percentage of income received), the uncertainty in application can come from some other term in the rule (e.g. disputes well known to tax and family law lawyers and scholars regarding what counts as 'income'; Marmor 2013). On the other hand, a legal norm might contain terms with uncertain meaning, but still have determinate applications due to aspects of law's systematic nature (e.g. through the application of other individual legal norms or interpretive norms of the system, including perhaps a prescription that individual legal norms be interpreted in a way that makes the legal system as a whole as coherent as possible, etc; e.g. Raz 2001, p. 418). Additionally, though

---

[1] See e.g. *Toussaint v. Toussaint*, 107 So. 3d 474 (Fla. Dist. Ct. App. 2013) (parol evidence was admissible to clarify a latent ambiguity; 'latent ambiguity...arises where the language employed is clear and intelligible and suggests but a single meaning, but some extrinsic fact or extraneous evidence creates a necessity for interpretation or choice among two or more possible meanings' (internal quotation marks removed)).

terms in a norm may be vague, they may give sufficient guidance in a particular context (Marmor 2014, p. 93, Soames 2011, pp. 31–2).

One way in which law differs from some other contexts of vagueness in prescriptions is that in other contexts one can return to the speaker for further clarification. This is generally not available for the application of legal norms (Soames 2011, pp. 35ff.) (though legislatures can respond to an interpretation of a statute they consider erroneous by an amendment that restores what they consider the correct interpretation). Additionally, a conversational context will often offer guidance for how to understand otherwise unclear terms or claims (Marmor 2014, p. 93). On the other hand, law does sometimes provide distinctive resources for responding to indeterminacy: for example, in American contract law (and especially with insurance policies), ambiguous provisions are to be construed against the drafter,[2] and some commentators claim that under the principle of 'lenity' uncertain provisions of criminal law statutes are to be construed in favour of the accused (Solan 2010, pp. 41–8).[3] There are also well-known 'canons' of interpretation for statutes, contracts, wills, trusts, and even constitutional provisions, which can help to resolve apparent uncertainties of meaning (Greenawalt 2010, 2013, Solan 2010).

What tends to occur in the legal context is that statutes or constitutional provisions with uncertain meaning or application are given judicial interpretations that make the meaning and application of the legal texts more precise (Soames 2011; see also Hart 2012, pp. 127–36). These interpretations are then binding on later courts (at least those at the same level or below the level of the court that makes the initial interpretation; Schauer 1987).

Solan has suggested that this process, of judicial interpretations that bind later courts, may be illegitimate, or at least inappropriate (Solan 2013). As the later court decisions will refer (and defer) to the earlier court decisions, rather than to the original statutory language, there seems to be, Solan argues, a case of judicial supremacy, with judges arrogating to themselves the law-making power that was properly vested with the legislatures. The courts, the argument goes, should stay to their proper role, subordinate to the legislature, 'faithful agents' following the direction (or lack thereof) of their masters. A somewhat different view is that judicial action clarifying ambiguities, filling in gaps, developing the common law in a 'doctrinal way' (Poscher 2012, p. 142), and even correcting some legal injustices and other mistakes, is commonly a duty, or at least an appropriate power, of judges within the legal system.

Especially when discussing vagueness (and other forms of uncertainty in meaning) in the context of law, it is crucial to distinguish semantic uncertainty from application uncertainty. In this context, semantic uncertainty can be understood broadly to be uncertainty regarding the meaning of a legal text, separate from any

---

[2] This is known as the principle of '*contra proferentem*'. See generally Farnsworth 2004, § 7.11, at pp. 459–61.
[3] The last statement is hedged because there are also commentators who claim that the existence of the interpretive principle of 'lenity' is more myth than reality, and that courts in fact do not generally construe criminal law norms in favour of the accused.

consideration of how it might or should be applied to the resolution of an actual or hypothetical legal dispute. For the reasons discussed throughout this chapter, a legal text can be *semantically uncertain* but have a certain legal application (e.g. due to resources in the law to resolve ambiguities, to reading legal texts in the light of other legal texts, and so on), and a *semantically certain* legal text can be applied in ways that differ (or appear to differ) from that certain meaning.

As already indicated, there are complications in considering semantic uncertainty in law, based on (e.g.) the role of context, purpose, the intentions of lawmakers, and the understandings of ratifiers (for constitutional provisions or other legal norms made valid by the votes of the general public or by lawmakers from another institution) in the understanding and application of legal norms. And the legal effect of any particular statute, administrative regulation, or constitutional provision will, of course, also depend both on comparable norms of the legal system with which the provision in question will be read, and also on the relevant norms of interpretation or application (e.g. Endicott 2005, p. 16).

A number of writers have noted the possible value of vagueness and other forms of indeterminacy within the law-making process. Indeterminate norms can be a way that the legislature delegates powers to administrative agencies, or to other legal actors who may have greater expertise, or who may use the discretion to make equitable judgments in individual cases (e.g. Endicott 2005, Marmor 2014, pp. 97–8).[4] Other commentators have argued that vagueness is simply a predictable (if not always inevitable) by-product of seeking the benefits that come with general or flexible language (e.g. Poscher 2012, pp. 142–3).[5]

Indeterminate norms may also simply be a way to avoid conflict among lawmakers or between contracting parties, who are unable to resolve their differences or simply do not want to take on the costs necessary to do so. With contracts, the parties might privately (and reasonably) hope that a dispute never arises that turns on the indeterminate term. With either contracts or legislation, one party (or both parties) might hope that a court would eventually side with that party's view of the term's meaning and application. In either sort of context, the benefits of not trying to resolve the dispute about an issue (and, in particular, not trying to force a resolution in one's favour) may be greater than the cost of the chance that the issue arises (and is resolved in the other side's favour) (e.g. Poscher 2012, pp. 143–4).

3. Hart, Dworkin, Precedent, and Judicial Choice

H.L.A. Hart (1958, pp. 606–11, 2012, pp. 124–36) famously argued that because words can give indeterminate guidance at times (they had, in a term he adapted

---

[4] See also Cohen-Eliya and Porat 2012, arguing that in considering the alternative ways to structure guidance, rules versus standards, one conclusion is that standards, because of their indeterminacy, delegate control to lower courts, while rules confine lower courts.

[5] The beneficial role of vagueness in creating flexibility has been noted by others (e.g. Tiersma 1999, pp. 79–85). It is also an aspect of H.L.A. Hart's analysis of 'open texture', discussed in section 3.

from Friedrich Waismann, 'open texture'), so could rules. His example was a statute declaring: 'No vehicles in the park'. Hart noted some uncertainties in the application of the word 'vehicle', though part of his discussion focused on the actual or likely intentions of the legislators rather than on semantic meaning. Hart indicated that where the application of a legal rule was uncertain, or where the law 'ran out', judges have to legislate, to 'make a fresh choice between open alternatives' (Hart 2012, p. 128). Hart indicated that because language was inevitably indeterminate in its application, so was law; he argued, however, that even if legal rules *could* be made fully determinate, this would actually be a loss rather than a gain, because the indeterminacy of rules gives the legal system flexibility to respond to new circumstances (Hart 2012, pp. 130–2).

When Hart's analysis slides from the 'open texture' of language to the 'open texture' of rules, and from a focus on semantic meaning to a focus on legislative intentions, this could (charitably) be read as an effort to show the complexity of the underlying problem: that in legal reasoning there are many different considerations we need to consider, and these different considerations may sometimes point in different directions: for example, where semantic meaning is indeterminate, legislative intentions may be determinate, and vice versa; and the meaning intended by the lawmakers may differ in important ways from the 'objective' or 'reasonable' semantic meaning.

Ronald Dworkin responded to Hart's views by arguing (famously, or perhaps notoriously)[6] that judges do not generally have discretion (at least in any philosophically interesting sense of discretion),[7] that there is always, or almost always, a right answer to legal questions, and that judges have an obligation to try to find that right answer, not to legislate anew (Dworkin 1977, 1978, pp. 14–45).[8]

In relation specifically to vagueness, Dworkin argued that vague language need not result in indeterminate law, because the legal system might have a rule that stated that the legal status quo is changed by a new (vague) statute only to the extent of the unambiguous meaning of that new statute (Dworkin 1977, p. 68). As Joseph Raz points out, Dworkin's argument here depends on a misunderstanding of vagueness—as vague terms tend to have not only indeterminate applications at their borders, but also indeterminate boundaries between clear and unclear applications (Raz 2009, pp. 72–4). Fortunately for Dworkin's position, he had other arguments for why indeterminate terms might not lead to indeterminate law: in particular, he

---

[6] Dworkin wrote: 'I myself am often accused of thinking that there is almost always a right answer to a legal question; the accusation suggests that if I were to confess to that opinion anything else I said about legal reasoning could safely be ignored' (Dworkin 1977, p. 58).

[7] Dworkin distinguishes between 'weak senses' of discretion, which would include occasions where a decision-maker must use his or her judgment in the application of criteria and occasions where the decision in question is unreviewable, and a 'strong sense' of discretion, under which the decision-maker determines which standard or criteria to apply. Dworkin argues that only discretion in the strong sense would fit the claims of Hart and other legal positivists, but he also rejected the idea that judges in fact had discretion in this 'strong' sense (Dworkin 1978, pp. 31–4).

[8] Dworkin consistently reaffirmed his belief in this right answer theory (e.g. Dworkin 2004, p. 388, Dworkin 2006, pp. 41–3, and Dworkin 2011, pp. 88–96).

argued that his approach to law and legal reasoning displayed the way that judges did and should choose among viable interpretations of the law the one that was morally best (Dworkin 1977, p. 68; see generally Dworkin 1978, pp. 81–130, and Dworkin 1986).

While Dworkin asserts that there is always (or almost always) a right answer to legal questions, he concedes that in the harder cases competent judges and lawyers will disagree on what the right answer is, and that there is no way for any judge (or lawyer or theorist) to demonstrate in an undeniable argument that the chosen outcome is the correct answer (Dworkin 1985, pp. 119–45).[9] However, this does not make the right answer theory (or assumption) without value or use. Even if a judge cannot be sure that the answer she reaches is the right one, the argument is that it is beneficial for judges and lawyers to be arguing about what the one right answer is, rather than immediately assuming in harder cases that there is no right (legal) answer, and making arguments about the best proposal for judicial legislation. Such judicial legislation, Dworkin argues, would both overstep the court's limited role within the legal system, and (for Dworkin, more importantly) would be legislation that would be imposed retroactively on the parties to the dispute, potentially undermining the right one party had under the existing law for the dispute to come out in her favour.[10] Some of the disputes between Hart, Dworkin, and later participants in the debates about the merits of legal positivism seemed to turn on the question of whether the norms courts had an obligation to apply were, for that reason alone, 'legal' norms (or, by contrast, whether it would make sense to say that a court had an obligation to apply norms that were nonetheless 'extralegal'; e.g. Dworkin 1983, pp. 260–3, Raz 1983, pp. 81–6). For our purposes, it is not important whether the right answer to legal disputes is grounded solely on legal norms the judge is obligated to apply or whether that same answer is (sometimes) grounded on a combination of legal and extra-legal norms the judge is obligated to apply. A different sort of problem is raised, however, with the objection (given by some of Dworkin's critics) that the factors and considerations the judge is obligated to apply in resolving some legal disputes are incommensurable, and therefore there will often not be a single right answer (Finnis 2011, pp. 290–5; cf. Raz 1999, pp. 46–66 and 182–201). That is, this analysis claims, the judge must ultimately choose between two (or more) equally legitimate outcomes.

Not to get too far off on the tangent of the determinacy or indeterminacy of law, but one should note the different sort of indeterminacy that one finds in common law legal systems (like the legal systems of the United States and England) involved in judicial decision making and precedent. It is an indeterminacy that does not fit

[9] Michael Moore has argued that Dworkin, to be consistent with his other views and claims, must accept that legal right answers must be demonstrable (Moore 1987, pp. 481–3), but that dispute takes us too far afield to discuss here.

[10] Gardner questions Dworkin's basic argument: 'Why should the fact that the law would inevitably fail to live up to certain ideals if [legal positivism] were true be a reason to deny [legal positivism], rather than a reason to admit that the law inevitably fails to live up to certain ideals, or perhaps a reason to wonder whether one has exaggerated the ideals themselves?' (Gardner 2012, p. 38, footnote omitted).

well under the categories of 'vagueness' or 'ambivalence', but it contains elements of each. The basic structure of common law precedent is that when a court decides a case, in subsequent cases decided by courts at the same level or a lower level in the judicial hierarchy the judges are bound by the earlier decision.[11] At the same time, what binds the courts in the later decisions is both limited and potentially very uncertain: the later court decision needs to be consistent only with the *outcome* of the prior case: that under certain facts, plaintiff (or defendant) prevails. No declarations by the judge(s) in the prior case regarding what justifies the outcome or even regarding which facts are crucial are binding, only the outcome (see generally Schauer 1987). Again, as with Dworkin's right answer theory, commentators differ on whether there is always (or almost always) a unique right way to understand and apply precedential cases; what is not seriously doubted is that reasonable judges, lawyers, and commentators frequently differ on the 'meaning' and application of prior cases to new or hypothetical disputes.

Thus, whether we are talking about legal reasoning generally, or common law precedential reasoning in particular, there is the strong suspicion that even if there are unique right answers to disputes about what the law requires, the intractable disagreements among reasonable and competent judges and practitioners leaves it to judges to choose among equally justifiable alternatives. Many commentators have argued that these choices are political in the narrow sense that judges whose personal political or ideological beliefs are liberal tend to make decisions favouring liberal outcomes, and judges whose personal political or ideological beliefs are conservative tend to make decisions favouring conservative outcomes.[12] However, even taking this correlation of judges' political views and outcome as proven, one need not conclude that judges are consciously legislating politically. One can follow the ideas of the American legal realists and, later, the critical legal theorists, in concluding that judges believe (perhaps wrongly) that there is one right answer, but their legal reasoning includes judgments that are affected (biased?) by their political and moral views (e.g. in regards to the 'reasonable' interpretations of statutes and constitutional provisions). A Dworkinian would go further and say that such views are *properly* part of legal interpretation—that judging *is* political, but only in a broad sense of political (not 'party political'), in that a judge must often make judgments regarding which otherwise reasonable interpretation of past official actions places those actions in the best light (in a moral-political sense) (Dworkin 1986).

To bring the discussion back to the topic at hand, when a judge must decide between two possible interpretations or applications of a vague or ambiguous legal text, the judge might choose one reading based on her conclusion that the alternative reading would be horrible or absurd, relative to her political and moral views.

---

[11] In many common law countries, some courts—most commonly, the highest courts in the jurisdiction—have the authority, in extreme circumstances, to overrule their own prior decisions.

[12] There are ample social scientific studies supporting these conclusions (most of which code the political views of the judge either using the party of the judge if the judge gained office through a state partisan election, or using the party affiliation of the President appointing the judge for federal judges).

And a judge may, for similarly political-legal reasons, choose an unlikely reading of a statutory text over an objectively more likely semantic reading.

Legal theorists as different as Karl Llewellyn (see Fuller 1934, p. 445) and Hans Kelsen (see Kelsen 1967, § 45, at pp. 348–51 and Kelsen 1992, § 38, at pp. 82–3) have argued that every application of a rule, however straightforward and uncontroversial, is the creation of a new norm, and one can find comparable ideas in hermeneutic theorists (Walshaw 2013). This is *not* the claim I am putting forward in this chapter. I want to distinguish also the important if nuanced point made by John Gardner, when he notes that 'the legislative text is not the *only* possible object of legislative interpretation. The law created by the statute—the statute's legal effect—is itself a second possible object of interpretation' (Gardner 2012, p. 58, emphasis in original).

The inquiry about vagueness and other forms of indeterminacy in legal reasoning may be similar to the claim by some theorists, that if judges or commentators only had the correct theory of language, we could overcome certain problems of legal reasoning. In general, the temptation seems strong for theorists to assert that if only the right theory of meaning, reference, semantics, pragmatics, vagueness, ambiguity, etc., were to be found, then issues of indeterminacy would disappear, and judges (and others) would discover and apply the one true law, finding the unique right answer in all disputes.

Some theorists in the area, especially those sympathetic to metaphysical realism or the more realist readings of Kripke/Putnam approaches to meaning and reference,[13] have urged reform in the way legal and judicial reasoning is done (and also in the way that it is understood), and have claimed or implied that once the proper approach to language, meaning, and reference becomes embedded in our legal practices, then legal indeterminacy would disappear, or sharply reduce. There are threshold problems with such an argument: as even Ronald Dworkin realized in connection with his 'right answer' theory, the existence of right answers is no guarantee that even the most competent commentators, lawyers, and judges will in fact converge on that answer, either immediately or over time.

Additionally, the right theory of language cannot make legal issues universally or fully determinate, because judges retain the authority and duty *to do justice between the parties* and *to make the best decision*, all things considered, in the application of legal (statutory, administrative, or constitutional) texts to the dispute before the court (Bix 2003).[14] One difficulty with many of the theories that seek legal determinacy through philosophy of language is that they assume a primacy to semantic meaning (or some analogous notion) when it is a common practice in law (some might even urge that this is an essential aspect of legal practice) to give weight to the choices of the lawmakers, even where those choices seem contrary to the ('objective' or 'ordinary person's') understanding of the terms used in the law (Bix 2003, pp. 286–93).

---

[13] I am thinking particularly of Michael Moore, Nicos Stavropoulos, and David Brink; see my discussion of their works in Bix 2003.

[14] Courts in common law countries and those in civil law countries generally vary in the extent to which their decisions create new law for later litigants.

There are a number of standard examples of judges interpreting legal texts contrary to their apparent clear meaning:

1. While the U.S. Sherman Antitrust Act invalidates all contracts in restraint of trade, the U.S. Supreme Court early on interpreted the text as invalidating only contracts that 'unreasonably' restrain trade (as almost all commercial contracts could be said to restrain trade to some extent).[15]

2. In the famous case of *Riggs v. Palmer*, the New York Court of Appeals read into the state's simple wills statute an exception that prevented an otherwise qualified grandson from inheriting from the grandfather he murdered.[16]

3. In a well-known U.S. Supreme Court case, *Church of the Holy Trinity v. United States*,[17] the Justices concluded that a pastor imported from Britain did not fall within statutory language forbidding the importation of foreigners 'to perform labor or service of any kind'.

4. In an influential case involving the interpretation in a contract law sale of goods cases, the Ninth Circuit Court of Appeals affirmed a decision concluding that a provision under which the buyer must pay the seller's 'posted price' in fact meant that the buyer must pay the posted price *unless* the price had just gone up, in which case the buyer would only have to pay the older price until any government construction contracts then under way were completed ('price protection').[18]

5. In a notorious nineteenth-century case, *Maurice v. Judd* (1818; discussed in O'Higgins 1970, p. 47), the court determined that though whales may not be 'fish' in the eyes of science, 'whale oil' is to be considered 'fish oil' for the purpose of determining whether an inspector was due a fee.

The judicial rhetoric in these sorts of cases varies. Sometimes the courts state that they are determining what the lawmakers or drafters *really meant*, or trying to reform language in light of the legislative purpose, or to avoid absurdity, or the like. (We can bracket for the moment whether the courts always believe the characterization they offer, or whether this may simply be a 'convention of presentation' or a standard way of avoiding controversy.) Whether the courts are merely making a complicated determination of what the law 'already is' or are developing the law in standard, doctrinal ways (cf. Gardner 2012, pp. 42–7), the point for our purposes remains the same: that semantic meaning and application regularly diverge, and that such divergence is part of the normal practice in our legal system (and many others).

---

[15] E.g. *Standard Oil v. United States*, 221 U.S. 1, 60 (1911).

[16] *Riggs v. Palmer*, 115 N.Y. 506, 22 N.E. 188 (1889). This is an example Ronald Dworkin often used to prove a different point about the nature of law and legal reasoning, e.g. Dworkin 1967, pp. 23–31; it was also an example important to the American legal realist, Benjamin Cardozo (Cardozo 1921, pp. 40–3), and the legal process scholars, Henry Hart and Albert Sacks (Hart and Sacks 1994, pp. 80–94).

[17] 143 U.S. 457 (1892).

[18] *Nanakuli Paving & Rock Co. v. Shell Oil Co.*, 664 F.2d 773 (9th Cir. 1981).

There are also well-known contexts where judges have developed the *legal* meaning of terms in a direction sharply different from the conventional meaning of the same terms: for example, where 'malice' in criminal law (and libel law) does not entail 'malevolent motive' as it does in conventional speech (Holmes 1897, p. 463).

As Marmor has argued, some situations where judges appear to be altering or adding to the semantic context of legal texts can be understood as judicial attempts to discern the implied content in the lawmakers' communication (Marmor 2011), though Marmor also recognizes that courts are quite inconsistent in their willingness or ability to locate and enforce such implied content (Marmor 2011, p. 101). This is a helpful reminder, but it likely explains only a fraction of the cases where court decisions diverge from the semantic content of the applicable legal norms.

4. Status of Claims

As one reader of a previous draft of this chapter pointed out, the claims offered here seem to wander across a wide range, from descriptive (this is what (U.S.) judges do) to conceptual or analytical (insinuating that these practices may somehow be intrinsic to legal reasoning generally or judicial reasoning in particular) to prescriptive (that whether current (American) judges follow these practices or not, it would be a good thing if they did). I do intend to make a descriptive claim, that the practices I describe are common, and generally accepted, in U.S. legal and judicial practice. I am *not* here making a conceptual or analytical claim; I think such claims for social practices are very difficult to justify even with what appear to be strong evidence and confident intuitions, and I do worry about the challenge of theorists who assert that one can *never* make conceptual claims about law (e.g. Leiter 2007, pp. 121–99). In any event, as I wrote elsewhere when discussing defeasibility and law (Bix 2012), forms of legal and judicial reasoning vary considerably across legal systems, and I see little reason to characterize dispute resolution systems that do not follow some common approach as being, for that reason, 'not legal' or in some way 'defective'. I can easily imagine a normative system and an associated dispute resolution system in which the norm-applying institutions tried never to alter the semantic meaning or the intended meaning ('speaker's meaning') of enacted legislation. I do not think that this would be a wise way to structure a normative system, but I see little reason to say that such a normative system could not be a '*legal* system'.

I *would* endorse the prescriptive claim, though this is not the proper occasion to attempt to justify that conclusion. I believe that it is, overall, a good thing that the courts have (or have taken) the limited authority to apply legal norms, on occasion, in a way that chooses among alternative possible meanings of legal texts, or that decides differently than would seem justified by the apparently clear meaning of the relevant legal texts. There are alternative and overlapping justifications for such powers, which can only be pointed to here: for example, the good consequences that can come from requiring, or at least authorizing, courts to try to improve the legal system (where improvement can mean making the norms individually or collectively more just, more coherent, or even more efficient), and the inherent (legal and moral) right and duty of judges to do justice between the parties in the course of resolving their disputes (cf. Raz 1994, pp. 310–24). Additionally, judges, like everyone else, have the (moral) obligation to do the (morally) right thing, all things considered, and for judges this will on some (generally rare) occasions entail changing, or in application temporarily deviating from, the semantic meaning of a legal text.

I should also make clear that I view such deviations from clear (or unclear) semantic meaning to be valuable only when used in exceptional circumstances, or, at least, when used only in moderation. There are obvious and important rule of law virtues to be protected,[19] and these tend to be promoted when the legal texts as applied reflect the reasonable understanding of those texts, and the relative certainty and predictability that are advanced by such practices (e.g. Fuller 1969, pp. 33–94, Marmor 2007, pp. 3–38). In general, there is much more than can and should be said on the normative case for deviating from semantic reason for moral and political reasons (and the appropriate limits of that case), but due to space constraints that discussion will have to await another occasion.

5. Conclusion

Vagueness and ambiguity involve the uncertain meaning, reference, and (thus) application of terms, but the implications for legal norms is far from straightforward. This is due to the fact that within law, the (normal) semantic content of legal norms must sometimes give way, either based on coherence with other legal norms, deference to the lawmakers' intentions, or the judge's duty or authority to do justice and (in common law countries) to improve the law.

In analysing legal reasoning within a legal system, it is important to distinguish indeterminacies that occur at the level of the semantic meaning of legal norms and the related but different issues that may arise at the point of applying legal norms. At the same time, one must recognize that the line between courts applying (their understanding of) a legal text's meaning and modifying the meaning to serve other purposes is not always clearly drawn or publicly expressed (as is true generally for the distinction between courts applying existing law and creating new law).

Legal theorists and practitioners have a great deal to learn from philosophers of language, meaning, and reference. However, we must also keep in mind how much of what courts do goes beyond semantic meaning, and involves considering modifying or overriding meaning in the name of morality, justice, or politics.

---

[19] In the criminal law, there would be especially strong justice reasons not to deviate from the semantic meaning in the direction of greater criminal liability, though these same reasons would obviously not apply, or apply less strongly, if the deviation were in the direction of less criminal liability.

References

Bix, Brian H. 2003. 'Can Theories of Meaning and Reference Solve the Problem of Legal Determinacy?' *Ratio Juris* 16(3): 281–95.

Bix, Brian H. 2012. 'Defeasibility and Open Texture'. In *The Logic of Legal Requirements*, edited by Jordi Ferrer Beltrán and Giovanni Battista Ratti, 193–201. Oxford: Oxford University Press.

Cardozo, Benjamin N. 1921. *The Nature of the Judicial Process*. New Haven (CT): Yale University Press.

Cohen-Eliya, Moshe and Iddo Porat. 2012. 'Judicial Minimalism and the Double Effect of Rules and Standards'. *Canadian Journal of Law and Jurisprudence* 25(2): 283–311.

Dworkin, Ronald. 1967. 'The Model of Rules'. *University of Chicago Law Review* 35(1): 14–46.

Dworkin, Ronald. 1977. 'No Right Answer?' In *Law, Morality and Society: Essays in Honour of H. L. A. Hart*, edited by Peter Hacker and Joseph Raz, 58–84. Oxford: Clarendon Press.

Dworkin, Ronald. 1978. *Taking Rights Seriously*. Cambridge (MA): Harvard University Press.

Dworkin, Ronald. 1983. 'A Reply by Ronald Dworkin'. In *Ronald Dworkin and Contemporary Jurisprudence*, edited by Marshall Cohen, 247–302. Totowa (NJ): Rowman & Allanheld.

Dworkin, Ronald. 1985. *A Matter of Principle*. Cambridge (MA): Harvard University Press.

Dworkin, Ronald. 1986. *Law's Empire*. Cambridge (MA): Harvard University Press.

Dworkin, Ronald. 2004. 'Ronald Dworkin Replies'. In *Dworkin and His Critics,* edited by Justine Burley, 339–95. Oxford: Blackwell Publishing.

Dworkin, Ronald. 2006. *Justice in Robes*. Cambridge (MA): Harvard University Press.

Dworkin, Ronald. 2011. *Justice for Hedgehogs*. Cambridge (MA): Harvard University Press.

Endicott, Timothy. 2005. 'The Value of Vagueness'. In *Vagueness in Normative Texts*, edited by Vijay K. Bhatia, Jan Engberg, Maurizio Gotti, and Dorothee Heller, 27–48. Bern: Peter Lang. Reprinted in Andrei Marmor and Scott Soames (eds). 2011. *The Philosophical Foundations of Language in the Law*, 14–30. New York: Oxford University Press.

Farnsworth, E. Allan. 2004. *Contracts*. 4th edn. New York: Aspen Publishing.

Finnis, John. 2011. *Philosophy of Law: Collected Essays: Vol. IV*. Oxford: Oxford University Press.

Fuller, Lon L. 1934. 'American Legal Realism'. *University of Pennsylvania Law Review* 82(5): 429–62.

Fuller, Lon L. 1969. *The Morality of Law*, rev. edn. New Haven: Yale University Press.

Gardner, John. 2012. *Law as a Leap of Faith*. Oxford: Oxford University Press.

Greenawalt, Kent. 2010. *Legal Interpretation: Perspectives from Other Disciplines and Private Texts*. Oxford: Oxford University Press.

Greenawalt, Kent. 2013. *Statutory and Common Law Interpretation*. Oxford: Oxford University Press.

Hart, H.L.A. 1958. 'Positivism and the Separation of Law and Morals'. *Harvard Law Review* 71(4): 593–629.

Hart, H.L.A. 2012. *The Concept of Law*, 3rd edn. Oxford: Oxford University Press.

Hart, Henry M., Jr and Albert M. Sacks. 1994. *The Legal Process*, edited by William N. Esckridge, Jr and Philip P. Frickey. Westbury (NY): Foundation Press.

Holmes, Oliver Wendell. 1897. 'The Path of the Law'. *Harvard Law Review* 10(8): 457–78.

Keefe, Rosanna and Peter Smith (eds). 1997. *Vagueness: A Reader.* Cambridge (MA): MIT Press.

Kelsen, Hans. 1967. *Pure Theory of Law.* Translated by Max Knight. Berkeley. California: University of California Press.

Kelsen, Hans. 1992. *Introduction to the Problems of Legal Theory.* Translated by Bonnie Litschewski Paulson and Stanley L. Paulson. Oxford: Clarendon Press.

Leiter, Brian. 2007. *Naturalizing Jurisprudence: Essays on American Legal Realism and Naturalism in Legal Philosophy.* Oxford: Oxford University Press.

Marmor, Andrei. 2007. *Law in the Age of Pluralism.* Oxford: Oxford University Press.

Marmor, Andrei. 2011. 'Can the Law Imply More Than It Says? On Some Pragmatic Aspects of Strategic Speech'. In *Philosophical Foundations of Language in the Law*, edited by Andrei Marmor and Scott Soames, 83–104. Oxford: Oxford University Press.

Marmor, Andrei. 2013. 'Truth in Law'. In *Current Legal Issues: Law and Language*, edited by Michael Freeman and Fiona Smith, 45–61. Oxford: Oxford University Press.

Marmor, Andrei. 2014. *The Language of Law.* Oxford: Oxford University Press.

Moore, Michael. 1987. 'Metaphysics, Epistemology, and Legal Theory'. *Southern California Law Review* 60(2): 453–506.

O'Higgins, Paul. 1970. 'William Sampson (1764–1836)'. *Dublin University Law Review* 2(1): 45–52.

Poscher, Ralf. 2012. 'Ambiguity and Vagueness in Legal Interpretation'. In *The Oxford Handbook of Language and Law*, edited by Lawrence Solan and Peter Tiersma, 128–44. Oxford: Oxford University Press.

Raz, Joseph. 1983. 'Legal Principles and the Limits of Law'. In *Ronald Dworkin and Contemporary Jurisprudence*, edited by Marshall Cohen, 73–87. Totowa (NJ): Rowman & Allanheld.

Raz, Joseph. 1994. *Ethics in the Public Domain.* Oxford: Clarendon Press.

Raz, Joseph. 1999. *Engaging Reason: On the Theory of Value and Action.* Oxford: Oxford University Press.

Raz, Joseph. 2001. 'Sorensen: Vagueness Has No Function in Law'. *Legal Theory* 7(4): 417–19.

Raz, Joseph. 2009. *The Authority of Law*, 2nd edn. Oxford: Oxford University Press.

Sainsbury, R.M. 1991. 'Is There Higher Order Vagueness?' *Philosophical Quarterly* 41(163): 167–82.

Schauer, Frederick. 1987. 'Precedent'. *Stanford Law Review* 39(3): 571–605.

Soames, Scott. 2011. 'What Vagueness and Inconsistency Tell Us About Interpretation'. In *Philosophical Foundations of Language in the Law*, edited by Andrei Marmor and Scott Soames, 31–57. Oxford: Oxford University Press.

Solan, Lawrence M. 2010. *The Language of Statutes: Law and Their Interpretation.* Chicago (IL): University of Chicago Press.

Solan, Lawrence M. 2013. 'Fear of Vagueness'. Paper presented at the AALS Conference (Panel on 'Interpretation and Uncertainty'), New Orleans, January 2013.

Tiersma, Peter M. 1999. *Legal Language.* Chicago (IL): University of Chicago Press.

Walshaw, Christopher. 2013. 'Interpretation is Understanding and Application: The Case for Concurrent Legal Interpretation'. *Statute Law Review* 34(2): 101–27.

Williamson, Timothy. 1992. 'Vagueness and Ignorance'. *Proceedings of the Aristotelian Society, Suppl. Vol.* 66: 145–62.

Williamson, Timothy. 1994. *Vagueness.* London: Routledge.

Wright, Crispin. 1992. 'Is Higher Order Vagueness Coherent?' *Analysis* 52(3): 129–39.

12

Non-Epistemic Uncertainty and the Problem of Legal Line Drawing

Leo Katz

1. Should Legal Concept Be More Scalar?

In a wonderfully provocative article called *Scalar Properties, Binary Judgments*, Larry Alexander raises a puzzle about law and morality: why do law and morality treat so many things that evidently lie on a continuum as binary? The article teems with interesting examples, but two should illustrate his point with sufficient clarity.

The first has to do with personhood. A person has a right not to be killed. But no one starts out as a person, or for that matter endures as a person forever. We start out as something very much less—a collection of cells—and end up as something very much less, a corpse. The transition from pre-personhood to personhood, and thence to post-personhood, is a continuous one, involving numerous intermediate stages. (It does not matter that at the back end the continuum will usually be traversed rather more quickly than at the front end. It still is a continuum, and people have, of course, been known to linger for extended periods of time at virtually all points of that continuum.) And yet both law and morality seem to insist that somewhere along that continuum there is a magical point at which one acquires, or loses, personhood—and thereby acquires or loses the right not to have certain things done to oneself. Is that really plausible, Alexander wonders? If so, where is that point? Surely it cannot be that we can just arbitrarily choose any old point. Given how much hangs on whether the creature we are dealing with is just below or just above that point, there must be some good reasons that would cause us to choose a particular location for it. Yet isn't it obvious that we in fact have no criteria for selecting such a location? And isn't the obvious lesson to draw from all of this that personhood does not really start at a particular point, but starts to come into being gradually, as well as expiring gradually, and that what we may do to a person similarly changes gradually?

He raises an analogous puzzle regarding consent. Consent is judged valid provided it is both informed and voluntary. And whether it was informed or voluntary are each regarded as binary judgements. Either the consenting party was informed or it was not; either he acted voluntarily or not. But being well informed or acting

Non-Epistemic Uncertainty and the Problem of Legal Line-Drawing. First Edition. Leo Katz. © Leo Katz 2016.
Published 2016 by Oxford University Press.

voluntarily, Alexander points out, seem to be matters of degree. To be sure, that does not exclude the possibility that there is a particular point at which the consenting party's level of ignorance or coercion exceeds some threshold such that we should say his consent no longer counts. But if there is, we should be able to say where that magic point lies. And once again, we seem to have no good criteria by which to decide when the degree of information or freedom required for valid consent is adequate. Since it is a very consequential matter where that point is located, it cannot be just arbitrarily chosen. And yet we seem to have no choice but to select it arbitrarily. And isn't the obvious lesson to draw the same one we drew with regard to personhood: that consent is not an all-or-nothing matter, but rather that consent becomes gradually more valid as the amount of information on which it is based and the freedom the consenting party enjoyed increase? Personhood and consent, as Alexander would put it, are scalar, not binary. That, in a nutshell, is Alexander's argument. There would not appear to be anything about it that would limit it to these particular examples, and Alexander's piece furnishes many more.

Let me restate Alexander's argument slightly, using the terminology coined by Ralf Poscher and Geert Keil. There are many situations in law, of which those involving the issue of personhood or consent happen to be particularly telling examples, in which a difficult line needs to be drawn—such as the line between being a person or not, consent being valid or not—but with regard to which we are in profound uncertainty as to where exactly that line ought to be drawn. What makes that uncertainty so profound is that we are usually not even in a position to say what it is that we would need to find out to let us resolve that uncertainty. In fact, in most such cases it looks as though there are no facts that we might conceivably find out which would allow us to settle the matter, even in principle. The uncertainty here, in other words, is *not* one of not having access to some crucial facts: hence the term 'non-epistemic uncertainty'. When we are in such a state of non-epistemic uncertainty with regard to a morally weighty matter such as personhood or consent, then that is strong evidence, perhaps even conclusive evidence, that we are wrong even to try to draw such a line. Instead it tells us that we are dealing with a scalar, not a binary, concept, and no line drawing should even be attempted.

There is considerable intuitive force to this argument. But is it right? And if not, what can be said in response to it?

Let me begin such a response by setting aside, at least for now, a relatively minor objection. Even if we decide that personhood and consent are scalar concepts, i.e. that personhood and valid consent come into being gradually rather than being either present or absent, this will not entirely rid us of the problem of non-epistemic uncertainty. There is after all the matter of mapping out the precise manner and rate at which personhood or consent accrete from zero to one hundred per cent. This too is morally consequential. Significant liability hangs on the exact nature of this mapping, and yet it is not easy to say how exactly it is to be accomplished, what facts or sets of facts would allow us to judge one such mapping inferior to another. Nevertheless, it is worth conceding that once we treat these concepts as scalar, the moral consequences certainly are less weighty, and our non-epistemic uncertainty therefore seems less of an argument against their existence or validity: even if we are wrong in thinking that in month four of a pregnancy, forty per cent of the creature's personhood has come into being, as opposed to just twenty per cent, that would have comparatively fewer significant consequences than if we decide that in month four personhood either exists, when it does not, or does not exist, when it does. The same for consent.

2. On the Obstinately Non-Scalar Character of Various Moral Doctrines

Alexander does not distinguish between moral and legal concepts, in making his argument. Indeed, there is nothing in his argument that would call for such a distinction. The moral concepts he considers, such as personhood and consent (though he considers many others, those are the only ones I have chosen to illustrate his argument with) play the same role in law and in morality. The law here closely tracks morality, or at least tries to do so. And the problem of non-epistemic uncertainty undermining the drawing of discontinuity-producing fine lines, and supporting a scalar version of the same doctrine, arises equally in law and morality. Nevertheless, for purposes of responding to his challenge it will serve us well to keep law and morality apart, and to begin by responding to his argument in the context of morality, before turning to the law.

What I will proceed to do in this section is to lay out a series of moral doctrines as non-scalar in character as personhood and consent, as plagued by non-epistemic uncertainty as they are, but nevertheless not ones which we are much tempted to 'scalarize' along the lines suggested by Alexander. With regard to the first few I will simply present them and note our reluctance to scalarize; with regard to the ones thereafter I will in fact be able to identify the causes of our reluctance to scalarize more precisely—that is, our reluctance to scalarize despite the presence of enormous non-epistemic uncertainty and despite our inability to explain where and why to draw the line where we are drawing it.

2.1 Prospect theory

A good place to begin is a famous example due to Amos Tversky and Daniel Kahneman, albeit one that was put to a somewhat different use in the context in which they first offered it (Tversky and Kahneman 1981). They asked their subjects (as it happened, a group of doctors, not that it mattered to the outcome) to consider what decision they would make when confronted by a certain difficult choice, to wit, 'an unusual Asian disease, which is expected to kill 600 people. Two alternative programs to combat the disease have been proposed.... If program A is adopted, 200 people will be saved. If program B is adopted, there is a 1/3 probability that 600 people will be saved, and 2/3 probability that no people will be saved. Which of the two programs would you favor?' By a substantial majority, the doctors preferred the 'sure thing' to the 'risky thing'. In other words, better to save the smaller number for sure, than maybe save everyone and perhaps save no one, at least with these particular odds. I trust that most readers will have the same reaction, because Tversky and Kahneman rightly claimed to have uncovered a rather deep-seated moral attitude toward risky choices under uncertainty: when we are choosing between a certain gain and an uncertain gamble with the statistically identical expected outcome, but consisting of a risky larger gain and the possibility of gaining nothing, we go for the first option, the certain gain.

There was an important second part to the experiment, in which a similar group of doctors was asked a slightly different question. Once again, the world was threatened by the aforementioned Asian disease. The doctors were once again asked to choose between two programs for combating the disease. About the first program, they were told that if it was adopted, 400 people would die. About the second program, they were told that if it ws adopted, there was a 1/3 probability that nobody would die, and a 2/3 probability that 600 people would die. Most doctors preferred the second program. In and of itself, that probably seems like it makes good sense, because it corresponds to yet another moral attitude we have towards risky choices under uncertainty: when we are choosing between a certain *loss* and an uncertain gamble, involving a risky larger loss and the possibility of not losing anything, but with the statistically identical expected outcome, we go for the gamble.

A problem, of course, arises because these choices are really the same. In one case the choice is described as one between prospective gains and in the other as one between prospective losses. Depending on one's vantage point, it is possible to describe something in one way as well as the other.

Now notice two crucial features of this example. First, we have here a moral doctrine, prescribing choices between certain and uncertain prospects, that has a distinctly discontinuous feature built into it, the radically different treatment we give a choice between uncertain and certain *gains*, on the one hand, and the treatment we give the choice between uncertain and certain *losses*. Yet there is no obvious reason in a lot of cases to categorize something as a choice between gains or a choice between losses. Both seem possible. Our reaction to learning this, certainly the doctors' reaction to learning this, was to be nonplussed. They were not led to question the doctrine, or to 'scalarize' it in some fashion—for example, by conceiving of there being a continuum between clear cases of gains and clear cases of losses, and treating in-between cases in an in-between fashion. Our commitment to this discontinuity persists despite the non-epistemic uncertainty we face in deciding whether something should be treated as a gain or as a loss.

2.2 Negligence

Another illuminating counter-example to Alexander's argument is the concept of negligence. The assessment of negligence, as it is commonly understood, in morality as well as law, involves a balancing of the risk someone imposes on others against the justification, the reasons for which he subjected others to that risk. Economists and utilitarians more generally, like to treat this balancing as a simple matter of cost–benefit calculation, but that is only one possible version of the balancing approach. Everyone recognizes that negligence has a sharp boundary: in the cost–benefit version of the concept, the defendant escapes blame and liability so long as the benefits generated by his risky action outweigh the costs, and he is liable and blameworthy if they do not. The breaking point is a point: a sharp discontinuity that occurs where costs and benefits precisely balance. That the boundary between negligence and prudence should be marked by such a discontinuity Alexander does not find puzzling. And superficially it seems as though we have an easy way of locating that point, the point at which negligence ends and prudence begins. It is the point where that balance is struck, where the costs balance the benefits. But once we try to operationalize the notion of costs and benefits, we discover that it is far from precise. It is plagued by indeterminacies, the resolution of which will be decisive for finding liability and blameworthiness or not. Once again non-epistemic uncertainty does not undermine the validity of a sharp distinction.

This may well be the context in which we find the co-existence of a sharp boundary and non-epistemic uncertainty about its precise boundary least troubling. That in turn should help us make the presence of a sharp boundary and non-epistemic uncertainty in at least some of the examples Alexander concerns himself with less troubling as well. One could think of the boundary marking the transition between life and death, or between personhood and non-personhood as involving a balancing of some sort. Indeed one could try to picture the assessment of whether someone is alive or not, as involving an assessment of the many ways in which he is still functional—a sort of balancing test that asks whether someone is more dead than alive, or the other way around. In conducting this balancing test, many indeterminacies will have to be settled, but are they so much worse than the indeterminacies that need to be settled in filling out the concept of negligence?

2.3 Temkin's spectrum cases

Here is an example, adapted from Larry Temkin, which comes close to offering a very direct argument as to why, in one of Alexander's most compelling cases, the line marking the beginning of personhood, non-epistemic uncertainty need not undermine the recognition of a sharp boundary (Temkin 2012).

Let us imagine a continuum of cases starting with an unfertilized egg at one end of the continuum and a freshly minted neonate at the other. There are cases representing all the stages in between: a partially fertilized egg, a fully fertilized egg, a composite of cells, homunculi of increasing degrees of maturity, and so on. This presumably is the continuum along which Alexander would want to say that personhood and the attendant right not to be killed gradually grow.

Now let us imagine having to make one of those classic triage choices: we are in a position to perform a life-saving operation either on a just-delivered neonate or on two about-to-be-born babies, in other words babies that are precisely a day younger than the neonate and are still in utero. This is not the kind of difficult choice where even a very non-consequentialist morality would tell us that we cannot sacrifice the one for the sake of the many, because the choice is simply between saving one or saving two, not between killing one and saving two. It seems pretty clear in this case that one should save the two, notwithstanding the fact that the two are a day younger than the one. Let us, provisionally, grant Alexander the assumption that, being a day younger, these creatures exhibit a little bit less personhood and for that reason are less meritorious of being rescued. Nevertheless, there being two of them, rather than one, that seems to easily dwarf the slight decrement in personhood.

Now repeat this process. Imagine the possibility of saving either two babies who are *one* day away from being born, or say, twenty babies who are *two* days about from being born. Once again, let's grant Alexander the assumption that being a little bit younger these creatures exhibit less personhood and are less deserving of being rescued. Still, the fact that there are so many more of these creatures seems to more than outweigh the fact that they are just a day younger than the two slightly older babies. And since the two babies merited rescue more than the one neonate, it follows that the twenty merit rescue more than the one neonate. Continue this process many times over and you will eventually arrive at the conclusion that some very large number of unfertilized eggs merits rescue more than a single neonate, and that seems rather absurd.

All right then, but if it is absurd where did things go awry? One of the steps on this chain of argument must not be correct. At some stage it must have been the case that we could not, by increasing the quantity of such creatures, make up for the fact that their personhood declined by another day's worth of growth. Presumably, that is the day at which personhood abruptly vanishes.

I don't know whether we necessarily have to designate the point at which this occurs as the one at which personhood begins, but it would not be implausible to do so. The doctrine that tells us that there is a sharp line between the point at which the weighing is conducted in one way and the point at which it is conducted in another, the point at which an accumulation of cells counts positively and the point at which it counts negatively, is no more or less plausible than the one that asserts that personhood arises at a particular point. But in this case we have not only a very strong intuition that there is such a point, but a very strong argument for backing up that intuition.

2.4 Broome's population ethics

My next example comes from John Broome's seminal book on population ethics, *Weighing Lives* (2004). One of the questions Broome takes up in that book is whether it is a good thing when extra people are born. With regard to this question, Broome points out that most of us have what he calls the 'neutrality intuition'. We think that it really makes no difference. To be sure, if the new person would be in extreme pain, then obviously it would be a bad thing. And if he would be ecstatically happy, then many would say that means it would be a good thing if he were born, a better thing than if he were not born, though they would not be sure. Many people have the neutrality intuition even with regard to that kind of case. But for the most part, we think that if someone's happiness level falls within a fairly wide range of happiness, short of ecstasy, and better than agony, it would neither improve nor worsen the world if he were born. This neutrality intuition actually plays a crucial part in the way in which economists make welfare calculations. When they project welfare into the future, they do not generally count it as a loss if a certain policy results in fewer births, or as a gain if it results in more births—except to the very limited extent that population size affects productivity or the average level of welfare. But if a policy simply deprives a country of some extra people who would have been as happy as those already around and would leave the welfare of those already around neither worsened nor improved, they would not count those people as a gain, or their failure to be born as something we are missing out on. All of that sounds eminently like common sense.

The problem is that it leads to paradox. One such paradox identified by Broome is the following. Consider the following three possible scenarios:

Scenario 1: We have a world of ten billion people, each at a welfare level of one unit.

Scenario 2: We have a world of eleven billion people, each at a welfare level of one unit.

Scenario 3: We have a world of eleven billion people, of whom ten billion are at a welfare level of one unit, and one billion of whom are at a welfare level of two units.

Now let's compare the three scenarios. Scenario 2 is no better than scenario 1 because of the 'neutrality intuition'. Scenario 3 is clearly better than scenario 2, since some of the people in it have a higher welfare level. But scenario 3 is not better than scenario 1 because of the neutrality intuition. We thus get an alarming, paradoxical intransitivity.

To avoid this intransitivity, we need to conclude that the neutrality intuition is wrong; that there is no range of welfare levels at which the production of extra people would not affect the welfare of the world. What we need to conclude instead is that there is a level below which adding extra people worsens things and above which it improves things. And that level is a precise level, not a range. The problem is, however, that we are here in a state of non-epistemic uncertainty about where that level lies, with no visible means for resolving that uncertainty. We have a binary distinction, which we are unable to locate except in a very rough-and-ready way.

3. The Source of Non-Epistemic Uncertainty

To recapitulate, Larry Alexander argued that moral and legal doctrines that try to create binary distinctions, when there seems no good way to locate the line where that distinction should be made, in other words in the face of profound non-epistemic uncertainty, are likely to be in error. What they reveal to us is that the underlying concept is really scalar, because by making it scalar we avoid the need to locate such a line. The above examples make it clear that at least in the moral realm, situations abound in which sharp lines need to be drawn because the concepts in question are definitely not scalar, even when faced with profound non-epistemic uncertainty about where that line should be drawn.

Alas, when we then try to operationalize that moral distinction by applying it, in other words, by turning it into law, we are kind of stuck.

Before turning to the question of how the law handles this uncertainty, I do want to pursue a little the question of the deeper roots of this non-epistemic uncertainty. If we are so sure that a sharp line should be drawn, it does seem in fact quite strange that we should not be in a better position to state on what basis it should be drawn. The situation really is paradoxical, as Alexander rightly insists.

John Broome surprisingly enough has little to say about this, beyond noting, correctly it seems, that such vagueness really is endemic to our moral thinking. It is what makes many moral questions so vexing. Indeed, it is what turns them into predicaments. He adds:

To say that [a] predicament is one of vagueness . . . does not make it trivial. It does not make it a mere matter of language, as though the problem would go away if only we organized our language better. It is in the nature of betterness that it is vague. This remark is independent of its metaphysical nature. Betterness is a concept of ours that has its role in our ethical thinking. Whether or not betterness belongs to the fabric of the world, it is an essential feature of our ethics that betterness is vague. It could not become precise without our ethics becoming something quite different from what it is.

(Broome 2004, p. 179)

He thinks that while the vagueness is irremediable, its boundaries may be more susceptible to specification, although he admits that he is not really up to that task either. ('There remains the problem of fixing the neutral level for existence. The neutral level is bound to be vague, so the problem is to set limits to its vagueness. This seems to me appallingly difficult . . .' (Broome 2004, p. 264).)

The philosopher Roy Sorensen is a bit more audacious in venturing a suggestion for the root cause of this kind of non-epistemic uncertainty (Sorensen 2001). The problem as he sees it is not unique to moral concepts, but afflicts all language. As he sees it, there is in fact a sharp boundary that separates the bald from the non-bald, the heap from the non-heap, even though we cannot say where that boundary is. But he is able to explain from whence that non-epistemic uncertainty about the precise place to draw the line comes.

Sorensen's explanation proceeds by analogy. He asks us to consider a variant of the liar's paradox: a card with two sides, labelled A and B. Side A of the card contains the following statement: 'The statement on Side B of this card is false.' Side B contains the statement: 'The statement on Side A of this card is false.' Although this sounds like the liar's paradox, it really is not, because unlike the liar's paradox, there is no necessary contradiction contained in these statements. In the liar's paradox, whatever we assume about the truth of one side of the card, will lead us to contradict the initial assumption. Here things go differently. Suppose we assume that the statement on Side A of the card is true. It would then follow that the statement on side B is false. In other words, the statement that 'The statement on Side A of this card is false' is false, which means that the statement on Side A is true, which is consistent with our initial assumption. So far there seems nothing troubling here. But suppose we had started out with the assumption that the statement on Side B of the card is true. Then we would have concluded that the statement on Side A is false, which is, of course, perfectly consistent with the assumption that the statement on Side B is true.

It seems possible, then, to assume that the Side A statement is true, and the Side B statement is false, and we will not be led to a contradiction. It also seems possible to assume the Side B statement is true, and the Side A statement is false, and that too will not lead to a contradiction. The one thing that we cannot, however, assume is that both statements are true, or that both statements are false. Only one of them can be false. But how should we choose between these two possibilities? Clearly we have nothing to go on. And yet we cannot simply conclude that neither of them is true and neither of them is false. Logic demands that each statement be either true or not true. If we cannot say that either of them is true and either of them is false, but we know that each of them has to be either true or false, the inescapable conclusion seems to be that the true answer is simply unknowable. It exists on what Sorensen likes to call an inaccessible 'epistemic island'. How else to account for our inability to know?

Sorensen suggests that the same is true in the sorites paradox. It is logically compelled that there is a bald man who differs by only a hair from a non-bald man, but we have no way of knowing what number constitutes the 'hair-trigger'. The exact number exists on an 'epistemic island' inaccessible to us.

4. How the Law Copes with Non-Epistemic Uncertainty: The 'Greediness' Problem

When the law encounters epistemic uncertainty, it has a relatively straightforward way of dealing with it. That's what our burden-of-proof rules are for. Epistemic uncertainty is the situation in which we simply don't know what the evidence establishes. We would like to have more facts, but we don't and so we are uncertain whether the plaintiff is right in claiming the defendant went through a red light when he hit him, or the defendant is right in claiming that he did not. The plaintiff has the burden of proof and therefore loses. He loses not because the defendant has proven that he acted without fault, but because we are uncertain whether he did, based on ignorance of certain facts that have remained stubbornly unascertainable.

Non-epistemic uncertainty we handle differently. Non-epistemic uncertainty is the question of where to draw the line between life and death and where to draw various other lines involved in mapping a moral doctrine onto the law. Why does the law do this? Why not confess ignorance, here too, and let the party that had the burden of proof win?

Broome's discussion of vagueness in the context of population ethics can, I think, shed considerable light on this. Broome identifies a fascinating phenomenon that he calls the 'greedy vagueness' problem. Suppose we have a population of ten million people living at a level that is possibly within the neutral range, but also quite possibly above it or below it. Imagine next a population of a hundred million people living below that level, but still within the neutral range. Is the second population worse or better than the first? The answer is, of course: we don't know. The addition of the extra people might have made things better or worse, depending on whether they fall below the neutral range or above. Lowering the standard of living of the first ten million makes it worse. As for the addition of the extra ninety million, we cannot say that it makes things better or worse because their standard of living is in the 'vague' range. Its being vague means that it could potentially be above the neutral level, in which case it potentially could compensate for the lowering of the standard of living by the addition of extra lives. But since it could just as well be below the neutral level, the opposite is possible as well. We simply don't know. And the reason we don't know is once again non-epistemic uncertainty.

There is a hidden punch to this example that only becomes apparent once we transpose it into other settings. The problem is that non-epistemic uncertainty is infectious. When we combine situations in which we have no such uncertainty with examples in which we do, an example results that is plagued by such uncertainty as well. Let's see concretely how this would play out if we acknowledged too readily our inability to judge negligence because the comparison between some benefits and some costs is just too non-epistemically uncertain. Taking a certain action has consequences $c1$, $c2$, $c3$, $c4$, and $c5$. Toting up the first four, we conclude that the balance of costs and benefits is negative. It is starting to look like negligence. But we are not sure how to value the balance of costs and benefits in consequence 5. That is likely to wreck the entire comparison. It is in that sense that non-epistemic uncertainty is infectious, or as Broome prefers to say, 'greedy'. It is usually possible to widen a comparative judgement to take in lots of irrelevant other stuff on the plus and on the minus side. Unless we are bold in declaring ourselves to be able to put a precise value on each of those plusses and minuses, whether we really can or not, we will thus disable ourselves from making any comparisons at all. Hence the courts' rightful reluctance to admit to the non-epistemic uncertainty they actually feel.

5. Some Lessons: The Problem of Transitional Justice

The problem of transitional justice is what to do with those who, acting in the name of laws we now consider grossly unjust, inflicted great harm on others. The problem arose after the collapse of the Third Reich and again after the collapse of Communism. Interestingly, it was viewed as something of a philosophical indulgence when applied to former Nazi officials administering Nazi laws, but as a serious concern when applied to former communist officials applying Communist laws. More than a serious concern—the predominant view was that it was a serious violation of the norm against retroactive laws to allow someone to be punished, or even just gently sanctioned, for administering what was good law at one time, however unjust it now seems.

Eric Posner and Adrian Vermeule published an article to which they gave the telling title *Transitional Justice as Ordinary Justice* (2004). Their point, nicely conveyed by the title, is that legal change happens in all legal regimes, that all justice is 'transitional' in the sense that we are retroactively applying norms adopted today to conduct that occurred yesterday. We may not do so openly, but we do it routinely. We do it frequently in civil law: the common law process almost by definition involves creating rules as a case arises, to be applied to this and all future cases. But even in the criminal law, which relies on statutes and forbids 'common law' law-making, retroactivity is commonplace. As Posner and Vermeule put it, 'legislatures and courts have ample leeway to adjust the *ex post facto* prohibition in pragmatic style'. They might extend a statute of limitations, for instance (although they shy away from doing so if the limitations period has already run); they might narrow and broaden various criminal defences; they might classify a new law as being 'procedural' rather than criminal (since retroactivity with regard to procedural laws is almost never a problem), or they might simply declare that the law they are making up really has been the law all along, but just has not been properly recognized as such.

Posner and Vermeule's defence of transitional justice is startling and original, but it is subject to some limitations that the foregoing analysis should help make more transparent. What they are really arguing is that retroactivity should be thought of as a scalar concept, which can exist in greater and lesser amounts, and the unfairness it gives rise to is similarly scalar, and is apt to be outweighed by the greater and lesser amounts of various practical, and collateral fairness-related advantages that flow from it. Now imagine we have reached the end of the continuum in which there is complete absence of a retroactivity ban. In other words, it would be fine if we decided today that selling alcohol to nineteen-year-olds last year was illegal, even though at that time it was not, and punished the person who consumed such alcohol accordingly. Under a scalar approach to retroactivity, it should be possible to render this case acceptable, indeed more than just one in which there is an absence of all retroactivity, so long as certain compensating advantages are injected into the situation. What would constitute such compensating advantages? Well, all the reasons that people have for wanting to inflict sanctions on the rulers of the ancien regime: that they behaved badly and deserve to suffer for it; that they profited from their wrongs and should be stripped of the profits they have accumulated; that it would help to deter future wrongdoing by others who have managed to gain control of a country's legal system and tried to use it abusively, to instil greater support and confidence in the new regime by the population at large, and so on.

Now imagine a slightly retroactive law—compensated for by some other advantage, that is—and assume that it is but very selectively enforced. As we make the law more retroactive, let us imagine that we 'compensate' for that injustice by making the law less selective, more universal in its enforcement. Selective enforcement is an evil; therefore making the enforcement less selective improves things, and let us suppose actually compensates, morally, for the slight increase in the degree of retroactivity of the law. Now imagine doing this repeatedly. We should then arrive at a situation in which we say that a law that is entirely *ex post facto* but which is applied truly universally is an improvement on the selective enforcement of a normal, non-*ex post facto* law. That surely is wrong. Where we went wrong is in not acknowledging a discontinuity. For laws at one end of the continuum, selective enforcement is good, and for laws at the other end of the continuum it is bad; and the transition between these two situations is like the transition from life to death, necessarily sudden. Of course, non-epistemic uncertainty keeps us from knowing where exactly that transition occurs, but that it occurs suddenly we can now see clearly.

At least some of the force of Posner and Vermeule's highly original take on the problem of transitional justice derives from their implicit assumption that the retroactivity norm operates in a scalar fashion. Although their use of the argument in this context is surprising and illuminating, a version of it is in fact a not uncommon form of legal argument: if someone objects to something, we argue that it differs only in degree from something else which he has no problem with, and that he should therefore temper his objection, and perhaps withdraw it entirely once he takes account of some special countervailing advantages. It is the inverse, in a way, of the slippery slope objection. But the underlying assumption that the norm operates in a scalar fashion we now know to be frequently unwarranted, and if it does not, the 'It's a mere difference in degree' argument loses a good deal of its force.

6. Conclusion

The boundaries of legal concepts are plagued by non-epistemic uncertainty. This fact has prompted many to suggest that we are simply misconceiving of these concepts as being binary, when they are really scalar. What I have tried to show is that the moral doctrines that the law here tracks are in fact binary in character, i.e. marked by sharp boundaries, though admittedly boundaries that are swathed in non-epistemic uncertainty. The roots of that epistemic uncertainty are somewhat obscure, although some highly original bold speculations about them have been offered. The law largely hides the non-epistemic uncertainty in its decision making, and for good reason. If admitted to, non-epistemic uncertainty would end up not only paralyzing the legal system as it tries to deal with such cases, but the paralysis would spread to many other cases and end up rendering almost all legal decision making impossible.

References

Alexander, Larry. 2008. 'Scalar Properties, Binary Judgements'. *Journal of Applied Philosophy* 25(2): 85–104.

Broome, John. 2004. *Weighing Lives*. Oxford: Oxford University Press.

Posner, Eric and Adrian Vermeule. 2004. 'Transitional Justice as Ordinary Justice'. *Harvard Law Rewiew* 117(3): 761–825.

Sorensen, Roy. 2001. *Vagueness and Contradiction.* Oxford: Oxford University Press.

Temkin, Larry. 2012. *Rethinking the Good: Moral Ideals and the Nature of Practical Reasoning.* Oxford: Oxford University Press.

Tversky, Amos and Daniel Kahneman. 1981. 'The Framing of Decisions and the Psychology of Choice'. *Science* 211(4481): 453–8.

13

Smoothing Vague Laws

*Adam J. Kolber**

It's no surprise that vague laws can have harsh consequences. Many jurisdictions, for example, provide a complete defence against criminal liability when using reasonable force in self-defence. Since the word 'reasonable' is vague, no one knows where to draw the line precisely. Two people who were equally reasonable in their use of force may nevertheless be treated differently in neighbouring courtrooms. One may walk out a free person, while the other is imprisoned for years.

What is more surprising is that *even if* we could agree about precisely where along the reasonableness spectrum some conduct falls, vague legal terms would still have harsh consequences because laws often draw sharp lines through features of the world best understood along spectra. A defender's level of caution can range anywhere from extremely cautious to entirely incautious. Since we draw a sharp line along this continuum, one person might use reasonable self-defence and have a complete justification for killing someone, while another might use deadly force with just a bit less caution and be imprisoned for murder. Though their reasonableness only varies slightly, the law treats them very differently.

When a vague legal term draws a line through a feature of the world best understood along a spectrum, we can often ease the severity of the line drawing by smoothing the law. A legal input and output have a 'smooth' relationship when, as the input gradually changes, the output gradually changes accordingly (Kolber 2014, p. 661). Smooth laws make the consequences of a law violation depend not on crossing some sharp boundary but on a feature that varies along a spectrum. So, for example, we could smoothly punish those who unreasonably use defensive force by increasing their sentences based on *how* unreasonable their use of force was. Indeed, some judges may punish in this smooth fashion. But structural sentencing impediments, such as statutory minimum sentences, can make smooth sentencing impossible, at least along certain parts of the continuum (Kolber 2016, pp. 877–9).

Many legal relationships are not smooth but 'bumpy'. An input and output have a bumpy relationship when a gradual change to the input sometimes dramatically

* For helpful comments, I thank Larry Alexander, Brian Bix, Leo Katz, Kathleen Reilly, Roy Sorensen, and Aaron Twerski, as well as participants in workshops at NYU School of Law and the University of Freiburg.

affects the output and sometimes has no effect at all (Kolber 2014, p. 662). For example, a reasonable driver who causes an accident will be deemed non-negligent and owe no damages, while a slightly less cautious driver may owe millions of dollars. Level of caution and damages owed have a bumpy relationship to each other because gradual changes to level of caution can dramatically affect damages (right on the border between negligence and non-negligence). And when level of caution falls below a critical level, it has no further impact on damages (at least until punitive damages kick in, if they are available at all).

Some scholars have discussed whether particular features of law and morality are continuous or discrete (or, if you prefer, scalar or binary),[1] but such terminology is inadequate. There is no dispute that variables like level of caution fall along a continuum. What is open to dispute is how changes in these variables ought to affect pertinent moral or legal outputs. Hence, I use the terms 'smooth' and 'bumpy' to capture certain relationships between a particular input and a particular output.[2] (Informally, we can speak about whether a law or body of law is smooth or bumpy based on the kind of relationships that predominate.)

In section 1, I argue that smooth laws frequently ameliorate the harms of legal vagueness while bumpy laws frequently augment them. While there are costs to smoothing the law that must be weighed against the benefits, we ought to look for good opportunities to make the law smoother than it is now. In section 2, I address recent work by Leo Katz defending the sharp lines drawn by the law (Katz 2011, pp. 139–81). Katz believes that many phenomena, such as birth and death and the giving of consent, warrant these sharp lines. More generally, he believes that attempts to make the law less all-or-nothing are doomed to fail. I raise doubts about whether Katz has demonstrated that these phenomena are truly all-or-nothing and argue that attempts to make the law less all-or-nothing are not only possible but often desirable.

1. Easing the Harms of Legal Vagueness

The law of criminal attempt illustrates how vague legal lines can have harsh consequences. We draw a sharp line between preparing to commit a crime and actually attempting a crime. At one extreme, a person might merely intend to commit a crime like murder but take no action to effectuate the plan.[3] In that case, he has not attempted a crime and will have no criminal liability whatsoever. At the other

---

[1] See e.g. Alexander 2008 (pp. 95–6), Bibas 2004 (p. 2487), Fennel 2012, Husak 1998 (p. 167), and Parchomovsky et al. 2007 (p. 738).

[2] Some legal concepts, such as tortious negligence, are 'theoretical intermediaries' (Kolber 2014, p. 660). They receive inputs about, say, how fast a person was driving, the nature of road conditions, and so on to compute some measure of how cautious or incautious a driver was. That determination then gets combined with others to determine whether or not damages are owed. Theoretical intermediaries can be analysed either as inputs or as outputs depending on the context.

[3] A person can also commit a crime by failing to take an action required by law. For simplicity, I discuss cases where a person must act in order to commit a crime.

extreme, a person might take every action he believes necessary to kill by: (1) developing the intention to kill; (2) purchasing a ski mask, gun, and ammunition; (3) driving to the intended victim's house; (4) breaking into his house in the middle of the night with the loaded gun; and (5) firing at the victim's head. If the bullet misses, the perpetrator could be convicted of attempted murder and spend many years in prison.

When did our hypothetical attempted murderer change from someone beyond the reach of the criminal law to someone subject to at least several years in prison under a statutory minimum sentence for attempted murder? To make matters harder, each of these steps could be further subdivided: did he cross the line when he drove a mile towards the victim's house or when he was a mile away from it? There is no obvious, natural demarcation between preparation and attempt.

Statutory language purporting to distinguish preparation and attempt is notoriously vague. In New York, for example, '[a] person is guilty of an attempt to commit a crime when, with intent to commit a crime', he engages in conduct which tends to effect the commission of such crime'.[4] The distinction is vague because it is hardly obvious when conduct all of a sudden 'tends to effect' the commission of a crime.

There is no widely accepted way to eliminate this vagueness. There are seemingly infinite ways to plot to kill someone, and it would be impossible to list them all in advance and decide precisely when in the course of each plan conduct switches from preparation to attempt. What is puzzling, however, is why the difficult task of distinguishing preparation and attempt has such dramatic consequences. Small differences in the culpability of people on each side of the line can mean the difference between exculpation and years in prison. If criminal law is supposed to punish people more when they are more culpable and if culpability gradually increases as one proceeds along a criminal path, we would expect those on either side of the line to have roughly the same culpability and receive roughly the same punishments. Nevertheless, we draw sharp lines: the mere preparer has no criminal liability while the attempter faces years in prison.

The problem I have demonstrated lies in the disconnect between the input–output relationships we think the law ought to have and the input–output relationships it actually has. If one's theory of punishment requires that small changes to some pertinent input (like how culpable a person is) should lead to small changes in some pertinent output (like how much punishment he deserves), then our approach to attempt law is likely to disappoint. Assuming there are only small changes in culpability as, say, the perpetrator gradually drives to his intended victim's home, there should only be small changes in the amount of punishment he receives.

When a small change to an input gradually changes an output, I say that the two have a smooth relationship. Many moral theorists likely believe that culpability and punishment ought to have a smooth relationship. The law, however, creates

---

[4] N.Y. Penal Law § 110 (2015).

a bumpy relationship between the two, at least right around the line that distinguishes preparation and attempt. Gradual changes to culpability can dramatically change levels of punishment, as when proceeding just slightly too far towards one's criminal goal suddenly translates into many years of incarceration.

The bumpy law of attempt exacerbates problems caused by legal vagueness. We don't know precisely when an attempt 'tends to effect the commission' of a crime. Thus, small errors can have disastrous consequences: some people who are quite culpable may receive no punishment whatsoever, while others who are just barely culpable may be deemed 'attempters' and get lumped in with those who are very culpable. In many jurisdictions, judges have discretion to more leniently punish a person who is just barely an attempter, but many jurisdictions also have mandatory minimum sentences. An attempt crime could have a mandatory minimum of several years in prison, tying the hands of judges who would have otherwise sentenced smoothly around the line dividing preparation and attempt. Moreover, even when judges have the flexibility to punish in smooth ways, we cannot be confident they will do so in the absence of legal norms inculcating the underlying smooth relationship. Thus, even though it is difficult to draw a non-vague line between preparation and attempt, we need not exacerbate the problem by giving the line such bumpy consequences.

One might object that culpability does not smoothly increase as one proceeds along a criminal path.[5] What changes, at least in some cases, is just *our evidence* of a person's culpability. If a person is wholeheartedly committed to some criminal enterprise, the mere happenstance of when he is arrested along that path reveals nothing about his culpability. If the objector believes that strength of evidence of culpability should correlate with punishment amount, however, then we are back to where we started: generally speaking, evidence that a person is attempting to commit a crime gradually increases as the crime proceeds. So we are still left wondering why criminal liability is bumpy.

Some may believe that neither culpability nor evidence of culpability should determine amounts of punishment. For example, some, like me, prefer to focus on consequentialist considerations, including the desire to deter crimes and incapacitate dangerous people. Many of my comments apply to such considerations: culpability and dangerousness are generally correlated, and there is typically no good reason to draw a sharp cut-off between a dangerous person and another slightly more or less so. Still, I don't argue that every important legal relationship is smooth—just that many important ones are. Here's the key point: if our best theory

---

[5] Larry Alexander and Kim Ferzan might deny that culpability gradually increases along a criminal path. They defend the uncommon view that an actor shouldn't be legally liable for pursuing a criminal path 'until the actor unleashes a risk of harm over which he no longer has complete control' (Alexander and Ferzan 2008, p. 379). For example, they would draw a sharp line between a person lying in wait who kills his target and the person lying in wait who has a heart attack and is whisked away by an ambulance moments before his target arrives. On their view, the former warrants serious punishment while the latter warrants none at all. I suspect most people believe that culpability increases more smoothly than Alexander and Ferzan do, but my main point is only that the law should generally match our views of the underlying moral relationships, cost and administrability permitting.

recommends that a particular relationship be smooth, then we have grounds to question laws that implement the relationship in a bumpy fashion.

Consider another illustration of the general point that vague legal terms often have unnecessarily bumpy effects. In the United States, federal law requires a minimum thirty-year sentence for 'using' a machine gun in a drug trafficking crime.[6] The Supreme Court has held that trading a firearm for drugs constitutes 'using' it,[7] even though such a use is likely to be much less culpable than firing or brandishing a firearm during a drug transaction. Though bartering a machine gun as part of a drug transaction is less culpable than the typical use of a machine gun in a drug transaction, we punish it as though it were one of the most serious of all criminal offences. Hence, in treating firearm bartering as a 'using', the law is bumpy to an extent that is hard to justify.

Similar concerns apply in self-defence contexts, as noted earlier. When we ask if a person who killed another engaged in reasonable self-defence, 'reasonable' is vague. Yet the reasonable killer will leave the courtroom a free person, while the just-slightly-unreasonable killer will be subject to at least the minimum sentence for murder. All of this is true, even when we know all the pertinent facts about a defendant's culpability.

Moreover, the problems caused by bumpiness extend far beyond the criminal law. In tort law, for example, a reasonable driver will owe no damages for a car accident he causes, while the just-slightly-unreasonable driver may owe millions. Vague expressions like 'reasonable', 'good faith', and 'aggravated' appear throughout the law and often have bumpy legal effects that are hard to justify in light of the underlying moral norms these expressions are meant to enforce.

Of course, not all indeterminacy in legal language can be ameliorated by making the law smoother. First, smooth laws will not resolve *ambiguous* statutes. A statute establishing an agency to regulate 'banks' could leave ambiguous whether the agency is supposed to regulate financial institutions or parcels of land adjacent to rivers.[8] Yet we cannot craft a smooth relationship to solve the problem. Presumably, we wouldn't create a single agency that splits its mission between regulating financial institutions and regulating riparian zones. Unlike the other examples I have given, the critical interpretive issue here does not involve a single continuous spectrum along which both kinds of banks can be arrayed.

Second, smooth laws are only appropriate when our underlying moral theory calls for them. For example, the Fifth Amendment to the U.S. Constitution provides that 'No person shall be…deprived of life…without due process of law.' But what qualifies as a 'person'? On one view, an entity is not a person until it is 'ensouled' by a divine entity. On this view, personhood is bivalent and vests instantaneously. On another view, personhood falls along a continuum from clear non-person, say a single sperm, to intermediate entities of gradually greater personhood like an embryo, a two-month-old foetus, a three-month-old foetus, and

---

[6] 18 U.S.C. § 924(c).   [7] *Smith v. United States*, 508 U.S. 223, 225 (1993).
[8] See e.g. Waldron 1994, p. 515.

so on until we reach a young child with clear personhood. Each moral theory likely dictates a different legal regime. Similarly, to pick up on an earlier example, we can debate whether culpability gradually increases as actors pursue a criminal path or whether it increases suddenly when some special line of demarcation is crossed. Absent good reasons to the contrary, however, one's underlying moral theories should dictate when the law uses smooth, bumpy, or other input–output relationships.[9]

Third, even when some underlying phenomenon is best understood in smooth terms, legal decision making may still require a choice among a small number of discrete options. For example, certain disputes can be brought in either state or federal court depending on whether the amount of money in controversy exceeds $75,000.[10] Even though little may distinguish a $75,000 case from a $75,001 case,[11] it is hard to imagine bringing suit in some entity that is, say, forty-nine per cent state court and fifty-one per cent federal court. Similarly, the U.S. Constitution requires that the president be at least thirty-five years old.[12] Even though nothing magical happens precisely when the age cut-off is reached, if age is a pertinent consideration at all, then perhaps it needs to have a bumpy relationship to presidential eligibility. After all, you cannot be a little bit president.

The set of situations requiring bumpy solutions—cases having what I call 'bumpy needs' (Kolber 2014, pp. 681–2)—may be relatively small, however. Even age and presidential eligibility can be smoothed somewhat by requiring candidates below a certain age to win by a supermajority of voters or by varying the powers of the presidency with the president's age. Nevertheless, there are instances where we must make discrete choices to admit or exclude evidence, deem a law constitutional or unconstitutional, and so on. In areas of law that primarily govern the operation of other laws, such as evidence law and constitutional law, we frequently have bumpy needs. These areas of law are not directed towards the kind of natural phenomena that tend to spread across spectra.

There is a fourth, more general consideration lurking here. Even when our best moral theory advises a smooth relationship, various practical considerations may nevertheless warrant bumpy laws. For example, perhaps bumpy laws are easier for people to remember or easier for judges and juries to apply. It may be easier to determine whether or not a defendant has crossed the line from preparation to attempt (vague as it may be) than to decide precisely how far along the path to murder he has progressed. When we are deciding disputes that are a safe distance from some critical cut-off point, bumpy decision making is cheaper and may better constrain discretion. Bumpy legislation may also be easier to enact because it hides the possibly controversial underlying theories that govern the relationship between inputs

---

[9] I describe some other possible relationships in Kolber 2014, pp. 664–6.
[10] 28 U.S.C. § 1332.
[11] See *Freeland v. Liberty Mutual Fire Insurance Co.*, 632 F 3d 250 (U.S. Court of Appeals (6th Cir.), 2011) (dismissing case for lack of jurisdiction where $75,000 amount in controversy did not *exceed* the $75,000 requirement for federal diversity jurisdiction).
[12] U.S. Constitution at Art. II, Section 1, Clause 5.

and outputs. Thus, a bumpy law may allow legislators to pitch legislation in different ways to different constituencies.[13]

Nevertheless, whenever we use a bumpy law to govern a smooth phenomenon, we are rounding a continuous result to some nearby discrete option. That rounding represents a deviation from what the law would ideally accomplish. Thus, while practical concerns may justify rounding, we shouldn't be too quick to assume that rounding is warranted.

For example, until recent decades, most jurisdictions followed bumpy principles of contributory negligence.[14] If a plaintiff was negligent at all in the circumstances that led to his injury, he would lose his lawsuit entirely. In recent decades, however, our bumpy contributory negligence regime has been largely supplanted by various types of comparative negligence.[15] In its purest form, comparative negligence smoothly reduces the plaintiff's recovery by the percentage of his injury attributable to his own negligence.

Comparative negligence may have seemed virtually impossible to implement when it was first considered. Surely it is much harder and more fact intensive to determine not whether a plaintiff was negligent at all but precisely how negligent the plaintiff was relative to the defendant. Nevertheless, comparative negligence has proven popular. Though it probably increases adjudication costs, many believe that justice is better served by it overall.

2. Response to Leo Katz

I have argued that we should look for opportunities to make the law smoother. Smoother laws can ease the harsh effects of line drawing and improve the fit between our laws and our underlying moral norms. We should not be blind to the costs of smooth laws: they are expensive to adjudicate and often grant substantial discretion to judges and other legal actors. But the cost of smooth laws will often be lower than the cost of bumpy rounding errors.

---

[13] [L]egislators may find that vagueness is essential to the process of building support for legislation: precisely drawn statutes may be more likely to concentrate interests, while vague statutes keep them diffuse. And as we know from public choice models of the legislative process, the likelihood of passing legislation diminishes as the forces opposed become more concentrated.... Legislators may draft vague statutes for... strategic reasons. Legislators may want to avoid responsibility for outcomes that excite public anger; vagueness facilitates their evasion of blame by allowing them to attribute bad outcomes to the resolution of vague terms by regulatory agencies or courts. Vagueness also allows legislators to represent the implications of legislation differently to different constituent groups and thus to satisfy a broader range of a heterogeneous population. In these contexts legislators value vagueness not as a tool in the design of socially optimal legal rules but rather as protection for their careers.

(Hadfield 1994, p. 550; footnotes omitted)

[14] See Restatement (First) of Torts § 467 (1934).
[15] 57B Am. Jur. 2D Negligence § 801 (2004).

Smoothing legal input–output relationships will often have the larger-scale effect of making the law less all or nothing. In his most recent book,[16] Leo Katz has argued against such changes. Katz believes that many phenomena that appear to stretch along continua, like becoming a person or dying or giving consent, are better understood as discrete events. He does not go so far as to 'defend the either/or character of legal doctrines', but he purports 'to show why any efforts to change things are doomed' (p. 157). He claims that 'most of the time either/ or can't be avoided, or more precisely, that if we tried to purge a doctrine of it, we would find that either/or has simply migrated to another part of the doctrine or has been replaced by some other, far more troublesome feature' (p. 157). In short, he writes, 'we can only affect where a sharp discontinuity will occur, not whether it will occur at all' (p. 157).[17] I now respond to Katz's claims that many phenomena important to the law are all or nothing and that the law cannot avoid sharp discontinuities.

2.1 Challenge #1: Birth and death are events, not processes

Katz acknowledges the initial appeal of understanding death as a continuous process rather than a discrete event: 'As we look more closely at the stages through which everyone passes as he moves from being fully alive to being fully dead, it starts to feel increasingly artificial to designate any one point in this progression as demarcating the boundary between life and death' (p. 158).

Despite its appeal, Katz defends a contrary view. He asks us to imagine the spectrum of how alive a person is broken up into about 1,000 increments (or any arbitrarily large number of increments). At one end is a person who is fully alive (H). Then comes another who is just one increment less alive (H - 1) and then another who is two increments less alive (H - 2). Eventually, we reach the last person who is just barely alive (H - 1,000).

Suppose we had to choose, Katz asks, between saving one person who is fully alive or two who are just a bit less alive. Surely, he says, we would choose two people who are just a bit less alive. The incremental reduction in life is very small, and we get to save two people rather than one. Similarly, we would choose to save three people who are two increments shy of being fully alive rather than two people who are one increment shy. Soon, though, we reach an odd conclusion. If '<' means less worthy of being saved, we get:

$$H < 2(H-1) < 3(H-2) < 4(H-3) < \ldots < 1001(H-1,000).$$

---

[16] Katz 2011. Unless otherwise noted, all further references are to this book. For a review of Katz's book, see Huang 2013.

[17] Interestingly, Katz denies that rule-of-law virtues like giving clear notice and avoiding arbitrary decisions justify the either/or nature of the law. 'On closer inspection', Katz argues, '[e]ither/ or does not necessarily, or even usually, result in bright-line rules. The boundaries of many doctrines are obscure. Yes, there is a fine line, but it is not a bright one—no one can comfortably predict where it lies, and so citizens do not in fact have notice and judges are not really constrained' (p. 145).

Katz claims that if we take this view to the extreme, it is better to save 1,001 people who are just barely alive than one fully alive human being. 'But this is absurd!' writes Katz. 'A single *H*-minus-1,000 is a collection of completely decomposed cells. How can a set of 1,001 such collections possibly trump a single living human being...? Something has gone wrong' (p. 160). Katz believes that the only way to avoid this conclusion is to identify some 'stunningly abrupt transition' where we can no longer 'compensate for a drop in quality by vastly upping the quantity of those inferior-grade Hs' (p. 160). Hence, he claims '[t]here is no gentle going into that good night, as it were. Death is a cliff, not a gentle slope' (p. 160).

In fact, however, Katz has not identified a 'stunningly abrupt transition'. He has described a gentle transition from very alive to somewhat alive to barely alive to completely dead. No quantity of bodies described merely as a 'collection of completely decomposed cells' will ever equal the value of a human life because such bodies are *already dead*. The problem is not that there is no continuum of life and death; it's that Katz is describing a body that has passed the end of the relevant spectrum.

Amounts of life can fall along a spectrum and still reach an endpoint when a body is not alive at all. Consider a property that indisputably falls along a continuum, like the temperature of ice. The continuum starts at absolute zero and gradually increases. But as the temperature rises above the melting point of water, we no longer have ice; we have liquid water. So though the temperature of ice is bounded in one direction by absolute zero and by the melting point of water in the other direction, there is an interesting range where the temperature of ice varies continuously. And just as ice can have an interesting range of temperatures bounded on two ends, human life has an interesting range of vital activity even though it, too, is bounded.

One reason Katz's hypothetical may lead us astray is that he proposes a continuum of life in biological terms. But his *reductio* argument concerns our beliefs not about how alive a being is but about the relative value of entities with different amounts of life. The valuation of a body need not correspond in obvious ways to the amount of life still in the body. The value of a life depends on the set of properties that give it value, not the number of cells it has that are still living.

For example, as an overly simplistic suggestion, suppose there is a relationship between the value of a person's life and his level of conscious awareness. Lives with more conscious awareness, on this view, would be valued more than lives with less conscious awareness. Katz might ask, 'Isn't a fully alive and conscious human being worth more than any number of people with just a minute quantity of conscious awareness?' So phrased, however, the answer depends quite a bit on the details. Faced with a tragic choice, we plausibly should save a large number of people with limited awareness (but whose lives still have value) over one person with full awareness. Katz's *reductio ad absurdum* has lost its *absurdum*.

If bodies can be assigned an amount of life from 0 to 1,000, it's true that there is a point where an abrupt transition occurs in our treatment of those bodies. A million or even a billion bodies assigned zero units of life will always generate less value than even a single non-zero-valued body. But there's nothing stunning about the transition from living to dead. Katz seems to move from the fact that there is a point at which a body has no life at all to the conclusion that there is no continuum of amounts of life. Consider, however, the set of real numbers—the archetypical case of a continuous range of numbers. We can say that there's a sharp transition between the set of positive real numbers and the set of non-positive real numbers. That is, we can craft a category that distinguishes numbers zero and lower from numbers greater than zero. But the fact that we can identify a property of real numbers that fits into a binary category doesn't alter the continuous nature of the numbers themselves. What marks a relevant discontinuity is a matter of perspective.

Recall the transition from contributory negligence to comparative negligence. Comparative negligence smoothed the law by more closely tying the reduction in plaintiffs' recoveries to the extent of their negligence. It surely made the law less either/or. True, we can imagine a sharp distinction between entirely non-negligent plaintiffs and those who are slightly negligent: no number of completely non-negligent plaintiffs will ever equal the negligence of one slightly negligent plaintiff. But this doesn't strike me as an interesting discontinuity. Comparative negligence smooths tort law variables that we actually care about, and were it beneficial to do so, we could make our treatment of death smoother as well.[18]

Katz offers some additional arguments to suggest that death is not a continuous process. Citing Peter Unger's work, Katz argues that we tend not to differentially value human lives based on their levels of ability and disability:

[W]e generally feel that the rights granted to all human beings should be the same regardless of abilities and disabilities. The progression from life to death is a progression from ability to disability. If we were to treat the dying differently depending on where they are located on that progression, it seems we ought to treat the fully alive differently...and most of us would feel loath to do that.

(p. 161)

We do strive to treat people the same regardless of their abilities. But, to reiterate, we must distinguish the claim that *life* is a matter of degree from the claim that *the value* of life is a matter of degree or that *particular rights* should be a matter of degree. Even if the value of a human body is either 'fully valued' or 'valueless' depending on whether it is alive, amounts of life may still be best understood in a continuous way. Furthermore, the fact that we strive to *treat* lives as equally valuable does not necessarily mean they are always deemed to have equal value. Most people would not be indifferent if they somehow aged ten years in an instant. Maybe lives do vary in value, but as a matter of public policy, we generally treat them as having equal value because any other scheme is too contentious, prone to error, or otherwise disadvantageous.[19]

Importantly, I do not seek to challenge Katz's underlying belief that death is a discrete event. Just as I allowed for the possibility that a foetus is ensouled at

---

[18] I have not argued that we *ought* to smooth our treatment of death. I have made the weaker claim that, contra Katz, we *could* smooth our treatment of death.

[19] See Harris 1999 for a discussion of some of the pertinent considerations.

some moment in time, I do not to purport to disprove the possibility that a life is 'disensouled' at some moment in time either. Moreover, even if death is a gradual process, there may still be practical reasons to treat death as a discrete event for legal purposes such that estates, for example, pass to heirs at a particular moment in time.[20] But Katz purports to show that any attempt to make the law less either/ or is doomed to fail or to merely shift the either/or feature of the law elsewhere, while I have argued that treating death as continuous need not implicate the serious problems Katz envisions.

After all, we often value lives differently. Health policy arguments that focus on quality-adjusted life years implicitly value younger lives more than older lives, all else being equal. If anything, health policy and bioethics are realms in which people are deeply torn as to whether the value of life should have a smooth or bumpy relationship with variables like age or expected remaining life span or have no relationship at all.[21]

Katz also claims that his argument that death is an event rather than a process can be applied in reverse to the beginning of life (p. 226 n. 7). Compare a newborn baby ('*neonate*') to a baby that is one day from being born ('*neonate* – 1') and so on until we reach the point of fertilization about 280 days earlier ('*neonate* – 280'). Katz suggests that those who believe the formation of life occurs along a spectrum would presumably believe that two *neonate* – 1's are more deserving of aid than one actual *neonate*. And using the logic previously described, we are led to the conclusion that 281 just-conceived foetuses are more deserving of being saved than one just-born baby. Katz says that 'this, too, is absurd'.[22]

Just as we can recognize an end to the continuum of dying, however, we can recognize a beginning to the continuum of becoming a person. Perhaps interests in life begin when a foetus reaches some level of intelligence or has some capacity to feel pain. Organisms with just a few cells lack such properties. Nevertheless, there may be periods of fetal development over which an entity does change in a continuous way with respect to some property associated with its moral or legal interests. The law governing reproductive rights in the U.S. arguably represents a

---

[20] In *Gulliver's Travels*, Jonathan Swift imagined immortals called Struldbruggs. Though they were immortal, their functionality declined to the point where they could barely speak a few words. Interestingly, at age eighty, they were 'looked on as dead in Law'. For example, their estates would transfer to their heirs, and they would become ineligible to purchase property or serve as witnesses in civil or criminal matters. At least in Swift's story, legal death is quite transparently separated from physical death (Swift 1996, pp. 154–60).

[21] John Harris, for example, generally favours no relationship between the value of a life and its age or remaining life span. 'Each person's desire to stay alive should be regarded as of the same importance and as deserving the same respect as that of anyone else, irrespective of the quality of their life or its expected duration' (Harris 1999, p. 372). He makes one very bumpy exception, however. There is 'some span of years that we consider a reasonable life', say seventy years (Harris 1999, p. 367). If we must give some scarce life-saving resource either to a person who has reached that age or someone who has not, Harris argues that we should give it to the younger person.

[22] Katz likely knows, though, that some people *actually would* endorse the alleged *reductio*. Initiatives in several U.S. states have sought constitutional amendments declaring that embryos are legal persons (Eckholm 2011, p. A16).

bumpy approximation of this view.[23] Thus, contra Katz, the law could (and in some respects does) understand the beginning and end of life in shades of grey rather than black and white.

2.2 Challenge #2: Consent is all-or-nothing

One way that consent can be imperfect is if it is secured through deception about material issues. A patient tricked into surgery with deliberately misleading risk information has not given fully valid consent. The extent to which a person is deceived can, of course, vary across a spectrum. We may sometimes find it helpful to speak about consent procured by deception as partial to varying degrees.

Katz focuses not on consent secured by deception but on consent secured through coercive pressure. For example, a person might threaten to reveal ever-so-slightly embarrassing information about a celebrity if the celebrity refuses to have sex with the threatener. In such cases, could the pressure partly invalidate consent? Or does pressure only invalidate consent when it crosses some critical threshold of coerciveness?

As a preliminary observation, not everyone agrees that the presence or absence of consent should matter to the criminal law. What clearly matters is a defendant's *belief* about whether someone else consented. It's true that, especially in the context of sexual assaults, many jurisdictions focus on the presence or absence of consent rather than the defendant's beliefs about consent (Cavallaro 1996, pp. 818–19). They may do so, in part, because it is difficult to read defendants' minds, and so the presence or absence of consent is a rough proxy for the defendant's beliefs about consent. To the extent what we really care about, however, are defendants' beliefs about consent, it is worth emphasizing that such beliefs are likely to spread across spectra. Defendants, for example, will have varying levels of confidence that another has consented to sex, and such beliefs should plausibly have a smooth effect on their culpability.

In any event, let us suppose, as Katz seems to, that the presence or absence of consent is independently relevant to criminal law. To show that consent is all-or-nothing, Katz asks us to consider cases in which a person says, 'Give me the $1,000 you have in your wallet', and couples the demand with one of five different threats:

Case 1: 'Or else I will kill you.'
Case 2: 'Or else I will destroy your treasured rosebushes.'
Case 3: 'Or else I will drive around your neighborhood with tortious negligence.'

---

[23] Looking at current law, one might say that a mother's interest in autonomy grows gradually weaker as her foetus's interests grow gradually stronger. Pre-viability, the mother retains a relatively strong constitutional right to abortion. At the point of viability, however, states can prohibit abortion, treating the infant's interests as almost as strong as the mother's (states cannot prohibit abortion even at viability when the pregnancy threatens the life or health of the mother) (see *Planned Parenthood v. Casey*, 505 U.S. 833, 846 (1992)). Finally, when a child is actually born, it receives full rights of personhood and has rights comparable to its mother's. See U.S. Const. amend. V ('No person shall be ... deprived of life, liberty, or property, without due process of law ...').

Case 4: 'Or else I will publicize your past relationship with me, which you would find highly
      embarrassing.'
Case 5: 'Or else I will end our friendship'

(pp. 164–6)

Katz argues that even though the amount of harm threatened in each case varies,
the blameworthiness of issuing the threat does not change gradually. In his view,
blameworthiness stays the same until case 5, when it disappears entirely. When a
person couples a demand with a threat, Katz argues (pp. 167–8), the blame for
doing so depends not on what the person threatens to do but on what he actually
does (in this case, inappropriately extract money from a person against his will). In
cases 1 to 4, the person inappropriately extracts the same thing: $1,000. Hence, he
is equally blameworthy in those cases no matter how coercive his threats were. By
contrast, in case 5 the threat is permissible, and so it generates little or no blameworthiness. Katz takes these cases to show that consent is all or nothing.

In real life, case 1 is much more traumatizing and hence more wrongful than the
others. But if we assume that the threatener poses no further threat once paid off,
as Katz surely intends, then perhaps he is right that cases 1 to 4 are equally wrongful. While I consider myself undecided, maybe it is the case that, even in the face
of varying amounts of pressure, the presence or absence of consent is binary. One's
attitude towards some transaction can plausibly be reduced to an all-or-nothing
question like: 'All things considered, do I want this transaction to proceed?'

In fact, if we modify Katz's example so that the demand and the threat are in
comparable units, we may think coercive pressure and consent really ought to have
a bumpy relationship. Suppose our bad guy says, 'Give me the $1,000 in your wal-
let', coupled with one of the following threats:

Case A: 'Or else I will take $10,000 from the open trunk of your car.'
Case B: 'Or else I will take $5,000 from the open trunk of your car.'
Case C: 'Or else I will take $500 from the open trunk of your car.'

Cases A and B may be equally wrongful. We might think that when a person threatens one of two wrongful actions (here, taking money from a wallet or from a car
trunk) and knows how aversive the options will be to the victim, the wrongfulness
of the threat depends primarily on the wrongfulness of the option the victim finds
least aversive. In A and B, the victim finds it less aversive to give $1,000 from his
wallet than to have any greater amount of money removed from his car. So no matter how much money the bad guy threatens to take from the trunk, it won't affect
whether or not the victim gives an overall thumbs up or down to the transaction.
What makes cases A and B equally wrongful is that the best option the bad guy
gives his victim in case A (the loss of $1,000) and in Case B (the loss of $1,000) are
equally aversive, and the bad guy knows it.

Returning to Katz's examples, he held wrongful harm constant in cases 1–4, so
we might take those to be equally aversive instances of non-consent. By case 5, the
threatened harm to friendship was no longer a wrongful harm in Katz's mind, and
so consent was no longer at issue. Similarly, in my case C, the least aversive option
involves the loss of $500. Were the victim in C to give $1,000, then all else being

equal, the transaction appears consensual, at least to the tune of the extra $500 he hands over. At most, the total wrongfulness of case C varies with the threat to take $500 from the trunk rather than the threat to take $1,000 from the wallet. So each set of examples could be interpreted to show a binary shift with respect to consent.

If we imagine measuring all transactions to assess their wrongful harm to a party, consent may be a special case where we treat wrongful harm as zero. If you genuinely consent to sex, we assume you are not averse to the activity. The consent inquiry plausibly asks a binary question like: 'Did you expect to be overall harmed or benefited by the interaction?'

But even if consent marks the transition from a person expecting to be harmed by a transaction to expecting to be benefited, it's not stunningly abrupt. After all, we often want to know *how much* a person was harmed (or benefited) by some criminal behaviour. So even if consent is binary, the wrongfulness of criminal behaviour still varies along a spectrum that depends on the *extent* to which a victim is harmed.[24]

For example, stealing a particular amount of money causes very different harms to different victims (Kolber 2011, pp. 627–32). For ultra-rich people, the loss may be trivial; for very poor people, it may be devastating. In keeping with his all-or-nothing approach, however, Katz denies the relevance of victim-specific evaluations of harm. He offers this interesting example (Katz 1998, pp. 145–50): Suppose a robber spots a potential victim and says, 'Give me your jewelry, or I will pummel you.' The victim says, 'Please sir, this cheap costume jewelry is of little value to you. But it has tremendous sentimental value to me. I would much prefer that you pummel me than take the jewelry.' Accommodating his victim's preference, the robber beats his victim but leaves the jewellery untouched.

Under the law, a non-violent robber who merely steals some cheap jewellery will generally be punished less severely than one who beats his victim. Katz points out, however, that in the hypothetical just described, the robber who accommodates his victim's preference for the beating has done something less harmful, as measured by victim aversiveness, than the robber who takes the jewellery. The one who takes the jewellery knowingly causes more harm to his victim than the one who beats him. But given that we would not punish the jewellery robber more than the battering robber, Katz seems to conclude, beliefs about victim aversiveness to criminal conduct are irrelevant to culpability (Katz 1998, p. 151). And since aversiveness is irrelevant, the fact that aversion comes in degrees is also irrelevant.

---

[24] And we should understand the extent of victim harm in a matter that is smooth rather than bumpy. Suppose some jurisdiction permits consent to relatively minor inflictions of pain during sado-masochistic sex but invalidates consent to more severe inflictions. Assume that, in this jurisdiction, X tries to consent to sadomasochistic injuries from Y that go beyond the legally permitted intensity. Ought Y be punished for the full extent of injuries X endures or only those exceeding the legally permitted consensual maximum?

The smoother approach strikes me as preferable: punish for injuries to the extent they exceed consented-to injuries. If a person receives ten inflictions that fall within permitted severity but the eleventh is too much, the perpetrator could be punished only for the eleventh. Similarly, if a victim receives ten inflictions each of which is ten per cent too intense, only the excess intensity should be considered.

I have an alternative explanation. If the perpetrator really believes the victim prefers to be beaten, then the perpetrator *really does* commit a more wrongful act by stealing his jewellery than by beating him. The criminal justice system may reach a different result only because it is too impractical to take victims' idiosyncratic preferences into account on a regular basis. Instead, we rely on rough proxy measures of victim aversiveness. Because violent crimes typically cause more harm and because we seek to give advance notice of the punishments associated with criminal conduct, we generally punish violent robberies more severely than non-violent ones. While we should consider perceived harms to victims where possible (Kolber 2011, pp. 627–32), absent good individualized data, we arguably do the best we can with rough proxies.

In this particular scenario, even an individualized assessment of culpability does not necessarily reveal that the battering robber deserves the *lighter* punishment that would normally go to the robber who takes the jewellery. Just as plausibly, the robber who takes the jewellery deserves the *severe* punishment that ordinarily goes to the robber who would beat the victim. In part because it is so difficult to firmly anchor punishments, we rely on pre-established, general rules of sentencing. But the convenience of our sentencing system hardly shows that we ought to ignore offenders' beliefs about the severity of the harms they cause.

Moreover, to the extent criminal justice is about preventing dangerous behaviour, we have additional grounds for punishing the battering robber more severely than the one who takes the jewellery. The one who takes the jewellery has demonstrated his willingness to cause more harm to his victim than the one who beats his victim. That makes the jewellery robber quite dangerous. But the jewellery robber may still be less dangerous than the robber who beats his victim. Though the battering robber shows an unusual willingness to accommodate his victim's preference, he also demonstrates a propensity to take pleasure in causing physical harm to others. His propensity to cause physical harm may outweigh whatever slight mitigation he deserves because of his willingness to accommodate his victim's preference.

Thus, we can explain away the discrepancy between our best theories of punishment and our actual treatment of the jewellery robber Katz describes by recognizing practical difficulties in making the criminal justice system consider beliefs about victim-measured harm. There is simply no plausible retributivist theory of punishment that is indifferent to the amount of harm a criminal culpably causes. Indeed, without the principle that culpability (or dangerousness) increases as offenders knowingly risk greater harms, it would be difficult to explain the relative punishments we assign to different crimes. Surely aggravated assaults receive higher punishments than simple assaults because the former foreseeably tend to cause more pain and suffering. And judges at sentencing certainly do take culpably caused victim harm into account, albeit in a bumpy fashion (Kolber 2011, pp. 628–34). Hence, even if there is some sense in which consent under coercive pressure is all-or-nothing, there is a related consideration—the perceived harmfulness of an act to the victim—that does affect culpability and dangerousness and which surely falls along a continuum.

2.3 Challenge #3: Multivariable criteria lead to important discontinuities

According to Katz, we must tolerate sharp discontinuities in the law because they can arise in any system that depends on multiple variables. He proposes an example similar to the following (pp. 176–81):[25] Suppose that we are planning a lakeside party and must decide precisely where along a circular lake to have it. Some parts of the lake are more convenient to people's homes than others. Each attendee votes for a precise location, and a substantial number of votes clusters right around the northernmost part of the lake. We can think of it as twelve noon on a clock face. Another substantial group of votes clusters around five o'clock. Under some schemes of aggregating all of these votes, we might pick a location that splits the difference, say, between two and three o'clock.

Now suppose that some who voted for the five o'clock region shift their preferences to eight o'clock. When we reaggregate preferences, we may plausibly find that the result suddenly jumps. Rather than averaging around the east side of the circular lake in the two to three range, we average around the west side of the lake in the nine to ten o'clock range. So, a small change in an input (the votes of just a few people), Katz suggests, suddenly has a dramatic change in the location of the party. Moreover, Katz believes that the problem represented here arises in lots of legal contexts where multiple variables are at play.

The example seems to be one where, in my terminology, we have bumpy needs. The circular nature of the lake prevents us from simply finding the point in space that minimizes deviation from each person's preference. Because we are forced to locate the party in a limited range of places along a circle, there will sometimes be physical discontinuities: we cannot have a party in the middle of the lake. The nature of the geographical terrain means that the optimal location will sometimes jump dramatically from place to place, just as jurisdiction over a case may jump dramatically from state to federal court when the interests in doing so are narrowly favoured. It is simply impractical to have hybrid courts with fifty-one per cent federal jurisdiction and forty-nine per cent state jurisdiction.

As Katz describes the problem, there is a discontinuity in the spatial coordinates of the party as we adjust one of the inputs. But Katz is focusing on an irrelevant output. The underlying theory, here, seems to take votes as inputs and then, through a process of aggregation, tries to minimize the spatial distance between each person's preferred location and the actual location. On that score, the jump from one end of the lake to the other is precisely what is required to minimize the continuous variable we really care about: the amount of preference deviation.

Thus, just because a system has either/or features doesn't mean that there is a troubling discontinuity. What matters is the relationship between the particular inputs and outputs we care about. For example, a plaintiff in a defamation lawsuit

---

[25] Katz cites Graciela Chichilnisky's work on social choice for inspiring the example (Chichilnisky 1982, p. 337).

may stand to receive slightly more or less than one million dollars in damages. Let us suppose the plaintiff will start some new and unrelated business venture only if he receives an award over one million dollars. In such a case, there would be a bumpy relationship between his potential award for damages and his business plan. But since there is no legal or moral connection between his success in the lawsuit and his business plan, the bumpiness is irrelevant. It's not the sort of relationship for which a theory of tort law needs to find a smooth explanation.

Similarly, Katz identifies a possible radical shift in the location of a party along a circle when location preferences change slightly. But that's because he is considering a variable—the angular coordinate of the party location—that doesn't ultimately concern us. The variable we do care about—the minimum deviation from party-goer preferences—does vary continuously as votes slightly change.

Consider, too, Katz's more real-world example of why multivariable systems cannot accommodate smoother principles. He notes that a valid contract has to satisfy requirements of both consideration (an exchange of something of value by each contracting party) and definiteness (sufficient specificity) and that these traits can plausibly fall along continua (pp. 179–81). Yet these traits, he claims, do not compensate for each other: raising the quantity of definiteness towards infinity cannot make up for a complete deficiency in consideration and vice versa.

The failure of multiple legal inputs to compensate for each other doesn't show that there are no such things as stronger or weaker contracts, however. Suppose we are trying to determine whether some words on a page represent a contract in a context where contracts must be legibly written down. No matter how clearly the stream of words is written, using the most durable paper and legible ink, it won't compensate for the fact that the writing consists only of gibberish. True, the 'Is it written down?' variable is very well satisfied. But the fact that some things in the world are not contracts at all doesn't mean that there isn't an interesting range of more or less well-formed contracts.

Moreover, even if Katz's contract law analysis is plausible, it's somewhat idiosyncratic. The law governing contracts concerns the operation of law on other laws (as with evidence law, constitutional law, and others). These laws do not govern the kind of phenomena that we expect to operate in smooth ways. Assuming we want contracts to be either valid or invalid, then we have bumpy needs that will lead to discontinuities. So, for example, it's true that the amount of consideration in a contract can vary along a spectrum. But we may artificially restrict analysis of contract validity to the mere presence or absence of consideration to reduce controversy and adjudication costs.

Undesirable as it may be, we could imagine a contract law regime with less bumpy needs where a contract that is not fully formed receives partial enforcement. There may even be a multivariable formula that determines the contract-like nature of an agreement and tells us how rigorously an agreement should be enforced. But such an approach might well increase legal uncertainty for little gain. The fact that sharp discontinuities are sometimes useful, however, doesn't show that we cannot or should not reduce many other discontinuities by smoothing the law.

2.4 Challenge #4: Discontinuities caused by partial defenses

As the prior section suggests, not all discontinuities are troublesome. It depends on what our underlying theories demand. For example, whenever we add up expected costs and benefits where each can fall along a continuum, we will find combinations around the zero point in which small shifts in costs or benefits will change an activity from harmful to neutral to beneficial. The discontinuities arise not because we are examining all-or-nothing phenomena but rather because we are considering more than one pertinent continuum.

Consider the possibility of allowing partial defences in criminal law that reduce sentences without eliminating criminal liability entirely (Husak 1998). Katz thinks 'there is nothing particularly wrong with' partial defences but believes they mask a lurking discontinuity (p. 168). He focuses on cases of duress, where, for example, a person robs a bank because someone threatened to harm his family if he did not participate. In such cases, when the coercive threat is insufficient for a complete defence, we might nevertheless consider the coercive pressure as part of a partial defence.

I will describe three duress-related scenarios similar to those Katz discusses. In each, I give a number from 1–100 that reflects the culpability a person would have had were he not under duress. To determine a person's total culpability, let us assume, we take his culpability for the crime charged minus credit deserved for avoiding the harm a bad guy threatens.

As a preliminary matter, notice that we would not necessarily punish someone just because his total culpability is positive. If we punished every person with any quantum of culpability, we might all have to spend time in prison. Rather, at low levels of culpability, the costs of punishment exceed the benefits. So let us make the further assumption that a person must have more than 15 units of culpability to warrant punishment.

In case one, a person commits a serious crime (+50) under modestly serious pressure (−30) and warrants a partial defence reflecting the difference between his crime and the pressure placed on him to commit the crime. His total culpability is 20 units. Since 20 units exceeds the 15-unit minimum, he warrants some modest punishment.

In case two, we increase both the seriousness of the crime (+60) and the pressure to commit it (−40) to get a person who is entitled to a partial defence reflecting the same magnitude of punishment as in case one. This person commits a very grave crime under rather serious pressure, but his total culpability is still twenty. Since twenty units exceeds the 15-unit minimum, he warrants the same modest punishment as in case one.

Finally, in case three, a person commits the same crime as in case two (+60), but received just a bit more pressure (−45) than in case two. Since his total culpability is 15, it does not exceed the punishment threshold, and so he warrants no actual punishment. Now, Katz emphasizes, there was a modest change in coercive pressure from case two to case three, but all of a sudden, we switch from giving the offender a partial defence to a complete defence.

Contra Katz, however, the use of partial defences did not lead us back to a disturbing discontinuity. The discontinuity fits with plausible approaches to punishment that take punishment costs into account. If we only seek to punish those above a certain net culpability threshold, then there will be some offenders whose treatment appears bumpy because, though they are only a bit less culpable than others, they receive no punishment at all. The bumpiness does not arise, however, from some important all-or-nothing feature of the law. It arises from the combination of one continuous consideration (the benefit of punishment) with another continuous consideration (the cost of punishment).

If one is especially concerned about the horizontal inequity of giving the slightly less culpable no punishment at all, we could eliminate the inequity simply by punishing all offenders only to the extent that their conduct exceeds the threshold. So, those in the first two cases would receive five units of punishment while the person in the third case would still receive no punishment. The five units of punishment that would differentiate those in cases one and two from the person in case three, however, would precisely equal the amount that the first two were more culpable. Thus, if we wanted to, we could entirely eliminate the lurking discontinuity Katz identifies.[26]

2.5 Challenge #5: Discontinuities when splitting recovered property

Katz purports to find a rather different discontinuity in efforts to smooth ownership interests in recovered stolen property. Consider a thief who sells stolen property to a person who is unaware that the merchandise was stolen (pp. 227–8 n. 9). When police later recover the property, courts struggle to determine whether the property should go back to the original owner or to the person who purchased the property in good faith. In the 1960s, John Coons suggested that courts should sometimes split the difference between the two parties, so that the one who receives the property might be required to compensate the other for half its value (Coons 1963).

Katz recognizes that Coons' split-the-value solution hardly makes the law less either/or, for it merely adds an additional option: the property goes to one party, the property goes to the other party, or they split it. But, Katz notes, 'the loss from the stolen goods' could be 'distributed in proportion to the relative fault of the two parties' (p. 228 n. 9). For example, the person whose property was stolen might have exercised insufficient caution to protect the property from theft or may have waited too long to notify authorities of its disappearance. Similarly, the good faith purchaser should, perhaps, have asked the thief more probing questions. So, as with comparative negligence, we could weigh all these factors. Such a solution might, at first, appear to reduce the either/or nature of the law. Katz argues, however, that this solution does not 'do away with all disturbing discontinuities.... For if one of

---

[26] Perhaps Katz's point is that our intuitive sense of culpability reflects a steep, rather than a smooth, drop in culpability as we move from cases 1 and 2 to case 3. If so, I simply do not share his intuition.

the parties exhibits even a tiny amount of fault, whereas the other party exhibits none, then suddenly we would switch from dividing the loss equally among them to putting the entire loss on the party at fault' (p. 228 n. 9).

I have two responses. First, even if Katz is right that his comparative fault solution fails to eliminate *all* discontinuities, it would appear to reduce discontinuity. Even if the law cannot be smoothed entirely, it would be odd to give up trying simply because some discontinuities are inevitable. Second, and more importantly, other approaches to dividing the loss can eliminate the discontinuity Katz identifies. Suppose that in cases like this, when parties have no fault at all, each is entitled to half the property. When one party is more at fault then another, its share is reduced by an amount that reflects its greater degree of fault, and the party less at fault receives a correspondingly larger share. If one party is faultless and another is a little bit at fault (the case Katz worries about), the party at fault might have its recovery reduced by an amount reflecting its modest deviation from reasonable conduct, and the faultless party's recovery could be increased accordingly. Maybe the faultless party would receive seventy-five per cent of the property's value while the other would receive twenty-five per cent. Just because one hypothetical approach to smoothing the law creates a disturbing discontinuity doesn't mean that others will have the same problem.

3. Conclusion

Morality is usually smooth, but the law is usually bumpy. Many aspects of our conduct are best understood along spectra that have smooth effects on our moral intuitions about praise and blame. The law, by contrast, tends to carve up our conduct into discrete categories. Conduct occurring somewhere along a spectrum either satisfies a vague statutory element or it doesn't. Such bumpiness often leads us to treat similar cases dissimilarly, causing unfairness and reductions in well-being in the process.

Not all phenomena of interest to the law are smooth. And even smooth phenomena sometimes require bumpy legal treatment due to the costs of adjudicating smooth laws or of granting legal actors too much discretion. But contra Katz, we can often make the law smoother, and we should when bumpy laws come at too high of a moral cost.

References

Alexander, Larry. 2008. 'Scalar Properties, Binary Judgements'. *Journal of Applied Philosophy* 25(2): 85–104.

Alexander, Larry and Kimberly K. Ferzan. 2008. 'Culpable Acts of Risk Creation'. *Ohio State Journal of Criminal Law* 5(2): 375–405.

Bibas, Stephanos. 2004. 'Plea Bargaining Outside the Shadow of Trial'. *Harvard Law Review* 117(8): 2463–547.

Cavallaro, Rosanna. 1996. 'A Big Mistake: Eroding the Defense of Mistake of Fact About Consent in Rape'. *Journal of Criminal Law and Criminology* 86(3): 818–60.

Chichilnisky, Graciela. 1982. 'Social Aggregation Rules and Continuity'. *Quarterly Journal of Economics* 97(2): 337–52.

Coons, John E. 1963. 'Approaches to Court Imposed Compromise—The Uses of Doubt and Reason'. *Northwestern University Law Review* 58(6): 750–94.

Eckholm, Erik. 2011. 'Push for "Personhood" Amendment Represents New Tack in Abortion'. *New York Times*, 25 October.

Fennel, Lee Anne. 2012. 'Lumpy Property'. *University of Pennsylvania Law Review* 160(7): 1955–93.

Hadfield, Gillian K. 1994. 'Weighing the Value of Vagueness: An Economic Perspective on Precision in the Law'. *California Law Review* 82(3): 541–54.

Harris, John. 1999. 'The Value of Life'. In *Bioethics: An Anthology*, edited by Helga Kuhse and Peter Singer, 365–72. Oxford: Blackwell.

Huang, Peter H. 2013. 'Review of Leo Katz, Why the Law is so Perverse'. *Journal of Legal Education* 63(1): 131–60.

Husak, Douglas N. 1998. 'Partial Defenses'. *Canadian Journal of Law and Jurisprudence* 11(1): 167–92.

Katz, Leo. 1998. *Ill-Gotten Gains: Evasion, Blackmail, Fraud, and Kindred Puzzles of the Law*. Chicago (IL): University of Chicago Press.

Katz, Leo. 2011. *Why the Law is So Perverse*. Chicago (IL): The University of Chicago Press.

Kolber, Adam J. 2011. 'The Experiential Future of the Law'. *Emory Law Journal* 60(3): 585–652.

Kolber, Adam J. 2014. 'Smooth and Bumpy Laws'. *California Law Review* 102(3): 655–90.

Kolber, Adam J. 2016. 'The Bumpiness of Criminal Law'. *Alabama Law Review* 67(3): 855–886.

Parchomovsky, Gideon, Peter Siegelman, and Steve Thel. 2007. 'Of Equal Wrongs and Half Rights'. *New York University Law Review* 82(3): 738–89.

Swift, Jonathan. 1726/1996. *Gulliver's Travels*. Dover (UK): Dover Publications.

Waldron, Jeremy. 1994. 'Vagueness in Law and Language: Some Philosophical Issues'. *California Law Review* 82(3): 509–40.

14

How Vagueness Makes Judges Lie

Roy Sorensen

Rome imported most of her gods from Greece. For instance the goddess of justice, Justitia, is the Greek goddess Themis. (Yes, that is the goddess ensconced in law school lobbies—blindfolded, balancing a scale, brandishing a sword.) Janus, the god of beginnings and transitions, was indigenous to Rome. My thesis is that those pledged to Justitia must pay homage to the two-faced Janus.

1. Two Senses of 'Vague'

'Vague' is ambiguous. Logicians focus on the sense that concerns the possession of borderline cases. When Janus stands at a threshold of a temple, is he in the temple or out? Our inability to answer cannot be remedied by linguistics, experiment, observation, or prayer. If an oracle answers that Janus is in the temple, then we will not be able to make sense of what we 'learned'. At best the oracle could only quiet our curiosity by mystification.

When borderline cases fall along a scale, they may launch a Sorites paradox. 'Excessive detention' is vague because there are preventative detentions for which there is no telling whether they are excessive. These borderline cases prevent detectable counterexamples to the induction step:

1. Base step: a detention of 52,596,000 minutes (about a century) is excessive.
2. Induction step: if a detention of n minutes is excessive, then so is a detention of n - 1 minutes.
3. Therefore, a detention of one minute is excessive.

The second sense of 'vague' concerns underspecificity. In this sense, vagueness varies inversely with certainty. The more vaguely you characterize the permissible limit, the more likely you are to avoid counterexample. Yet these sketchier detention limits become less informative for those wishing to specify a permissible detention.

Police find underspecificity tactically useful. A criminal might leak guilty knowledge of the murder weapon. A dubious confession can be exposed by the confessor's ignorance of details that would be known by the perpetrator.

How Vagueness Makes Judges Lie. First Edition. Roy Sorensen. © Roy Sorensen 2016. Published 2016 by Oxford University Press.

This sense of 'vague' cannot drive a sorites paradox, so logicians have no interest in it—aside from preventing equivocations (Sorensen 1989 and 2001, s. IV). Yet this is the sense that receives the most explicit commentary from legal theorists. Underspecific statutes are struck down for being 'void for vagueness'. This formal requirement substantially limits what can be outlawed. Obscenity laws must specify the words that ought not to be publicly mentioned. Yet this public statement violates the law and so printers may be obliged not to disseminate the obscene law.

When two rules conflict, the *lex specialis* principle gives precedence to the more specific rule (in the same spirit as *lex posterior* gives precedence to the later rule and *lex superior* favours the higher ranking rule). The common law doctrine of *stare decisis* steadily adds content through precedents. As legal systems mature, they become more precise—in the sense of specificity.

My thesis is that *both* senses of 'vague' systematically precipitate moral dilemmas for judges. Each sense creates predicaments in which the judge has an obligation to lie and an obligation to refrain from that lie. Often, neither obligation overrides the other. Consequently, the judge inevitably violates an obligation.

I develop this moral dilemma with the help of 'The Umpire's Dilemma'. This puzzle, posed by Colin Radford (1985), arises when an adjudicator knows an infraction has occurred but does not know the particular infraction. One solution to the dilemma is to abandon the requirement of adjudicative specificity. The hitch is that a specific judgment is needed to satisfy the following causal requirement: a verdict is just only if it is an appropriate effect of the infraction it alleges (Sorensen 2006). 'Appropriate' is spelled out along the lines familiar from the causal theory of perception, especially Fred Dretske's account of 'non-epistemic seeing' (Dretske 1969).

2. The Borderline Path to Lying

In *Vagueness Has No Function in Law* I argued that borderline cases pressure judges into disingenuous verdicts. In this section, I revisit this path to insincerity. I reverse the trek to find a fork leading to another path by which vagueness leads to judicial prevarication. That fork is marked by performatives.

Charles Peirce influentially characterized borderline cases in terms of inquiry resistance; no amount of conceptual or empirical investigation can resolve the question (Peirce 1902, p. 748). Most borderline cases are merely relative to a contextually specified method of inquiry. Peirce defined vagueness in terms of absolute unknowability. We do not know what would count as discovering the threshold.

The silver lining in this dark cloud of ignorance is conflict resolution. A debate is rendered moot by persuading the parties that they are debating a borderline case. This insight reduces partisans to agnostics. An abstemious consensus is achieved. The problem is dissolved rather than solved.

One legacy of Peirce is that most commentators accept the verdict exclusion principle: applying a predicate to one of its (absolute) borderline cases yields an unknowable proposition. If Jaffa cakes are borderline biscuits, then no one can know whether Jaffa cakes are biscuits. If commanded to prove or disprove 'Jaffa cakes are biscuits', you would object that the task is impossible. At best, you could only go through the motions.

Impossible tasks systematically appear on the 'To do' list of the judiciary. British tax authorities claimed that Jaffa cakes are subject to the value added tax on biscuits. The vendors countered that Jaffa cakes are cakes rather than biscuits. The tribunal had to answer the question—and not by a flip of a coin. A verdict must be based on evidence.

This evidential requirement removes the option of characterizing the issue as an absolute borderline case. Judges are forced to characterize 'Are Jaffa cakes biscuits?' as a problem to be solved (not a pseudo-problem to be dissolved on grounds of indeterminacy). Accordingly, all of Ronald Dworkin's (1977) 'hard cases' are *relative* borderline cases. There is always an answer (in a mature legal system such as found in the United Kingdom and the United States). So Dworkin concludes that Hart (1961) was mistaken in thinking there is a role for judicial discretion.

Hart is right *de facto*. In the absence of a feasible answer, judges pursue ends that are feasible. They will help the more sympathetic litigant or try their hand at social policy. When compelled to answer a question that the judge deems as bereft of a true answer, he concentrates on the effect of the answer. What else is there to think about?

Dworkin, however, is right *de jure*. The judge will wrap his social work in the black robe of principle and precedent. Just as Dworkin requires, the tribunal gave a principled verdict. In a nuanced nine-point decision, they sided with the vendors.[1]

Thomas Nagel measures absurdity by the distance between aspiration and reality (as when your pants fall down while being knighted) (Nagel 1971). Judges take themselves seriously—and insist on respect from others (punishing contempt of court with fines and detention). One can reduce Nagelian absurdity by either lowering the aspiration or raising reality to aspiration. Perhaps some members of the tribunal became more optimistic about the feasibility of discovering whether Jaffa cakes are biscuits. My focus is on judges who resolved the absurdity by privately distinguishing between what they assert and what they believe. The public was amused by the spectacle. But what were the judges to do? Although the indeterminacy is manifest, the tribunal was forced to treat the question as answer*able*—and to answer!

Lawyers claim that their role as advocates licenses them to argue insincerely (Solan 2011). Judges lack this shield. Their reasoning must be credible in their own eyes. Silly lies are an occupational hazard of judges. Serious lies are also part of the job. The judge must sometimes assert, hand over his heart, that a borderline murder is murder.

Jeremy Bentham *blamed* judges for lying. He believed that legal fictions are convenient lies. They could be replaced by literal truths. But the judges and legislators

---

[1] United Biscuits (UK) Ltd [1991], VAT decision 6344. Available at <http://www.hmrc.gov.uk/manuals/vfoodmanual/vfood6260.htm>.

are too lazy and corrupt. In his *Rationale of Judicial Evidence* (1827), Bentham proposes that judges be banned from testifying on grounds of habitual mendacity.

The judicial lies induced by vagueness do not arise from a vice. They are side effects of conscientious adjudication. If I were a judge, I would fall into the same moral dilemma.

I concentrate on verdicts, but legal proceedings require many procedural calls that involve borderline cases. The judge must make these judgments quickly so as to not throw off the rhythm of the proceedings. A judge who recognizes the borderline status of the issue need not answer arbitrarily. Umpires tend to resolve borderline cases in favour of the weaker team to keep the contest interesting (especially if there is a threat of a 'blow-out'). Or the umpire may favour the side that has suffered a string of unfavourable calls (to appear balanced).

Judges want *stable* verdicts. Since appeals come from the losing side, a judge can avoid being reversed by favouring losers on procedural matters. Favouring losers keeps them losers. (As Oscar Wilde observed, one should play fairly—when you have the winning cards. Indeed, the holder of the winning cards should also tolerate some minor cheating.) Of course, the judge cannot admit to this strategic manipulation of borderline cases. Each call will be presented as definite—even if difficult.

3. The Performadox Response

One may hope to rescue the judges by emphasizing J.L. Austin's insight that verdicts are *performatives*. If the judge says 'My verdict is that Jaffa cakes are not biscuits', he is merely *reporting* his verdict. Since this self-referential report is true, the judge is not lying.

Austin would be chagrined by this application of his theory of a performative. He introduced the concept as a challenge to the hegemony of description. Prior to ordinary language philosophy, the central function of language was thought to be reporting facts. This conforms to the stereotypical contrast between words and deeds. In *How to Do Things with Words*, Austin challenged the dichotomy with a *detailed* account of how we perform actions through speech. Characterizing performatives as self-verifying reports of one's own speech act would be a relapse into the old hegemony of description.

Initially, Austin denied that performatives have truth-values. This suggests a different performative rescue. If lies must be false (or at least have a truth-value), then no verdict could be a lie. At worst, verdicts could be infelicitous. However, Austin soon admitted that *assertion* passes all the tests of being a performative, such as the hereby test: 'I hereby state that I have never been a Communist' (often addressed, under subpoena, to the House Un-American Activities Committee in Austin's era). Professor Austin also acknowledged that the action element of performatives is compatible with sensitivity to evidence. Indeed, Austin's taxonomy of performatives is partly based on the degree to which they depend on evidence. Commissives (promising, proposing, contracting) are commitments that need not be based on evidence. Exercitives (voting, appointing, proclaiming) are exercisings of power and are also relatively unencumbered. But verdictives (acquitting, diagnosing, grading) consist of findings based on evidence: 'Verdictives have obvious connexions with truth and falsity, soundness and unsoundness, and fairness and unfairness. That the content of a verdict is true or false is shown, for example, in a dispute over an umpire's calling "Out", "Three strikes", or "Four balls" ' (Austin 1962, p. 153).

As noted by Jonathan Cohen (1964), there is an interesting problem about the truth conditions of sentences such as 'I state that I have never been a Communist.' Does the statement entail the complement clause that I have never been a Communist? Or is the statement made true by the very act of stating it? Austin must have been tempted to answer that 'I state that' merely flags the nature of the performative in the way grammar flags the nature of the speech act without becoming part of the content. (The interrogative mood signals the speech act of asking without describing the speaker as asking.) After all, a former Communist could not avoid a perjury charge by claiming that he only testified to *stating* that he had never been a Communist. Yet we do not really bracket the performatory preface. If the speaker adds, 'so help me God', he had better not be an atheist!

Kent Bach and Robert Harnish analyse performatives as involving two speech acts (Bach and Harnish 1992). The first is the trivial assertion that one is performing the speech act. The second is the substantive deed corresponding to the complement clause. Thus the defendant is both describing himself as stating and is stating that he has never been a communist. On William Lycan's paratactic account, the complement is a specimen: 'I have never been a Communist. That is what I assert' (Lycan 1984, ch. 6). Although the specimen is not the primary assertion, the speaker is semantically committed to it. A similar point extends to 'My verdict is that Jaffa cakes are not biscuits.' The judge is committed to Jaffa cakes not being biscuits, not just to his finding that Jaffa cakes are not biscuits. Since the performative is a verdictive, the judge is also committed to there being sufficient evidence for Jaffa cakes not being biscuits.

4. The Relocation Effect

Some resist the verdict exclusion principle by introducing tie-breaking rules such as 'Borderline cases are to be precisified in favor of the defense.' One might also suggest adoption of the Scottish 'Not proven' as a third verdict. Recognition of why these reforms are futile is illustrated by a proposal made by a member of the Baltimore Orioles baseball team: 'They should move first base back a step to eliminate all the close plays.'[2]

Relocation will also occur when more precise terms are used because there will be residual vagueness. For instance, instead of using 'adult' one might try 'eighteen-year-old'. But there will still be borderline cases that exploit the vagaries of

---

[2] John Lowenstein as reported by the *Detroit Free Press* (27 April 1984, at F1).

measurement. One day before his eighteenth birthday Paul Johnson committed a robbery. The prosecution charged him as an adult: 'A person is in existence on the day of his birth. On the first anniversary he or she has lived one year and one day.' (When this reached the California Court of Appeal, Justice William Channell overruled the prior decisions and had Johnson tried as a juvenile.)

Relocation also affects proposals to reinterpret verdicts as carrying qualifications such as '*According to the admissible evidence*, the defendant is guilty.' Throwing out evidence allows us to side step some borderline cases but forces us to step into other borderline cases.

5. The Underspecific Path to Lying

In law, disjunctive indictments are forbidden. Knowing that the defendant is guilty of either A or B is not sufficient to justify a guilty verdict. If neither alternative can be proved individually, then the defendant prevails. This standard of proof, reminiscent of intuitionism in mathematics, violates an attractive moral principle: 'Known criminals ought to be punished for their crimes.'

An influential fraction of twentieth-century Americans will sign on to the principle only when they read it narrowly as *legally acquired* knowledge. In 1914 the United States Supreme Court gave teeth to the Fourth Amendment when it handed down its decision in *Weeks v. United States*.[3] Weeks involved the appeal of a defendant who had been convicted based on evidence that had been seized by a federal agent without a warrant or other constitutional justification. The Supreme Court reversed the defendant's conviction, thereby creating what is known as the 'exclusionary rule'. In *Mapp v. Ohio*,[4] the Supreme Court made the exclusionary rule applicable to the states.

The exclusionary rule has survived intense criticism and weakening by exceptions and loopholes. The rule is widely subverted by 'testilying'. Police routinely lie to keep evidence admissible, often claiming, with mechanical phraseology, that the defendant made the incriminating evidence visible by dropping it. Prosecutors and judges are aware of 'dropsy' perjury. However, they wish to keep a smooth working relationship with the police. Commentators on the exclusionary rule worry that prosecutors and judges have become complicit in the perjury. High standards of specificity in the indictment lead prosecutors to make assertions that are more specific than their evidence warrants. The high standard also quashes sincerity-preserving hedges by witnesses, police, experts, and the judge who oversees the proceedings.

There is a *little* slack. The law is stricter with verbs than adverbs. Jurors do not need to specify whether the defendant murdered his victim loudly rather than quietly, politely rather than rudely, cheaply rather than expensively. The what-question takes precedence over the how-question. The modality of the

---

[3] 232 U.S. 383 (1914).   [4] 367 U.S. 643 (1961).

crime is irrelevant. U.S. Supreme Court Justice Antonin Scalia illustrates with a hypothetical case: a woman's body is found in the remains of a burned down house. The jurors disagree over whether the defendant first murdered the woman and then burned down the house to conceal the crime or knocked her unconscious and then set fire to the house to kill her. Disagreement on the modality of murder does not prevent the jury from finding the man guilty. Yet Scalia goes on to emphasize that the jury cannot convict a defendant of a general felony: 'We would not permit...an indictment charging that the defendant assaulted either X on Tuesday or Y on Wednesday, despite the "moral equivalence" of those two acts.'[5]

A bill of indictment can list a range of charges that the jury can choose to pursue (typically along a scale such as murder, manslaughter, assault). The restriction is that a specific charge must be proven. Proof of the disjunction of charges is not enough.

Law is complicated. Philosophers therefore gravitate toward the simplicity of games. Indeed, they simplify further with *thought experiments* about the game. This was Colin Radford's strategy in *The Umpire's Dilemma* (Radford 1985). Surprisingly, his hypothetical episode of armchair cricket became actual during the first innings of the final Ashes Test of 2009. Ricky Ponting faced a ball that was somehow deflected into the wicket keeper's hands. The bowler's side contended Ponting was therefore out. The umpire, Asad Rauf, began protracted deliberation. To avoid 'dead air' the game commentator, Jonathan Agnew thought aloud: 'Either the ball hit Ponting's bat or it hit his pads. If it hit his bat, he is out caught behind. If it hit his pads, he is out lbw [leg before the wicket]. So, either way, he is out.' The hitch was that umpires must give the benefit of the doubt to the batsman. This means the umpire must be in a position to specify the basis for the out (a basis which fans record on their score cards). When asked 'How is the batsman out?' the umpire must single out the type of out from an exhaustive list of options: bowled, timed out, caught, handled the ball, hit the ball twice, hit wicket, lbw, obstructing the field, run out, and stumped. Since Rauf did not know the specific basis for the out, he eventually ruled that Ponting was not out.

Colin Radford's original thesis is that this dilemma reveals something deficient in intuitionism—the logic L.E.J. Brouwer unravelled from Immanuel Kant and then applied to proof practices in mathematics. Brouwer associates truth with provability and provability with constructability. Radford's objection is that intuitionism is insensitive to the dilemma. If intuitionism were correct, then it would not be true that Ponting was out. Ponting would be definitely not out because there was no way to prove he was out. Umpire Rauf's verdict would have been clearly correct; he would only be guilty of answering too slowly.

Defenders of intuitionism have countered that their founder, L.E.J. Brouwer, only requires truths to be prov*able*. In principle, one could ascertain what deflected the ball. Indeed, Ponting probably knew. Radford's critique can be rescued with an alternative scenario in which the ball was a borderline case of 'deflected by a pad and caught out'. All the classical logician needs is a case that is borderline between deflection by the kneepad and deflection by the bat.

6. Rumfitt's Defence of the Umpire

Even without the repair, Radford has posed an interesting professional dilemma for adjudicators. Here is Simon Beck's formulation of the umpire's dilemma:

… he must rule either Out or Not (to do nothing is in effect to rule Not out). If he rules Not out on the grounds that he is not certain which law was broken, then he does something unfair to the fielding side since 'surely the batsman *was* out one way or the other.' There is no way of being out 'lbw or caught'—the laws are exclusive and exhaustive. Either 'lbw' or 'cause' must be entered into the scorebook. Since the umpire does not know which it is, if he rules Out then he will have to tell a lie and break the laws himself—the very laws it is his duty to see uphold.

(Beck 2008, p. 321)

To clear Rauf of the accusation of lying, Ian Rumfitt distinguishes between being out and being correctly dismissed. To be out 'is such that a condition specified by the Laws of Cricket as sufficient for giving a batsman out obtains'. So although Rauf knew that Ponting was out, this did not put him in a position to dismiss him as out. In particular, Law 27 of the Marylebone Cricket Club 2008 says that 'to be dismissed, the batsman must be out under some Law', where this is understood as requirement to specify the law. Thus Rumfitt approves of Rauf's decision to call Ponting not out even though Rauf knew that Ponting was out.

Rumfitt goes on to endorse the parallel behaviour of judges who acquit criminals even when certain that they are guilty. In a footnote, he acknowledges some distinguished disagreement on the matter:

Joseph Raz (personal communication) believes that Rauf should have plumped for one of the grounds and given Ponting out on that ground. He points out that, in criminal appeals, the appellant loses even if the decision is shown to be faulty, so long as the fault did not cause any injustice. Justice is rarely pristine, and a no-nonsense judge might well cut through the problem in the way Raz suggests. But those of a more delicate sensibility may still admire Rauf's scrupulousness in resisting the temptation to do the right thing for the wrong reason.

(Rumfitt 2010, p. 209 fn)

I take Raz to be strengthening the case for the option that Beck described as lying. If the lie is not unjust and prevents an unjust outcome (acquitting a criminal who is known to be guilty), then the lie is justified. Almost no philosopher will condemn the Razian lie by applying the premise that *all* lying is wrong (Immanuel Kant being a notorious exception to the rule). If any sternness is in order, Raz's logic points in the direction of the lie being obligatory rather than supererogatory. Given that judicial lying is justified (as opposed to be merely excusable) it can be done repeatedly and the judge can urge his colleagues to do the same.

Rumfitt esteems the scrupulousness of a judge who refrains from doing 'the right thing for the wrong reason'. But this admiration is hostage to the type of wrongdoer. Releasing a known serial killer does not stimulate admiration for judicial scrupulousness. 'Acquitting the guilty and condemning the innocent—the Lord detests them both' (*Proverbs* 17:15). The Lord's loathing must intensify when the judge acquits those he *knows* to be guilty.

But we need not bring in consequences to feel the force of Raz's solution. The utilitarian has no monopoly on the slogan 'The end justifies the means.' Retributivists hunger for justice in the product sense more keenly than the process sense. Career burglars are sometimes punished for burglaries they did not commit. When the mistake is discovered, the public is consoled by the fact that the burglar was guilty of other crimes of exactly the same sort. The burglar is getting what he deserved but through a deviant path. It is rough justice.

7. Forced Assertion and Inevitable Lying

Both Simon Beck and Ian Rumfitt have insights that strengthen our grasp of the umpire's dilemma. My reservation about Beck's formulation is that one horn of the dilemma is not sharp enough. I agree that the umpire lies if he insincerely specifies an infraction. The umpire also lies if he says that the batsman is not out when he knows that he is out. The dilemma is an effect of a forced assertion. It is as if the umpire is answering a multiple-choice test in which all of the answers are known to be false.

The dilemma is not avoided by the presence of an answer that will be accepted by authorities. When Christopher Hitchens was taking his citizenship test on the U.S. Constitution (Hitchens 2010, p. 252), he was asked, 'What did the Emancipation Proclamation do?' He knew that 'It freed the slaves' would be marked correct (even though the true answer is that the Thirteenth Amendment freed the slaves). So he construed his task as providing accepted answers rather than true answers. Thus the anti-religious Hitchens edged towards the Catholic doctrine of mental reservation to avoid characterizing his insincere answer as a lie.

Ian Rumfitt is located along the same edge when he distinguishes between asserting Ponting is out and correctly dismissing Ponting as out. The umpire could not declare 'Ponting is out but I hereby rule that he is not out.' He has mis-graded if he gives credit for a true answer that is not in the answer key. Rauf cannot avoid lying. So I disagree with Rumfitt's assumption that there is an option that does not involve a dirty hand. Rauf's 'not out' verdict was a lie. The verdict was false and Rauf knew it. As Rumfitt concedes, 'not out' is not a self-referential remark about the umpire's mental state. It is an objective assessment that must be based on empirical conditions and the rules of the game.

8. Knowledge by Fiction?

Rumfitt concedes that English law sometimes permits the disjunctive reasoning execrated by the Laws of Cricket. He cites *Giannetto*.[6] Here a defendant was convicted despite uncertainty as to whether he personally murdered his wife or hired another party to do it. The defendant appealed on the grounds that the jury should have been instructed that they must all agree he was the killer or all agree that another person killed his wife. The Court of Appeals dismissed the appeal by relying on the Accessories and Abettors Act of 1861. It endorses the legal fiction that anyone who encourages a murder is a murderer. More precisely, anyone who shall 'aid, abet, counsel or procure the commission of any indictable offence...shall be liable to be tried, indicted and punished as a principal offender'.

The upshot is that while the grounds for attributing the murder were disjunctive, the charge was not. So what the law forbids are disjunctive *indictments*. Disjunctive reasoning can get smuggled in by introducing legal fictions that unify disparate crimes. The Court of Appeals did not object to the trial judge's observation that just nodding in response to someone's announcement that he was going off to commit murder makes one liable to a mandatory life sentence—even if the nod makes no causal difference.

9. Rumfitt's Disjunctivist Proposal

Rumfitt laments this contrived indifference to whether one is a principal or an accessory. He recommends a legal reform that would explicitly permit disjunctive indictments:

For in a case where there was insufficient evidence to convict A of the principal offense, and insufficient evidence to convict him of being an accessory, the prosecution could still put to the jury the question 'Is the following disjunction true: A is either the principal offender or an accessory?'...Disjunctive indictments would need to be used with caution: it would be oppressive if prosecutors could lay a charge that disjoined all the offences in the criminal code. (Although perhaps article 6(3)(a) of the European Convention on Human Rights, which requires that a defendant be informed 'in detail of the nature and cause of the allegation against him' already precludes that.) Moreover, judges would need special rules for sentencing those convicted of such disjunctive charges: a plausible rule is that the sentence handed down should not exceed the lower of the maxima that Parliament will have specified for each disjunct.

(Rumfitt 2010, pp. 208–9)

Rumfitt's proposal is most plausible for disjunctive indictments that are not too disjunctive. Best are cases in which a single individual is involved with two qualitatively identical possible crimes. For instance, if someone has testified in two trials in such a way as to make it plain that he committed perjury at least once, then Rumfitt's reform will easily let us convict—despite ignorance of which trial involved perjury.

[6] 1 Cr. App. Rep. 1 (1997).

Further down the slippery slope are wildly disjunctive crimes. If we have decisive evidence that one twin embezzled while the other committed a murder, but cannot tell which twin committed which crime, then we may indict them of murderezzlement.

10. Criminal Natural Kinds

Quine defended our aversion to 'grue' on the grounds that it is not close to being a natural kind. 'Green' is close enough to support inductive reasoning. Better yet is the terminology based on the electromagnetic spectrum. If crimes formed natural kinds, perhaps on analogy with diseases, then one might have a basis for insisting that indictments be non-disjunctive. Natural kinds let us, with the same breath, predict and convict. The inventor of the 'new riddle of induction', Nelson Goodman, was a conventionalist who instead appealed to the greater entrenchment of 'green' over 'grue'. Goodman regarded belief in natural kinds as a projection of familiarity on to nature.

Intuitions about naturalness are affected by familiarity. At first glance, a crime such as theft appears to 'cut nature at the joint'. But legal scholars object that the appearance of unity disintegrates under closer inspection. For instance, Leo Katz challenges the reader to define 'theft' (Katz 1987). Is it any crime against property? No, that is too broad because it would include arson. Is theft any involuntary transfer of property? No, that would overextend the term to foreclosure. We also need to rule out robbery, blackmail, and the passing of bad cheques. Katz asserts that no one has succeeded in defining 'theft'.

Katz grants that common law has successfully defined more specific crimes: Larceny is 'the trespassory taking and carrying away of personal property of another with intent to steal it'. Embezzlement is 'the fraudulent conversion of the property of another by one who is already in lawful possession of it'. False pretenses is 'a false representation of a material present or past fact which causes the victim to pass title to his property to the wrongdoer who knows his presentation to be false and intends thereby to defraud the victim' (Katz 1987, pp. 90–2). So Katz does not share Ludwig Wittgenstein's pessimism about definition. Katz emphasizes the contrast between some well-defined crimes and crimes that lack an essential definition.

So where did 'theft' come from? Katz traces it to *Commonwealth v. O'Malley*.[7] A Boston family paid Bridget McDonald her wage of thirty-eight dollars. Since she was an illiterate servant, Martin O'Malley asked her to let him take the money to be counted. When she acquiesced, he refused to return the bills. She locked a door to prevent his escape. But he threatened to burn the money. Bridget opened the door and off O'Malley went. When Martin O'Malley was prosecuted for larceny, the trial court said he should have charged with embezzlement. After all, he had not taken the money from Bridget. He merely kept

---

[7] 97 Mass. 584 (1867).

it against her will. O'Malley was acquitted. A jury then convicted O'Malley of embezzlement. He appealed on the ground that he actually had committed larceny. Since there is no further record of O'Malley he apparently went free. As a remedy for this injustice, some legislatures combined larceny, embezzlement, and false pretences into a single disjunctive offence called 'theft'. Katz objects:

Under the common law, fairness requires that a defendant be told whether he or she is charged with larceny, or embezzlement, or false pretenses in order to prepare the appropriate defense and that he or she be convicted only if a jury can agree upon which of the three was committed. Doesn't fairness require that a defendant be told with which kind of theft he or she is charged?

(Katz 1987, p. 92)

The defender of disjunctive charges can reply that the charge is clear enough: the defendant committed at least one of the deeds on the specified list. Once the disjunctive legislation is in place, the problem is not fair warning. The problem is that the defence's burden has been greatly increased.

Katz's appeal to the principle of fair notice can be seen as linkage with the 'void-for-vagueness' doctrine. We object to vague laws because they fail to give due notice of what is prohibited, they are capriciously enforced, and they usurp the role of legislators. However, these reservations could be circumvented by a long list of precise disjuncts. The precedent could be the physician's *Diagnostic and Statistical Manual*. It achieves greater precision and consensus in diagnosis by operationalism; the disease is ascribed exactly if it satisfies a quota of verifiable symptoms. The defendant's concern with long but specific disjunctive indictments would not be with the unclarity. It would be with the broadening of guilt. The law errs on the side of acquitting the guilty. But once guilt is established, the defendant can only rely on the weaker bias against over-punishing the guilty.

Vagueness does affect sentencing. Hegel concedes that

Reason cannot determine...whether justice requires...(1) a...punishment of forty lashes or thirty-nine, or (2) a fine of 5 dollars or four dollars ninety three, or (3) imprisonment of a year or of three hundred sixty four days. And yet injustice is done if there is one lash [or dollar or day] too many...Here the interest...is that something be actually done, that the matter be settled, and decided somehow, no matter how (within a certain limit).

(Hegel 1821/1967, s. 214 and Zusatz to 214)

Over-punishing the guilty is not as bad as punishing the innocent. So broad indictments, by making guilt much more probable, reduce the bias favouring defendants.

Katz's emphasis on real definition suggests a more metaphysical objection to disjunctive indictments. There is no natural kind corresponding to theft. Disjunctive indictments resemble 'gerrymanders'. In 1812 a cartoonist criticized the state senate redistricting instigated by Massachusetts Governor Gerry by blending his name with 'salamander' (Figure 14.1):

Figure 14.1 'The Gerrymander' *Boston Gazette*, 26 March 1812
<https://www.loc.gov/exhibits/treasures/trr113.html>.

Notice that the gerrymandered districts score well on the criterion of precision. The district lines are not blurred. There are plenty of clear boundaries. The concern lies in how the lines are drawn. Instead of following natural contours, the governor has contrived categories to maximize his political representation.

Only gerrymandering will capture *all* the crimes that concern Rumfitt. If we decide to pursue only some of the disjunctive crimes, then which ones? If there is no principled basis then our solution will share much of the arbitrariness that it sought to remedy.

11. Criticism of Minimax Sentencing

Rumfitt's utilitarian concern about the oppressiveness of disjunctive indictments is in tension with his Rawlsian minimax rule for sentencing (minimize the maximum penalty). Very general crimes do not require minimizing the maximum for the least bad species of the crime. For instance, 'rape' is highly general because of the great variety of ways in which there can be sex without consent. Since disjunctiveness is just another form of generality, why apply a minimax rule for some species of generality rather than others?

There is no minimax rule for the other sense of 'vague'. Judges do not search for the most lenient precisification. Whereas ambiguity in contracts is interpreted against the drafter, vagueness in legislation is interpreted by the intent of the legislators. Since the legislators aim to penalize known criminals, judges do not gravitate to the lightest sentence.

Indeed, many judges openly exert ingenuity to impose heavier sentences. Consider a case concerning the extra penalty drug dealers suffer for selling within 1,000 feet of a school. In March 2002, James Robbins was arrested on the corner of Eighth Avenue and 40th Street in Manhattan for selling drugs to an undercover police officer. The nearest school, Holy Cross, is located on 43rd Street between Eighth and Ninth Avenues. The distance is more than 1,000 feet by foot because buildings block the direct path. However, the law enforcement officers said the correct measure was 'as the crow flies'. Accordingly, they calculated the straight-line distance with the Pythagorean theorem, yielding 907.63 feet. The New York Court of Appeals unanimously upheld Robbins' conviction: 'Plainly, guilt under the statute cannot depend on whether a particular building in a person's path to a school happens to be open to the public or locked at the time of a drug sale' (Chief Judge Judith S. Kaye).

12. Disjunctive Performatives?

My second objection to Rumfitt's proposal is that a disjunctive indictment would be a disjunctive performative. All disjunctive performatives violate an overtness requirement. A performative works by the speaker showing what he had in mind. With performatives such as promising, saying so makes it so. Anyone who says he promises, promises—even if he breaks the promise. Other performatives can only be performed by those in a position of authority. A teacher can dismiss a class by saying, 'Class dismissed!' A student cannot. A mother can name her child. Her congressman cannot. I can transubstantiate bread and wine into garbage by declaring it garbage. However, I cannot make biscuits by declaring 'These lumps of dough are biscuits.' Garbage is a state of mind. Biscuits are not.

An indictment is an act of self-expression by an appropriate authority. 'You are hereby charged with either murder or embezzlement' fails to evince a legally relevant state of mind. It is like 'I hereby insinuate that you embezzled.'

Oaths show the same resistance to disjunction. When called to jury duty, I wanted to avoid the standard oath (ending with performative supplement 'So help me God'). I had been warned that judges in Brooklyn process potential jurors at an industrial scale. A soft-spoken atheist might wind up swearing to God *by default*! Working up my nerve, I interrupted the judge with a premeditated shout from the crowd: 'I WANT TO AFFIRM!'. As feared, a hundred eyes passed from the judge to me and then back at the judge. The judge was momentarily stunned. The machine ground to a halt. Silence. Regaining his composure, the judge continued, 'Very well, EVERYBODY repeat after me: I hereby either swear to God or

AFFIRM that…'. The judge had stunned me right back! I had assumed I would be separately sworn in. Flustered, I meekly repeated the oath or 'oath'. What had just happened? Had I sworffirmed?

13. The Causal Theory of Verdicts

My third and main objection to Rumfitt's proposal is that disjunctive verdicts are never just—even if they are expedient and even if we should sometimes act unjustly. Verdictives purport to be direct effects of what they represent. The umpire's motto is 'I call them as I see them.' He needs special training to see them just as we need special training to read. But the point of the training is to make the judgment automatic.

Fred Dretske contrasted the belief-dependency of epistemic seeing (seeing that *p* is the case) with non-epistemic seeing (the sense in which a judge and his dog see a gavel) (Dretske 1969). Typically, we both see and see that something is the case. The point is that non-epistemic seeing does not rely on belief. This gives perception the objectivity needed to arbitrate between hypotheses. If seeing depended on beliefs, there would be a worrisome circularity in using observation to test theories. This circularity would extend to verdictives. Each verdictive purports to be an appropriate effect of what it found. 'Appropriate' is vague but past work on other causal theories (perception, memory, names, etc.) provides guidance.

The key difference for my purposes is that epistemic seeing tolerates disjunctions. When you see a baby, *you see that* it is either a boy or a girl but you do not *see* a disjunctive fact. You are responding to its babyhood, not its boyhood or its girlhood. The cause of what you are seeing is its being baby, not its being a mammal. The causal relation requires the appropriate grain of specificity.

In the umpire's dilemma, the umpire is supposed to be exercising a special perceptual skill. He learns how to tell whether a pitch is a strike or a ball and then can make the judgement automatically—as an observation. The dilemma arises for Rauf because he sees that Ponting is out despite not seeing the out. The situation is morally awkward because a verdict is an assertion; the umpire appears doomed to lie.

People can be trained to see institutional facts. Teachers learn how to tell the difference between a pass and a fail. They are supposed to give their verdict on the basis of this learned ability. To facilitate this ability, they organize the course so that it is easier to tell the difference between a pass and a fail.

The directness of verdicts is obscured in law because the hard cases get most of the attention. But lawyers are trained to detect legality just as language learners are trained to detect grammaticality. The non-epistemic nature of verdictives prevents them from being based on evidence that supports disjunctive judgments. Since the verdict is supposed to be non-epistemic, the initial charge must reflect this non-epistemic nature. To set up a successful verdict, one must solve a Goldilocks problem. It must not be too specific nor too underspecific.

14. Rationale for the Causal Requirement

Hunter-gatherer societies regard eyewitness testimony as the best type of evidence. Inferential justifications are weaker. This ranking is reflected in ordinary English. You will be more confident if I report 'Your passport is in the glove compartment' than if I report 'Your passport must be in the glove compartment.' For the 'must' signals an inference. We do not use 'must' when we see or when we are relying on testimony.

The causal requirement explains why a professor cannot justifiably grade examinations by throwing them on a staircase and grading in accordance with their altitude. Even if this random procedure happens to match student performance, the process fails to make the grades appropriate effects of student performance. The causal requirement also explains why there is no pre-punishment for future crimes (Sorensen 2006). A just verdict must be an *effect* of the crime. Even if the judge foresees the crime with certainty, he cannot rule that the defendant is guilty.

Since there are no disjunctive causes, the requirement also precludes the justification of disjunctive verdictives. For instance, if Jesse robs a bank in Lancaster while his identical twin coincidentally robs a bank in Oxford, then a judge cannot compensate for his uncertainty as to which twin robbed which bank by finding Jesse guilty of either robbing the Lancaster bank or robbing the Oxford bank. If the prosecutor cannot specify which twin robbed which bank, then both twins are acquitted.

A verdict can have the sort of generality that determinables have to their determinates. Consider Stephen Yablo's example of Sophie—a pigeon that has been trained to peck at red triangles to the exclusion of all other colours (Yablo 1992). Sophie will peck at a scarlet triangle. But this does not mean that the triangle being scarlet (rather than crimson or vermillion or burgundy) caused Sophie's pecking. She would have pecked at any red triangle. Causation goes to the most specific property *that makes a difference*. Sophie would not have pecked at a blue triangle even though blue and red are equally determinates of the determinable *coloured*. The redness of the triangle caused Sophie to peck, not the underspecific property of being coloured and not the overspecific property of being scarlet. Being coloured does not screen off being red but red screens off being scarlet. Red solves the Goldilocks problem by being neither too vague nor too precise. If theft stands to larceny as red stands to scarlet, then theft can be a cause of punishment. The fact that we cannot define 'theft' would be no more troublesome than the fact that we cannot define 'red'.

Verdicts, as 'findings of guilt', sound very epistemological. These precede the conviction (the stage at which legal status changes, a stage normally delayed to permit legal manoeuvres for the defence). Verdicts do not entail punishment (which routinely precedes conviction thanks to the practice of giving credit for time served awaiting trial). However, verdicts stand to knowledge only as perception stands to knowledge. Perception is a means of generating knowledge and is guided by knowledge. However, perception does not entail knowledge. I might learn someone committed a crime by a guilty verdict. But a guilty verdict can be just without itself being an instance of knowledge.

You perceive an object by virtue of having an appropriate causal connection with it. That is why no one in 2006 could see the Prime Minister of Poland Jarosław Kaczyński by seeing his identical twin, Lech Kaczyński, the President of Poland. When Jarosław skipped the inauguration ceremony of his brother (to avoid visual confusion), the audience had all they needed to know what Jarosław looked like. But they did not see Jarosław.

Perception does not require knowledge. Consider Carl Ginet's fake barn scenario. A father is driving along pointing out barns for the edification of his son. Unbeknownst to him, the pair has entered a county in which it is the practice to erect barn facades. Fortunately, the barns singled out by the father are genuine. But there was too much luck involved for the father to have known the building was a barn. So the fake barn scenario undermines knowledge and thus is a counterexample to the causal theory of knowledge. Nevertheless, the fake barn scenario is not a counterexample to the causal theory of perception. There was an appropriate causal connection. The father saw the barn. He just did not get perceptual knowledge from the experience.

Fake barn scenarios also preserve the justice of verdicts. If a verdict is obtained in the normal way in a region that happens to harbour many fake trials, then the verdict is just despite the fact that no one involved in the trial knew they were participating in a genuine trial.

15. An Analogy with Episodic Memory

The same point holds for personal, episodic memory. The father remembers the barn even though he did not know it was a barn.

Memory can survive epistemic reversals. If a psychologist deceives a research subject into thinking she confabulated a conversation with his secretary, then the subject does not know the conversation took place. But she still remembers the conversation.

People sometimes are remembering when they think they are imagining. This leads them to overestimate their creativity with respect to melodies and stories. A painter who thinks he imagines a house may come to suspect he remembered if the depicted house bears a remarkable resemblance. But sheer resemblance is not enough. There must a causal path from the house to the painter.

Personal, episodic memory is the basis for autobiographical narrative constructions. Recognition of the causal connection requirement forces us to respect chronological order. For the subject to conceive of himself as remembering, he must trace 'a continuous spatio-temporal route through all the narratives of memory, a route continuous with the present and future location of the remembering subject' (Campbell 1997, p. 110).

The justification of a verdict imposes the same plot requirements. As in memory, the judge can be aware that the narrative is gappy and selective. But this modesty evinces the presupposition of connectedness. Those trying to influence the verdict will naturally develop competing narratives.

The story-telling aspect does not mesh with knowledge-based accounts of verdicts. Memory is narrower than knowledge in some respects, broader in others. There can be justified verdicts without knowledge of guilt and justified verdicts of non-guilt despite knowledge of guilt. Knowledge of guilt and innocence is only indirectly relevant to verdicts. Just as inquiry can show that the causal connection condition was not satisfied for memory, it can show that it was not satisfied for a verdict.

In some ways, memory is easier than knowledge. In those cases, the verdicts will appear unjustified to those who think verdicts are primarily epistemic. Whereas the simple causal theory of knowledge mistakenly implies that we have no knowledge of the future or of general statements or mathematical statements, the simple causal theory of *verdicts* welcomes the implication that there can be no just verdicts about future events or abstract entities or generalities. The causal theory of verdicts enjoys the same success as causal theories of perception and memory. Each of these theories states a necessary condition, not a sufficient condition. Specifically, judges strive to make their verdicts *appropriate* effects of past crimes.

All of these causal theories exclude deviant causal chains. For instance, veridical frame-ups do not generate just verdicts. The demand for causal evidence excludes several forms of attractive reasoning. Consider appeal to duplicates. The revelation that we have convicted the identical twin of the real perpetuator forces a whole new trial for the new suspect. The prosecution cannot avoid the expense by proving the first trial would have had the same outcome if the correct twin had been tried.

The demand for causal evidence also exerts *de facto* pressure on the defence's reasoning. If the accused rapist merely wishes to create doubt, then he should concede as little as he can while adding as many imaginative counter-explanations as he can muster: either there was no sex or it was consensual or I was a thousand miles away or I was entrapped or I was insane. From a logical point of view, the more disjuncts the accused introduces, the higher the probability that the disjunction is true. So if the defence's task were merely to preclude knowledge of guilt, disjuncts should be maximized. But instead of complimenting the attorney for his zeal, the judge will disallow the defence as 'inconsistent' (Nagle 1981). Judges, who tend to be former prosecutors, prefer that an innocent verdict be based on an exonerating cause rather than a lack of proved guilt. Judges only grudgingly allow disjuncts. The judicially preferred format of alternative pleading is conditional arguing. The defence sets up a fallback argument that only takes effect if the primary argument is rejected. If the primary argument is accepted, then it is as if the secondary argument had never been mentioned. A hierarchy of potential arguments allows each argument be causal. The modular construction also allows the judge to consider a sequence of simple arguments instead of a large argument. Although human beings perform much parallel processing unconsciously, conscious thought is always sequential.

According to Armstrong 1961, the point of perception is acquiring knowledge—reliable true beliefs. But most theorists think perception is only indirectly related to knowledge. Perceptual processes are modular. Modular systems are designed to deliver quick, reliable judgments on a narrowly circumscribed evidential basis. As illustrated by the tenacity of optical illusions, perception is cognitively impenetrable. It does not obey the total evidence requirement.

In 1966 the U.S. Supreme Court wrote, 'The basic purpose of a trial is the determination of truth.' Larry Laudan (2006) cites this as the guiding premise of his book *Truth, Error, and Criminal Law: An Essay in Legal Epistemology*. But the legal aversion to disjunctive indictments suggests that verdicts only have as much relationship to knowledge as perception.

I have argued for four theses. First, the two senses of 'vague' generate parallel moral dilemmas for judges about lying. Second, the umpire's dilemma cannot be resolved by permitting disjunctive indictments because they are systematically unjust. Third, this injustice is explained by the causal theory of verdicts. Fourth, the causal theory correctly characterizes verdicts as akin to perception rather than to open-minded inquiry.

References

Armstrong, David. 1961. *Perception and the Physical World*. London: Routledge & Kegan Paul.

Austin, J.L. 1962. *How to Do Things with Words*. Cambridge (MA): Harvard University Press.

Bach, Kent and Robert M. Harnish. 1992. 'How Performatives Really Work: A Reply to Searle'. *Linguistics and Philosophy* 15(1): 93–110.

Beck, Simon. 2008. 'Intuitionism, Constructive Interpretation, and Cricket'. *Philosophical Perspectives* 37(2): 319–31.

Bentham, Jeremy. 1827. *Rationale of Judicial Evidence, Specially Applied to English Practice*. Vol. 5. London: Hunt and Clarke.

Campbell, John. 1997. 'The Structure of Time in Autobiographical Memory'. *European Journal of Philosophy* 5(2): 105–18.

Cohen, L.J. 1964. 'Do Illocutionary Forces Exist?' *Philosophical Quarterly* 14(55): 118–37.

Dretske, Fred. 1969. *Seeing and Knowing*. Chicago (IL): University of Chicago Press.

Dworkin, Ronald. 1977. *Taking Rights Seriously*. Cambridge (MA): Harvard University Press.

Hart, H.L.A. 1961. *The Concept of Law*. Oxford: Oxford University Press.

Hegel, G.W.F. 1821/1967. *The Philosophy of Right*, edited by T.M. Knox. London: Oxford University Press.

Hitchens, Christopher. 2010. *Hitch-22: A Memoir*. New York: Twelve.

Katz, Leo. 1987. *Bad Acts and Guilty Minds*. Chicago (IL): University of Chicago Press.

Laudan, Larry. 2006. *Truth, Error, and Criminal Law: An Essay in Legal Epistemology*. Cambridge: Cambridge University Press.

Lycan, William. 1984. *The Logical Form of Natural Language*. Cambridge: MIT Press.

Nagel, Thomas. 1971. 'The Absurd'. *The Journal of Philosophy* 68(20): 716–27.

Nagle, James F. 1981. 'Inconsistent Defenses in Criminal Cases'. *Military Law Review* 92: 77–128.

Peirce, C.S. 1902. 'Vague'. In *Dictionary of Philosophy and Psychology*, Vol. 2, edited by James M. Baldwin, p. 748. New York: MacMillan.

Radford, Colin. 1985. 'The Umpire's Dilemma'. *Analysis* 45(2): 109–11.

Rumfitt, Ian. 2010. 'Ricky Ponting and the Judges'. *Analysis* 70(2): 205–10.

Solan, Larry. 2011. 'Lawyers as Insincere (But Truthful) Actors'. *Journal of the Legal Profession* 36(2): 487–527.

Sorensen, Roy. 1989. 'The Ambiguity of Vagueness and Precision'. *Pacific Philosophical Quarterly* 70(2): 174–83.

Sorensen, Roy. 2001. 'Vagueness Has No Function in Law'. *Legal Theory* 7(4): 385–415.

Sorensen, Roy. 2006. 'Future Law: Prepunishment and the Causal Theory of Verdicts'. *Noûs* 40(1): 166–83.

Yablo, Stephen. 1992. 'Mental Causation'. *Philosophical Review* 101: 245–80.

15

Clarity, Thoughtfulness, and the Rule of Law

Jeremy Waldron

1.

Section 61–8–303(1) of the Montana Code—the part of Montana's law dealing with speed limits—used to provide as follows:

[α] A person operating or driving a vehicle of any character on a public highway of this state shall drive the vehicle in a careful and prudent manner and at a rate of speed no greater than is reasonable and proper under the conditions existing at the point of operation, taking into account the amount and character of traffic, condition of brakes, weight of vehicle, grade and width of highway, condition of surface, and freedom of obstruction to the view ahead. The person operating or driving the vehicle shall drive the vehicle so as not to unduly or unreasonably endanger the life, limb, property, or other rights of a person entitled to the use of the street or highway.

But it now specifies numerical speed limits:

[β] the speed limit for vehicles traveling: (a) on a federal-aid interstate highway outside an urbanized area of 50,000 population or more is 75 miles an hour at all times and the speed limit for vehicles traveling on federal-aid interstate highways within an urbanized area of 50,000 population or more is 65 miles an hour at all times; (b) on any other public highway of this state is 70 miles an hour during the daytime and 65 miles an hour during the night-time; (c) in an urban district is 25 miles an hour.

The reason that Section 61–8–303(1) now specifies numerical speed limits is that in 1998, in a case called *State v. Stanko*, the Montana Supreme Court, by a vote of four to three, struck down the earlier version 'void for vagueness on its face and in violation of the Due Process Clause of the Montana Constitution'.[1]

    The Court explained why it struck the statute down in terms provided by the federal void-for-vagueness doctrine:

As generally stated, the void-for-vagueness doctrine requires that a penal statute define the criminal offense with sufficient definiteness that ordinary people can understand what

---

[1] *State v. Stanko*, 292 Mont. 192, 974 P.2d 1132 (Mont., 1998).

conduct is prohibited and in a manner that does not encourage arbitrary and discriminatory enforcement.[2]

And it cited an earlier judgment of the U.S. Supreme Court: 'If arbitrary and discriminatory enforcement is to be prevented, laws must provide explicit standards for those who apply them.'[3]

The problem appears to have been that Mr Stanko would have no idea of which of a variety of possible conceptions of *reasonable speed* he would be at the mercy of, so far as his interactions with the law were concerned. And on the Court, the position of the majority was that he was entitled to know this, so he could adjust his behaviour accordingly.

2.

I have labelled these versions of the Montana speed limit as [α] and [β], respectively. Version [β] casts the speed limit in the form of a rule, using mostly numerical predicates along with references to various types of roadway. This was the version adopted after *Stanko* was decided, in order to avoid the problems that the pre-*Stanko* standard ran into. True, version [β] refers to 'daytime' and 'nighttime', but the apparent vagueness of these terms is offset by subsequent language in the section: '(5) "Daytime" means from one-half hour before sunrise to one-half hour after sunset. "Nighttime" means at any other hour.'

Version [α] by contrast—i.e. the provision under which Mr Stanko was charged—was cast as a standard using all sorts of terms that seem to require judgment on the part of anyone applying them: 'in a careful and prudent manner', 'at a rate of speed no greater than is reasonable and proper under the conditions', and 'to unduly or unreasonably endanger the life, limb, property, or other rights of a person entitled to the use of the street or highway'. Some of the terms used in traffic laws are no doubt vague in some familiar sense: they suffer from sorites vagueness, which occurs when the law confronts a continuous spectrum with its binary logic; and some of them may suffer from Wittgensteinian vagueness—indeterminacy of criteria—like 'vehicle'. But the vagueness of the terms used in version [α] is not of that sort—at least not in the first instance; I shall say something in a moment about the entanglement of various different forms of vagueness. The Montana Supreme Court was particularly exercised by the phrase '...at a rate of speed no greater than is reasonable and proper under the conditions existing at the point of operation....' Consider 'reasonable' in this predicate. The primary difficulty here is not that velocities form a continuum that does not disclose any bright line between the reasonable and unreasonable: that would be sorites vagueness. The primary difficulty is that the ordinary citizen has no idea of what conception of reasonableness is

---

[2] *Kolender v. Lawson*, 461 U.S. 352, 357–8 (1983).
[3] *Grayned v. City of Rockford*, 408 U.S. 104 (1972).

being invoked here. This is not really a matter of vagueness, at least not in anything the philosopher's sense of vagueness. It is a matter of competing conceptions.

To make this problem vivid, I am going to exaggerate a little, endowing Mr Stanko with a set of rather Nietzschean views about driving. Mr Stanko, I will say, may have considered the issue of *reasonable speed* in terms that took account of the particular joys of driving fast on relatively deserted highways—the wind in your hair, the sense of freedom, even perhaps the exhilaration of a certain amount of risk. But the Stanko conception of reasonable speed is not universally shared. The officer who pulled Mr Stanko over, Officer Breidenbach, may have developed a conception of reasonable speed in ways that were oriented mostly to safety and the avoidance of the death and mayhem that are all too often features of the experiences that confront law-enforcement officers on highways with speeding drivers. These disparate conceptions of *reasonable speed* may overlap in large areas of conduct. And, whatever conception one is using, one is directed by the Montana statute to refer to factors like the amount and character of traffic, condition of brakes, weight of vehicle, grade and width of highway, condition of surface, and freedom of obstruction to the view ahead. Even so, Mr Stanko's driving at 85 mph in a new and mechanically perfect car on a sunny day on a road that was, for all practical purposes, clear of any other traffic, is exactly the kind of case to pose an issue between these two conceptions of reasonable speed. Apparently the road afforded an unobstructed view for some 300 feet; that was how far Breidenbach was behind Stanko and he never lost sight of him. But it was a mountain road and there were some broad and challenging curves: exactly the sort of road to generate what we may call Stanko-exhilaration of the most delightful sort. It was the sort of road that separates the good drivers from the bad and Stanko may have been proud of his excellent driving. Officer Breidenbach might say there were risks associated with Stanko's driving. And so there certainly were: a person stepping onto the road from a concealed position might be mowed down by a vehicle approaching at 85 mph. But the event was unlikely; it was a wilderness area. And anyway the statute did not direct the elimination of risk: it instructed the driver 'not to unduly or unreasonably endanger the life, limb, property, or other rights of a person entitled to the use of the street or highway', and the two conceptions of *reasonable speed* are likely to differ in their assessment of which abstract possibilities of endangerment are undue or unreasonable.

3.

I talked earlier about the entanglement of different kinds of vagueness. The fact that there is a choice to be made between the Breidenbach and the Stanko conceptions of *reasonable speed* is not a matter of vagueness. But the application of *either one* of these conceptions might involve vagueness of the sorites kind. For Stanko's conception still generates some sense of unreasonable speed—where the exhilaration gives way to terror, the wind rips rather than ruffles one's hair, and the risk to other road-users is massive. But where Stanko-reasonableness fades into

Stanko-unreasonableness will be quite indeterminate. There will be grey areas; it will be impossible to draw a bright line. And there will be similar issues for Officer Breidenbach's more cautious conception. His conception too will array velocities on a continuum and it will not determine a bright line separating Breidenbach-reasonableness from Breidenbach-unreasonableness. But we are not called to confront these issues of vagueness until we have chosen between the two conceptions.

The same may be said about any element of Wittgensteinian vagueness in my story. For example, the application of Officer Breidenbach's conception of reasonable speed may not involve checking off any tidy set of necessary and sufficient conditions. Judging two different vehicles to be each travelling at a reasonable speed may, in Breidenbach's view, involve the application of different sets of criteria that bear at best a family resemblance relationship to one another.

All in all, this business of reasonable speed will often be a complex and delicate matter of judgement that is difficult to articulate. Backing up Officer Breidenbach at the hearing in *Stanko*, the Montana Attorney-General said this, when he was asked what speed would be reasonable in the circumstances in which Mr Stanko was pulled over:

> Again, that would be depending upon the—it will always be a question of judgment at the time based on the conditions at the time, if there were heavier traffic. I cannot give you a number that would have been reasonable and prudent at that—it ultimately may come down to a question to be determined by the jury. The officer will exercise his best judgment in applying the statute.

But what I am arguing here is that it is possible to separate the background question of general evaluation that the use of a term like 'reasonable speed' involves from the difficult matters of judgment and line drawing that are involved in the application of a given conception of reasonableness.

4.

The idea of there being different conceptions of a given concept is familiar from the work of Ronald Dworkin (1978). I hope it is not too challenging for my philosophical colleagues. It is a fairly straightforward idea. The application of certain value-laden predicates often involves the use of something like a normative theory or a principle, which one takes to be indicated by the use of the term.

Anyone who is trying to figure out what is reasonable in some domain has to have a sense of the sort of reasons that are important to take into account and the weight to be given to them when they pull in different directions. The concept of *the reasonable*—or, in our case, of *a reasonable speed*—doesn't tell them much beyond this, except that the concept of what it is reasonable for me to do does not neglect the interests of others and requires some fair balance among the interests of all affected.[4] A conception of the reasonable in some sphere fills out this

----

[4] Cf. the discussion in Rawls 1993/2005, pp. 48–54.

schema, by indicating the interests that are to be particularly taken into account, the weight to be accorded to them, and the idea of a fair balance among them. Officer Breidenbach's conception of a reasonable speed differs from Mr Stanko's conception, in my story, by not according much weight to the exhilaration factor.

Some value-concepts that are used in law afford greater initial guidance than *reasonableness* does. Consider, for example, the use of the term 'cruel' (as applied to possible punishments) in the 8th Amendment to the U.S. Constitution and in Article 12 of the Canadian Charter of Rights and Freedoms. When we try to apply it to possible punishments—such as solitary confinement or capital punishment—we are aware that 'cruel' is concerned with the extent of suffering and the attitude towards suffering evinced by persons involved in its infliction.[5] Beyond that, different users have to develop different theories of how, through the use of this term, an upper limit on the harshness or painfulness of punishment is to be established. One theory might rivet its attention on the unhealthy and sadistic attitudes that can all too easily be associated with the intentional infliction of discomfort and distress that punishment inevitably involves. Another theory might focus on the occurrence of suffering that seems to be in excess of what is required as punishment, whether this occurrence is the result of anyone's intention or not. These generate disparate conceptions of cruelty. My point is that the concept of cruelty already sets us off along certain lines, but within those lines we may move in somewhat different directions. The 8th Amendment does not require us to make a general evaluation (or just any old evaluation) of punishment; it is not concerned, for example, with the expensiveness or inefficiency of a form of punishment as a criterion of limitation.[6] So the predicate already frames and channels the work that we do under the auspices of this provision. This, of course, is what thick moral predicates do: their use requires an evaluation, but they channel and direct the evaluation that is required to a certain extent. The thicker the term, the greater the degree of channelling and direction. But it is seldom enough to eliminate the possibility of rival conceptions.

One additional complicating point is this. The use of a thick moral term already intimates a certain sort of evaluation, even if it does not settle its exact character. But the sort of evaluation it intimates may not command the support of those to whom the provision that uses the term is addressed. If a law is enacted that says 'Women should not wear outfits that are unchaste', many of those to whom it is addressed (many women, for example) may not accept any norms of the sort that are embodied in the term 'chaste'. Even among those who do accept norms of this kind, there will be disparate conceptions of what chastity requires. But the disparity, the indeterminacy, will be heightened by some people offering and using

---

⁵ See Waldron 2010, pp. 299–302.
⁶ Even when a court reaches the conclusion that (say) disproportionate punishments fall foul of such a norm, they do so not because the norm invites us (under the auspices of 'cruel') to consider everything that might be relevant to the assessment of the punishment in question (including proportionality), but because we have a theory that a punishment becomes cruel when there is, so to speak, a surplus of suffering gratuitously inflicted that bears no proportional relation to reasonable penal goals.

conceptions whose aim it is to dilute the impact of the sort of norms traditionally embodied in the term. They may even essay what C.L. Stevenson called persuasive definitions of the term, like 'Daring is the new chaste' (Stevenson 1938), etc.

One reason for using rules rather than standards is to avoid this sort of thing. One commands a certain speed limit, or a certain determinate limit on punishment, or a certain length for women's skirts—and requires people to observe the rule, whether they agree with what they may think of as the underlying policy or not. But with a standard—whether it uses 'reasonable' or 'cruel' or 'chaste'—one cannot avoid the fact that users have to develop and apply a conception, and that conception may be informed not only by their particular take on how best to elaborate the standard but also by their particular view about the desirability of the norms that the standard appears to embody.

5.

I want to return now to my speeding example from Montana. I spoke about Officer Breidenbach's conception of *a reasonable speed* and Mr Stanko's conception. Many of us will think that (in my story) Mr Stanko's conception of reasonable speed is in error and that Officer Breidenbach's conception is closer to the truth. There is no difficulty with using notions of correctness and error here; we can easily think of conceptions of *reasonable speed* that would be plainly erroneous. What should we say about the possibility that some people will approach the application of predicates like 'reasonable' thinking in terms of the objective truth about reasonable speed and right answers and moral reality and so on?

One thing we might say is that the prospect of different people coming up with disparate conceptions of reasonable speed does not affect the point that one of these might be the right conception. Probably Mr Stanko thinks his is the right conception; if he didn't think that, he would hold a different conception. And something similar may be said for Officer Breidenbach. The disparity of their conceptions is not incompatible with the point that one of them may be correct. And of course equally the fact that there may be one correct conception doesn't allay the difficulties—if any—that the disparity of conceptions gives rise to.

Or does it? Some will say that a norm whose application admits of a right answer cannot be invidiously indeterminate, any more than a rule can. There are right answers for the application of what I called version [β] of the Montana speed limit. If someone is going 80 mph on the open highway he is breaking the law, and if he knows that is his speed, then he knows he is breaking the law, and so do the police if they have an accurate speed-detector and the judge if he is presented with accurate evidence. Of course, people may lie or misread their instruments, and evidence may be distorted: innocent people may be convicted and they may not know in advance whose flawed evidence they will be at the mercy of. But this is not what we mean by linguistic indeterminacy. And similarly—it may be said—people may use the wrong conception of reasonable speed under version [α] but that doesn't make version [α] of the Montana speed limit indeterminate.

I am not sure what to think about this line of argument. One difficulty is that right answers to the questions posed by [α] are not self-certifying and there is no easy, agreed, or operationalized way of getting to them. Under normal conditions the right answer does not sit up and display itself as such. So, following the line of argument above, if Mr Stanko is convicted because his conception of reasonable speed is regarded as incorrect, he may well think of himself as being in a position analogous to someone wrongfully convicted under version [β] because of a faulty radar gun.

It is interesting, at any rate, that the Court showed no interest in the prospect of right answers to the evaluative questions posed by version [α] of the speed limit. Their concern was the possible proliferation of conceptions each claiming to be the right answer and Mr Stanko's inability to know which of these claimants he would be at the mercy of.

6.

The decision of the Montana Supreme Court in the *Stanko* case was not unanimous. Three of the justices voted to convict Mr Stanko. Two of them said that his speed was so excessive that he lacked standing to impugn version [α] of the speed limit for vagueness: I guess the idea was that a whole array of conceptions of *reasonable speed* would overlap in condemning his velocity,[7] so that *as applied* to his case the standard was not vague.

The other dissenting judge, Chief Justice Turnage, was quite impatient with Mr Stanko's complaint about version [α] along different lines.

This important statutory provision of our motor vehicle traffic regulations has been the law of Montana since it was enacted by the legislature in 1955.... This important traffic regulation has remained unchanged as the law of Montana... since that time. Appellant Rudy Stanko challenged this statute as being unconstitutional in 1998 because of vagueness. Apparently for the past forty-three years, other citizens driving upon our highways had no problem in understanding this statutory provision. Section 61–8–303(1) is not vague and most particularly is not unconstitutional as a denial of due process. Therefore, I dissent.

That was all he wrote. Now, not only did Chief Justice Turnage suggest that the alleged indeterminacy of version [α] had never proved a problem for generations of Montanan drivers, he also suggested that the version was—as phrased—an '*important* statutory provision of our motor vehicle traffic regulations'. Why might he have thought that?

---

[7] Justice Regnier, dissenting:

In my view, Stanko's speed on the roadway where he was arrested clearly falls within the behavior proscribed by the statute. Operating a vehicle at 85 miles per hour on a two-lane highway with frost heaves, steep hills, and curves, where farm vehicles may unexpectedly appear, is not reasonable and proper under the conditions. Therefore, I conclude that Stanko has no standing to attack the facial validity of this statute.

The Chief Justice did not elaborate. But in a much earlier case (*State v. Schaeffer*, from 1917), another state Supreme Court, this time in Ohio,[8] said this about a *reasonable speed* provision:

The Legislature... in this instance, saw fit to fix no definite rate of speed for the car.... [A] rate of speed dangerous in one situation would be quite safe in another situation, and if the rate of speed were definitely fixed, naturally it would have to be the minimum speed at which cars might be safely driven, because that speed would have to be a safeguard against every possible situation.... There is no place in all the public [roads] where a situation is not constantly changing from comparatively no traffic to a most congested traffic; from no foot travelers to a throng of them; from open and clear intersections, private drives, and street crossings, to those that are crowded; from free and unobstructed streets to streets filled with crowds of foot travelers and others getting off and on street cars and other vehicles. In order to meet these varying situations, and impose upon the automobilist [*sic*] the duty of anticipating them and guarding against the dangers that arise out of them, this statute was evidently passed in the interests of the public safety in a public highway.

And the court went on to say that it was precisely the statute's 'adaptability to meet every dangerous situation' that commends it as a valid enactment.

Notice, in this regard, the court's emphasis on the role of the driver ('the automobilist') in anticipating the varying situations that arise and adjusting his speed accordingly. When we discuss these situations of vagueness, it is tempting to say that the allegedly vague law is 'applied' by law enforcement officials and courts and to neglect the initial role of 'self-application' by the primary subject of the law—the driver.[9] But the driver is the first addressee of any traffic law and, for most of the cases to which the law applies, it is the driver's judgement, and only the driver's judgement, that is relied upon. The legislature determines that the objects of traffic policy will be better safeguarded in a varying environment by trusting to the judgement of the driver—with his or her eyes and ears there on the spot—to determine a reasonable speed, than to try to determine this itself from its lofty vantage point in the State Capitol. That's how standards work: they represent a determination that some of the judgements that the law requires are better made downstream from the legislature, at street level (as it were) than upstream in the legislative chamber itself; that's why they use value language like 'reasonable' to indicate to the citizen that it is for him to make a judgement about the matter. The use of this language guides the driver's action, not directly by telling him exactly what the upper speed limit should be, but by instructing him that an exercise of judgement on his part is called for; this is guidance too.[10]

Now, in the *Stanko* case—the case we began with—the Montana Supreme Court did notice that a standard, such as version [*a*] of the Montana speed limit, transfers

---

[8] *State v. Schaeffer*, 96 Ohio St. 215; 117 N.E. 220 (1917). I have discussed this case extensively in Waldron 2011a.

[9] For the idea of self-application as a most important moment in the legal process, see Hart and Sacks 1958/1994, p. 120.

[10] This was my argument in Waldron 2011a.

judgment downstream, out of the legislative chamber. But it saw this only as an unconstitutional delegation to law enforcement authorities. It said,

A vague law impermissibly delegates basic policy matters to policemen, judges, and juries for resolution on an ad hoc and subjective basis, with the attendant dangers of arbitrary and discriminatory application.

The trouble with this is that it entirely neglects the first moment of application: self-application of the norm by the driver. What it says about Montana drivers' self-application of version [α] is that 'the average motorist in Montana would have *no idea* of the speed at which he or she could operate his or her motor vehicle on this State's highways without violating Montana's "basic rule"' (my emphasis). Really? No idea at all? One is reminded of an observation by John Stuart Mill in his essay on *Utilitarianism*: 'There is no difficulty in proving any ethical standard whatever to work ill, if we suppose universal idiocy to be conjoined with it' (Mill 1861/1987, pp. 296). But, on any hypothesis short of that, most actual drivers will have some working hunches about reasonable speeds in various circumstances. And this presumably is what Chief Justice Turnage meant in his dissent, when he said that 'apparently for the past forty-three years, other citizens driving upon our highways had no problem in understanding this statutory provision'.

7.

Of course, a difficulty arises when the driver's hypothesis about reasonable speed turns out to be incompatible with the views of law enforcement and the courts. Law involves layers of application: the driver self-applies the standard; the police officer applies it in swearing out a complaint; and the judge applies it in convicting or acquitting the defendant.

In some cases, we might expect considerable variation. Three possibilities spring to mind. (i) In a pluralistic society, there may be areas of life where there are radically disparate ways of doing things, leading to radically disparate convictions about what is reasonable and unreasonable conduct in that area. (ii) In other cases, the views of a court, say, on what is reasonable and unreasonable may be informed by information which in the nature of things the individual cannot have; so there would be an element of unfairness in judging the individuals' assessment of reasonableness by the court's rather differently informed conception.[11] (iii) In still other cases, applications by individual law-enforcement officers may be contaminated by prejudice leading them to apply differential standards to members of different groups in the community. The court in *Stanko* hinted at this when it worried about 'dangers of arbitrary and discriminatory application'.

---

[11] Cf. the discussion of *Cline v. Frink Dairy Co.*, 274 U.S. 445 (1927) in Post 1994. In *Cline*, individual dairymen had to work out what a 'reasonable profit' was on their products; but the state's assessment of a reasonable profit involved macro-economic data that the individual dairymen could not have access to.

These possibilities help us understand the case against using value-predicates: in some areas of life and law, it may be difficult to align or coordinate the self-application of these norms with their secondary application by law enforcement officials and judges. They work better where there is substantial reason to expect such alignment, worse where there is good reason not to.

The Court in *Stanko* exaggerated the difficulties of using a *reasonable speed* statute. And I played along with that, by imagining a quite considerable ethical disparity between Mr Stanko's Nietzschean conception of *reasonable speed*—wind in the hair, living on the edge, etc.—and Officer Breidenbach's more safety-oriented conception. I did that so that, in section 3, I could illustrate the difference between indeterminacy arising out of multiple conceptions of *reasonable speed* and indeterminacy arising out of the vagueness (the sorites vagueness or the Wittgensteinian vagueness) of any one of these conceptions.

8.

But there are ways of minimizing the disparities between the various conceptions in play here. Drivers have to remember that when they are implicitly invited by the law to apply a conception of reasonable speed, they are not asked to do this as a parlour game. They are invited to do this *as a matter of law*: it is law, they are self-applying, something that is supposed to represent not just their own idiosyncratic views, but a view that can stand, even in their own self-application of it, in the name of the whole community. So if Mr Stanko is aware of the idiosyncrasy of his personal conception of *reasonable speed*, he may want to think twice before he self-applies this as a community norm (albeit a community-norm that is, for the time being, in his hands). This is not just a matter of prudence—though a prudent driver will give some thought to the views that police officers are likely to have on the matter. (We all do this when we drive over the limit but within what we take to be the margin of tolerance—12–15 mph over the limit—on the New York State Thruway.) As I say, it is a matter of maintaining awareness that this is law, for the community, that we are talking about. Apart from anything else, it is important that drivers orient their sense of reasonable speed to one another's driving on the same roadways. Drivers have to share the road and it is desirable for them to share a sense of how this norm that they have is to be self-administered among them.

Officer Breidenbach must reflect on this too; perhaps his conception of *reasonable speed* has been too greatly informed by the traumas of the accident scenes he has attended, giving him a distorted view of the dangers of driving (say) above 65 mph. He has to enforce version [α] of the speed limit for the community, not just for himself; and he must ponder what conceptions of *reasonable speed* good and thoughtful drivers in his jurisdiction are likely to have come up with, and what outer limits of this shared sense of reasonableness he ought to regard himself as responsible for patrolling.

I think this issue of reasonableness being treated as a legal standard and thus as a shared standard, not just a matter of individual ethical conviction, is very important.

How does it stand in relation to the objective, moral realist approach I mentioned in section 5? Does that help reduce the possible disparity among people's conceptions of reasonable speed? Maybe. If people approach the matter in a fallibilist spirit, and if they approach it also as though everyone's job is to ask himself or herself scrupulously the same question—what is reasonable in this instance, *really?*—then maybe version [α] can work well. It is, however, important to note that the objective approach will not work well without the specific legal orientation towards a shared norm that I have been talking about. Cut loose of that, the objective approach is as likely to be invoked in order to underwrite individuals' idiosyncratic conceptions and to bring those conceptions into closer relation with one another. We all know self-proclaimed realist moral philosophers who use the rhetoric of objectivity in what the English call a bloody-minded way, simply to reinforce their own views with an insistence that any attempt to relate them to the possibility of social consensus would be a treacherous concession to relativism. In traffic law, consensus matters often more than truth, for it is our acting together that law concerns itself with—in coordinating our driving, and in protecting people from disparities between self-application and official application.

9.

The advertised title of this chapter was originally 'Clarity, Thoughtfulness and the Rule of Law'. I have tried to show that the use of terms like 'reasonable' in some of the laws that apply to us should not be seen simply as instances of objectionable vagueness or indeterminacy. On the contrary, these standards often help to sponsor thoughtfulness and reflection in the law, on the part of those who are called on to apply it (including its primary addresses). People who are instructed to drive at a reasonable speed are credited with the ability to develop a conception of reasonableness in this regard and to apply it themselves to the diverse circumstances that led the legislature to refrain from issuing a numerical rule.

Elsewhere I have argued that the sponsorship of this thoughtfulness is entirely compatible with the political ideal of the Rule of Law. People have questioned this. They say that the use of terms like 'reasonable' yields norms that suffer from a deficit of clarity—'[t]he desideratum of clarity', said Lon Fuller, 'represents one of the most essential ingredients of legality' (Fuller 1969, p. 63)—and that therefore it detracts from or undermines the Rule of Law, because such norms do not let people know in advance exactly where they stand, they don't offer determinate guidance, and they empower those entrusted with the application of the law to impose their own judgments in a way that is not legally controlled, or at least not tightly controlled by law. People then seem to be at the mercy of the value judgements (the discretion) of officials and courts, second-guessing their own futile attempts to figure out how these norms will be authoritatively applied. For example, it is

F.A. Hayek's opinion, expressed in *The Road to Serfdom*, that '[o]ne could write a history of the decline of the Rule of Law...in terms of the progressive introduction of these vague formulas [like "reasonableness"] into legislation and of the increasing arbitrariness and uncertainty that results' (Hayek 1944, p. 78). I hope I have made clear why I disagree with this. It is true that the Rule of Law looks for some degree of certainty and predictability in the actions of the state, so that expectations can be nurtured and respected and so that people can know with some degree of assurance what rights they can count on and what their obligations are. In some areas this matters more than in others.[12] But I have argued that we should avoid any conception of the Rule of Law that requires law to be mechanically applicable in all circumstances, and that we should not diminish the role of law in focusing intelligence and facilitating the use of reasons, including moral reason, among its participants (Waldron 2011b). The use of standards as well as rules is one of the ways in which law does this.

So: I think we should resist the view that when standards are in play—norms like version [α] of the Montana traffic law—we might as well not have law at all, or that the thoughtfulness which is sponsored in the use of standards represents the opposite of the Rule of Law. It is a mistake to regard these norms as simply blank cheques for discretion, as though the most they told the person that they were addressed to was to prepare themselves for the arbitrary imposition of a value judgement by those in power. In fact the use of standards clearly represents an exercise in legal guidance. Think back to version [α]. Is it really the case that it gives the drivers of Montana no guidance? Only on the crudest behavioural conception of what it is to guide someone's action. Having one's action guided by a norm is not just a matter of finding out about the norm and conforming one's behaviour to its specifications. It can involve a more complex engagement of practical reason than that. The use of a standard credits a human agent not just with the ability to comply with instructions but with the capacity to engage in practical deliberation. The sign that says 'Drive at a reasonable speed in the circumstances' tells the driver 'Now is the time to check the weather and the road conditions and relate that information to your speed and moderate your behaviour accordingly. Now is the time to focus on this and do the thinking that the application of the standard requires.' It mobilizes the resources of practical intelligence possessed by the norm subject—a mobilization that might not take place if the lawmaker had not promulgated the standard. It guides his agency in that way, even if it leaves it up to him to determine the appropriate behaviour. It is law that requires and triggers thoughtfulness, rather than law that supersedes thoughtfulness.

---

[12] The most important thing, we are told, that people need from the law that governs them is predictability in the conduct of their lives and businesses. Tom Bingham quoted Lord Mansfield:

> In all mercantile transactions the great object should be certainty: and therefore it is of more consequence that a rule should be certain, than whether the rule is established one way rather than the other.

> (Bingham 2010, p. 38)

Bingham went on to observe in his own voice that '[n]o one would choose to business, perhaps involving large sums of money, in a country where parties rights and obligations were undecided'.

10.

I have focused most of this discussion on standards that use broad evaluative terms like 'reasonable'. In section 4, I briefly discussed the use of thicker terms like 'cruel' in the 8th Amendment. I want to conclude by summarize three of the points I have made by reference to this class of value-terms.

First, I think we can see clearly in the case of the prohibition on cruel punishment the distinction between possible indeterminacy resulting from disparate conceptions of *cruelty* and possible indeterminacy resulting from the vagueness of any given conception of it. Indeed, it is probably easier to see this in the case of *cruel punishment* than in the case of *reasonable speed*: there was something artificial about the rival Stanko- and Breidenbach-conceptions that I manufactured for the latter. As I said in section 4, we all know that cruelty is about inappropriate attitudes towards others' suffering. But some may have conceptions of this that are informed by a savage retributivism and regard nothing as cruel unless it goes beyond the demands of, say, *lex talionis*, while others may operate with an equation of cruel punishment with the infliction or toleration of suffering that is unnecessary in light of a more humane penology. Clearly, once we have chosen one of these—and there are many other available conceptions—we will face further questions, which may be questions of vagueness, about their application. But the first step—the development of a working conception of cruel punishment—is not in itself the resolution of a vagueness problem.

A second point I made about reasonable speed is that the application of this norm is entrusted in the first instance to its primary addressees—drivers. Police and courts come later. Exploration of analogous points for the 8th Amendment prohibition is interesting. In an exact analogy with version [α] of the Montana speed limit, it is a mistake to say that the 8th Amendment is directed primarily to courts and that the problem with it is that it doesn't give enough guidance to judges. The 8th Amendment is directed in the first instance to legislators. It is a constitutional provision and they are its primary addressees (along with prison officials who may be capable on occasion of acting cruelly without legislative authorization). Legislators are the ones who are to take care that the punishments they authorize are not cruel. In an interesting asymmetry, the analogue of the Officer Breidenbach figure will be some private petitioner, who claims he is being cruelly treated. He and his lawyers make a complaint to the court about what the legislator has authorized, and the federal courts responds to that complaint (just as the Montana courts responded to Officer Breidenbach's complaint about Rudy Stanko).

Once again the possible disparity between the conception of *cruelty* held by the legislative majority, the conception of *cruelty* held by the petitioner, and the conception of *cruelty* held by the court may pose a problem. But it is a problem that can be mitigated in a number of ways, not least by the feedback given by the courts to legislators and potential petitioners through constitutional *stare decisis*.

I also believe that the point I made in section 7 about appealing not just to one's own personal and perhaps idiosyncratic conception of the concept being used in the law is particularly important here. In an article entitled 'Cruel, Inhuman and Degrading Treatment: The Words Themselves' (Waldron 2008), I tried to distinguish the approach I am recommending here from the 'moral reading' of provisions like the 8th Amendment recommended by Ronald Dworkin. Dworkin's approach seems to suggest that each norm-applier should ask himself as honestly as he can and in as objective a spirit as he can muster certain quite specific evaluative questions: 'What attitudes towards suffering really are seriously inappropriate? What really is cruel?' On Dworkin's approach, the norm-applier is to ask these questions as complicated moral questions, and to try to get to the objective right answer—that is, to the moral truth about cruelty, inhumanity, and degradation and about the other moral issues that they embed. Any sensible person will recognize, of course, that as with all objective inquiries, what you get is the speaker's best opinion, and opinions will differ. But the formation of the opinion is supposed to be governed by the discipline of presenting the question and the answer in an objective spirit.

On Dworkin's account, the norm-applier engages his or her own critical views on what counts as inhuman and degrading. On the account I have suggested, one should be trying to articulate a conception of cruelty that can work for us all, as a standard for common conscience. Some may go further and say that these provisions they purport elicit some shared sense of positive morality, some 'common conscience' we already share, some code that already exists or resonates among us.[13] (Maybe the conjunction of 'unusual' with 'cruel' in the 8th Amendment points us in that direction.) I have toyed with that position in the past, but I think it goes too far. But I do want to insist that there is a difference between one's own personal view of what makes a punishment cruel and a view that one articulates (as a legislator, as a petitioner, or as a judge) as something that can stand and be applied as constitutional law in the name of us all.

Of course, even within this framework, there are plenty of options. All of the conceptions of cruel punishment I have mentioned—here and in section 4—could work as attempts to articulate a conception of cruelty that can work as law. So we still have to face the question of indeterminacy at this level.

This brings me to my third and final point, which is, again, about the Rule of Law and thoughtfulness. I acknowledged in section 8 that the Rule of Law sometimes has to insist on clarity and predictability, which might call into question the use of evaluative terms like those I have been considering in this chapter. But in some cases the craving for certainty matters less than the need for reflection, flexibility, reason, and thought, sponsored by the law through its use of standards rather than rules. I can imagine an argument that traffic law is an area where clarity is important, though I tried to state the opposite case in section 6. I cannot imagine

---

[13] We sometimes think of these standards as prohibiting conduct that 'shocks the conscience'. Again, I prefer to think of that not as an appeal to the moral sensibility of the solitary individual, but to the possibility of establishing some sort of shared conscience ('con-science' in the etymological sense of 'knowing together').

anyone saying that it is more important to be able to say with certainty what the punishment is for an offence than to suffer the indeterminacy occasioned by the use of predicates like 'cruel' in constitutional provisions.

For one thing, the primary addressee of these provisions is not an individual as in the traffic case, but a legislature; and it is hard to get a sense of what the interest or expectation of predictability amounts to in this matter. It is not the predictability that a businessman craves or the predictability needed for the autonomy of a Hayekian individual.

For another thing, it is the job of a legislature to deliberate thoughtfully and at length on the constitutional character of the laws that it passes. (It's a mistake to think this is only the function of the courts, not the legislature. Some countries— New Zealand, the United Kingdom—require the Attorney-General to certify that a proposed bill is compatible with the constitution or the Bill of Rights and if necessary to open a debate devoted to this very issue.) True, legislatures are perfectly capable of generating thought and debate when left to their own devices. But the legislative advantage of the 8th Amendment is that it requires the legislature to address the question of the cruelty of the punishments it ordains, whatever else it talks about. You may say that, in light of the indeterminacy as between rival possible conceptions of cruel punishment, that will be an inconclusive debate, with members often talking at cross purposes, precisely because the crucial term is unclear; and if it is conclusive, it will yield different and incompatible results depending on whose conception of cruel punishment is in the majority.

Maybe so. But it is a mistake to think that the only value of such a debate lies in the clarity of its terms and the determinate and consistent conclusiveness of its outcomes. Sometimes, what matters is just that there should be a debate on cruelty, within at least the terms of reference that the concept affords, whether or not it is conclusive. The passage of a penal statute is better when it is accompanied by a debate about cruelty in these indeterminate terms, for the indeterminacy of the terms does not mean that the debate might as well not take place at all. Law can sponsor thoughtfulness of certain sorts—here thoughtfulness about cruelty in the legislature—even when law does not tell us determinately what exactly to think about it.

References

Bingham, Tom. 2010. *The Rule of Law*. London: Allen Lane.
Dworkin, Ronald. 1978. *Taking Rights Seriously*. Harvard: Harvard University Press.
Fuller, Lon L. 1969. *The Morality of Law*, rev. edn. New Haven: Yale University Press.
Hart, Henry M. and Albert M. Sacks. 1958/1994. *The Legal Process: Basic Problems in the Making and Application of Law*. New York: Foundation Press.
Hayek, Friedrich August von. 1944. *The Road to Serfdom*. Chicago (IL): University of Chicago Press.
Mill, John Stuart. 1861/1987. 'Utilitarianism'. In *Utilitarianism and Other Essays*, edited by Alan Ryan, 272–338. Harmondsworth: Penguin Books.

Post, Robert C. 1994. 'Reconceptualizing Vagueness: Legal Rules and Social Orders'. *California Law Review* 82(3): 491–507.

Rawls, John. 1993/2005. *Political Liberalism*, 2nd edn. New York: Columbia University Press.

Stevenson, Charles Leslie. 1938. 'Persuasive Definition'. *Mind* 47(187): 331–50.

Waldron, Jeremy. 2008. 'Cruel, Inhuman, and Degrading Treatment: The Words Themselves'. *New York University Public Law and Legal Theory Working Papers*. Paper 98. Available at <http://lsr.nellco.org/nyu_plltwp/98>. Reprinted in Jeremy Waldron. 2010. *Torture, Terror and Trade-Offs*. Oxford: Oxford University Press.

Waldron, Jeremy. 2010. *Torture, Terror and Trade-Offs*. Oxford: Oxford University Press.

Waldron, Jeremy. 2011a. 'Vagueness and the Guidance of Action'. In *Philosophical Foundations of Language in the Law*, edited by Andrei Marmor and Scott Soames, 58–81. Oxford: Oxford University Press.

Waldron, Jeremy. 2011b. 'Thoughtfulness and the Rule of Law'. *British Academy Review* 18: 1–11.

Index

Weber, Marc Andree 4, 16, 189–203
Wechsler, Stephen 232
Wellmann, Carl 157
West, Robin 128
whole act rule 240–1
whole code rule 240
Williams, Bernard 214
Williamson, Timothy 2, 25, 35, 78, 86, 112, 166, 178, 206, 222
Wise, Virginia 180

Wittgenstein, Ludwig 7, 73, 84, 131, 194, 198, 213, 307, 318, 320, 326
Wittgensteinian vagueness, *see* indeterminacy of criteria
Wright, Crispin 3, 23, 207–8, 211, 248

Yablo, Stephen 312

Zippelius, Reinhold 239